W9-BYY-676

6th Edition

by Barry Burd, PhD

Java® For Dummies®, 6th Edition

Published by: **John Wiley & Sons, Inc.,** 111 River Street, Hoboken, NJ 07030-5774, www.wiley.com

Copyright © 2015 by John Wiley & Sons, Inc., Hoboken, New Jersey

Published simultaneously in Canada

For general information on our other products and services, please contact our Customer Care Department within the U.S. at 877-762-2974, outside the U.S. at 317-572-3993, or fax 317-572-4002. For technical support, please visit www.wiley.com/techsupport.

Wiley publishes in a variety of print and electronic formats and by print-on-demand. Some material included with standard print versions of this book may not be included in e-books or in print-on-demand. If this book refers to media such as a CD or DVD that is not included in the version you purchased, you may download this material at http://booksupport.wiley.com. For more information about Wiley products, visit www.wiley.com.

Library of Congress Control Number: 2013954105

ISBN 978-1-119-17569-8

Contents at a Glance

Table of Contents

Introduction

. . . .

*J*ava is good stuff. I've been using it for years. I like Java because it's very orderly. Almost everything follows simple rules. The rules can seem intimidating at times, but this book is here to help you figure them out. So, if you want to use Java and want an alternative to the traditional techie, soft-cover book, sit down, relax, and start reading *Java For Dummies,* 6th Edition.

How to Use This Book

I wish I could say, "Open to a random page of this book and start writing Java code. Just fill in the blanks and don't look back." In a sense, this is true. You can't break anything by writing Java code, so you're always free to experiment.

But let me be honest. If you don't understand the bigger picture, writing a program is difficult. That's true with any computer programming language — not just Java. If you're typing code without knowing what it's about, and the code doesn't do exactly what you want it to do, you're just plain stuck.

So, in this book, I divide Java programming into manageable chunks. Each chunk is (more or less) a chapter. You can jump in anywhere you want — Chapter 5, Chapter 10, or wherever. You can even start by poking around in the middle of a chapter. I've tried to make the examples interesting without making one chapter depend on another. When I use an important idea from another chapter, I include a note to help you find your way around.

In general, my advice is as follows:

- ✔ If you already know something, don't bother reading about it.
- ✔ If you're curious, don't be afraid to skip ahead. You can always sneak a peek at an earlier chapter if you really need to do so.

Conventions Used in This Book

Almost every technical book starts with a little typeface legend, and *Java For Dummies,* 6th Edition, is no exception. What follows is a brief explanation of the typefaces used in this book:

- ✔ New terms are set in *italics*.

- ✔ If you need to type something that's mixed in with the regular text, the characters you type appear in bold. For example: "Type **MyNewProject** in the text field."

- ✔ You also see this `computerese` font. I use computerese for Java code, filenames, web page addresses (URLs), onscreen messages, and other such things. Also, if something you need to type is really long, it appears in computerese font on its own line (or lines).

- ✔ You need to change certain things when you type them on your own computer keyboard. For instance, I may ask you to type

```
public class Anyname
```

which means that you type **public class** and then some name that you make up on your own. Words that you need to replace with your own words are set in *`italicized computerese`*.

What You Don't Have to Read

Pick the first chapter or section that has material you don't already know and start reading there. Of course, you may hate making decisions as much as I do. If so, here are some guidelines that you can follow:

- ✔ If you already know what kind of an animal Java is and know that you want to use Java, skip Chapter 1 and go straight to Chapter 2. Believe me, I won't mind.

- ✔ If you already know how to get a Java program running, and you don't care what happens behind the scenes when a Java program runs, then skip Chapter 2 and start with Chapter 3.

- ✔ If you write programs for a living but use any language other than C or C++, start with Chapter 2 or 3. When you reach Chapters 5 and 6, you'll probably find them to be easy reading. When you get to Chapter 7, it'll be time to dive in.

- ✔ If you write C (not C++) programs for a living, start with Chapters 2, 3, and 4 but just skim Chapters 5 and 6.

- ✔ If you write C++ programs for a living, glance at Chapters 2 and 3, skim Chapters 4 through 6, and start reading seriously in Chapter 7. (Java is a bit different from C++ in the way it handles classes and objects.)

- ✔ If you write Java programs for a living, come to my house and help me write *Java For Dummies,* 7th Edition.

If you want to skip the sidebars and the Technical Stuff icons, please do. In fact, if you want to skip anything at all, feel free.

Foolish Assumptions

In this book, I make a few assumptions about you, the reader. If one of these assumptions is incorrect, you're probably okay. If all these assumptions are incorrect . . . well, buy the book anyway.

- ✔ **I assume that you have access to a computer.** Here's the good news: You can run most of the code in this book on almost any computer. The only computers that you can't use to run this code are ancient things that are more than ten years old (give or take a few years).

- ✔ **I assume that you can navigate through your computer's common menus and dialog boxes.** You don't have to be a Windows, Linux, or Macintosh power user, but you should be able to start a program, find a file, put a file into a certain directory . . . that sort of thing. Most of the time, when you practice the stuff in this book, you're typing code on your keyboard, not pointing and clicking your mouse.

  On those rare occasions when you need to drag and drop, cut and paste, or plug and play, I guide you carefully through the steps. But your computer may be configured in any of several billion ways, and my instructions may not quite fit your special situation. So, when you reach one of these platform-specific tasks, try following the steps in this book. If the steps don't quite fit, consult a book with instructions tailored to your system.

- ✔ **I assume that you can think logically.** That's all there is to programming in Java — thinking logically. If you can think logically, you've got it made. If you don't believe that you can think logically, read on. You may be pleasantly surprised.

- ✔ **I make very few assumptions about your computer programming experience (or your lack of such experience).** In writing this book, I've tried to do the impossible. I've tried to make the book interesting for experienced programmers, yet accessible to people with little or no programming experience. This means that I don't assume any particular programming background on your part. If you've never created a loop or indexed an array, that's okay.

  On the other hand, if you've done these things (maybe in Visual Basic, COBOL, or C++), you'll discover some interesting plot twists in Java. The developers of Java took the best ideas in object-oriented programming, streamlined them, reworked them, and reorganized them into a sleek, powerful way of thinking about problems. You'll find many new, thought-provoking features in Java. As you find out about these features, many of them will seem very natural to you. One way or another, you'll feel good about using Java.

How This Book Is Organized

This book is divided into subsections, which are grouped into sections, which come together to make chapters, which are lumped finally into five parts. (When you write a book, you get to know your book's structure pretty well. After months of writing, you find yourself dreaming in sections and chapters when you go to bed at night.) The parts of the book are listed here.

Part I: Getting Started with Java

This part is your complete, executive briefing on Java. It includes some "What is Java?" material and a jump-start chapter — Chapter 3. In Chapter 3, you visit the major technical ideas and dissect a simple program.

Part II: Writing Your Own Java Program

Chapters 4 through 6 cover the fundamentals. These chapters describe the things that you need to know so you can get your computer humming along.

If you've written programs in Visual Basic, C++, or any another language, some of the material in Part II may be familiar to you. If so, you can skip some sections or read this stuff quickly. But don't read too quickly. Java is a little different from some other programming languages, especially in the things that I describe in Chapter 4.

Part III: Working with the Big Picture: Object-Oriented Programming

Part III has some of my favorite chapters. This part covers the all-important topic of object-oriented programming. In these chapters, you find out how to map solutions to big problems. (Sure, the examples in these chapters aren't big, but the examples involve big ideas.) In bite-worthy increments, you discover how to design classes, reuse existing classes, and construct objects.

Have you read any of those books that explain object-oriented programming in vague, general terms? I'm very proud to say that *Java For Dummies,* 6th Edition, isn't like that. In this book, I illustrate each concept with a simple-yet-concrete program example.

Part IV: Savvy Java Techniques

If you've tasted some Java and want more, you can find what you need in this part of the book. This part's chapters are devoted to details — the things that you don't see when you first glance at the material. So, after you read the earlier parts and write some programs on your own, you can dive in a little deeper by reading Part IV.

Part V: The Part of Tens

The Part of Tens is a little Java candy store. In the Part of Tens, you can find lists — lists of tips for avoiding mistakes, for finding resources, and for all kinds of interesting goodies.

Icons Used in This Book

If you could watch me write this book, you'd see me sitting at my computer, talking to myself. I say each sentence in my head. Most of the sentences I mutter several times. When I have an extra thought, a side comment, or something that doesn't belong in the regular stream, I twist my head a little bit. That way, whoever's listening to me (usually nobody) knows that I'm off on a momentary tangent.

Of course, in print, you can't see me twisting my head. I need some other way of setting a side thought in a corner by itself. I do it with icons. When you see a Tip icon or a Remember icon, you know that I'm taking a quick detour.

Here's a list of icons that I use in this book:

A tip is an extra piece of information — something helpful that the other books may forget to tell you.

Everyone makes mistakes. Heaven knows that I've made a few in my time. Anyway, when I think people are especially prone to make a mistake, I mark it with a Warning icon.

Question: What's stronger than a Tip, but not as strong as a Warning?

Answer: A Remember icon.

"If you don't remember what *such-and-such* means, see *blah-blah-blah*," or "For more information, read *blahhity-blah-blah*."

This icon calls attention to useful material that you can find online. (You don't have to wait long to see one of these icons. I use one at the end of this introduction!)

Occasionally, I run across a technical tidbit. The tidbit may help you understand what the people behind the scenes (the people who developed Java) were thinking. You don't have to read it, but you may find it useful. You may also find the tidbit helpful if you plan to read other (more geeky) books about Java.

Beyond the Book

I've written a lot of extra content that you won't find in this book. Go online to find the following:

- **Cheat Sheet:** Check out www.dummies.com/cheatsheet/java.

- **Online Articles:** On several of the pages that open each of this book's parts, you can find links to what the folks at *For Dummies* call Web Extras, which expand on some concept I've discussed in that particular section. You can find them at www.dummies.com/extras/java.

Where to Go from Here

If you've gotten this far, you're ready to start reading about Java application development. Think of me (the author) as your guide, your host, your personal assistant. I do everything I can to keep things interesting and, most importantly, to help you understand.

If you like what you read, send me a note. My e-mail address, which I created just for comments and questions about this book, is JavaForDummies@ allmycode.com. If e-mail and chat aren't your favorites, you can reach me instead on Twitter (@allmycode) and on Facebook (www.facebook.com/ allmycode). And don't forget — for the latest updates, visit this book's website. The site's address is www.allmycode.com/JavaForDummies.

Part I

Getting Started with Java

In this part . . .

- ✔ Find out about the tools you need for developing Java programs.
- ✔ Find out how Java fits into today's technology scene.
- ✔ See your first complete Java program.

Chapter 1

All about Java

Say what you want about computers. As far as I'm concerned, computers are good for just two simple reasons:

✔ **When computers do work, they feel no resistance, no stress, no boredom, and no fatigue.** Computers are our electronic slaves. I have my computer working 24/7 doing calculations for Cosmology@Home — a distributed computing project to investigate models describing the universe. Do I feel sorry for my computer because it's working so hard? Does the computer complain? Will the computer report me to the National Labor Relations Board? No.

I can make demands, give the computer its orders, and crack the whip. Do I (or should I) feel the least bit guilty? Not at all.

✔ **Computers move ideas, not paper.** Not long ago, when you wanted to send a message to someone, you hired a messenger. The messenger got on his or her horse and delivered your message personally. The message was on paper, parchment, a clay tablet, or whatever physical medium was available at the time.

This whole process seems wasteful now, but that's only because you and I are sitting comfortably in the electronic age. Messages are ideas, and physical things like ink, paper, and horses have little or nothing to do with real ideas; they're just temporary carriers for ideas (even though people used them to carry ideas for several centuries). Nevertheless, the ideas themselves are paperless, horseless, and messengerless.

The neat thing about computers is that they carry ideas efficiently. They carry nothing but the ideas, a couple of photons, and a little electrical power. They do this with no muss, no fuss, and no extra physical baggage.

When you start dealing efficiently with ideas, something very nice happens. Suddenly, all the overhead is gone. Instead of pushing paper and trees, you're pushing numbers and concepts. Without the overhead, you can do things much faster and do things that are far more complex than ever before.

What You Can Do with Java

It would be so nice if all this complexity were free, but unfortunately, it isn't. Someone has to think hard and decide exactly what to ask the computer to do. After that thinking, someone has to write a set of instructions for the computer to follow.

Given the current state of affairs, you can't write these instructions in English or any other language that people speak. Science fiction is filled with stories about people who say simple things to robots and get back disastrous, unexpected results. English and other such languages are unsuitable for communication with computers for several reasons:

- ✔ **An English sentence can be misinterpreted.** "Chew one tablet three times a day until finished."

- ✔ **It's difficult to weave a very complicated command in English.** "Join flange A to protuberance B, making sure to connect only the outermost lip of flange A to the larger end of the protuberance B, while joining the middle and inner lips of flange A to grommet C."

- ✔ **An English sentence has lots of extra baggage.** "Sentence has unneeded words."

- ✔ **English is difficult to interpret.** "As part of this Publishing Agreement between John Wiley & Sons, Inc. ('Wiley') and the Author ('Barry Burd'), Wiley shall pay the sum of one-thousand-two-hundred-fifty-seven dollars and sixty-three cents ($1,257.63) to the Author for partial submittal of *Java For Dummies,* 6th Edition ('the Work')."

To tell a computer what to do, you have to use a special language to write terse, unambiguous instructions. A special language of this kind is called a *computer programming language.* A set of instructions written in such a language is called a *program.* When looked at as a big blob, these instructions are called *software* or *code.* Here's what code looks like when it's written in Java:

```java
public class PayBarry {
    public static void main(String args[]) {

        double checkAmount = 1257.63;
        System.out.print("Pay to the order of ");
        System.out.print("Dr. Barry Burd ");
        System.out.print("$");
        System.out.println(checkAmount);
    }
}
```

Why You Should Use Java

It's time to celebrate! You've just picked up a copy of *Java For Dummies*, 6th Edition, and you're reading Chapter 1. At this rate, you'll be an expert Java programmer in no time at all, so rejoice in your eventual success by throwing a big party.

To prepare for the party, I'll bake a cake. I'm lazy, so I'll use a ready-to-bake cake mix. Let me see . . . add water to the mix and then add butter and eggs . . . Hey, wait! I just looked at the list of ingredients. What's MSG? And what about propylene glycol? That's used in antifreeze, isn't it?

I'll change plans and make the cake from scratch. Sure, it's a little harder, but that way I get exactly what I want.

Computer programs work the same way. You can use somebody else's program or write your own. If you use somebody else's program, you use whatever you get. When you write your own program, you can tailor the program especially for your needs.

Writing computer code is a big, worldwide industry. Companies do it, freelance professionals do it, hobbyists do it — all kinds of people do it. A typical big company has teams, departments, and divisions that write programs for the company. But you can write programs for yourself or someone else, for a living or for fun. In a recent estimate, the number of lines of code written each day by programmers in the United States alone exceeds the number of methane molecules on the planet Jupiter.* Take almost anything that can be done with a computer. With the right amount of time, you can write your own program to do it. (Of course, the "right amount of time" may be very long, but that's not the point. Many interesting and useful programs can be written in hours or even minutes.)

Getting Perspective: Where Java Fits In

Here's a brief history of modern computer programming:

✔ **1954–1957: FORTRAN is developed.**

   FORTRAN was the first modern computer programming language. For scientific programming, FORTRAN is a real racehorse. Year after year, FORTRAN is a leading language among computer programmers throughout the world.

---

*I made up this fact all by myself.

✔ **1959: Grace Hopper at Remington Rand develops the COBOL programming language.**

The letter *B* in COBOL stands for *Business,* and business is just what COBOL is all about. The language's primary feature is the processing of one record after another, one customer after another, or one employee after another.

Within a few years after its initial development, COBOL became the most widely used language for business data processing. Even today, COBOL represents a large part of the computer programming industry.

✔ **1972: Dennis Ritchie at AT&T Bell Labs develops the C programming language.**

The "look and feel" that you see in this book's examples comes from the C programming language. Code written in C uses curly braces, `if` statements, `for` statements, and so on.

In terms of power, you can use C to solve the same problems that you can solve by using FORTRAN, Java, or any other modern programming language. (You can write a scientific calculator program in COBOL, but doing that sort of thing would feel really strange.) The difference between one programming language and another isn't power. The difference is ease and appropriateness of use. That's where the Java language excels.

✔ **1986: Bjarne Stroustrup (again at AT&T Bell Labs) develops C++.**

Unlike its C language ancestor, the language C++ supports object-oriented programming. This support represents a huge step forward. (See the next section in this chapter.)

✔ **May 23, 1995: Sun Microsystems releases its first official version of the Java programming language.**

Java improves upon the concepts in C++. Java's "Write Once, Run Anywhere" philosophy makes the language ideal for distributing code across the Internet.

Additionally, Java is a great general-purpose programming language. With Java, you can write windowed applications, build and explore databases, control handheld devices, and more. Within five short years, the Java programming language had 2.5 million developers worldwide. (I know. I have a commemorative T-shirt to prove it.)

✔ **November 2000: The College Board announces that, starting in the year 2003, the Computer Science Advanced Placement exams will be based on Java.**

Wanna know what that snot-nosed kid living down the street is learning in high school? You guessed it — Java.

✔ **2002: Microsoft introduces a new language named C#.**

Many of the C# language features come directly from features in Java.

✔ **June 2004: Sys-Con Media reports that the demand for Java programmers tops the demand for C++ programmers by 50 percent** (`http://java.sys-con.com/node/48507`).

And there's more! The demand for Java programmers beats the combined demand for C++ and C# programmers by 8 percent. Java programmers are more employable than VB (Visual Basic) programmers by a whopping 190 percent.

✔ **2007: Google adopts Java as the primary language for creating apps on Android mobile devices.**

✔ **January 2010: Oracle Corporation purchases Sun Microsystems, bringing Java technology into the Oracle family of products.**

✔ **June 2010: eWeek ranks Java first among its "Top 10 Programming Languages to Keep You Employed"** (`www.eweek.com/c/a/Application-Development/Top-10-Programming-Languages-to-Keep-You-Employed-719257`).

✔ **August 2013: Java runs on more than 1.1 billion desktop computers** (`http://java.com/en/about`) **and Android Java runs on 250 million mobile phones** (`www.mobiledevicemanager.com/mobile-device-statistics/250-million-android-devices-in-use`).

Additionally, Java technology provides interactive capabilities to all Blu-ray devices and is the most popular programming language in the TIOBE Programming Community Index (`www.tiobe.com/index.php/content/paperinfo/tpci`), on PYPL: the PopularitY of Programming Language Index (`http://sites.google.com/site/pydatalog/pypl/PyPL-PopularitY-of-Programming-Language`), and on other indexes.

Well, I'm impressed.

Object-Oriented Programming (OOP)

It's three in the morning. I'm dreaming about the history course that I failed in high school. The teacher is yelling at me, "You have two days to study for the final exam, but you won't remember to study. You'll forget and feel guilty, guilty, guilty."

Suddenly, the phone rings. I'm awakened abruptly from my deep sleep. (Sure, I disliked dreaming about the history course, but I like being awakened even less.) At first, I drop the telephone on the floor. After fumbling to pick it up, I issue a grumpy, "Hello, who's this?" A voice answers, "I'm a reporter from *The New York Times*. I'm writing an article about Java, and I need to know all about the programming language in five words or less. Can you explain it?"

My mind is too hazy. I can't think. So I say the first thing that comes to my mind and then go back to sleep.

Come morning, I hardly remember the conversation with the reporter. In fact, I don't remember how I answered the question. Did I tell the reporter where he could put his article about Java?

I put on my robe and rush to the front of my house's driveway. As I pick up the morning paper, I glance at the front page and see the two-inch headline:

Burd Calls Java "A Great Object-Oriented Language"

Object-oriented languages

Java is object-oriented. What does that mean? Unlike languages, such as FORTRAN, that focus on giving the computer imperative "Do this/Do that" commands, object-oriented languages focus on data. Of course, object-oriented programs still tell the computer what to do. They start, however, by organizing the data, and the commands come later.

Object-oriented languages are better than "Do this/Do that" languages because they organize data in a way that helps people do all kinds of things with it. To modify the data, you can build on what you already have rather than scrap everything you've done and start over each time you need to do something new. Although computer programmers are generally smart people, they took a while to figure this out. For the full history lesson, see the sidebar "The winding road from FORTRAN to Java" (but I won't make you feel guilty if you don't read it).

Objects and their classes

In an object-oriented language, you use objects *and* classes to organize your data.

Imagine that you're writing a computer program to keep track of the houses in a new condominium development (still under construction). The houses differ only slightly from one another. Each house has a distinctive siding color, an indoor paint color, a kitchen cabinet style, and so on. In your object-oriented computer program, each house is an object.

But objects aren't the whole story. Although the houses differ slightly from one another, all the houses share the same list of characteristics. For instance, each house has a characteristic known as *siding color*. Each house has another characteristic known as *kitchen cabinet style*. In your object-oriented program, you need a master list containing all the characteristics that a house object can possess. This master list of characteristics is called a *class*.

The winding road from FORTRAN to Java

In the mid-1950s, a team of people created a programming language named FORTRAN. It was a good language, but it was based on the idea that you should issue direct, imperative commands to the computer. "Do this, computer. Then do that, computer." (Of course, the commands in a real FORTRAN program were much more precise than "Do this" or "Do that.")

In the years that followed, teams developed many new computer languages, and many of the languages copied the FORTRAN "Do this/Do that" model. One of the more popular "Do this/Do that" languages went by the one-letter name *C*. Of course, the "Do this/Do that" camp had some renegades. In languages named SIMULA and Smalltalk, programmers moved the imperative "Do this" commands into the background and concentrated on descriptions of data. In these languages, you didn't come right out and say, "Print a list of delinquent accounts." Instead, you began by saying, "This is what it means to be an account. An account has a name and a balance." Then you said, "This is how you ask an account whether it's delinquent." Suddenly, the data became king. An account was a thing that had a name, a balance, and a way of telling you whether it was delinquent.

Languages that focus first on the data are called *object-oriented* programming languages. These object-oriented languages make excellent programming tools. Here's why:

✔ Thinking first about the data makes you a good computer programmer.

✔ You can extend and reuse the descriptions of data over and over again. When you try to teach old FORTRAN programs new tricks, however, the old programs show how brittle they are. They break.

In the 1970s, object-oriented languages, such as SIMULA and Smalltalk, were buried in the computer hobbyist magazine articles. In the meantime, languages based on the old FORTRAN model were multiplying like rabbits.

So in 1986, a fellow named Bjarne Stroustrup created a language named C++. The C++ language became very popular because it mixed the old C language terminology with the improved object-oriented structure. Many companies turned their backs on the old FORTRAN/C programming style and adopted C++ as their standard.

But C++ had a flaw. Using C++, you could bypass all the object-oriented features and write a program by using the old FORTRAN/C programming style. When you started writing a C++ accounting program, you could take either fork in the road:

✔ You could start by issuing direct "Do this" commands to the computer, saying the mathematical equivalent of "Print a list of delinquent accounts, and make it snappy."

✔ You could take the object-oriented approach and begin by describing what it means to be an account.

Some people said that C++ offered the best of both worlds, but others argued that the first world (the world of FORTRAN and C) shouldn't be part of modern programming. If you gave a programmer an opportunity to write code either way, the programmer would too often choose to write code the wrong way.

So in 1995, James Gosling of Sun Microsystems created the language named *Java*. In creating Java, Gosling borrowed the look and feel of C++. But Gosling took most of the old "Do this/Do that" features of C++ and threw them in the trash. Then he added features that made the development of objects smoother and easier. All in all, Gosling created a language whose object-oriented philosophy is pure and clean. When you program in Java, you have no choice but to work with objects. That's the way it should be.

So there you have it. Object-oriented programming is misnamed. It should really be called "programming with classes and objects."

Now notice that I put the word *classes* first. How dare I do this! Well, maybe I'm not so crazy. Think again about a housing development that's under construction. Somewhere on the lot, in a rickety trailer parked on bare dirt, is a master list of characteristics known as a blueprint. An architect's blueprint is like an object-oriented programmer's class. A blueprint is a list of characteristics that each house will have. The blueprint says, "siding." The actual house object has gray siding. The blueprint says, "kitchen cabinet." The actual house object has Louis XIV kitchen cabinets.

The analogy doesn't end with lists of characteristics. Another important parallel exists between blueprints and classes. A year after you create the blueprint, you use it to build ten houses. It's the same with classes and objects. First, the programmer writes code to describe a class. Then when the program runs, the computer creates objects from the (blueprint) class.

So that's the real relationship between classes and objects. The programmer defines a class, and from the class definition, the computer makes individual objects.

What's so good about an object-oriented language?

Based on the previous section's story about home building, imagine that you've already written a computer program to keep track of the building instructions for houses in a new development. Then, the big boss decides on a modified plan — a plan in which half the houses have three bedrooms and the other half have four.

If you use the old FORTRAN/C style of computer programming, your instructions look like this:

```
Dig a ditch for the basement.
Lay concrete around the sides of the ditch.
Put two-by-fours along the sides for the basement's frame.
. . .
```

This would be like an architect creating a long list of instructions instead of a blueprint. To modify the plan, you have to sort through the list to find the instructions for building bedrooms. To make things worse, the instructions could be scattered among pages 234, 394–410, 739, 10, and 2. If the builder had to decipher other peoples' complicated instructions, the task would be ten times harder.

Starting with a class, however, is like starting with a blueprint. If you decide to have both three- and four-bedroom houses, you can start with a blueprint called the *house* blueprint that has a ground floor and a second floor, but has no indoor walls drawn on the second floor. Then you make two more second-floor blueprints — one for the three-bedroom house and another for the four-bedroom house. (You name these new blueprints the *three-bedroom house* blueprint and the *four-bedroom house* blueprint.)

Your builder colleagues are amazed with your sense of logic and organization, but they have concerns. They pose a question. "You called one of the blueprints the 'three-bedroom house' blueprint. How can you do this if it's a blueprint for a second floor and not for a whole house?"

You smile knowingly and answer, "The three-bedroom house blueprint can say, 'For info about the lower floors, see the original house blueprint.' That way, the three-bedroom house blueprint describes a whole house. The four-bedroom house blueprint can say the same thing. With this setup, we can take advantage of all the work we already did to create the original house blueprint and save lots of money."

In the language of object-oriented programming, the three- and four-bedroom house classes are *inheriting* the features of the original house class. You can also say that the three- and four-bedroom house classes are *extending* the original house class. (See Figure 1-1.)

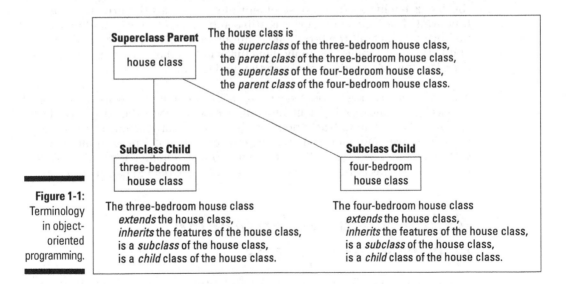

Superclass Parent
house class

The house class is
the *superclass* of the three-bedroom house class,
the *parent class* of the three-bedroom house class,
the *superclass* of the four-bedroom house class,
the *parent class* of the four-bedroom house class.

Subclass Child
three-bedroom house class

Subclass Child
four-bedroom house class

Figure 1-1:
Terminology in object-oriented programming.

The three-bedroom house class
extends the house class,
inherits the features of the house class,
is a *subclass* of the house class,
is a *child* class of the house class.

The four-bedroom house class
extends the house class,
inherits the features of the house class,
is a *subclass* of the house class,
is a *child* class of the house class.

The original house class is called the *superclass* of the three- and four-bedroom house classes. In that vein, the three- and four-bedroom house classes are *subclasses* of the original house class. Put another way, the original house class is called the *parent class* of three- and four-bedroom house classes. The three- and four-bedroom house classes are *child classes* of the original house class. (See Figure 1-1.)

Needless to say, your homebuilder colleagues are jealous. A crowd of homebuilders is mobbing around you to hear about your great ideas. So, at that moment, you drop one more bombshell: "By creating a class with subclasses, we can reuse the blueprint in the future. If someone comes along and wants a five-bedroom house, we can extend our original house blueprint by making a five-bedroom house blueprint. We'll never have to spend money for an original house blueprint again."

"But," says a colleague in the back row, "what happens if someone wants a different first-floor design? Do we trash the original house blueprint or start scribbling all over the original blueprint? That'll cost big bucks, won't it?"

In a confident tone, you reply, "We don't have to mess with the original house blueprint. If someone wants a Jacuzzi in his living room, we can make a new, small blueprint describing only the new living room and call this the *Jacuzzi-in-living-room house* blueprint. Then, this new blueprint can refer to the original house blueprint for info on the rest of the house (the part that's not in the living room)." In the language of object-oriented programming, the Jacuzzi-in-living-room house blueprint still *extends* the original house blueprint. The Jacuzzi blueprint is still a subclass of the original house blueprint. In fact, all the terminology about superclass, parent class, and child class still applies. The only thing that's new is that the Jacuzzi blueprint *overrides* the living room features in the original house blueprint.

In the days before object-oriented languages, the programming world experienced a crisis in software development. Programmers wrote code, then discovered new needs, and then had to trash their code and start from scratch. This problem happened over and over again because the code that the programmers were writing couldn't be reused. Object-oriented programming changed all this for the better (and, as Burd said, Java is "A Great Object-Oriented Language").

Refining your understanding of classes and objects

When you program in Java, you work constantly with classes and objects. These two ideas are really important. That's why, in this chapter, I hit you over the head with one analogy after another about classes and objects.

Close your eyes for a minute and think about what it means for something to be a chair. . . .

A chair has a seat, a back, and legs. Each seat has a shape, a color, a degree of softness, and so on. These are the properties that a chair possesses. What I describe is *chairness* — the notion of something being a chair. In object-oriented terminology, I'm describing the Chair class.

Now peek over the edge of this book's margin and take a minute to look around your room. (If you're not sitting in a room right now, fake it.)

Several chairs are in the room, and each chair is an object. Each of these objects is an example of that ethereal thing called the Chair class. So that's how it works — the class is the idea of *chairness,* and each individual chair is an object.

A class isn't quite a collection of things. Instead, a class is the idea behind a certain kind of thing. When I talk about the class of chairs in your room, I'm talking about the fact that each chair has legs, a seat, a color, and so on. The colors may be different for different chairs in the room, but that doesn't matter. When you talk about a class of things, you're focusing on the properties that each of the things possesses.

It makes sense to think of an object as being a concrete instance of a class. In fact, the official terminology is consistent with this thinking. If you write a Java program in which you define a Chair class, each actual chair (the chair that you're sitting on, the empty chair right next to you, and so on) is called an *instance* of the Chair class.

Here's another way to think about a class. Imagine a table displaying all three of your bank accounts. (See Table 1-1.)

Table 1-1	A Table of Accounts	
Account Number	*Type*	*Balance*
16-13154-22864-7	Checking	174.87
1011 1234 2122 0000	Credit	−471.03
16-17238-13344-7	Savings	247.38

Think of the table's column headings as a class, and think of each row of the table as an object. The table's column headings describe the Account class.

According to the table's column headings, each account has an account number, a type, and a balance. Rephrased in the terminology of object-oriented programming, each object in the Account class (that is, each instance of the Account class) has an account number, a type, and a balance. So, the bottom row of the table is an object with account number *16-17238-13344-7*. This same object has type *Savings* and a balance of *247.38*. If you opened a new account, you would have another object, and the table would grow an additional row. The new object would be an instance of the same Account class.

What's Next?

This chapter is filled with general descriptions of things. A general description is good when you're just getting started, but you don't really understand things until you get to know some specifics. That's why the next several chapters deal with specifics.

So please, turn the page. The next chapter can't wait for you to read it.

Chapter 2

All about Software

. . . .

In This Chapter

▶ Understanding the roles of the software development tools

▶ Selecting the version of Java that's right for you

▶ Preparing to write and run Java programs

. . . .

*T*he best way to get to know Java is to do Java. When you're doing Java, you're writing, testing, and running your own Java programs. This chapter gets you ready to do Java by describing the *general* software setup — the software that you must have on your computer whether you run Windows, Mac, Linux, or Joe's Private Operating System. This chapter *doesn't* describe the specific setup instructions for Windows, for a Mac, or for any other system.

For setup instructions that are specific to your system, visit this book's website (www.allmycode.com/JavaForDummies).

Quick-Start Instructions

If you're a seasoned veteran of computers and computing (whatever that means), and if you're too jumpy to get detailed instructions from this book's website, you can try installing the required software by following this section's general instructions. The instructions work for many computers, but not all. And this section provides no detailed steps, no if-this-then-do-that alternatives, and no this-works-but-you're-better-off-doing-something-else tips.

To prepare your computer for writing Java programs, follow these steps:

1. **Visit Java.com.**

   Follow the instructions at http://java.com to download and install Java.

2. **Optionally, visit** `www.oracle.com/technetwork/java/javase/downloads`.

   Follow the instructions at that website to download and install the Java SE documentation (also known as the *Javadoc pages* or the *Java SE API Docs*).

3. **Visit Eclipse.org.**

   Follow the instructions at `http://eclipse.org/downloads` to download and install Eclipse.

   Eclipse's download page offers several different packages, including Eclipse Classic, Eclipse for Java EE, Eclipse for JavaScript, and others. To run this book's examples, you need a relatively small Eclipse package — the Eclipse IDE for Java Developers.

4. **Test your installed software.**

   a. Launch Eclipse.

   b. In Eclipse, create a new Java project.

   c. Within the Java project, create a new Java class named Displayer.

   d. Edit the new `Displayer.java` *file by typing the code from Listing 3-1 (the first code listing in Chapter 3). Type the code in Eclipse's editor pane.*

   e. Run `Displayer.java` *and check to make sure that the run's output reads* `You'll love Java!`.

That's it! But remember, not everyone (computer geek or not) can follow these skeletal instructions flawlessly. So you have several alternatives:

✔ **Visit this book's website.**

   Do not pass "go." Do not try this section's quick-start instructions. Follow the more detailed instructions that you find at `www.allmycode.com/JavaForDummies`.

✔ **Try this section's quick-start instructions.**

   You can't hurt anything by trying. If you accidentally install the wrong software, you can probably leave the wrong software on your computer. (You don't have to uninstall it.) If you're not sure whether you've installed the software correctly, you can always fall back on my website's detailed instructions.

✔ **E-mail your questions to me at** `JavaForDummies@allmycode.com`.

✔ **Tweet me at** `@allmycode`.

✔ **Visit my** `/allmycode` **Facebook page.**

   I like hearing from readers.

What You Install on Your Computer

I once met a tool and die maker. He used tools to make tools (and dies). I was happy to meet him because I knew that, one day, I'd make an analogy between computer programmers and tool and die makers.

A computer programmer uses existing programs as tools to create new programs. The existing programs and new programs might perform very different kinds of tasks. For example, a Java program (a program that you create) might keep track of a business's customers. To create that customer-tracking program, you might use an existing program that looks for errors in your Java code. This general-purpose error-finding program can find errors in any kind of Java code — customer-tracking code, weather-predicting code, gaming code, or the code for an app on your mobile phone.

So how many tools do you need for creating Java programs? As a novice, you need three tools:

✔ **You need a *compiler*.**

A compiler takes the Java code that you write and turns that code into something that can run on your computer.

✔ **You need a *Java Virtual Machine* (JVM).**

A Java Virtual Machine runs your code (and other peoples' Java code) on your computer.

✔ **You need an *integrated development environment* (IDE).**

An integrated development environment helps you manage your Java code and provides convenient ways for you to write, compile, and run your code.

To be honest, you don't actually *need* an integrated development environment. In fact, some developers take pride in using plain, old text editors such as Windows Notepad or the vi editor in Unix. But, as a novice developer, a full-featured IDE makes your life much, much easier.

The World Wide Web has free, downloadable versions of each of these tools. For example, the quick-start instructions near the beginning of this chapter advise you to visit Java.com and Eclipse.org. By clicking a button on a Java.com page, you install a Java Virtual Machine on your computer. At Eclipse.org, you download the Eclipse integrated development environment, which comes with its own built-in Java compiler. (You get two of the three tools in one download. Not bad!)

The rest of this chapter describes compilers, JVMs, and IDEs.

This chapter provides background information about software you need on your computer. But the chapter contains absolutely no detailed instructions to help you install the software. For detailed instructions, visit this book's website (www.allmycode.com/JavaForDummies).

What is a compiler?

"A compiler takes the Java code that you write and turns that code into something that can run on your computer."

–Barry Burd, *Java For Dummies,* 6th Edition

You're a human being. (Sure, every rule has exceptions. But if you're reading this book, you're probably human.) Anyway, humans can write and comprehend the code in Listing 2-1.

Listing 2-1: Looking for a Vacant Room

```
// This is part of a Java program
// (not a complete Java program).
roomNum = 1;
while (roomNum < 100) {
    if (guests[roomNum] == 0) {
        out.println("Room " + roomNum
                + " is available.");
        exit(0);
    } else {
        roomNum++;
    }
}
out.println("No vacancy");
```

The Java code in Listing 2-1 checks for vacancies in a small hotel (a hotel with room numbers 1 to 99). You can't run the code in Listing 2-1 without adding several additional lines. But here in Chapter 2, those additional lines aren't important. What's important is that, by staring at the code, squinting a bit, and looking past all the code's strange punctuation, you can see what the code is trying to do:

```
Set the room number to 1.
As long as the room number is less than 100,
    Check the number of guests in the room.
    If the number of guests in the room is 0, then
        report that the room is available,
        and stop.
    Otherwise,
        prepare to check the next room by
        adding 1 to the room number.
If you get to the non-existent room number 100, then
    report that there are no vacancies.
```

If you don't see the similarities between Listing 2-1 and its English equivalent, don't worry. You're reading *Java For Dummies,* 6th Edition, and like most human beings, you can learn to read and write the code in Listing 2-1. The code in Listing 2-1 is called *Java source code.*

So here's the catch: Computers aren't human beings. Computers don't normally follow instructions like the instructions in Listing 2-1. That is, computers don't follow Java source code instructions. Instead, computers follow cryptic instructions like the ones in Listing 2-2.

Listing 2-2:   Listing 2-1 Translated into Java Bytecode

```
aload_0
iconst_1
putfield Hotel/roomNum I
goto 32
aload_0
getfield Hotel/guests [I
aload_0
getfield Hotel/roomNum I
iaload
ifne 26
getstatic java/lang/System/out Ljava/io/PrintStream;
new java/lang/StringBuilder
dup
ldc "Room "
invokespecial java/lang/StringBuilder/<init>(Ljava/lang/String;)V
aload_0
getfield Hotel/roomNum I
invokevirtual java/lang/StringBuilder/append(I)Ljava/lang/StringBuilder;
ldc " is available."
invokevirtual
   java/lang/StringBuilder/append(Ljava/lang/String;)Ljava/lang/StringBuilder;
invokevirtual java/lang/StringBuilder/toString()Ljava/lang/String;
invokevirtual java/io/PrintStream/println(Ljava/lang/String;)V
iconst_0
invokestatic java/lang/System/exit(I)V
goto 32
aload_0
dup
getfield Hotel/roomNum I
iconst_1
iadd
putfield Hotel/roomNum I
aload_0
getfield Hotel/roomNum I
bipush 100
if_icmplt 5
getstatic java/lang/System/out Ljava/io/PrintStream;
ldc "No vacancy"
invokevirtual java/io/PrintStream/println(Ljava/lang/String;)V
return
```

The instructions in Listing 2-2 aren't Java source code instructions. They're *Java bytecode* instructions. When you write a Java program, you write source code instructions (like the instructions in Listing 2-1). After writing the source code, you run a program (that is, you apply a tool) to your source code. The program is a *compiler.* The compiler translates your source code instructions into Java bytecode instructions. In other words, the compiler takes code that you can write and understand (like the code in Listing 2-1) and translates it into code that a computer can execute (like the code in Listing 2-2).

You might put your source code in a file named `Hotel.java`. If so, the compiler probably puts the Java bytecode in another file named `Hotel.class`. Normally, you don't bother looking at the bytecode in the `Hotel.class` file. In fact, the compiler doesn't encode the `Hotel.class` file as ordinary text, so you can't examine the bytecode with an ordinary editor. If you try to open `Hotel.class` with Notepad, TextEdit, KWrite, or even Microsoft Word, you'll see nothing but dots, squiggles, and other gobbledygook. To create Listing 2-2, I had to apply yet another tool to my `Hotel.class` file. That tool displays a text-like version of a Java bytecode file. I used Ando Saabas's Java Bytecode Editor (`www.cs.ioc.ee/~ando/jbe`).

No one (except for a few crazy developers in some isolated labs in faraway places) writes Java bytecode. You run software (a compiler) to create Java bytecode. The only reason to look at Listing 2-2 is to understand what a hard worker your computer is.

What is a Java Virtual Machine?

> *"A Java Virtual Machine runs your code (and other peoples' Java code) on your computer."*
>
> –Barry Burd, *Java For Dummies,* 6th Edition

In the preceding "What is a compiler?" section, I make a big fuss about computers following instructions like the ones in Listing 2-2. As fusses go, it's a very nice fuss. But if you don't read every fussy word, you may be misguided. The exact wording is "... computers follow cryptic instructions *like* the ones in Listing 2-2." The instructions in Listing 2-2 are a lot like instructions that a computer can execute, but generally, computers don't execute Java bytecode instructions. Instead, each kind of computer processor has its own set of executable instructions, and each computer operating system uses the processor's instructions in a slightly different way.

Here's a hypothetical situation: Imagine that you run the Linux operating system on a computer that has an old Pentium processor. Your friend runs Linux on a computer with a different kind of processor — a PowerPC processor. (In the 1990s, Intel Corporation made Pentium processors, and IBM made PowerPC processors.)

Listing 2-3 contains a set of instructions to display Hello world! on the computer screen.[*] The instructions work on a Pentium processor running the Linux operating system.

Listing 2-3: A Simple Program for a Pentium Processor

```
.data

msg:
        .ascii  "Hello, world!\n"
        len = . - msg

.text

    .global _start

_start:

        movl    $len,%edx
        movl    $msg,%ecx
        movl    $1,%ebx
        movl    $4,%eax
        int     $0x80


        movl    $0,%ebx
        movl    $1,%eax
        int     $0x80
```

Listing 2-4 contains another set of instructions to display Hello world! on the screen.[**] The instructions in Listing 2-4 work on a PowerPC processor running Linux.

---

[*] I paraphrase these Intel instructions from Konstantin Boldyshev's *Linux Assembly HOWTO* (http://tldp.org/HOWTO/Assembly-HOWTO/hello.html).

[**] I paraphrase the PowerPC code from Hollis Blanchard's PowerPC Assembly page (www.ibm.com/developerworks/library/1-ppc). Hollis also reviewed and critiqued this "What is a Java Virtual Machine?" section for me. Thank you, Hollis.

Listing 2-4: A Simple Program for a PowerPC Processor

```
.data

msg:
        .string "Hello, world!\n"
        len     = . - msg

.text

        .global _start
_start:

        li      0,4
        li      3,1

        lis     4,msg@ha
        addi    4,4,msg@l
        li      5,len
        sc


        li      0,1
        li      3,1
        sc
```

The instructions in Listing 2-3 run smoothly on a Pentium processor. But these instructions mean nothing to a PowerPC processor. Likewise, the instructions in Listing 2-4 run nicely on a PowerPC, but these same instructions are complete gibberish to a computer with a Pentium processor. So your friend's PowerPC software might not be available on your computer. And your Intel computer's software might not run at all on your friend's computer.

Now go to your cousin's house. Your cousin's computer has a Pentium processor (just like yours), but your cousin's computer runs Windows instead of Linux. What does your cousin's computer do when you feed it the Pentium code in Listing 2-3? It screams, "Not a valid Win32 application" or "Windows can't open this file." What a mess!

Java bytecode creates order from all this chaos. Java bytecode is something like the code in Listings 2-3 and 2-4, but Java bytecode isn't specific to one kind of processor or to one operating system. Instead, a set of Java bytecode instructions runs on any computer. If you write a Java program and compile that Java program into bytecode, then your computer can run the bytecode, your friend's computer can run the bytecode, your grandmother's supercomputer can run the bytecode, and with any luck, your cellphone or tablet can run the bytecode.

For a look at some Java bytecode, see Listing 2-2. But remember, you never have to write or decipher Java bytecode. Writing bytecode is the compiler's job. Deciphering bytecode is the Java Virtual Machine's job.

With Java, you can take a bytecode file that you created with a Windows computer, copy the bytecode to who-knows-what kind of computer, and then run the bytecode with no trouble at all. That's one of the many reasons why Java has become popular so quickly. This outstanding feature, which gives you the ability to run code on many different kinds of computers, is called *portability*.

What makes Java bytecode so versatile? This fantastic universality enjoyed by Java bytecode programs comes from the Java Virtual Machine. The Java Virtual Machine is one of those three tools that you must have on your computer.

Imagine that you're the Windows representative to the United Nations Security Council. (See Figure 2-1.) The Macintosh representative is seated to your right, and the Linux representative is on your left. (Naturally, you don't get along with either of these people. You're always cordial to one another, but you're never sincere. What do you expect? It's politics!) The distinguished representative from Java is at the podium. The Java representative is speaking in bytecode, and neither you nor your fellow ambassadors (Mac and Linux) understand a word of Java bytecode.

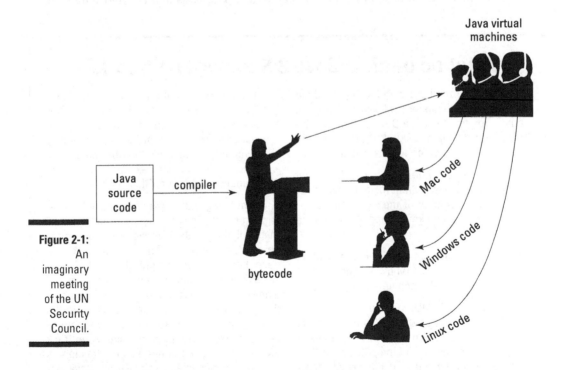

Figure 2-1:
An imaginary meeting of the UN Security Council.

But each of you has an interpreter. Your interpreter translates from bytecode to Windows while the Java representative speaks. Another interpreter translates from bytecode to Macintosh-ese. And a third interpreter translates bytecode into Linux-speak.

Think of your interpreter as a virtual ambassador. The interpreter doesn't really represent your country, but the interpreter performs one of the important tasks that a real ambassador performs. The interpreter listens to bytecode on your behalf. The interpreter does what you would do if your native language were Java bytecode. The interpreter pretends to be the Windows ambassador, and sits through the boring bytecode speech, taking in every word, and processing each word in some way or other.

You have an interpreter — a virtual ambassador. In the same way, a Windows computer runs its own bytecode-interpreting software. That software is the Java Virtual Machine.

A Java Virtual Machine is a proxy, an errand boy, a go-between. The JVM serves as an interpreter between Java's run-anywhere bytecode and your computer's own system. While it runs, the JVM walks your computer through the execution of bytecode instructions. The JVM examines your bytecode, bit by bit, and carries out the instructions described in the bytecode. The JVM interprets bytecode for your Windows system, your Mac, or your Linux box, or for whatever kind of computer you're using. That's a good thing. It's what makes Java programs more portable than programs in any other language.

What on earth is Java 2 Standard Edition 1.2?

If you poke around the web looking for Java tools, you find things with all kinds of strange names. You find the Java Development Kit, the Software Development Kit, the Java Runtime Environment, and other confusing names.

✔ The names *Java Development Kit* (JDK) and *Software Development Kit* (SDK) stand for different versions of the same toolset — a toolset whose key component is a Java compiler.

✔ The name *Java Runtime Environment* (JRE) stands for a toolset whose key component is a Java Virtual Machine.

If you install the JDK on your computer, the JRE comes along with it. You can also get the JRE on its own. In fact, you can have many combinations of the JDK and JRE on your computer. For example, my Windows computer currently has JDK 1.6, JDK 1.8, and JRE 8 in its `c:\program files\Java` directory and has JRE 7 in its `c:\program files (x86)\Java` directory. Only occasionally do I run into any version conflicts. If you suspect that you're experiencing a version conflict, it's best to uninstall all JDK and JRE versions except the latest (for example, JDK 1.8 or JRE 8).

The numbering of Java versions can be confusing. Instead of "Java 1," "Java 2," and "Java 3," the numbering of Java versions winds through an obstacle course. This sidebar's figure describes the development of new Java versions over time. Each Java version has several names. The *product version* is an official name that's used for the world in general, and the *developer version* is a number that identifies versions so that programmers can keep track of them. (In casual conversation, developers use all kinds of names for the various Java versions.) The *code name* is a more playful name that identifies a version while it's being created.

Platform	Codename	Features
1995 (Beta)		
1996 JDK* 1.0		
1997 JDK 1.1		Inner classes, Java Beans, Reflection
1998 J2SE* 1.2	Playground	Swing classes for creation of GUI interfaces
1999		
2000 J2SE 1.3	Kestrel	Java Naming and Directory Interface (JNDI)
2001		
2002 J2SE 1.4	Merlin	New I/O, regular expressions, XML parsing
2003		
2004 J2SE 5.0	Tiger	Generic types, annotations, enum types, varargs, enhanced for
2005		statement, static imports, new concurrency classes
2006 Java SE* 6	Mustang	Scripting language support, performance enhancements
2007		
2008		
2009		
2010		
2011 Java SE 7	Dolphin	Strings in switch statement, catching multiple exceptions
2012		try statement with resources, integration with JavaFX
2013		
2014 Java SE 8		Lambda expressions

The asterisks in the figure mark changes in the formulation of Java product-version names. Back in 1996, the product versions were *Java Development Kit 1.0* and *Java Development Kit 1.1*. In 1998, someone decided to christen the product *Java 2 Standard Edition 1.2*, which confuses everyone to this day. At the time, anyone using the term *Java Development Kit* was asked to use *Software Development Kit* (SDK) instead.

In 2004 the *1.* business went away from the platform version name, and in 2006 Java platform names lost the *2* and the *.0*.

By far the most significant changes for Java developers came about in 2004. With the release of J2SE 5.0, the overseers of Java made changes to the language by adding new features — features such as generic types, annotations, and the enhanced for statement. (To see Java annotations in action, go to Chapters 8 and 9. For examples of the use of the enhanced for statement and generic types, see Chapters 11 and 12.)

Most of the programs in this book run only with Java 5.0 or later. They don't run with any version earlier than Java 5.0. Particularly, they don't run with Java 1.4 or Java 1.4.2. A few of this book's examples don't run with Java 8 or lower. But don't worry too much about Java version numbers. Java 6 or 7 is better than no Java at all. You can learn a lot about Java without having the latest Java version.

Developing software

"All this has happened before, and it will all happen again."

—*Peter Pan* (J.M. Barrie) and *Battlestar Galactica*
(2003–2009, NBC Universal)

When you create a Java program, you repeat the same steps over and over again. Figure 2-2 illustrates the cycle.

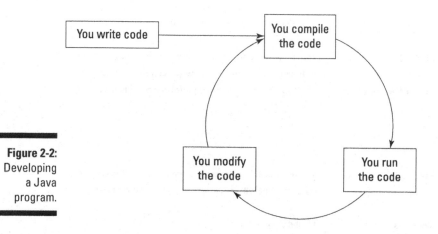

Figure 2-2:
Developing
a Java
program.

First, you write a program. After writing the first draft, you repeatedly compile, run, and modify the program. With a little experience, the compile and run steps become very easy. In many cases, one mouse click starts the compilation or the run.

However, writing the first draft and modifying the code are not one-click tasks. Developing code requires time and concentration.

Never be discouraged when the first draft of your code doesn't work. For that matter, never be discouraged when the 25th draft of your code doesn't work. Rewriting code is one of the most important things you can do (aside from ensuring world peace).

For detailed instructions on compiling and running Java programs, visit this book's website (www.allmycode.com/JavaForDummies).

When people talk about writing programs, they use the wording in Figure 2-2. They say, "You compile the code" and "You run the code." But the "you" isn't always accurate, and the "code" differs slightly from one part of the cycle to the next. Figure 2-3 describes the cycle from Figure 2-2 in a bit more detail.

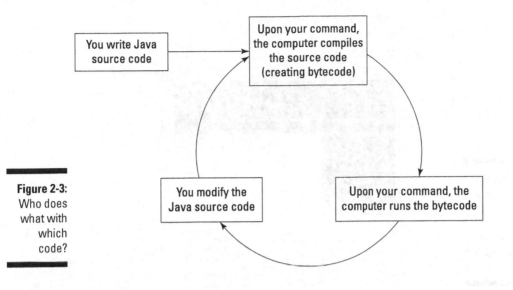

Figure 2-3:
Who does
what with
which
code?

For most people's needs, Figure 2-3 contains too much information. If I click a Run icon, I don't have to remember that the computer runs code on my behalf. And for all I care, the computer can run my original Java code or some bytecode knock-off of my original Java code. The details in Figure 2-3 aren't important. The only use for Figure 2-3 is to help you if the loose wording in Figure 2-2 confuses you. If Figure 2-2 doesn't confuse you, then ignore Figure 2-3.

What is an Integrated Development Environment?

"An integrated development environment helps you manage your Java code and provides convenient ways for you to write, compile, and run your code."

–Barry Burd, *Java For Dummies*, 6th Edition

In the olden days, writing and running a Java program involved opening several windows — a window for typing the program, another window for running the program, and maybe a third window to keep track of all the code that you've written. (See Figure 2-4.)

An integrated development environment seamlessly combines all this functionality into one well-organized application. (See Figure 2-5.)

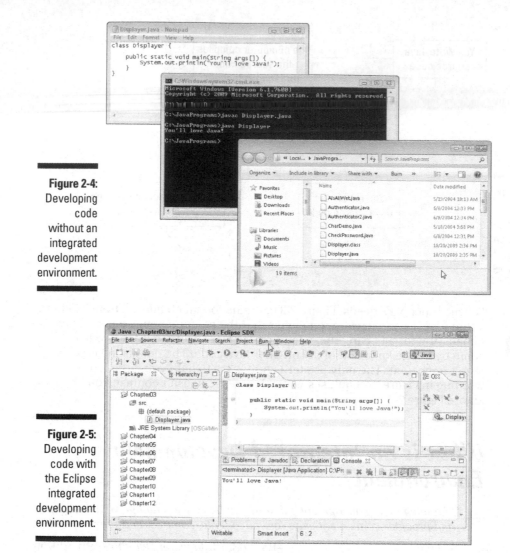

Figure 2-4:
Developing code without an integrated development environment.

Figure 2-5:
Developing code with the Eclipse integrated development environment.

Java has its share of integrated development environments. Some of the more popular products include Eclipse, IntelliJ IDEA, and NetBeans. Some fancy environments even have drag-and-drop components so that you can design your graphical interface visually. (See Figure 2-6.)

Figure 2-6:
Using the
drag-and-
drop Swing
GUI Builder
in the
NetBeans
IDE.

To run a program, you might click a toolbar button or choose Run from a menu. To compile a program, you might not have to do anything at all. (You might not even have to issue a command. Some IDEs compile your code automatically while you type it.)

For help with installing and using an integrated development environment, see this book's website (www.allmycode.com/JavaForDummies).

Chapter 3

Using the Basic Building Blocks

In This Chapter

▶ Speaking the Java language: the API and the Language Specification

▶ Understanding the parts of a simple program

▶ Documenting your code

"Все мысли, которые имеют огромные последствия всегда просты. (All great ideas are simple.)"

— Leo Tolstoy

The quotation applies to all kinds of things — things like life, love, and computer programming. That's why this chapter takes a multilayered approach. In this chapter, you get your first details about Java programming. And in discovering details, you'll see the simplicities.

Speaking the Java Language

If you try to picture in your mind the entire English language, what do you see? Maybe you see words, words, words. (That's what Hamlet saw.) Looking at the language under a microscope, you see one word after another. The bunch-of-words image is fine, but if you step back a bit, you may see two other things:

✔ The language's grammar

✔ Thousands of expressions, sayings, idioms, and historical names

The first category (the grammar) includes rules like, "The verb agrees with the noun in number and person." The second category (expressions, sayings, and stuff) includes knowledge like, "Julius Caesar was a famous Roman emperor, so don't name your son Julius Caesar, unless you want him to get beaten up every day after school."

The Java programming language has all the aspects of a spoken language like English. Java has words, grammar, commonly used names, stylistic idioms, and other such things.

The grammar and the common names

The people at Sun Microsystems who created Java thought of Java as having two parts. Just as English has its grammar and commonly used names, the Java programming language has its specification (its grammar) and its Application Programming Interface (its commonly used names). Whenever I write Java programs, I keep two important pieces of documentation — one for each part of the language — on my desk:

- ✔ **The Java Language Specification:** This documentation includes rules like, "Always put an open parenthesis after the word *for*" and "Use an asterisk to multiply two numbers."

- ✔ **The Application Programming Interface:** Java's Application Programming Interface (API) contains thousands of tools that were added to Java after the language's grammar was defined. These tools range from the commonplace to the exotic. For instance, the tools include a routine named *pow* that can raise 5 to the 10th power for you. A more razzle-dazzle tool (named JFrame) displays a window on your computer's screen. Other tools listen for the user's button clicks, query databases, and do all kinds of useful things.

You can download the Language Specification, the API documents, and all the other Java documentation (or view the documents online) by poking around at `http://docs.oracle.com/javase/specs`. But watch out! This web page is a moving target. By the time you read this book, the link in this paragraph will probably be out of date. The safest thing to do is to start at Java.Sun.com and then look for links to things like "Java SE" (short for "Java Standard Edition") and "reference" or "documentation."

The first part of Java, the Language Specification, is relatively small. That doesn't mean you won't take plenty of time finding out how to use the rules in the Language Specification. Other programming languages, however, have double, triple, or ten times the number of rules.

The second part of Java — the API — can be intimidating because it's so large. The API contains nearly 4,000 tools and keeps growing with each new Java language release. Pretty scary, eh? Well, the good news is that you don't have to memorize anything in the API. Nothing. None of it. You can look up the stuff you need to use in the documentation and ignore the stuff you don't need. What you use often, you'll remember. What you don't use often, you'll forget (like any other programmer).

No one knows all there is to know about the Java API. If you're a Java programmer who frequently writes programs that open new windows, you know how to use the API JFrame class. If you seldom write programs that open windows, the first few times you need to create a window, you can look up the JFrame class in the API documentation. My guess is that if you took a typical Java programmer and kept that programmer from looking up anything in the API documentation, the programmer would be able to use less than 2 percent of all the tools in the Java API.

You may love the _For Dummies_ style, but unfortunately, Java's official API documentation isn't written that way. The API documentation is both concise and precise. For some help deciphering the API documentation's language and style, see this book's website (www.allmycode.com/JavaForDummies).

In a way, nothing about the Java API is special. Whenever you write a Java program — even the smallest, simplest Java program — you create a class that's on par with any of the classes defined in the official Java API. The API is just a set of classes and other tools that were created by ordinary programmers who happen to participate in the official Java Community Process (JCP) and in the OpenJDK Project. Unlike the tools that you create, the tools in the API are distributed with every version of Java. (I'm assuming that you, the reader, are not a participant in the Java Community Process or the OpenJDK Project. But, with a fine book like _Java For Dummies,_ 6th Edition, one never knows.)

If you're interested in the JCP's activities, visit www.jcp.org. If you're interested in the OpenJDK Project, visit http://openjdk.java.net.

The folks at the JCP don't keep the Java programs in the official Java API a secret. If you want, you can look at all these programs. When you install Java on your computer, the installation puts a file named src.zip on your hard drive. You can open src.zip with your favorite unzipping program. There, before your eyes, is all the Java API code.

The words in a Java program

A hard-core Javateer will say that the Java programming language has two kinds of words: keywords and identifiers. This is true. But the bare truth, without any other explanation, is sometimes misleading. So I recommend dressing up the truth a bit and thinking in terms of three kinds of words: keywords, identifiers that ordinary programmers like you and I create, and identifiers from the API.

The differences among these three kinds of words are similar to the differences among words in the English language. In the sentence "Sam is a person," the word *person* is like a Java keyword. No matter who uses the word *person,* the word always means roughly the same thing. (Sure, you can think of bizarre exceptions in English usage, but please don't.)

The word *Sam* is like a Java identifier because Sam is a name for a particular person. Words like *Sam, Dinswald,* and *McGillimaroo* aren't prepacked with meaning in the English language. These words apply to different people depending on the context and become names when parents pick one for their newborn kid.

Now consider the sentence "Julius Caesar is a person." If you utter this sentence, you're probably talking about the fellow who ruled Rome until the Ides of March. Although the name *Julius Caesar* isn't hard-wired into the English language, almost everyone uses the name to refer to the same person. If English were a programming language, the name *Julius Caesar* would be an API identifier.

So here's how I, in my mind, divide the words in a Java program into categories:

- **Keywords:** A *keyword* is a word that has its own special meaning in the Java programming language, and that meaning doesn't change from one program to another. Examples of keywords in Java include if, else, and do.

  The JCP committee members, who have the final say on what constitutes a Java program, have chosen all the Java keywords. If you think about the two parts of Java, which I discuss earlier in the "The grammar and the common names" section, the Java keywords belong solidly to the Language Specification.

- **Identifiers:** An *identifier* is a name for something. The identifier's meaning can change from one program to another, but some identifiers' meanings tend to change more.

  - *Identifiers created by you and me:* As a Java programmer (yes, even as a novice Java programmer), you create new names for classes and other things that you describe in your programs. Of course, you may name something Prime, and the guy writing code two cubicles down the hall can name something else Prime. That's okay because Java doesn't have a predetermined meaning for Prime. In your program, you can make Prime stand for the Federal Reserve's prime rate. And the guy down the hall can make Prime stand for the "bread, roll, preserves, and prime rib." A conflict doesn't arise, because you and your co-worker are writing two different Java programs.

- *Identifiers from the API:* The JCP members have created names for many things and thrown almost 40,000 of these names into the Java API. The API comes with each version of Java, so these names are available to anyone who writes a Java program. Examples of such names are `String`, `Integer`, `JWindow`, `JButton`, `JTextField`, and `File`.

Strictly speaking, the meanings of the identifiers in the Java API aren't cast in stone. Although you can make up your own meanings for `JButton` or `JWindow`, this isn't a good idea. If you did, you would confuse the dickens out of other programmers, who are used to the standard API meanings for these familiar identifier names. But even worse, when your code assigns a new meaning to an identifier like `JButton`, you lose any computational power that was created for the identifier in the API code. The programmers of Sun Microsystems, the Java Community Process, and the OpenJDK Project did all the work writing Java code to handle buttons. If you assign your own meaning to `JButton`, you're turning your back on all the progress made in creating the API.

To see the list of Java keywords, visit this book's website (`www.allmycode.com/JavaForDummies`).

Checking Out Java Code for the First Time

The first time you look at somebody else's Java program, you tend to feel a bit queasy. The realization that you don't understand something (or many things) in the code can make you nervous. I've written hundreds (maybe thousands) of Java programs, but I still feel insecure when I start reading someone else's code.

The truth is that finding out about a Java program is a bootstrapping experience. First, you gawk in awe of the program. Then you run the program to see what it does. Then you stare at the program for a while or read someone's explanation of the program and its parts. Then you gawk a little more and run the program again. Eventually, you come to terms with the program. (Don't believe the wise guys who say they never go through these steps. Even the experienced programmers approach a new project slowly and carefully.)

In Listing 3-1, you get a blast of Java code. (Like all novice programmers, you're expected to gawk humbly at the code.) Hidden in the code, I've placed some important ideas, which I explain in detail in the next section. These ideas include the use of classes, methods, and Java statements.

Listing 3-1: The Simplest Java Program

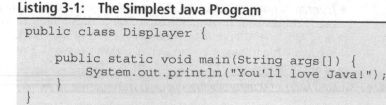

```java
public class Displayer {

    public static void main(String args[]) {
        System.out.println("You'll love Java!");
    }

}
```

You don't have to type the code in Listing 3-1 (or in any of this book's listings). To download all the code in this book, visit the book's website (www.allmycode.com/JavaForDummies).

When you run the program from Listing 3-1, the computer displays You'll love Java! (Figure 3-1 shows the output of the Displayer program when you use the Eclipse IDE.) Now, I admit that writing and running a Java program is a lot of work just to get You'll love Java! to appear on somebody's computer screen, but every endeavor has to start somewhere.

Figure 3-1:
I use Eclipse to run the program in Listing 3-1.

```
📺 Console ⊠
<terminated> Displayer [Java
You'll love Java!
```

To learn how to run the code in Listing 3-1, visit this book's website (www.allmycode.com/JavaForDummies).

In the following section, you do more than just admire the program's output. After you read the following section, you actually understand what makes the program in Listing 3-1 work.

Understanding a Simple Java Program

This section presents, explains, analyzes, dissects, and otherwise demystifies the Java program shown previously in Listing 3-1.

The Java class

Because Java is an object-oriented programming language, your primary goal is to describe classes and objects. (If you're not convinced about this, read the sections on object-oriented programming in Chapter 1.)

On those special days when I'm feeling sentimental, I tell people that Java is more pure in its object-orientation than most other so-called object-oriented languages. I say this because, in Java, you can't do anything until you create a class of some kind. It's like being on *Jeopardy!* and hearing Alex Trebek say, "Let's go to a commercial" and then interrupting him by saying, "I'm sorry, Alex. You can't issue an instruction without putting your instruction inside a class."

In Java, the entire program is a class. I wrote the program, so I get to make up a name for my new class. I chose the name `Displayer` because the program displays a line of text on the computer screen. That's why the first line in Listing 3-1 contains the words `class Displayer`. (See Figure 3-2.)

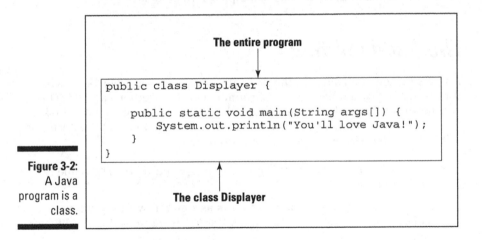

The entire program

```
public class Displayer {

    public static void main(String args[]) {
        System.out.println("You'll love Java!");
    }
}
```

The class Displayer

Figure 3-2:
A Java
program is a
class.

The first two words in Listing 3-1, `public` and `class`, are Java keywords. (See the section "The words in a Java program," earlier in this chapter.) No matter who writes a Java program, the words `public` and `class` are always used the same way. On the other hand, `Displayer` in Listing 3-1 is an identifier. I made up the word `Displayer` while I was writing this chapter. `Displayer` is the name of a particular class — the class that I'm creating by writing this program.

This book is filled with talk about classes, but for the best description of a Java class (the reason for using the word `class` in Listing 3-1) visit Chapter 7. The word `public` means (roughly) that other Java programs can use the features declared in Listing 3-1. For more details about the meaning of `public` and the use of the word `public` in a Java program, see Chapters 7 and 14.

tHE JAVA PROGRAMMING LANGUAGE IS cASe-sEnsITiVE. If you change a lowercase letter in a word to an UpperCase letter, you can change the word's meaning. cHANGING case can make the entire word go from being meaningful to being meaningless. In the first line of Listing 3-1, you can't replace `class` with `Class`. iF YOU DO, THE WHOLE PROGRAM STOPS WORKING. The same holds true, to some extent, for the name of a file containing a particular class. For example, the name of the class in Listing 3-1 is `Displayer`, starting with an uppercase letter D. So it's a good idea to save the code of Listing 3-1 in a file named `Displayer.java`, starting with an uppercase letter D.

Normally, if you define a class named `DogAndPony`, the class's Java code goes in a file named `DogAndPony.java`, spelled and capitalized exactly the same way that the class name is spelled and capitalized. In fact, this file-naming convention is mandatory for most examples in this book.

The Java method

You're working as an auto mechanic in an upscale garage. Your boss, who's always in a hurry and has a habit of running words together, says, "fixThe Alternator on that junkyOldFord." Mentally, you run through a list of tasks. "Drive the car into the bay, lift the hood, get a wrench, loosen the alternator belt," and so on. Three things are going on here:

- **You have a name for the thing you're supposed to do.** The name is *fixTheAlternator.*

- **In your mind, you have a list of tasks associated with the name *fixTheAlternator.*** The list includes "Drive the car into the bay, lift the hood, get a wrench, loosen the alternator belt," and so on.

- **You have a grumpy boss who's telling you to do all this work.** Your boss gets you working by saying, "fixTheAlternator." In other words, your boss gets you working by saying the name of the thing you're supposed to do.

In this scenario, using the word *method* wouldn't be a big stretch. You have a method for doing something with an alternator. Your boss calls that method into action, and you respond by doing all the things in the list of instructions that you associate with the method.

If you believe all that (and I hope you do), then you're ready to read about Java methods. In Java, a *method* is a list of things to do. Every method has a name, and you tell the computer to do the things in the list by using the method's name in your program.

I've never written a program to get a robot to fix an alternator. But, if I did, the program might include a fixTheAlternator method. The list of instructions in my fixTheAlternator method would look something like the text in Listing 3-2.

Don't scrutinize Listings 3-2 and 3-3 too carefully. All the code in Listings 3-2 and 3-3 is fake! I made up this code so that it looks a lot like real Java code, but it's not real. What's more important, the code in Listings 3-2 and 3-3 isn't meant to illustrate all the rules about Java. So, if you have a grain of salt handy, take it with Listings 3-2 and 3-3.

Listing 3-2:   A Method Declaration

```
void fixTheAlternator() {
    driveInto(car, bay);
    lift(hood);
    get(wrench);
    loosen(alternatorBelt);
    ...
}
```

Somewhere else in my Java code (somewhere outside of Listing 3-2), I need an instruction to call my fixTheAlternator method into action. The instruction to call the fixTheAlternator method into action may look like the line in Listing 3-3.

Listing 3-3:   A Method Call

```
fixTheAlternator(junkyOldFord);
```

Now that you have a basic understanding of what a method is and how it works, you can dig a little deeper into some useful terminology:

- ✔ If I'm being lazy, I refer to the code in Listing 3-2 as a *method*. If I'm not being lazy, I refer to this code as a *method declaration*.

- ✔ The method declaration in Listing 3-2 has two parts. The first line (the part with fixTheAlternator in it, up to but not including the open curly brace) is a *method header*. The rest of Listing 3-2 (the part surrounded by curly braces) is a *method body*.

- ✔ The term *method declaration* distinguishes the list of instructions in Listing 3-2 from the instruction in Listing 3-3, which is known as a *method call*.

A *method's declaration* tells the computer what happens if you call the method into action. A *method call* (a separate piece of code) tells the computer to actually call the method into action. A method's declaration and the method's call tend to be in different parts of the Java program.

The main method in a program

Figure 3-3 has a copy of the code from Listing 3-1. The bulk of the code contains the declaration of a method named `main`. (Just look for the word *main* in the code's method header.) For now, don't worry about the other words in the method header — `public`, `static`, `void`, `String`, and `args`. I explain these words in the next several chapters.

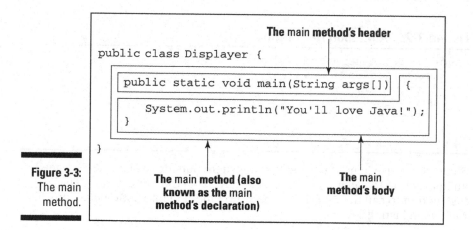

Figure 3-3:
The main method.

Like any Java method, the `main` method is a recipe.

```
How to make biscuits:
    Heat the oven.
    Roll the dough.
    Bake the rolled dough.
```

or

```
How to follow the main instructions for a Displayer:
    Print "You_ll love Java!" on the screen.
```

The word *main* plays a special role in Java. In particular, you never write code that explicitly calls a main method into action. The word *main* is the name of the method that is called into action automatically when the program begins running.

So look back at Figure 3-1. When the Displayer program runs, the computer automatically finds the program's main method and executes any instructions inside the method's body. In the Displayer program, the main method's body has only one instruction. That instruction tells the computer to print You'll love Java! on the screen. So in Figure 3-1, You'll love Java! appears on the computer screen.

The instructions in a method aren't executed until the method is called into action. But, if you give a method the name *main,* that method is called into action automatically.

Almost every computer programming language has something akin to Java's methods. If you've worked with other languages, you may remember things like subprograms, procedures, functions, subroutines, subprocedures, or PERFORM statements. Whatever you call it in your favorite programming language, a method is a bunch of instructions collected and given a new name.

How you finally tell the computer to do something

Buried deep in the heart of Listing 3-1 is the single line that actually issues a direct instruction to the computer. The line, which is highlighted in Figure 3-4, tells the computer to display You'll love Java! This line is a *statement.* In Java, a statement is a direct instruction that tells the computer to do something (for example, display this text, put 7 in that memory location, make a window appear).

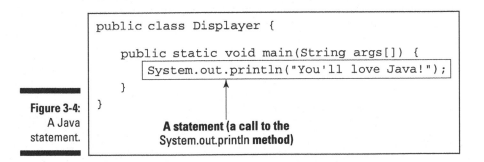

Figure 3-4:
A Java
statement.

In `System.out.println`, the next-to-last character is a lowercase letter *l*, not a digit *1*.

Of course, Java has different kinds of statements. A method call, which I introduce in the earlier "The Java method" section, is one of the many kinds of Java statements. Listing 3-3 shows you what a method call looks like, and Figure 3-4 also contains a method call that looks like this:

```
System.out.println("You'll love Java!");
```

When the computer executes this statement, the computer calls a method named `System.out.println` into action. (Yes, in Java, a name can have dots in it. The dots mean something.)

I said it already, but this is worth repeating: In `System.out.println`, the next-to-last character is a lowercase letter *l (as in the word "line"),* not a digit *1 (as in the number "one").* If you use a digit *1,* your code won't work. Just think of `println` as a way of saying "print line," and you won't have any problem.

To learn the meaning behind the dots in Java names, see Chapter 9.

Figure 3-5 illustrates the `System.out.println` situation. Actually, two methods play active roles in the running of the `Displayer` program. Here's how they work:

✔ **There's a declaration for a `main` method.** I wrote the `main` method myself. This `main` method is called automatically whenever I run the `Displayer` program.

✔ **There's a call to the `System.out.println` method.** The method call for the `System.out.println` method is the only statement in the body of the `main` method. In other words, calling the `System.out.println` method is the only thing on the `main` method's to-do list.

The declaration for the `System.out.println` method is buried inside the official Java API. For a refresher on the Java API, see the sections "The grammar and the common names" and "The words in a Java program," earlier in this chapter.

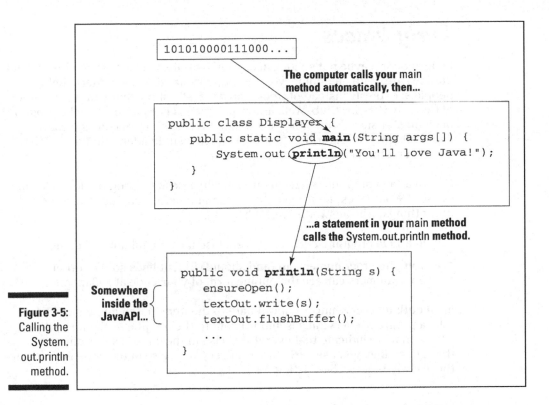

101010000111000...

The computer calls your main
method automatically, then...

```
public class Displayer {
    public static void main(String args[]) {
        System.out.println("You'll love Java!");
    }
}
```

...a statement in your main method
calls the System.out.println method.

**Somewhere
inside the
JavaAPI...**

```
public void println(String s) {
    ensureOpen();
    textOut.write(s);
    textOut.flushBuffer();
    ...
}
```

Figure 3-5:
Calling the
System.
out.println
method.

When I say things like, "System.out.println is buried inside the API," I'm not
doing justice to the API. True, you can ignore all the nitty-gritty Java code
inside the API. All you need to remember is that `System.out.println` is
defined somewhere inside that code. But I'm not being fair when I make the
API code sound like something magical. The API is just another bunch of Java
code. The statements in the API that tell the computer what it means to carry
out a call to `System.out.println` look a lot like the Java code in Listing 3-1.

In Java, each statement (like the boxed line in Figure 3-4) ends with a semicolon. Other lines in Figure 3-4 don't end with semicolons, because the
other lines in Figure 3-4 aren't statements. For instance, the method header
(the line with the word *main* in it) doesn't directly tell the computer to do
anything. The method header announces, "Just in case you ever want to do
`main`, the next few lines of code tell you how to do it."

Every complete Java statement ends with a semicolon.

Curly braces

Long ago, or maybe not so long ago, your schoolteachers told you how useful outlines are. With an outline, you can organize thoughts and ideas, help people see forests instead of trees, and generally show that you're a member of the Tidy Persons Club. Well, a Java program is like an outline. The program in Listing 3-1 starts with a big header line that says, "Here comes a class named Displayer." After that first big header, a subheader announces, "Here comes a method named main."

Now, if a Java program is like an outline, why doesn't a program look like an outline? What takes the place of the Roman numerals, capital letters, and other things? The answer is twofold:

- In a Java program, curly braces enclose meaningful units of code.

- You, the programmer, can (and should) indent lines so that other programmers can see the outline form of your code at a glance.

In an outline, everything is subordinate to the item in Roman numeral I. In a Java program, everything is subordinate to the top line — the line with class in it. To indicate that everything else in the code is subordinate to this class line, you use curly braces. Everything else in the code goes inside these curly braces. (See Listing 3-4.)

Listing 3-4: Curly Braces for a Java Class

```
public class Displayer {

    public static void main(String args[]) {
        System.out.println("You'll love Java!");
    }
}
```

In an outline, some stuff is subordinate to a capital letter *A* item. In a Java program, some lines are subordinate to the method header. To indicate that something is subordinate to a method header, you use curly braces. (See Listing 3-5.)

Listing 3-5: Curly Braces for a Java Method

```
public class Displayer {

    public static void main(String args[]) {
        System.out.println("You'll love Java!");
    }
}
```

In an outline, some items are at the bottom of the food chain. In the `Displayer` class, the corresponding line is the line that begins with `System.out.println`. Accordingly, this `System.out.println` line goes inside all the other curly braces and is indented more than any other line.

Never lose sight of the fact that a Java program is, first and foremost, an outline.

If you put curly braces in the wrong places or omit curly braces where the braces should be, your program probably won't work at all. If your program works, it'll probably work incorrectly.

If you don't indent lines of code in an informative manner, your program will still work correctly, but neither you nor any other programmer will be able to figure out what you were thinking when you wrote the code.

If you're a visual thinker, you can picture outlines of Java programs in your head. One friend of mine visualizes an actual numbered outline morphing into a Java program. (See Figure 3-6.) Another person, who shall remain nameless, uses more bizarre imagery. (See Figure 3-7.)

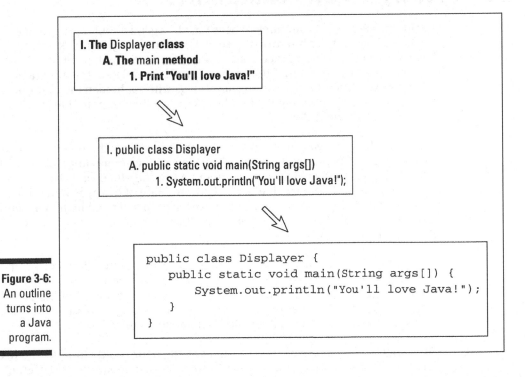

Figure 3-6:
An outline turns into a Java program.

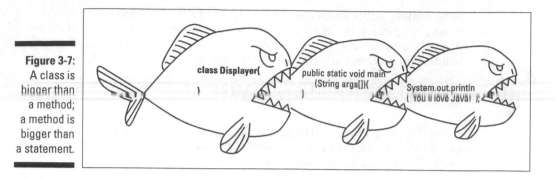

Figure 3-7:
A class is
bigger than
a method;
a method is
bigger than
a statement.

I appreciate a good excuse as much as the next guy, but failing to indent your Java code is inexcusable. In fact, many Java IDEs have tools to indent your code automatically. Visit this book's website (www.allmycode.com/JavaForDummies) for more information.

And Now, a Few Comments

People gather around campfires to hear the old legend about a programmer whose laziness got her into trouble. To maintain this programmer's anonymity, I call her Jane Pro. Jane worked many months to create the holy grail of computing — a program that thinks on its own. If completed, this program could work independently, learning new things without human intervention. Day after day, night after night, she labored to give the program that spark of creative, independent thought.

One day, when she was almost finished with the project, she received a disturbing piece of paper mail from her health insurance company. No, the mail wasn't about a serious illness. It was about a routine office visit. The insurance company's claim form had a place for her date of birth, as if her date of birth had changed since the last time she sent in a claim. She had absent-mindedly scribbled 2014 as her year of birth, so the insurance company refused to pay the bill.

Jane dialed the insurance company's phone number. Within 20 minutes, she was talking to a live person. "I'm sorry," said the live person. "To resolve this issue you must dial a different number." Well, you can guess what happened next. "I'm sorry. The other operator gave you the wrong number." And then, "I'm sorry. You must call back the original phone number."

Five months later, Jane's ear ached, but after 800 hours on the phone, she had finally gotten a tentative promise that the insurance company would eventually reprocess the claim. Elated as she was, she was anxious to get back to her programming project. Could she remember what all those lines of code were supposed to be doing?

No, she couldn't. She stared and stared at her own work and, like a dream that doesn't make sense the next morning, the code was completely meaningless to her. She had written a million lines of code, and not one line was accompanied by an informative explanatory comment. She had left no clues to help her understand what she'd been thinking, so in frustration, she abandoned the whole project.

Adding comments to your code

Listing 3-6 has an enhanced version of this chapter's sample program. In addition to all the keywords, identifiers, and punctuation, Listing 3-6 has text that's meant for human beings to read.

Listing 3-6: **Three Kinds of Comments**

```
/*
 * Listing 3-6 in "Java For Dummies, 6th Edition"
 *
 * Copyright 2014 Wiley Publishing, Inc.
 * All rights reserved.
 */

/**
 * The Displayer class displays text
 * on the computer screen.
 *
 * @author  Barry Burd
 * @version 1.0 10/24/13
 * @see     java.lang.System
 */
public class Displayer {

    /**
     * The main method is where
     * execution of the code begins.
     *
     * @param  args    (See Chapter 11.)
     */
    public static void main(String args[]) {
        System.out.println("I love Java!");  //I? You?
    }
}
```

A *comment* is a special section of text inside a program whose purpose is to help people understand the program. A comment is part of a good program's documentation.

The Java programming language has three kinds of comments:

✔ **Traditional comments:** The first five lines of Listing 3-6 form one *traditional* comment. The comment begins with /* and ends with */. Everything between the opening /* and the closing */ is for human eyes only. No information about "Java For Dummies, 6th Edition" or Wiley Publishing, Inc. is translated by the compiler.

To read about compilers, see Chapter 2.

The second, third, fourth, and fifth lines in Listing 3-6 have extra asterisks (*). I call them extra because these asterisks aren't required when you create a comment. They just make the comment look pretty. I include them in Listing 3-6 because, for some reason that I don't entirely understand, most Java programmers add these extra asterisks.

✔ **End-of-line comments:** The text //I? You? in Listing 3-6 is an *end-of-line* comment. An end-of-line comment starts with two slashes and goes to the end of a line of type. Once again, the compiler doesn't translate the text inside the end-of-line comment.

✔ **Javadoc comments:** A *javadoc* comment begins with a slash and two asterisks (/**). Listing 3-6 has two javadoc comments — one with the text The Displayer class...and another with the text The main method is where....

A javadoc comment is a special kind of traditional comment. A javadoc comment is meant to be read by people who never even look at the Java code. But that doesn't make sense. How can you see the javadoc comments in Listing 3-6 if you never look at Listing 3-6?

Well, a certain program called *javadoc* (what else?) can find all the javadoc comments in Listing 3-6 and turn these comments into a nice-looking web page. Figure 3-8 shows the page.

Javadoc comments are great. Here are several great things about them:

✔ The only person who has to look at a piece of Java code is the programmer who writes the code. Other people who use the code can find out what the code does by viewing the automatically generated web page.

✔ Because other people don't look at the Java code, other people don't make changes to the Java code. (In other words, other people don't introduce errors into the existing Java code.)

✔ Because other people don't look at the Java code, other people don't have to decipher the inner workings of the Java code. All these people need to know about the code is what they read on the code's web page.

✔ The programmer doesn't create two separate things — some Java code over here and some documentation about the code over there. Instead, the programmer creates one piece of Java code and embeds the documentation (in the form of javadoc comments) right inside the code.

✔ Best of all, the generation of web pages from javadoc comments is automatic. So everyone's documentation has the same format. No matter whose Java code you use, you find out about that code by reading a page like the one in Figure 3-8. That's good because the format in Figure 3-8 is familiar to anyone who uses Java.

You can generate your own web pages from the javadoc comments that you put in your code. To discover how, visit this book's website (`www.allmycode.com/JavaForDummies`).

Package **Class** Tree Deprecated Index Help
PREV CLASS NEXT CLASS   FRAMES   NO FRAMES
SUMMARY: NESTED | FIELD | CONSTR | METHOD   DETAIL: FIELD | CONSTR | METHOD

Class Displayer

```
java.lang.Object
   └─Displayer
```

```
public class Displayer
extends java.lang.Object
```

The Displayer class displays text on the computer screen.

See Also:
    System

Constructor Summary

`Displayer()`

Method Summary

| static void | `main(java.lang.String[] args)` The main method is where execution of the code begins. |

Methods inherited from class java.lang.Object

`clone, equals, finalize, getClass, hashCode, notify, notifyAll, toString, wait, wait, wait`

Constructor Detail

Displayer

`public Displayer()`

Method Detail

main

`public static void main(java.lang.String[] args)`

    The main method is where execution of the code begins.

    Parameters:
        args - (See Chapter 11.)

Package **Class** Tree Deprecated Index Help
PREV CLASS NEXT CLASS   FRAMES   NO FRAMES
SUMMARY: NESTED | FIELD | CONSTR | METHOD   DETAIL: FIELD | CONSTR | METHOD

Figure 3-8:
The javadoc page generated from the code in Listing 3-6.

What's Barry's excuse?

For years, I've been telling my students to put comments in their code, and for years, I've been creating sample code (like the code in Listing 3-1) with no comments in it. Why?

Three little words: "Know your audience." When you write complicated, real-life code, your audience is other programmers, information technology managers, and people who need help deciphering what you've done. When I write simple samples of code for this book, my audience is you — the novice Java programmer. Instead of reading my comments, your best strategy is to stare at my Java statements — the statements that Java's compiler deciphers. That's why I put so few comments in this book's listings.

Besides, I'm a little lazy.

Using comments to experiment with your code

You may hear programmers talk about *commenting out* certain parts of their code. When you're writing a program and something's not working correctly, it often helps to try removing some of the code. If nothing else, you find out what happens when that suspicious code is removed. Of course, you may not like what happens when the code is removed, so you don't want to delete the code completely. Instead, you turn your ordinary Java statements into comments. For instance, you turn the statement

```
System.out.println("I love Java!");
```

into the comment

```
// System.out.println("I love Java!");
```

This change keeps the Java compiler from seeing the code while you try to figure out what's wrong with your program.

Traditional comments aren't very useful for commenting out code. The big problem is that you can't put one traditional comment inside of another. For instance, suppose you want to comment out the following statements:

```
System.out.println("Parents,");
System.out.println("pick your");
/*
 * Intentionally displays on four separate lines
 */
System.out.println("battles");
System.out.println("carefully!");
```

If you try to turn this code into one traditional comment, you get the following mess:

```
/*
  System.out.println("Parents,");
  System.out.println("pick your");
  /*
   * Intentionally displays on four separate lines
   */
  System.out.println("battles");
  System.out.println("carefully!");
*/
```

The first */ (after Intentionally displays) ends the traditional comment prematurely. Then the battles and carefully statements aren't commented out, and the last */ chokes the compiler. You can't nest traditional comments inside one another. Because of this, I recommend end-of-line comments as tools for experimenting with your code.

Most IDEs can comment out sections of your code for you automatically. For details, visit this book's website (www.allmycode.com/JavaForDummies).

Part II
Writing Your Own Java Programs

Before executing
amountInAccount =
        amountInAccount + 1000000.00;

amountInAccount

```
50.22
```

After executing
amountInAccount =
        amountInAccount + 1000000.00;

amountInAccount

```
50.22
1000050.22
```

Trees are precious. I can't put all of Java's features in a printed book. A few features that belong in Part II just didn't make the cut! Visit www.dummies.com/extras/java to read about some of these features.

In this part . . .

- ✔ Create new values and modify existing values.
- ✔ Put decision-making into your application's logic.
- ✔ Repeat things as needed when your program runs.

Chapter 4

Making the Most of Variables and Their Values

he following conversation between Mr. Van Doren and Mr. Barasch never took place:

> *Charles:* A sea squirt eats its brain, turning itself from an animal into a plant.
>
> *Jack:* Is that your final answer, Charles?
>
> *Charles:* Yes, it is.
>
> *Jack:* How much money do you have in your account today, Charles?
>
> *Charles:* I have fifty dollars and twenty-two cents in my checking account.
>
> *Jack:* Well, you better call the IRS, because your sea squirt answer is correct. You just won a million dollars to add to your checking account. What do you think of that, Charles?
>
> *Charles:* I owe it all to honesty, diligence, and hard work, Jack.

Some aspects of this dialogue can be represented in Java by a few lines of code.

Varying a Variable

No matter how you acquire your million dollars, you can use a variable to tally your wealth. Listing 4-1 shows the code.

Listing 4-1:   Using a Variable

```
amountInAccount = 50.22;
amountInAccount = amountInAccount + 1000000.00;
```

You don't have to type the code in Listing 4-1 (or in any of this book's listings). To download all the code in this book, visit the book's website (www. allmycode.com/JavaForDummies).

The code in Listing 4-1 makes use of the amountInAccount variable. A *variable* is a placeholder. You can stick a number like 50.22 into a variable. After you place a number in the variable, you can change your mind and put a different number into the variable. (That's what varies in a variable.) Of course, when you put a new number in a variable, the old number is no longer there. If you didn't save the old number somewhere else, the old number is gone.

Figure 4-1 gives a before-and-after picture of the code in Listing 4-1. After the first statement in Listing 4-1 is executed, the variable amountInAccount has the number 50.22 in it. Then, after the second statement of Listing 4-1 is executed, the amountInAccount variable suddenly has 1000050.22 in it. When you think about a variable, picture a place in the computer's memory where wires and transistors store 50.22, 1000050.22, or whatever. On the left side of Figure 4-1, imagine that the box with 50.22 in it is surrounded by millions of other such boxes.

Before executing
amountInAccount =
   amountInAccount + 1000000.00;

amountInAccount

| 50.22 |

After executing
amountInAccount =
   amountInAccount + 1000000.00;

amountInAccount

| ~~50.22~~ 1000050.22 |

Figure 4-1: A variable (before and after).

Now you need some terminology. The thing stored in a variable is a *value*. A variable's value can change during the run of a program (when Jack gives you a million bucks, for instance). The value that's stored in a variable isn't necessarily a number. (For instance, you can create a variable that always stores a letter.) The kind of value that's stored in a variable is a variable's *type*.

You can read more about types in the section "Understanding the Types of Values That Variables May Have," later in this chapter.

A subtle, almost unnoticeable difference exists between a variable and a variable's *name*. Even in formal writing, I often use the word *variable* when I mean *variable name*. Strictly speaking, amountInAccount is a variable name, and all the memory storage associated with amountInAccount (including the type that amountInAccount has and whatever value amountInAccount currently represents) is the variable itself. If you think this distinction between *variable* and *variable name* is too subtle for you to worry about, join the club.

Every variable name is an identifier — a name that you can make up in your own code. In preparing Listing 4-1, I made up the name *amountInAccount*.

For more information on the kinds of names in a Java program, see Chapter 3.

Before the sun sets on Listing 4-1, you need to notice one more part of the listing. The listing has 50.22 and 1000000.00 in it. Anybody in his or her right mind would call these things *numbers,* but in a Java program it helps to call these things *literals.*

And what's so literal about 50.22 and 1000000.00? Well, think about the variable amountInAccount in Listing 4-1. The variable amountInAccount stands for 50.22 some of the time, but it stands for 1000050.22 the rest of the time. You could use the word *number* to talk about amountInAccount. But really, what amountInAccount stands for depends on the fashion of the moment. On the other hand, 50.22 literally stands for the value $50\,^{22}/_{100}$.

A variable's value changes; a literal's value doesn't.

Starting with Java 7, you can add underscores to your numeric literals. Instead of using the plain old 1000000.00 in Listing 4-1, you can write amountInAccount = amountInAccount + 1_000_000.00. Unfortunately, you can't easily do what you're most tempted to do. You can't write 1,000,000.00 (as you would in the United States), nor can you write 1.000.000,00 (as you would in Germany). If you want to write 1,000,000.00, you have to use some fancy formatting tricks. For more information about formatting, check Chapters 10 and 11.

Assignment Statements

Statements like the ones in Listing 4-1 are called *assignment statements.* In an assignment statement, you assign a value to something. In many cases, this something is a variable.

I recommend getting into the habit of reading assignment statements from right to left. Figure 4-2 illustrates the action of the first line in Listing 4-1.

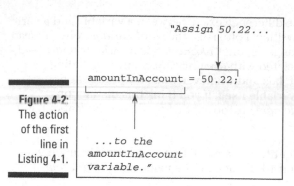

Figure 4-2:
The action
of the first
line in
Listing 4-1.

The second line in Listing 4-1 is just a bit more complicated. Figure 4-3 illustrates the action of the second line in Listing 4-1.

In an assignment statement, the thing being assigned a value is always on the left side of the equal sign.

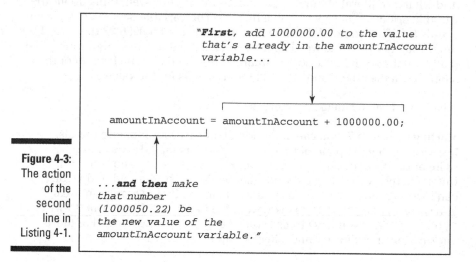

Figure 4-3:
The action
of the
second
line in
Listing 4-1.

Understanding the Types of Values That Variables May Have

Have you seen the TV commercials that make you think you're flying around among the circuits inside a computer? Pretty cool, eh? These commercials show 0s (zeros) and 1s (ones) sailing by because 0s and 1s are the only things that computers can really deal with. When you think a computer is storing the letter *J*, the computer is really storing 01001010. Everything inside the computer is a sequence of 0s and 1s. As every computer geek knows, a 0 or 1 is called a *bit*.

As it turns out, the sequence 01001010, which stands for the letter *J,* can also stand for the number 74. The same sequence can also stand for $1.0369608636003646 \times 10^{-43}$. In fact, if the bits are interpreted as screen pixels, the same sequence can be used to represent the dots shown in Figure 4-4. The meaning of 01001010 depends on the way the software interprets this sequence of 0s and 1s.

Figure 4-4:
An extreme
close-up of
eight black
and white
screen
pixels.

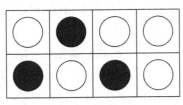

So how do you tell the computer what 01001010 stands for? The answer is in the concept of *type.* The type of a variable is the range of values that the variable is permitted to store.

I copied the lines from Listing 4-1 and put them into a complete Java program. The program is in Listing 4-2. When I run the program in Listing 4-2, I get the output shown in Figure 4-5.

Listing 4-2:   A Program Uses amountInAccount

```java
public class Millionaire {
    public static void main(String args[]) {
        double amountInAccount;

        amountInAccount = 50.22;
        amountInAccount = amountInAccount + 1000000.00;

        System.out.print("You have $");
        System.out.print(amountInAccount);
        System.out.println("in your account.");
    }
}
```

Figure 4-5:
Running the
program in
Listing 4-2.

```
Console ☒                                    ▣ ✖ ✖
<terminated> Millionaire [Java Application] C:\Program Files
You have $1000050.22 in your account.
```

Most of the programs in this book are text-based. A text-based program has no windows, no dialog boxes — nothing of that kind. All you see is line after line of plain, unformatted text. The user types something, and the computer displays a response beneath each line of input. As visually unexciting as such programs may be, they contain the basic concepts for all computer programming. They're also easier for the novice programmer to read, write, and understand. So in this book I take a two-pronged approach. The examples in the printed book are mostly text-based, but you can find fancier versions of most examples on this book's website (www.allmycode.com/JavaForDummies). These fancier versions have windows, buttons, text fields, and other elements of a typical *graphical user interface* (GUI).

In Listing 4-2, look at the first line in the body of the `main` method.

```
double amountInAccount;
```

This line is called a *variable declaration.* Putting this line in your program is like saying, "I'm declaring my intention to have a variable named *amountInAccount* in my program." This line reserves the name *amountInAccount* for your use in the program.

In this variable declaration, the word *double* is a Java keyword. This word *double* tells the computer what kinds of values you intend to store in `amountInAccount`. In particular, the word *double* stands for numbers between -1.8×10^{308} and 1.8×10^{308}. (These are enormous numbers with 308 zeros before the decimal point. Only the world's richest people write checks with 308 zeros in them. The second of these numbers is one-point-eight gazazzo-zillion-kaskillion. The number 1.8×10^{308}, a constant defined by the International Bureau of Weights and Measures, is the number of eccentric computer programmers between Sunnyvale, California, and the M31 Andromeda Galaxy.)

More important than the humongous range of the `double` keyword's numbers is the fact that a `double` value can have digits beyond the decimal point. After you declare `amountInAccount` to be of type `double`, you can store all sorts of numbers in `amountInAccount`. You can store 50.22, 0.02398479, or –3.0. In Listing 4-2, if I hadn't declared `amountInAccount` to be of type `double`, I may not have been able to store 50.22. Instead, I would have had to store plain old 50, without any digits beyond the decimal point.

Another type — type `float` — also allows you to have digits beyond the decimal point. But `float` values aren't as accurate as `double` values.

In many situations, you have a choice. You can declare certain values to be either `float` values or `double` values. But don't sweat the choice between `float` and `double`. For most programs, just use `double`. With today's fancy processors, the space that you save using the `float` type is almost never worth the loss of accuracy. (For more details, see the nearby sidebar, "Digits beyond the decimal point.")

Digits beyond the decimal point

Java has two different types that have digits beyond the decimal point: type double and type float. So what's the difference? When you declare a variable to be of type double, you're telling the computer to keep track of 64 bits when it stores the variable's values. When you declare a variable to be of type float, the computer keeps track of only 32 bits.

You could change Listing 4-2 and declare amountInAccount to be of type float.

```
float amountInAccount;
```

Surely, 32 bits are enough to store a small number like 50.22, right? Well, they are and they aren't. You could easily store 50.00 with only 32 bits. Heck, you could store 50.00 with only 6 bits. The size of the number doesn't matter. The accuracy matters. In a 64-bit double variable, you're using most of the bits to store stuff beyond the decimal point. To store the .22 part of 50.22, you need more than the measly 32 bits that you get with type float.

Do you really believe what you just read — that it takes more than 32 bits to store .22? To help convince you, I made a few changes to the code in Listing 4-2. I made amountInAccount be of type float. I changed the first three statements inside the main method as follows:

```
float amountInAccount;

amountInAccount = 50.22F;
amountInAccount = amountInAccount + 1000000.00F;
```

(To understand why I used the letter F in 50.22F and 1000000.00F, see Table 4-1.) The output I got was

```
You have $1000050.25 in your account.
```

Compare this with the output in Figure 4-5. When I switch from type double to type float, Charles has an extra three cents in his account. By changing to the 32-bit float type, I've clobbered the accuracy in the amountInAccount variable's hundredths place. That's bad.

Another difficulty with float values is purely cosmetic. Look again at the literals, 50.22 and 1000000.00, in Listing 4-2. The Laws of Java say that literals like these take up 64 bits each. This means that if you declare amountInAccount to be of type float, you're going to run into trouble. You'll have trouble stuffing those 64-bit literals into your little 32-bit amountInAccount variable. To compensate, you can switch from double literals to float literals by adding an F to each double literal, but a number with an extra F at the end looks funny.

```
float amountInAccount;
amountInAccount = 50.22F;
amountInAccount = amountInAccount + 1000000.00F;
```

To experiment with numbers, visit http://babbage.cs.qc.edu/IEEE-754. The page takes any number that you enter and shows you how the number would be represented as 32 bits and as 64 bits.

The big million-dollar jackpot in Listing 4-2 is impressive. But Listing 4-2 doesn't illustrate the best way to deal with dollar amounts. In a Java program, the best way to represent currency is to shun the double and float types and opt instead for a type named BigDecimal. For more information, see this book's website (www.allmycode.com/JavaForDummies).

Displaying Text

The last three statements in Listing 4-2 use a neat formatting trick. You want to display several different things on a single line on the screen. You put these things in separate statements. All but the last of the statements are calls to System.out.print. (The last statement is a call to System.out.println.) Calls to System.out.print display text on part of a line and then leave the cursor at the end of the current line. After executing System.out.print, the cursor is still at the end of the same line, so the next System.out.*whatever* can continue printing on that same line. With several calls to print capped off by a single call to println, the result is just one nice-looking line of output. (Refer to Figure 4-5.)

A call to System.out.print writes some things and leaves the cursor sitting at the end of the line of output. A call to System.out.println writes things and then finishes the job by moving the cursor to the start of a brand-new line of output.

Numbers without Decimal Points

"In 1995, the average family had 2.3 children."

At this point, a wise guy always remarks that no real family has exactly 2.3 children. Clearly, whole numbers have a role in this world. Therefore, in Java, you can declare a variable to store nothing but whole numbers. Listing 4-3 shows a program that uses whole number variables.

Listing 4-3:   Using the int Type

```
public class ElevatorFitter {

    public static void main(String args[]) {
        int weightOfAPerson;
        int elevatorWeightLimit;
        int numberOfPeople;

        weightOfAPerson = 150;
        elevatorWeightLimit = 1400;
```

```
        numberOfPeople =
            elevatorWeightLimit / weightOfAPerson;

        System.out.print("You can fit");
        System.out.print(numberOfPeople);
        System.out.println("people on the elevator.");
    }
}
```

The story behind the program in Listing 4-3 takes some heavy-duty explaining. So here goes:

You have a hotel elevator whose weight capacity is 1,400 pounds. One weekend, the hotel hosts the Brickenchicker family reunion. A certain branch of the Brickenchicker family has been blessed with identical dectuplets (ten siblings, all with the same physical characteristics). Normally, each of the Brickenchicker dectuplets weighs exactly 145 pounds. But on Saturday, the family has a big catered lunch, and, because lunch included strawberry shortcake, each of the Brickenchicker dectuplets now weighs 150 pounds. Immediately after lunch, all ten of the Brickenchicker dectuplets arrive at the elevator at exactly the same time. (Why not? All ten of them think alike.) So, the question is, how many of the dectuplets can fit on the elevator?

Now remember, if you put one ounce more than 1,400 pounds of weight on the elevator, the elevator cable breaks, plunging all dectuplets on the elevator to their sudden (and costly) deaths.

The answer to the Brickenchicker riddle (the output of the program of Listing 4-3) is shown in Figure 4-6.

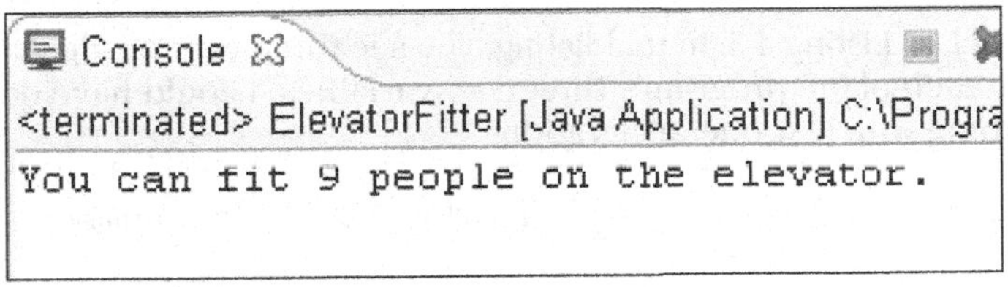

Figure 4-6: Save the Brickenchickers.

```
Console ☒                                        ■   ✕
<terminated> ElevatorFitter [Java Application] C:\Progra
You can fit 9 people on the elevator.
```

At the core of the Brickenchicker elevator problem, you have whole numbers — numbers with no digits beyond the decimal point. When you divide 1,400 by 150, you get 9⅓, but you shouldn't take the ⅓ seriously. No matter how hard you try, you can't squeeze an extra 50 pounds worth of Brickenchicker dectuplet onto the elevator. This fact is reflected nicely in Java. In Listing 4-3, all three variables (`weightOfAPerson`, `elevatorWeightLimit`, and `numberOfPeople`) are of type `int`. An `int` value is a whole number. When you divide one `int` value by another

Four ways to store whole numbers

Java has four types of whole numbers. The types are byte, short, int, and long. Unlike the complicated story about the accuracy of types float and double, the only thing that matters when you choose among the whole number types is the size of the number that you're trying to store. If you want to use numbers larger than 127, don't use byte. To store numbers larger than 32767, don't use short.

Most of the time, you'll use int. But if you need to store numbers larger than 2147483647, forsake int in favor of long. (A long number can be as big as 9223372036854775807.) For the whole story, see Table 4-1.

(as you do with the slash in Listing 4-3), you get another int. When you divide 1,400 by 150, you get 9 — not 9⅓. You see this in Figure 4-6. Taken together, the following statements display 9 onscreen:

```
numberOfPeople =
    elevatorWeightLimit / weightOfAPerson;

System.out.print(numberOfPeople);
```

Combining Declarations and Initializing Variables

Look back at Listing 4-3. In that listing, you see three variable declarations — one for each of the program's three int variables. I could have done the same thing with just one declaration:

```
int weightOfAPerson, elevatorWeightLimit, numberOfPeople;
```

If two variables have completely different types, you can't create both variables in the same declaration. For instance, to create an int variable named *weightOfFred* and a double variable named *amountInFredsAccount,* you need two separate variable declarations.

You can give variables their starting values in a declaration. In Listing 4-3 for instance, one declaration can replace several lines in the main method (all but the calls to print and println).

```
int weightOfAPerson = 150, elevatorWeightLimit = 1400,
  numberOfPeople = elevatorWeightLimit/weightOfAPerson;
```

When you do this, you don't say that you're assigning values to variables. The pieces of the declarations with equal signs in them aren't really called assignment statements. Instead, you say that you're *initializing* the variables. Believe it or not, keeping this distinction in mind is helpful.

Like everything else in life, initializing a variable has advantages and disadvantages:

- **When you combine six lines of Listing 4-3 into just one declaration, the code becomes more concise.** Sometimes, concise code is easier to read. Sometimes it's not. As a programmer, it's your judgment call.

- **By initializing a variable, you might automatically avoid certain programming errors.** For an example, see Chapter 7.

- **In some situations, you have no choice. The nature of your code forces you either to initialize or not to initialize.** For an example that doesn't lend itself to variable initialization, see the deleting-evidence program in Chapter 6.

The Atoms: Java's Primitive Types

The words *int* and *double* that I describe in the previous sections are examples of *primitive types* (also known as *simple* types) in Java. The Java language has exactly eight primitive types. As a newcomer to Java, you can pretty much ignore all but four of these types. (As programming languages go, Java is nice and compact that way.) Table 4-1 shows the complete list of primitive types.

Table 4-1	Java's Primitive Types	
Type Name	*What a Literal Looks Like*	*Range of Values*
Whole number types		
byte	(byte)42	−128 to 127
short	(short)42	−32768 to 32767
int	42	−2147483648 to 2147483647
long	42L	−9223372036854775808 to 9223372036854775807
Decimal number types		
float	42.0F	-3.4×10^{38} to 3.4×10^{38}
double	42.0	-1.8×10^{308} to 1.8×10^{308}

(continued)

Table 4-1 *(continued)*

Type Name	What a Literal Looks Like	Range of Values
Character type		
char	'A'	Thousands of characters, glyphs, and symbols
Logical type		
boolean	true	true, false

The types that you shouldn't ignore are int, double, char, and boolean. Previous sections in this chapter cover the int and double types. So, this section covers char and boolean types.

The char type

Not so long ago, people thought computers existed only for doing big number-crunching calculations. Nowadays, with word processors, nobody thinks that way anymore. So, if you haven't been in a cryogenic freezing chamber for the last 20 years, you know that computers store letters, punctuation symbols, and other characters.

The Java type that's used to store characters is called *char*. Listing 4-4 has a simple program that uses the char type. Figure 4-7 shows the output of the program in Listing 4-4.

Listing 4-4:   Using the char Type

```
public class CharDemo {

  public static void main(String args[]) {
    char myLittleChar = 'b';
    char myBigChar = Character.toUpperCase(myLittleChar);
    System.out.println(myBigChar);
  }
}
```

In Listing 4-4, the first initialization stores the letter *b* in the variable myLittleChar. In the initialization, notice how *b* is surrounded by single quote marks. In Java, every char literal starts and ends with a single quote mark.

In a Java program, single quote marks surround the letter in a char literal.

If you need help sorting out the terms *assignment, declaration,* and *initialization,* see the "Combining Declarations and Initializing Variables" section, earlier in this chapter.

Figure 4-7:
An exciting
run of the
program of
Listing 4-4 as
it appears in
the Eclipse
Console
view.

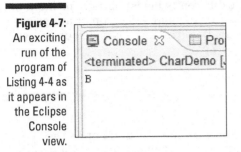

In the second initialization of Listing 4-4, the program calls an API method whose name is *Character.toUpperCase*. The `Character.toUpperCase` method does just what its name suggests — the method produces the uppercase equivalent of the letter *b*. This uppercase equivalent (the letter *B*) is assigned to the `myBigChar` variable, and the *B* that's in `myBigChar` prints onscreen.

For an introduction to the Java Application Programming Interface (API), see Chapter 3.

If you're tempted to write the following statement,

```
char myLittleChars = 'barry';  //Don't do this
```

please resist the temptation. You can't store more than one letter at a time in a `char` variable, and you can't put more than one letter between a pair of single quotes. If you're trying to store words or sentences (not just single letters), you need to use something called a *String*.

For a look at Java's `String` type, see the section "The Molecules and Compounds: Reference Types," later in this chapter.

If you're used to writing programs in other languages, you may be aware of something called ASCII Character Encoding. Most languages use ASCII; Java uses Unicode. In the old ASCII representation, each character takes up only 8 bits, but in Unicode, each character takes up 8, 16, or 32 bits. Whereas ASCII stores the letters of the familiar Roman (English) alphabet, Unicode has room for characters from most of the world's commonly spoken languages. The only problem is that some of the Java API methods are geared specially toward 16-bit Unicode. Occasionally, this bites you in the back (or it bytes you in the back, as the case may be). If you're using a method to write `Hello` on the screen and `H e l l o` shows up instead, check the method's documentation for mention of Unicode characters.

It's worth noticing that the two methods, `Character.toUpperCase` and `System.out.println`, are used quite differently in Listing 4-4. The method `Character.toUpperCase` is called as part of an initialization or an assignment statement, but the method `System.out.println` is called on its own. To find out more about this, see Chapter 7.

The boolean type

A variable of type `boolean` stores one of two values — `true` or `false`. Listing 4-5 demonstrates the use of a `boolean` variable. Figure 4-8 shows the output of the program in Listing 4-5.

Listing 4-5: Using the boolean Type

```
public class ElevatorFitter2 {

    public static void main(String args[]) {
        System.out.println("True or False?");
        System.out.println("You can fit all ten of the");
        System.out.println("Brickenchicker dectuplets");
        System.out.println("on the elevator:");
        System.out.println();

        int weightOfAPerson = 150;
        int elevatorWeightLimit = 1400;
        int numberOfPeople =
            elevatorWeightLimit / weightOfAPerson;

        boolean allTenOkay = numberOfPeople >= 10;

        System.out.println(allTenOkay);
    }
}
```

Figure 4-8:
The
Bricken-
chicker
dectuplets
strike again.

```
True or False?
You can fit all ten of the
Brickenchicker dectuplets
on the elevator:

false
```

In Listing 4-5, the `allTenOkay` variable is of type `boolean`. To find a value for the `allTenOkay` variable, the program checks to see whether `numberOfPeople` is greater than or equal to ten. (The symbols `>=` stand for *greater than or equal to*.)

At this point, it pays to be fussy about terminology. Any part of a Java program that has a value is an *expression*. If you write

```
weightOfAPerson = 150;
```

then `150` is an expression (an expression whose value is the quantity `150`). If you write

```
numberOfEggs = 2 + 2;
```

then `2 + 2` is an expression (because 2 + 2 has the value 4). If you write

```
int numberOfPeople =
    elevatorWeightLimit / weightOfAPerson;
```

then `elevatorWeightLimit / weightOfAPerson` is an expression. (The value of the expression `elevatorWeightLimit / weightOfAPerson` depends on whatever values the variables `elevatorWeightLimit` and `weightOfAPerson` have when the code containing the expression is executed.)

Any part of a Java program that has a value is an *expression*.

In Listing 4-5, the code `numberOfPeople >= 10` is an expression. The expression's value depends on the value stored in the `numberOfPeople` variable. But, as you know from seeing the strawberry shortcake at the Brickenchicker family's catered lunch, the value of `numberOfPeople` isn't greater than or equal to ten. As a result, the value of `numberOfPeople >= 10` is `false`. So, in the statement in Listing 4-5, in which `allTenOkay` is assigned a value, the `allTenOkay` variable is assigned a `false` value.

In Listing 4-5, I call `System.out.println()` with nothing inside the parentheses. When I do this, Java adds a line break to the program's output. In Listing 4-5, `System.out.println()` tells the program to display a blank line.

The Molecules and Compounds: Reference Types

By combining simple things, you get more complicated things. That's the way things always go. Take some of Java's primitive types, whip them together to make a primitive type stew, and what do you get? A more complicated type called a *reference type*.

The program in Listing 4-6 uses reference types. Figure 4-9 shows you what happens when you run the program in Listing 4-6.

Listing 4-6: Using Reference Types

```
import javax.swing.JFrame;

public class ShowAFrame {

    public static void main(String args[]) {
        JFrame myFrame = new JFrame();
        String myTitle = "Blank Frame";

        myFrame.setTitle(myTitle);
        myFrame.setSize(300, 200);
        myFrame.setDefaultCloseOperation
            (JFrame.EXIT_ON_CLOSE);
        myFrame.setVisible(true);
    }
}
```

The program in Listing 4-6 uses two references types. Both types are defined in the Java API. One of the types (the one that you'll use all the time) is called *String*. The other type (the one that you can use to create GUIs) is called *JFrame*.

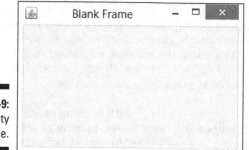

Figure 4-9:
An empty
frame.

A `String` is a bunch of characters. It's like having several `char` values in a row. So, with the `myTitle` variable declared to be of type `String`, assigning `"Blank Frame"` to the `myTitle` variable makes sense in Listing 4-6. The `String` class is declared in the Java API.

In a Java program, double quote marks surround the letters in a `String` literal.

A Java *JFrame* is a lot like a window. (The only difference is that you call it a JFrame instead of a window.) To keep Listing 4-6 short and sweet, I decided not to put anything in my frame — no buttons, no fields, nothing.

Even with a completely empty frame, Listing 4-6 uses tricks that I don't describe until later in this book. So don't try reading and interpreting every word of Listing 4-6. The big thing to get from Listing 4-6 is that the program has two variable declarations. In writing the program, I made up two variable names — myTitle and myFrame. According to the declarations, myTitle is of type String, and myFrame is of type JFrame.

You can look up String and JFrame in Java's API documentation. But, even before you do, I can tell you what you'll find. You'll find that String and JFrame are the names of Java classes. So, that's the big news. Every class is the name of a reference type. You can reserve amountInAccount for double values by writing

```
double amountInAccount;
```

or by writing

```
double amountInAccount = 50.22;
```

You can also reserve myFrame for a JFrame value by writing

```
JFrame myFrame;
```

or by writing

```
JFrame myFrame = new JFrame();
```

To review the notion of a Java class, see the sections on object-oriented programming (OOP) in Chapter 1.

Every Java class is a reference type. If you declare a variable to have some type that's not a primitive type, the variable's type is (most of the time) the name of a Java class.

Now, when you declare a variable to have type int, you can visualize what that declaration means in a fairly straightforward way. It means that, somewhere inside the computer's memory, a storage location is reserved for that variable's value. In the storage location is a bunch of bits. The arrangement of the bits ensures that a certain whole number is represented.

That explanation is fine for primitive types like int or double, but what does it mean when you declare a variable to have a reference type? What does it mean to declare variable myFrame to be of type JFrame?

Well, what does it mean to declare *i thank You God* to be an E. E. Cummings poem? What would it mean to write the following declaration?

```
EECummingsPoem ithankYouGod;
```

It means that a class of things is `EECummingsPoem`, and `ithankYouGod` refers to an instance of that class. In other words, `ithankYouGod` is an object belonging to the `EECummingsPoem` class.

Because `JFrame` is a class, you can create objects from that class. (See Chapter 1.) Each object (each instance of the `JFrame` class) is an actual frame — a window that appears on the screen when you run the code in Listing 4-6. By declaring the variable `myFrame` to be of type `JFrame`, you're reserving the use of the name `myFrame`. This reservation tells the computer that `myFrame` can refer to an actual `JFrame`-type object. In other words, `myFrame` can become a nickname for one of the windows that appears on the computer screen. Figure 4-10 illustrates the situation.

When you declare `ClassName variableName;`, you're saying that a certain variable can refer to an instance of a particular class.

In Listing 4-6, the phrase `JFrame myFrame` reserves the use of the name `myFrame`. On that same line of code, the phrase `new JFrame()` creates a new object (an instance of the `JFrame` class). Finally, that line's equal sign makes `myFrame` refer to the new object. Knowing that the two words `new JFrame()` create an object can be very important. For a more thorough explanation of objects, see Chapter 7.

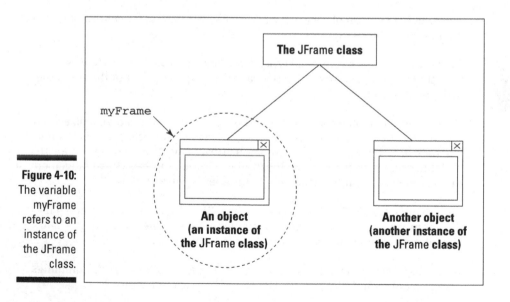

Figure 4-10:
The variable
myFrame
refers to an
instance of
the JFrame
class.

Primitive type stew

While I'm on the subject of frames, what's a frame anyway? A *frame* is a window that has a certain height and width and a certain location on your computer's screen. Therefore, deep inside the declaration of the `Frame` class, you can find variable declarations that look something like this:

```
int width;
int height;
int x;
int y;
```

Here's another example — `Time`. An instance of the `Time` class may have an hour (a number from 1 to 12), a number of minutes (from 0 to 59), and a letter (*a* for a.m.; *p* for p.m.).

```
int hour;
int minutes;
char amOrPm;
```

Notice that this high and mighty thing called a Java API class is neither high nor mighty. A class is just a collection of declarations. Some of those declarations are the declarations of variables. Some of those variable declarations use primitive types, and other variable declarations use reference types. These reference types, however, come from other classes, and the declarations of those classes have variables. The chain goes on and on. Ultimately, everything comes, in one way or another, from the primitive types.

An Import Declaration

It's always good to announce your intentions up front. Consider the following classroom lecture:

> *"Today, in our History of Film course, we'll be discussing the career of actor* **Lionel Herbert Blythe Barrymore**.
>
> *"Born in Philadelphia,* **Barrymore** *appeared in more than 200 films, including* It's a Wonderful Life, Key Largo, *and* Dr. Kildare's Wedding Day. *In addition,* **Barrymore** *was a writer, composer, and director.* **Barrymore** *did the voice of Ebenezer Scrooge every year on radio. . . ."*

Interesting stuff, heh? Now compare the paragraphs above with a lecture in which the instructor doesn't begin by introducing the subject:

> *"Welcome once again to the History of Film.*
>
> *"Born in Philadelphia,* **Lionel Barrymore** *appeared in more than 200 films, including It's a* Wonderful Life, Key Largo, *and* Dr. Kildare's Wedding Day. *In addition,* **Barrymore (not Ethel, John, or Drew)** *was a writer, composer, and director.* **Lionel Barrymore** *did the voice of Ebenezer Scrooge every year on radio. . . ."*

Without a proper introduction, a speaker may have to remind you constantly that the discussion is about Lionel Barrymore and not about some other Barrymore. The same is true in a Java program. Look again at Listing 4-6:

```
import javax.swing.JFrame;

public class ShowAFrame {

    public static void main(String args[]) {
        JFrame myFrame = new JFrame();
```

In Listing 4-6, you announce in the introduction (in the *import declaration*) that you're using JFrame in your Java class. You clarify what you mean by JFrame with the full name javax.swing.JFrame. (Hey! Didn't the first lecturer clarify with the full name "Lionel Herbert Blythe Barrymore?") After announcing your intentions in the import declaration, you can use the abbreviated name *JFrame* in your Java class code.

If you don't use an import declaration, then you have to repeat the full javax.swing.JFrame name wherever you use the name *JFrame* in your code. For example, without an import declaration, the code of Listing 4-6 would look like this:

```
public class ShowAFrame {

    public static void main(String args[]) {
        javax.swing.JFrame myFrame =
            new javax.swing.JFrame();
        String myTitle = "Blank Frame";

        myFrame.setTitle(myTitle);
        myFrame.setSize(3200, 200);
        myFrame.setDefaultCloseOperation
            (javax.swing.JFrame.EXIT_ON_CLOSE);
        myFrame.setVisible(true);
    }
}
```

The details of this import stuff can be pretty nasty. But fortunately, many IDEs have convenient helper features for import declarations. For details, see this book's website (www.allmycode.com/JavaForDummies).

No single section in this book can present the entire story about import declarations. To begin untangling some of the import declaration's subtleties, see Chapters 5, 9, and 10.

Creating New Values by Applying Operators

What could be more comforting than your old friend, the plus sign? It was the first thing that you learned about in elementary school math. Almost everybody knows how to add 2 and 2. In fact, in English usage, adding 2 and 2 is a metaphor for something that's easy to do. Whenever you see a plus sign, a cell in your brain says, "Thank goodness — it could be something much more complicated."

So Java has a plus sign. You can use it for several purposes. You can use the plus sign to add two numbers, like this:

```
int apples, oranges, fruit;
apples = 5;
oranges = 16;
fruit = apples + oranges;
```

You can also use the plus sign to paste `String` values together:

```
String startOfChapter =
    "It's three in the morning. I'm dreaming about the"+
    "history course that I failed in high school.";
System.out.println(startOfChapter);
```

This can be handy because in Java, you're not allowed to make a `String` straddle from one line to another. In other words, the following code wouldn't work at all:

```
String thisIsBadCode =
    "It's three in the morning. I'm dreaming about the
     history course that I failed in high school.";
System.out.println(thisIsBadCode);
```

The correct way to say that you're pasting `String` values together is to say that you're *concatenating* `String` values.

You can even use the plus sign to paste numbers next to `String` values.

```
int apples, oranges, fruit;
apples = 5;
oranges = 16;
fruit = apples + oranges;
System.out.println("You have" + fruit +
                   "pieces of fruit.");
```

Of course, the old minus sign is available, too (but not for `String` values).

```
apples = fruit - oranges;
```

Use an asterisk (*) for multiplication and a slash (/) for division.

```
double rate, pay;
int hours;

rate = 6.25;
hours = 35;
pay = rate * hours;
System.out.println(pay);
```

For an example using division, refer to Listing 4-3.

When you divide an `int` value by another `int` value, you get an `int` value. The computer doesn't round. Instead, the computer chops off any remainder. If you put `System.out.println(11 / 4)` in your program, the computer prints 2, not 2.75. To get past this, make either (or both) of the numbers you're dividing `double` values. If you put `System.out.println(11.0 / 4)` in your program, the computer prints 2.75.

Another useful arithmetic operator is called the *remainder* operator. The symbol for the remainder operator is the percent sign (%). When you put `System.out.println(11 % 4)` in your program, the computer prints 3. It does this because 4 goes into 11 who-cares-how-many times with a remainder of 3. The remainder operator turns out to be fairly useful. Listing 4-7 has an example.

Listing 4-7: Making Change

```
import static java.lang.System.out;

public class MakeChange {

    public static void main(String args[]) {
        int total = 248;
        int quarters = total / 25;
        int whatsLeft = total % 25;

        int dimes = whatsLeft / 10;
        whatsLeft = whatsLeft % 10;

        int nickels = whatsLeft / 5;
        whatsLeft = whatsLeft % 5;

        int cents = whatsLeft;

        out.println("From" + total + "cents you get");
        out.println(quarters + "quarters");
        out.println(dimes + "dimes");
        out.println(nickels + "nickels");
        out.println(cents + "cents");
    }
}
```

Figure 4-11 shows a run of the code in Listing 4-7. You start with a total of 248 cents. Then

```
quarters = total / 25
```

divides 248 by 25, giving 9. That means you can make 9 quarters from 248 cents. Next,

```
whatsLeft = total % 25
```

divides 248 by 25 again, and puts only the remainder, 23, into `whatsLeft`. Now you're ready for the next step, which is to take as many dimes as you can out of 23 cents.

Import declarations: The ugly truth

Notice the import declaration at the top of Listing 4-7:

```
import static java.lang.
    System.out;
```

Compare this with the import declaration at the top of Listing 4-6:

```
import javax.swing.JFrame;
```

By adding the `import static java.lang.System.out;` line to Listing 4-7, I can make the rest of the code a bit easier to read, and I can avoid having long Java statements that start on one line and continue on another. But you never have to do that. If you remove the `import static java.lang.System.out;` line and pepper the code liberally with `System.out.println`, and then the code works just fine.

Here's a question: Why does one declaration include the word *static,* while the other declaration doesn't? Well, to be honest, I wish I hadn't asked!

For the real story about *static,* you have to read part of Chapter 10. And frankly, I don't recommend skipping ahead to that chapter's *static* section if you take medicine for a heart condition, if you're pregnant or nursing, or if you have no previous experience with object-oriented programming. For now, rest assured that Chapter 10 is easy to read after you've made the journey through Part III of this book. And when you have to decide whether to use the word *static* in an import declaration, remember these hints:

- ✔ The vast majority of import declarations in Java program do not use the word *static.*

- ✔ In this book, I never use *import static* to import anything except `System.out`. (Well, almost never. . . .)

- ✔ Most import declarations don't use the word *static* because most declarations import classes. Unfortunately, `System.out` is not the name of a class.

The code in Listing 4-7 makes change in U.S. currency with the following coin denominations: 1 cent, 5 cents (one nickel), 10 cents (one dime), and 25 cents (one quarter). With these denominations, the MakeChange class gives you more than simply a set of coins adding up to 248 cents. The MakeChange class gives you the *smallest number of coins* that add up to 248 cents. With some minor tweaking, you can make the code work in any country's coinage. You can always get a set of coins adding up to a total. But, for the denominations of coins in some countries, you won't always get the *smallest number of coins* that add up to a total. In fact, I'm looking for examples. If your country's coinage prevents MakeChange from always giving the best answer, please, send me an e-mail (JavaForDummies@allmycode.com).

Figure 4-11:
Change for
$2.48.

```
From 248 cents you get
9 quarters
2 dimes
0 nickels
3 cents
```

Initialize once, assign often

Listing 4-7 has three lines that put values into the variable whatsLeft:

```java
int whatsLeft = total % 25;

whatsLeft = whatsLeft % 10;

whatsLeft = whatsLeft % 5;
```

Only one of these lines is a declaration. The other two lines are assignment statements. That's good because you can't declare the same variable more than once (not without creating something called a *block*). If you goof and write

```java
int whatsLeft = total % 25;

int whatsLeft = whatsLeft % 10;
```

in Listing 4-7, you see an error message (whatsLeft is already defined) when you try to compile your code.

To find out what a block is, see Chapter 5. Then, for some honest talk about redeclaring variables, see Chapter 10.

The increment and decrement operators

Java has some neat little operators that make life easier (for the computer's processor, for your brain, and for your fingers). Altogether, four such operators exist — two increment operators and two decrement operators.

The increment operators add 1, and the decrement operators subtract 1. The increment operators use double plus signs (++), and the decrement operators use double minus signs (– –). To see how they work, you need some examples. The first example is in Figure 4-12.

Figure 4-13 shows a run of the program in Figure 4-12. In this horribly uneventful run, the count of bunnies prints three times.

The double plus signs go by two names, depending on where you put them. When you put the ++ before a variable, the ++ is called the *preincrement* operator. (The *pre* stands for *before*.)

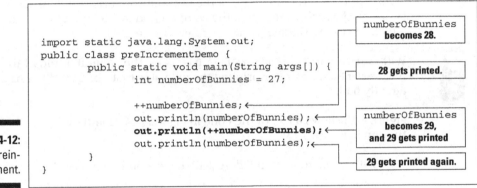

Figure 4-12:
Using preincrement.

```
import static java.lang.System.out;
public class preIncrementDemo {
        public static void main(String args[]) {
                int numberOfBunnies = 27;

                ++numberOfBunnies;
                out.println(numberOfBunnies);
                out.println(++numberOfBunnies);
                out.println(numberOfBunnies);
        }
}
```

numberOfBunnies becomes 28.

28 gets printed.

numberOfBunnies becomes 29, and 29 gets printed

29 gets printed again.

Figure 4-13:
A run of the code in Figure 4-12.

Console ✕
<terminated> Preincrer
28
29
29

The word *before* has two meanings:

- ✔ You put ++ before the variable.
- ✔ The computer adds 1 to the variable's value before the variable is used in any other part of the statement.

To understand this, look at the bold line in Figure 4-12. The computer adds 1 to numberOfBunnies (raising the value of numberOfBunnies to 29) and then prints 29 onscreen.

With `out.println(++numberOfBunnies)`, the computer adds 1 to `numberOfBunnies` before printing the new value of `numberOfBunnies` onscreen.

An alternative to preincrement is *postincrement*. (The *post* stands for *after*.) The word *after* has two different meanings:

- ✔ You put `++` after the variable.
- ✔ The computer adds 1 to the variable's value after the variable is used in any other part of the statement.

To see more clearly how postincrement works, look at the bold line in Figure 4-14. The computer prints the old value of `numberOfBunnies` (which is 28) on the screen, and then the computer adds 1 to `numberOfBunnies`, which raises the value of `numberOfBunnies` to 29.

With `out.println(numberOfBunnies++)`, the computer adds 1 to `numberOfBunnies` after printing the old value that `numberOfBunnies` already had.

Figure 4-15 shows a run of the code in Figure 4-14. Compare Figure 4-15 with the run in Figure 4-13:

- ✔ With preincrement in Figure 4-13, the second number is 29.
- ✔ With postincrement in Figure 4-15, the second number is 28.

  In Figure 4-15, 29 doesn't show onscreen until the end of the run, when the computer executes one last `out.println(numberOfBunnies)`.

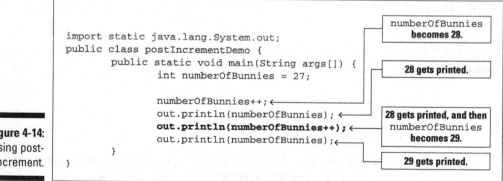

Figure 4-14: Using post-increment.

```
import static java.lang.System.out;
public class postIncrementDemo {
    public static void main(String args[]) {
        int numberOfBunnies = 27;

        numberOfBunnies++;
        out.println(numberOfBunnies);
        out.println(numberOfBunnies++);
        out.println(numberOfBunnies);
    }
}
```

numberOfBunnies **becomes 28.**

28 gets printed.

28 gets printed, and then numberOfBunnies **becomes 29.**

29 gets printed.

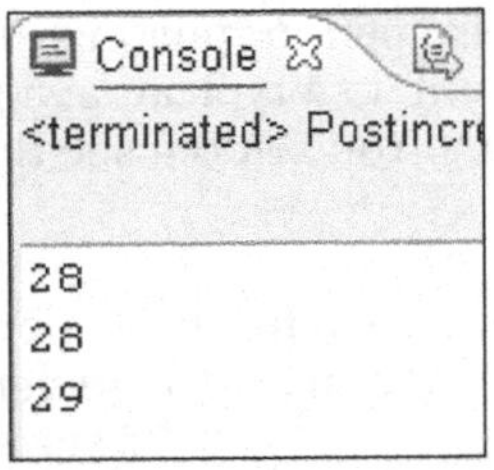

Figure 4-15:
A run of
the code in
Figure 4-14.

```
Console 
<terminated> Postincr

28
28
29
```

Statements and expressions

You can describe the pre- and postincrement and pre- and postdecrement operators in two ways: the way everyone understands them and the right way. The way that I explain the concept in most of this section (in terms of time, with *before* and *after*) is the way that everyone understands it. Unfortunately, the way everyone understands the concept isn't really the right way. When you see ++ or --, you can think in terms of time sequence. But occasionally some programmer uses ++ or -- in a convoluted way, and the notions of *before* and *after* break down. So, if you're ever in a tight spot, think about these operators in terms of statements and expressions.

First, remember that a statement tells the computer to do something, and an expression has a value. (I discuss statements in Chapter 3, and I describe expressions elsewhere in this chapter.) Which category does numberOfBunnies++ belong to? The surprising answer is both. The Java code numberOfBunnies++ is both a statement and an expression.

Assume that, before the computer executes the code out.println(numberOf Bunnies++), the value of numberOf Bunnies is 28.

✔ As a statement, numberOfBunnies++ tells the computer to add 1 to number OfBunnies.

✔ As an expression, the value of number OfBunnies++ is 28, not 29.

So, even though the computer adds 1 to numberOfBunnies, the code out. println(numberOfBunnies++) really means out.println(28).

Now, almost everything you just read about numberOfBunnies++ is true about ++numberOfBunnies. The only difference is that as an expression, ++numberOfBunnies behaves in a more intuitive way.

✔ As a statement, ++numberOfBunnies tells the computer to add 1 to number OfBunnies.

✔ As an expression, the value of ++number OfBunnies is 29.

So, with out.println(++numberOf Bunnies), the computer adds 1 to the variable numberOfBunnies, and the code out.println(++numberOfBunnies) really means out.println(29).

Are you trying to decide between using preincrement or postincrement? Try no longer. Most programmers use postincrement. In a typical Java program, you often see things like `numberOfBunnies++`. You seldom see things like `++numberOfBunnies`.

In addition to preincrement and postincrement, Java has two operators that use `--`. These operators are called *predecrement* and *postdecrement*.

- With predecrement (`--numberOfBunnies`), the computer subtracts 1 from the variable's value before the variable is used in the rest of the statement.

- With postdecrement (`numberOfBunnies--`), the computer subtracts 1 from the variable's value after the variable is used in the rest of the statement.

Instead of writing `++numberOfBunnies`, you could achieve the same effect by writing `numberOfBunnies = numberOfBunnies + 1`. So some people conclude that Java's `++` and `--` operators are for saving keystrokes — to keep those poor fingers from overworking themselves. This is entirely incorrect. The best reason for using `++` is to avoid the inefficient and error-prone practice of writing the same variable name, such as `numberOfBunnies`, twice in the same statement. If you write `numberOfBunnies` only once (as you do when you use `++` or `--`), the computer has to figure out what `numberOfBunnies` means only once. On top of that, when you write `numberOfBunnies` only once, you have only one chance (instead of two chances) to type the variable name incorrectly. With simple expressions like `numberOfBunnies++`, these advantages hardly make a difference. But with more complicated expressions, such as `inventoryItems[(quantityReceived--*itemsPerBox+17)]++`, the efficiency and accuracy that you gain by using `++` and `--` are significant.

Assignment operators

If you read the preceding section, which is about operators that add 1, you may be wondering whether you can manipulate these operators to add 2 or add 5 or add 1000000. Can you write `numberOfBunnies++++` and still call yourself a Java programmer? Well, you can't. If you try it, an error message appears when you try to compile your code.

So what can you do? As luck would have it, Java has plenty of assignment operators that you can use. With an *assignment operator,* you can add, subtract, multiply, or divide by anything you want. You can do other cool operations, too. Listing 4-8 has a smorgasbord of assignment operators (the things with equal signs). Figure 4-16 shows the output from running Listing 4-8.

Listing 4-8: **Assignment Operators**

```java
public class UseAssignmentOperators {

    public static void main(String args[]) {
        int numberOfBunnies = 27;
        int numberExtra = 53;

        numberOfBunnies += 1;
        System.out.println(numberOfBunnies);

        numberOfBunnies += 5;
        System.out.println(numberOfBunnies);

        numberOfBunnies += numberExtra;
        System.out.println(numberOfBunnies);

        numberOfBunnies *= 2;
        System.out.println(numberOfBunnies);

        System.out.println(numberOfBunnies -= 7);

        System.out.println(numberOfBunnies = 100);
    }
}
```

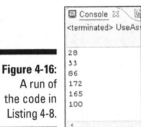

Figure 4-16:
A run of
the code in
Listing 4-8.

Listing 4-8 shows how versatile Java's assignment operators are. With the assignment operators, you can add, subtract, multiply, or divide a variable by any number. Notice how `+= 5` adds 5 to `numberOfBunnies`, and how `*= 2` multiplies `numberOfBunnies` by 2. You can even use another expression's value (in Listing 4-8, `numberExtra`) as the number to be applied.

The last two lines in Listing 4-8 demonstrate a special feature of Java's assignment operators. You can use an assignment operator as part of a larger Java statement. In the next to last line of Listing 4-8, the operator subtracts 7 from `numberOfBunnies`, decreasing the value of `numberOfBunnies` from `172` to `165`. Then the whole assignment business is stuffed into a call to `System.out.println`, so 165 prints onscreen.

Lo and behold, the last line of Listing 4-8 shows how you can do the same thing with Java's plain-old equal sign. The thing that I call an assignment statement near the start of this chapter is really one of the assignment operators that I describe in this section. Therefore, whenever you assign a value to something, you can make that assignment be part of a larger statement.

Each use of an assignment operator does double duty as a statement and an expression. In all cases, the expression's value equals whatever value you assign. For example, before executing the code `System.out.println(numberOfBunnies -= 7)`, the value of `numberOfBunnies` is `172`. As a statement, `numberOfBunnies -= 7` tells the computer to subtract 7 from `numberOfBunnies` (so the value of `numberOfBunnies` goes from `172` to `165`). As an expression, the value of `numberOfBunnies -= 7` is `165`. So the code `System.out.println(numberOfBunnies -= 7)` really means `System.out.println(165)`. The number 165 displays on the computer screen.

For a richer explanation of this kind of thing, see the sidebar "Statements and expressions," earlier in this chapter.

Chapter 5

Controlling Program Flow with Decision-Making Statements

. . . .

. . . .

*T*he TV show *Dennis the Menace* aired on CBS from 1959 to 1963. I remember one episode in which Mr. Wilson was having trouble making an important decision. I think it was something about changing jobs or moving to a new town. Anyway, I can still see that shot of Mr. Wilson sitting in his yard, sipping lemonade, and staring into nowhere for the whole afternoon. Of course, the annoying character Dennis was constantly interrupting Mr. Wilson's peace and quiet. That's what made this situation funny.

What impressed me about this episode (the reason why I remember it so clearly even now) was Mr. Wilson's dogged intent in making the decision. This guy wasn't going about his everyday business, roaming around the neighborhood, while thoughts about the decision wandered in and out of his mind. He was sitting quietly in his yard, making marks carefully and logically on his mental balance sheet. How many people actually make decisions this way?

At that time, I was still pretty young. I'd never faced the responsibility of making a big decision that affected my family and me. But I wondered what such a decision-making process would be like. Would it help to sit there like a stump for hours on end? Would I make my decisions by the careful weighing and tallying of options? Or would I shoot in the dark, take risks, and act on impulse? Only time would tell.

Making Decisions (Java if Statements)

When you're writing computer programs, you're constantly hitting forks in roads. Did the user correctly type his or her password? If yes, let the user work; if no, kick the bum out. So the Java programming language needs a way of making a program branch in one of two directions. Fortunately, the language has a way: It's called an if statement.

Guess the number

Listing 5-1 illustrates the use of an if statement. Two runs of the program in Listing 5-1 are shown in Figure 5-1.

Listing 5-1:   A Guessing Game

```java
import static java.lang.System.out;
import java.util.Scanner;
import java.util.Random;

public class GuessingGame {

    public static void main(String args[]) {
        Scanner keyboard = new Scanner(System.in);

        out.print("Enter an int from 1 to 10: ");

        int inputNumber = keyboard.nextInt();
        int randomNumber = new Random().nextInt(10) + 1;

        if (inputNumber == randomNumber) {
            out.println("**********");
            out.println("*You win.*");
            out.println("**********");
        } else {
            out.println("You lose.");
            out.print("The random number was ");
            out.println(randomNumber + ".");
        }

        out.println("Thank you for playing.");

        keyboard.close();
    }
}
```

```
Enter an int from 1 to 10: 2
**********
*You win.*
**********
Thank you for playing.


Enter an int from 1 to 10: 4
You lose.
The random number was 10.
Thank you for playing.
```

Figure 5-1:
Two runs of
the guessing
game.

The program in Listing 5-1 plays a guessing game with the user. The program gets a number (a guess) from the user and then generates a random number between 1 and 10. If the number that the user entered is the same as the random number, the user wins. Otherwise, the user loses, and the program tells the user what the random number was.

She controlled keystrokes from the keyboard

Taken together, the lines

```
import java.util.Scanner;

        Scanner keyboard = new Scanner(System.in);

        int inputNumber = keyboard.nextInt();
```

in Listing 5-1 get whatever number the user types on the computer's keyboard. The last of the three lines puts this number into a variable named *inputNumber*. If these lines look complicated, don't worry. You can copy these lines almost word for word whenever you want to read from the keyboard. Include the first two lines (the `import` and `Scanner` lines) just once in your program. Later in your program, wherever the user types an `int` value, include a line with a call to `nextInt` (as in the last of the preceding three lines of code).

Of all the names in these three lines of code, the only two names that I coined myself are *inputNumber* and *keyboard*. All the other names are part of Java. So, if I want to be creative, I can write the lines this way:

```
import java.util.Scanner;

        Scanner readingThingie = new Scanner(System.in);

        int valueTypedIn = readingThingie.nextInt();
```

I can also beef up my program's import declarations, as I do later on in Listings 5-2 and 5-3. Other than that, I have very little leeway.

As you read on in this book, you'll start recognizing the patterns behind these three lines of code, so I don't clutter up this section with all the details. For now, you can just copy these three lines and keep the following in mind:

- ✔ **When you import `java.util.Scanner`, you don't use the word *static*.**

  But importing `Scanner` is different from importing `System.out`. When you import `java.lang.System.out`, you use the word *static*. (Refer to Listing 5-1.) The difference creeps into the code because `Scanner` is the name of a class, and `System.out` isn't the name of a class.

  For a quick look at the use of the word *static* in import declarations, see one of the sidebars in Chapter 4. For a more complete story about the word, see Chapter 10.

- ✔ **Typically (on a desktop or laptop computer) the name *System.in* stands for the keyboard.**

  To get characters from some place other than the keyboard, you can type something other than `System.in` inside the parentheses.

  What else can you put inside the parentheses? For some ideas, see Chapter 8.

  In Listing 5-1, I make the arbitrary decision to give one of my variables the name `keyboard`. The name `keyboard` reminds you, the reader, that this variable refers to a bunch of plastic buttons in front of your computer. Naming something `keyboard` doesn't tell Java anything about plastic buttons or about user input. On the other hand, the name `System.in` always tells Java about those plastic buttons. The code `Scanner keyboard = new Scanner(System.in)` in Listing 5-1 connects the name `keyboard` with the plastic buttons that we all know and love.

- ✔ **When you expect the user to type an `int` value (a whole number of some kind), use `nextInt()`.**

  If you expect the user to type a `double` value (a number containing a decimal point), use `nextDouble()`. If you expect the user to type **true** or **false**, use `nextBoolean()`. If you expect the user to type a word like *Barry, Java,* or *Hello,* use `next()`.

  Decimal points vary from one country to another. In the United States, *10.5* (with a period) represents ten and a half, but in France, *10,5* (with a comma) represents ten and a half. In the Persian language, a decimal point looks like a slash (but it sits a bit lower than the digit characters). Your computer's operating system stores information about the country you live in, and Java reads that information to decide what *ten and a half*

looks like. If you run a program containing a `nextDouble()` method call, and Java responds with an `InputMismatchException`, check your input. You might have input `10.5` when your country's conventions require 10,5 (or some other way of representing *ten and a half*).

For an example in which the user types a word, see Listing 5-3 later in this chapter. For an example in which the user types a single character, see Listing 6-4 in Chapter 6. For an example in which a program reads an entire line of text (all in one big gulp), see Chapter 8.

✔ **You can get several values from the keyboard, one after another.**

To do this, use the `keyboard.nextInt()` code several times.

To see a program that reads more than one value from the keyboard, go to Listing 5-4 later in this chapter.

✔ Whenever you use Java's `Scanner`, you should call the `close` method after your last `nextInt` call (or your last `nextDouble` call, or your last next*Whatever* call).

In Listing 5-1, the `main` method's last statement is

```
keyboard.close();
```

This statement does some housekeeping to disconnect the Java program from the computer keyboard. (The amount of required housekeeping is more than you might think!) If I omit this statement from Listing 5-1, nothing terrible happens. Java's Virtual Machine usually cleans up after itself very nicely. But using `close()` to explicitly detach from the keyboard is good practice, and some IDEs display warnings if you omit the `keyboard.close()` statement. So in this book's example, I always remember to close my `Scanner` variables.

In Chapter 13, I show you a more reliable way to incorporate the `keyboard.close()` statement in your Java program.

When your program calls `System.out.println`, your program uses the computer's screen. So why don't you call a `close` method after all your `System.out.println` calls? The answer is subtle. In Listing 5-1, your own code connects to the keyboard by calling `new Scanner(in)`. So, later in the program, your code cleans up after itself by calling the `close` method. But with `System.out.println`, your own code doesn't create a connection to the screen. (The `out` variable refers to a `PrintStream`, but you don't call `new PrintStream()` to prepare for calling `System.out.println`.) Instead, the Java Virtual Machine connects to the screen on your behalf. The Java Virtual Machine's code (which you never have to see) contains a call to `new PrintStream()` in preparation for your calling `System.out.println`. So, being a well-behaved piece of code, the Java Virtual Machine eventually calls `out.close()` without any effort on your part.

Creating randomness

Achieving real randomness is surprisingly difficult. Mathematician Persi Diaconis says that if you flip a coin several times, always starting with the head side up, you're likely to toss heads more often than tails. If you toss several more times, always starting with the tail side up, you'll likely toss tails more often than heads. In other words, coin tossing isn't really fair.*

Computers aren't much better than coins and human thumbs. A computer mimics the generation of random sequences, but in the end, the computer just does what it's told and does all this in a purely deterministic fashion. So in Listing 5-1, when the computer executes

```
import java.util.Random;

        int randomNumber = new Random().nextInt(10) + 1;
```

the computer appears to give us a randomly generated number — a whole number between 1 and 10. But it's all a fake. The computer just follows instructions. It's not really random, but without bending a computer over backwards, it's the best that anyone can do.

Once again, I ask you to take this code on blind faith. Don't worry about what `new Random().nextInt` means until you have more experience with Java. Just copy this code into your own programs and have fun with it. And if the numbers from 1 to 10 aren't in your flight plans, don't fret. To roll an imaginary die, write the statement

```
int rollEmBaby = new Random().nextInt(6) + 1;
```

With the execution of this statement, the variable `rollEmBaby` gets a value from 1 to 6.

The if statement

At the core of Listing 5-1 is a Java `if` statement. This `if` statement represents a fork in the road. (See Figure 5-2.) The computer follows one of two prongs — the prong that prints `You win` or the prong that prints `You lose`. The computer decides which prong to take by testing the truth or falsehood of a *condition*. In Listing 5-1, the condition being tested is

```
inputNumber == randomNumber
```

---

* Diaconis, Persi. "The Search for Randomness." American Association for the Advancement of Science annual meeting. Seattle. 14 Feb. 2004.

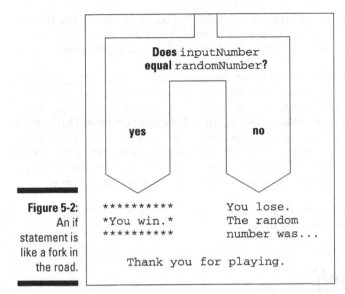

Figure 5-2:
An if
statement is
like a fork in
the road.

```
Does inputNumber
equal randomNumber?



yes                    no



* * * * * * * * * *     You lose.
*You win.*             The random
* * * * * * * * * *     number was...

Thank you for playing.
```

Does the value of inputNumber equal the value of randomNumber? When
the condition is true, the computer does the stuff between the condition and the
word *else*. When the condition turns out to be false, the computer does the
stuff after the word *else*. Either way, the computer goes on to execute the last
println call, which displays Thank you for playing.

The condition in an if statement must be enclosed in parentheses. However,
a line like if (inputNumber == randomNumber) is not a complete statement (just as "If I had a hammer" isn't a complete sentence). So this line if
(inputNumber == randomNumber) shouldn't end with a semicolon.

Sometimes, when I'm writing about a condition that's being tested, I slip into
using the word *expression* instead of *condition*. That's okay because every
condition is an expression. An expression is something that has a value and,
sure enough, every condition has a value. The condition's value is either
true or false. (For revealing information about expressions and values
like true and false, see Chapter 4.)

The double equal sign

In Listing 5-1, in the if statement's condition, notice the use of the double
equal sign. Comparing two numbers to see whether they're the same isn't the
same as setting something equal to something else. That's why the symbol to
compare for equality isn't the same as the symbol that's used in an assignment

or an initialization. In an `if` statement's condition, you can't replace the double equal sign with a single equal sign. If you do, your program just won't work. (You almost always get an error message when you try to compile your code.)

On the other hand, if you never make the mistake of using a single equal sign in a condition, you're not normal. Not long ago, while I was teaching an introductory Java course, I promised that I'd swallow my laser pointer if no one made the single equal sign mistake during any of the lab sessions. This wasn't an idle promise. I knew I'd never have to keep it. As it turned out, even if I had ignored the first ten times anybody made the single equal sign mistake during those lab sessions, I would still be laser-pointer free. Everybody mistakenly uses the single equal sign several times in his or her programming career.

The trick is not to avoid making the single equal sign mistake; the trick is to catch the mistake whenever you make it.

Brace yourself

The `if` statement in Listing 5-1 has two halves — a top half and a bottom half. I have names for these two parts of an `if` statement. I call them the *if part* (the top half) and the *else part* (the bottom half).

The `if` part in Listing 5-1 seems to have more than one statement in it. I make this happen by enclosing the three statements of the `if` part in a pair of curly braces. When I do this, I form a *block*. A block is a bunch of statements scrunched together by a pair of curly braces.

With this block, three calls to `println` are tucked away safely inside the `if` part. With the curly braces, the rows of asterisks and the words `You win` display only when the user's guess is correct.

This business with blocks and curly braces applies to the `else` part as well. In Listing 5-1, whenever `inputNumber` doesn't equal `randomNumber`, the computer executes three `print`/`println` calls. To convince the computer that all three of these calls are inside the `else` clause, I put these calls into a block. That is, I enclose these three calls in a pair of curly braces.

Strictly speaking, Listing 5-1 has only one statement between the `if` and the `else` statements and only one statement after the `else` statement. The trick is that when you place a bunch of statements inside curly braces, you get a block; and a block behaves, in all respects, like a single statement. In fact, the official Java documentation lists blocks as one of the many kinds of statements. So, in Listing 5-1, the block that prints `You win` and asterisks is a single statement that has, within it, three smaller statements.

Indenting if statements in your code

Notice how, in Listing 5-1, the `print` and `println` calls inside the `if` statement are indented. (This includes both the `You win` and `You lose` statements. The `print` and `println` calls that come after the word *else* are still part of the `if` statement.) Strictly speaking, you don't have to indent the statements that are inside an `if` statement. For all the compiler cares, you can write your whole program on a single line or place all your statements in an artful, misshapen zigzag. The problem is that neither you nor anyone else can make sense of your code if you don't indent your statements in some logical fashion. In Listing 5-1, the indenting of the `print` and `println` statements helps your eye (and brain) see quickly that these statements are subordinate to the overall `if`/`else` flow.

In a small program, unindented or poorly indented code is barely tolerable. But in a complicated program, indentation that doesn't follow a neat, logical pattern is a big, ugly nightmare.

Many Java IDEs have tools to indent your code automatically. In fact, code indentation is one of my favorite IDE features. So don't walk — run — to a computer, and visit this book's website (`www.allmycode.com/JavaForDummies`) for more information on what Java IDEs can offer.

When you write `if` statements, you may be tempted to chuck all the rules about curly braces out the window and just rely on indentation. Unfortunately, this seldom works. If you indent three statements after the word *else* and forget to enclose those statements in curly braces, the computer thinks that the `else` part includes only the first of the three statements. What's worse, the indentation misleads you into believing that the `else` part includes all three statements. This makes it more difficult for you to figure out why your code isn't behaving the way you think it should. So watch those braces!

Elseless in Ifrica

Okay, so the title of this section is contrived. Big deal! The idea is that you can create an `if` statement without the `else` part. Take, for instance, the code in Listing 5-1, shown earlier. Maybe you'd rather not rub it in whenever the user loses the game. The modified code in Listing 5-2 shows you how to do this (and Figure 5-3 shows you the result).

Listing 5-2: A Kinder, Gentler Guessing Game

```java
import static java.lang.System.in;
import static java.lang.System.out;
import java.util.Scanner;
import java.util.Random;

public class DontTellThemTheyLost {

    public static void main(String args[]) {
        Scanner keyboard = new Scanner(in);

        out.print("Enter an int from 1 to 10: ");

        int inputNumber = keyboard.nextInt();
        int randomNumber = new Random().nextInt(10) + 1;

        if (inputNumber == randomNumber) {
            out.println("*You win.*");
        }

        out.println("That was a very good guess :-)");
        out.print("The random number was ");
        out.println(randomNumber + ".");
        out.println("Thank you for playing.");

        keyboard.close();
    }
}
```

```
Enter an int from 1 to 10: 4
*You win.*
That was a very good guess :-)
The random number was 4.
Thank you for playing.


Enter an int from 1 to 10: 4
That was a very good guess :-)
The random number was 6.
Thank you for playing.
```

Figure 5-3:
Two runs of
the game in
Listing 5-2.

The if statement in Listing 5-2 has no else part. When inputNumber is the same as randomNumber, the computer prints You win. When inputNumber is different from randomNumber, the computer doesn't print You win.

Listing 5-2 illustrates another new idea. With an import declaration for System. in, I can reduce new Scanner(System.in) to the shorter new Scanner(in). Adding this import declaration is hardly worth the effort. In fact, I do more typing with the import declaration than without it. Nevertheless, the code in Listing 5-2 demonstrates that it's possible to import System.in.

Forming Conditions with Comparisons and Logical Operators

The Java programming language has plenty of little squiggles and doodads for your various condition-forming needs. This section tells you all about them.

Comparing numbers; comparing characters

Table 5-1 shows you the operators that you can use to compare one thing with another.

Table 5-1	Comparison Operators	
Operator Symbol	**Meaning**	**Example**
==	is equal to	`numberOfCows == 5`
!=	is not equal to	`buttonClicked != panicButton`
<	is less than	`numberOfCows < 5`
>	is greater than	`myInitial > 'B'`
<=	is less than or equal to	`numberOfCows <= 5`
>=	is greater than or equal to	`myInitial >= 'B'`

You can use all Java's comparison operators to compare numbers and characters. When you compare numbers, things go pretty much the way you think they should go. But when you compare characters, things are a little strange. Comparing uppercase letters with one another is no problem. Because the letter *B* comes alphabetically before *H,* the condition `'B' < 'H'` is true. Comparing lowercase letters with one another is also okay. What's strange is that when you compare an uppercase letter with a lowercase letter, the uppercase letter is always smaller. So, even though `'Z' < 'A'` is false, `'Z' < 'a'` is true.

Under the hood, the letters *A* through *Z* are stored with numeric codes 65 through 90. The letters *a* through *z* are stored with codes 97 through 122. That's why each uppercase letter is smaller than each lowercase letter.

Be careful when you compare two numbers for equality (with `==`) or inequality (with `!=`). After doing some calculations and obtaining two `double` values or two `float` values, the values that you have are seldom dead-on equal to one another. (The problem comes from those pesky digits beyond the decimal point.) For instance, the Fahrenheit equivalent of 21 degrees Celsius is

69.8, and when you calculate `9.0 / 5 * 21 + 32` by hand, you get 69.8. But the condition `9.0 / 5 * 21 + 32 == 69.8` turns out to be false. That's because, when the computer calculates `9.0 / 5 * 21 + 32`, it gets 69.80000000000001, not 69.8.

Comparing objects

When you start working with objects, you find that you can use `==` and `!=` to compare objects with one another. For instance, a button that you see on the computer screen is an object. You can ask whether the thing that was just mouse-clicked is a particular button on your screen. You do this with Java's equality operator.

```
if (e.getSource() == bCopy) {
    clipboard.setText(which.getText());
```

To find out more about responding to button clicks, read Chapter 15.

The big gotcha with Java's comparison scheme comes when you compare two strings. (For a word or two about Java's `String` type, see the section about reference types in Chapter 4.) When you compare two strings with one another, you don't want to use the double equal sign. Using the double equal sign would ask, "Is this string stored in exactly the same place in memory as that other string?" Usually, that's not what you want to ask. Instead, you usually want to ask, "Does this string have the same characters in it as that other string?" To ask the second question (the more appropriate question) Java's `String` type has a method named *equals*. (Like everything else in the known universe, this `equals` method is defined in the Java API, short for Application Programming Interface.) The `equals` method compares two strings to see whether they have the same characters in them. For an example using Java's `equals` method, see Listing 5-3. (Figure 5-4 shows a run of the program in Listing 5-3.)

Figure 5-4:
The results
of using `==`
and using
Java's
equals
method.

```
What's the password? swordfish
You typed >>swordfish<<

The word you typed is not
stored in the same place as
the real password, but that's
no big deal.

The word you typed has the
same characters as the real
password. You can use our
precious system.
```

Listing 5-3:   Checking a Password

```java
import static java.lang.System.*;
import java.util.Scanner;

public class CheckPassword {

    public static void main(String args[]) {

        out.print("What's the password?");

        Scanner keyboard = new Scanner(in);
        String password = keyboard.next();

        out.println("You typed >>" + password + "<<");
        out.println();

        if (password == "swordfish") {
            out.println("The word you typed is stored");
            out.println("in the same place as the real");
            out.println("password. You must be a");
            out.println("hacker.");
        } else {
            out.println("The word you typed is not");
            out.println("stored in the same place as");
            out.println("the real password, but that's");
            out.println("no big deal.");
        }
        out.println();

        if (password.equals("swordfish")) {
            out.println("The word you typed has the");
            out.println("same characters as the real");
            out.println("password. You can use our");
            out.println("precious system.");
        } else {
            out.println("The word you typed doesn't");
            out.println("have the same characters as");
            out.println("the real password. You can't");
            out.println("use our precious system.");
        }

        keyboard.close();
    }
}
```

In Listing 5-3, the call `keyboard.next()` grabs whatever word the user types on the computer keyboard. The code shoves this word into the variable named *password*. Then the program's `if` statements use two different techniques to compare `password` with `"swordfish"`.

The examples in the printed book are mostly text-based, but you can find fancier versions of most examples on this book's website (www.allmycode.com/JavaForDummies). These fancier versions have windows, buttons, text fields, and other elements of a typical *graphical user interface* (GUI).

The more appropriate of the two techniques uses Java's equals method. The equals method looks funny because when you call it, you put a dot after one string and put the other string in parentheses. But that's the way you have to do it.

In calling Java's equals method, it doesn't matter which string gets the dot and which gets the parentheses. For instance, in Listing 5-3, you could have written

```
if ("swordfish".equals(password))
```

The method would work just as well.

A call to Java's equals method looks imbalanced, but it's not. There's a reason behind the apparent imbalance between the dot and the parentheses. The idea is that you have two objects: the password object and the "swordfish" object. Each of these two objects is of type String. (However, password is a variable of type String, and "swordfish" is a String literal.) When you write password.equals("swordfish"), you're calling an equals method that belongs to the password object. When you call that method, you're feeding "swordfish" to the method as the method's parameter (pun intended).

You can read more about methods belonging to objects in Chapter 7.

When comparing strings with one another, use the equals method — not the double equal sign.

Importing everything in one fell swoop

The first line of Listing 5-3 illustrates a lazy way of importing both System.out and System.in. To import everything that System has to offer, you use the asterisk wildcard character (*). In fact, importing java.lang.System.* is like having about 30 separate import declarations, including System.in, System.out, System.err, System.nanoTime, and many other System things.

The use of an asterisk in an `import` declaration is generally considered bad programming practice, so I don't do it often in this book's examples. But for larger programs — programs that use dozens of names from the Java API — the lazy asterisk trick is handy.

You can't toss an asterisk anywhere you want inside an `import` declaration. For example, you can't import everything starting with java by writing `import java.*`. You can substitute an asterisk only for the name of a class or for the name of something static that's tucked away inside a class. For more information about asterisks in `import` declarations, see Chapter 9. For information about static things, see Chapter 10.

Java's logical operators

Mr. Spock would be pleased. Java has all the operators that you need for mixing and matching logical tests. The operators are shown in Table 5-2.

Table 5-2		Logical Operators
Operator Symbol	*Meaning*	*Example*
`&&`	and	`5 < x && x < 10`
`||`	or	`x < 5 || 10 < x`
`!`	not	`!password.equals("swordfish")`

You can use these operators to form all kinds of elaborate conditions. Listing 5-4 has an example.

Listing 5-4:   Checking Username and Password

```java
import javax.swing.JOptionPane;

public class Authenticator {

    public static void main(String args[]) {

        String username =
            JOptionPane.showInputDialog("Username:");
        String password =
            JOptionPane.showInputDialog("Password:");

        if (
            username != null &&
```

(continued)

Listing 5-4 *(continued)*

```
            password != null &&
            (
                (username.equals("bburd") &&
                 password.equals("swordfish")) ||
                (username.equals("hritter") &&
                 password.equals("preakston"))
            )
        )
    {
        JOptionPane.showMessageDialog
            (null, "You're in.");
    } else {
        JOptionPane.showMessageDialog
            (null, "You're suspicious.");
    }
    }
}
```

Several runs of the program of Listing 5-4 are shown in Figure 5-5. When the username is *bburd* and the password is *swordfish* or when the username is *hritter* and the password is *preakston,* the user gets a nice message. Otherwise, the user is a bum who gets the nasty message that he or she deserves.

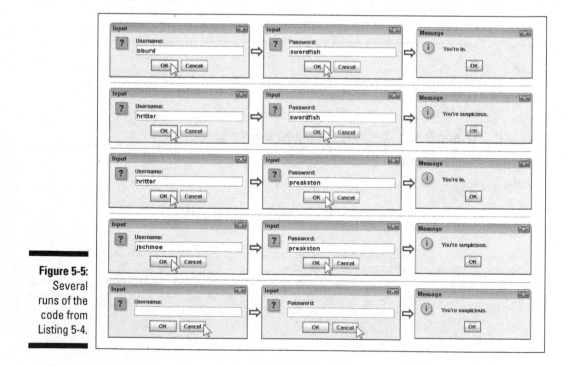

Figure 5-5:
Several runs of the code from Listing 5-4.

Confession: Figure 5-5 is a fake! To help you read the usernames and passwords, I added an extra statement to Listing 5-4. The extra statement (`UIManager.put("TextField.font", new Font("Dialog", Font.BOLD, 14))`) enlarges each text field's font size. Yes, I modified the code before creating the figure. Shame on me!

Listing 5-4 illustrates a new way to get user input; namely, to show the user an input dialog. The statement

```
String password =
    JOptionPane.showInputDialog("Password:");
```

in Listing 5-4 performs more or less the same task as the statement

```
String password = keyboard.next();
```

from Listing 5-3. The big difference is, while `keyboard.next()` displays dull-looking text in a console, `JOptionPane.showInputDialog("Username:")` displays a fancy dialog box containing a text field and buttons. (Compare Figures 5-4 and 5-5.) When the user clicks OK, the computer takes whatever text is in the text field and hands that text over to a variable. In fact, Listing 5-4 uses `JOptionPane.showInputDialog` twice — once to get a value for the `username` variable and a second time to get a value for the `password` variable.

Near the end of Listing 5-4, I use a slight variation on the `JOptionPane` business,

```
JOptionPane.showMessageDialog
    (null, "You're in.");
```

With `showMessageDialog`, I show a very simple dialog box — a box with no text field. (Again, see Figure 5-5.)

Like thousands of other names, the name `JOptionPane` is defined in Java's API. (To be more specific, `JOptionPane` is defined inside something called `javax.swing`, which in turn is defined inside Java's API.) So to use the name `JOptionPane` throughout Listing 5-4, I import `javax.swing.JOptionPane` at the top of the listing.

In Listing 5-4, `JOptionPane.showInputDialog` works nicely because the user's input (username and password) are mere strings of characters. If you want the user to input a number (an `int` or a `double`, for example), you have to do some extra work. For example, to get an `int` value from the user, type something like `int numberOfCows = Integer.parseInt(JOptionPane.showInputDialog("How many cows?"))`. The extra `Integer.parseInt`

stuff forces your text field's input to be an `int` value. To get a `double` value from the user, type something like `double fractionOfHolsteins = Double.parseDouble(JOptionPane.showInputDialog("Holsteins:"))`. The extra `Double.parseDouble` business forces your text field's input to be a `double` value.

Vive les nuls!

The French translations of *For Dummies* books are books *Pour les Nuls.* So a "dummy" in English is a "nul" in French. But in Java, the word `null` means "nothing." When you see

```
if (
    username != null
```

in Listing 5-4, you can imagine that you see

```
if (
    username isn't nothing
```

or

```
if (
    username has any value at all
```

To find out how `username` can have no value, see the last row in Figure 5-5. When you click Cancel in the first dialog box, the computer hands `null` to your program. So in Listing 5-4, the variable `username` becomes `null`. The comparisons `username != null` checks to make sure that you haven't clicked Cancel in the program's first dialog box. The comparison `password != null` performs the same kind of check for the program's second dialog box. When you see the `if` statement in Listing 5-4, you can imagine that you see the following:

```
if (
    you didn't press Cancel in the username dialog and
    you didn't press Cancel in the password dialog and
    (
      (you typed "bburd" in the username dialog) and
       you typed "swordfish" in the password dialog)) or
      (you typed "hritter" in the username dialog) and
       you typed "preakston" in the password dialog))
    )
  )
```

In Listing 5-4, the comparisons `username != null` and `password != null` are not optional. If you forget to include these and click Cancel when the program runs, you get a nasty `NullPointerException` message, and the program comes crashing down before your eyes. The word `null` represents *nothing*, and in Java, you can't compare *nothing* to a string like `"bburd"` or `"swordfish"`. In Listing 5-4, the purpose of the comparison `username != null` is to prevent Java from moving on to check `username.equals("bburd")` whenever you happen to click Cancel. Without this preliminary `username != null` test, you're courting trouble.

The last couple of `null`s in Listing 5-4 are different from the others. In the code `JOptionPane.showMessageDialog (null, "You're in.")`, the word `null` stands for "no other dialog box." In particular, the call `showMessageDialog` tells Java to pop up a new dialog box, and the word `null` indicates that the new dialog box doesn't grow out of any existing dialog box. One way or another, Java insists that you say something about the origin of the newly popped dialog box. (For some reason, Java doesn't insist that you specify the origin of the `showInputDialog` box. Go figure!) Anyway, in Listing 5-4, having a `showMessageDialog` box pop up from nowhere is quite useful.

(Conditions in parentheses)

Keep an eye on those parentheses! When you're combining conditions with logical operators, it's better to waste typing effort and add unneeded parentheses than to goof up your result by using too few parentheses. Take, for example, the expression

```
2 < 5 || 100 < 6 && 27 < 1
```

By misreading this expression, you might conclude that the expression is false. That is, you could wrongly read the expression as meaning `(something-or-other) && 27 < 1`. Because 27 < 1 is false, you would conclude that the whole expression is false. The fact is that, in Java, any `&&` operator is evaluated before any `||` operator. So the expression really asks if `2 < 5 || (something-or-other)`. Because 2 < 5 is true, the whole expression is true.

To change the expression's value from `true` to `false`, you can put the expression's first two comparisons in parentheses, like this:

```
(2 < 5 || 100 < 6) && 27 < 1
```

Java's || operator is *inclusive*. This means that you get a true value whenever the thing on the left side is true, the thing on the right side is true, or both things are true. For instance, the expression 2 < 10 || 20 < 30 is true.

In Java, you can't combine comparisons the way you do in ordinary English. In English, you may say, "We'll have between three and ten people at the dinner table." But in Java, you get an error message if you write 3 <= people <= 10. To do this comparison, you need something like 3 <= people && people <= 10.

In Listing 5-4, the if statement's condition has more than a dozen parentheses. What happens if you omit two of them?

```
if (
    username != null &&
    password != null &&
    // open parenthesis omitted
        (username.equals("bburd") &&
         password.equals("swordfish")) ||
        (username.equals("hritter") &&
         password.equals("preakston"))
    // close parenthesis omitted
    )
```

Java tries to interpret your wishes by grouping everything before the "or" (the || operator):

```
if (
    username != null &&
    password != null &&
    (username.equals("bburd") &&
     password.equals("swordfish"))

    ||

    (username.equals("hritter") &&
     password.equals("preakston"))
    )
```

When the user clicks Cancel and username is null, Java says, "Okay! The stuff before the || operator is false, but maybe the stuff after the || operator is true. I'll check the stuff after the || operator to find out whether it's true." (Java often talks to itself. The psychiatrists are monitoring this situation.)

Anyway, when Java finally checks username.equals("hritter"), your program aborts with an ugly NullPointerException message. You've made Java angry by trying to apply .equals to a null username. (Psychiatrists have recommended anger management sessions for Java, but Java's insurance plan refuses to pay for the sessions.)

Building a Nest

Have you seen those cute Russian Matryoshka nesting dolls? Open one, and another one is inside. Open the second, and a third one is inside it. You can do the same thing with Java's if statements. (Talk about fun!) Listing 5-5 shows you how.

Listing 5-5:   Nested if Statements

```
import static java.lang.System.out;
import java.util.Scanner;

public class Authenticator2 {

    public static void main(String args[]) {
        Scanner keyboard = new Scanner(System.in);

        out.print("Username: ");
        String username = keyboard.next();

        if (username.equals("bburd")) {
            out.print("Password: ");
            String password = keyboard.next();

            if (password.equals("swordfish")) {
                out.println("You're in.");
            } else {
                out.println("Incorrect password");
            }

        } else {
            out.println("Unknown user");
        }

        keyboard.close();
    }
}
```

Figure 5-6 shows several runs of the code in Listing 5-5. The main idea is that to log on, you have to pass two tests. (In other words, two conditions must be true.) The first condition tests for a valid username; the second condition tests for the correct password. If you pass the first test (the username test), you march right into another if statement that performs a second test (the password test). If you fail the first test, you never make it to the second test. Figure 5-7 shows the overall plan.

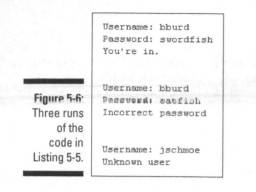

Figure 5-6:
Three runs
of the
code in
Listing 5-5.

```
Username: bburd
Password: swordfish
You're in.


Username: bburd
Password: catfish
Incorrect password


Username: jschmoe
Unknown user
```

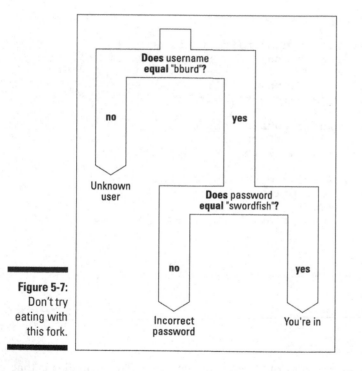

Figure 5-7:
Don't try
eating with
this fork.

The code in Listing 5-5 does a good job with nested `if` statements, but it does a terrible job with real-world user authentication. First, never show a password in plain view (without asterisks to masquerade the password). Second, don't handle passwords without encrypting them. Third, don't tell the malicious user which of the two words (the username or the password) was entered incorrectly. Fourth . . . well I could go on and on. The code in Listing 5-5 just isn't meant to illustrate good username/password practices.

Choosing among Many Alternatives (Java switch Statements)

I'm the first to admit that I hate making decisions. If things go wrong, I would rather have the problem be someone else's fault. Writing the previous sections (on making decisions with Java's if statement) knocked the stuffing right out of me. That's why my mind boggles as I begin this section on choosing among many alternatives. What a relief it is to have that confession out of the way!

Your basic switch statement

Now, it's time to explore situations in which you have a decision with many branches. Take, for instance, the popular campfire song "Al's All Wet." (For a review of the lyrics, see the sidebar.) You're eager to write code that prints this song's lyrics. Fortunately, you don't have to type all the words over and over again. Instead, you can take advantage of the repetition in the lyrics.

A complete program to display the "Al's All Wet" lyrics won't come until Chapter 6. In the meantime, assume that you have a variable named *verse*. The value of verse is 1, 2, 3, or 4, depending on which verse of "Al's All Wet" you're trying to print. You could have a big, clumsy bunch of if statements that checks each possible verse number.

```
if (verse == 1) {
    out.println("That's because he has no brain.");
}
if (verse == 2) {
    out.println("That's because he is a pain.");
}
if (verse == 3) {
    out.println("'Cause this is the last refrain.");
}
```

But that approach seems wasteful. Why not create a statement that checks the value of verse just once and then takes an action based on the value that it finds? Fortunately, just such a statement exists. It's called a *switch* statement. Listing 5-6 has an example of a switch statement.

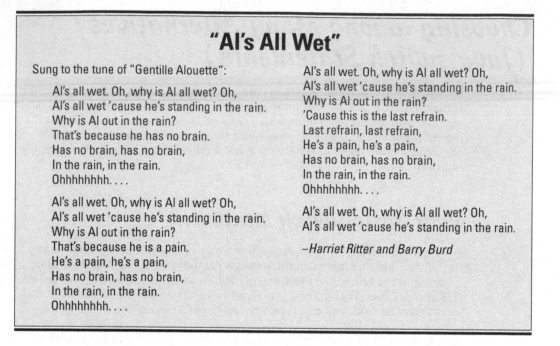

"Al's All Wet"

Sung to the tune of "Gentille Alouette":

Al's all wet. Oh, why is Al all wet? Oh,
Al's all wet 'cause he's standing in the rain.
Why is Al out in the rain?
That's because he has no brain.
Has no brain, has no brain,
In the rain, in the rain.
Ohhhhhhhh. . . .

Al's all wet. Oh, why is Al all wet? Oh,
Al's all wet 'cause he's standing in the rain.
Why is Al out in the rain?
That's because he is a pain.
He's a pain, he's a pain,
Has no brain, has no brain,
In the rain, in the rain.
Ohhhhhhhh. . . .

Al's all wet. Oh, why is Al all wet? Oh,
Al's all wet 'cause he's standing in the rain.
Why is Al out in the rain?
'Cause this is the last refrain.
Last refrain, last refrain,
He's a pain, he's a pain,
Has no brain, has no brain,
In the rain, in the rain.
Ohhhhhhhh. . . .

Al's all wet. Oh, why is Al all wet? Oh,
Al's all wet 'cause he's standing in the rain.

—Harriet Ritter and Barry Burd

Listing 5-6: A switch Statement

```java
import static java.lang.System.out;
import java.util.Scanner;

public class JustSwitchIt {

    public static void main(String args[]) {
        Scanner keyboard = new Scanner(System.in);
        out.print("Which verse? ");
        int verse = keyboard.nextInt();

        switch (verse) {
        case 1:
            out.println("That's because he has no brain.");
            break;
        case 2:
            out.println("That's because he is a pain.");
            break;
        case 3:
            out.println("'Cause this is the last refrain.");
            break;
        default:
            out.println("No such verse. Please try again.");
```

```
        break;
    }

    out.println("Ohhhhhhhh . . . .");

    keyboard.close();
    }
}
```

Figure 5-8 shows two runs of the program in Listing 5-6. (Figure 5-9 illustrates the program's overall idea.) First, the user types a number, like the number 2. Then, execution of the program reaches the top of the switch statement. The computer checks the value of the verse variable. When the computer determines that the verse variable's value is 2, the computer checks each case of the switch statement. The value 2 doesn't match the topmost case, so the computer proceeds on to the middle of the three cases. The value posted for the middle case (the number 2) matches the value of the verse variable, so the computer executes the statements that come immediately after case 2. These two statements are

```
out.println("That's because he is a pain.");
break;
```

Figure 5-8:
Running
the code of
Listing 5-6
two times.

```
Which verse? 2
That's because he is a pain.
Ohhhhhhhh. . . .


Which verse? 6
No such verse. Please try again.
Ohhhhhhhh. . . .
```

The first of the two statements displays the line That's because he is a pain. on the screen. The second statement is called a *break* statement. (What a surprise!) When the computer encounters a break statement, the computer jumps out of whatever switch statement it's in. So, in Listing 5-6, the computer skips right past the case that would display 'Cause this is the last refrain. In fact, the computer jumps out of the entire switch statement and goes straight to the statement just after the end of the switch statement. The computer displays Ohhhhhhhh. . . . because that's what the statement after the switch statement tells the computer to do.

If the pesky user asks for verse 6, the computer responds by dropping past cases 1, 2, and 3. Instead, the computer does the default. In the default, the computer displays No such verse. Please try again, and then breaks out of the switch statement. After the computer is out of the switch statement, the computer displays Ohhhhhhhh. . . .

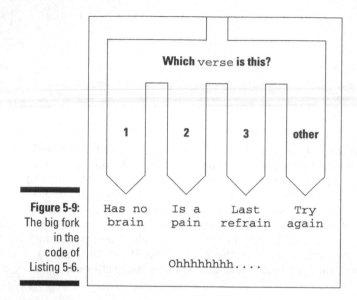

Figure 5-9:
The big fork
in the
code of
Listing 5-6.

You don't really need to put a break at the very end of a switch statement. In Listing 5-6, the last break (the break that's part of the default) is just for the sake of overall tidiness.

To break or not to break

In every Java programmer's life, a time comes when he or she forgets to use break statements. At first, the resulting output is confusing, but then the programmer remembers fall-through. The term *fall-through* describes what happens when you end a case without a break statement. What happens is that execution of the code falls right through to the next case in line. Execution keeps falling through until you eventually reach a break statement or the end of the entire switch statement.

Usually, when you're using a switch statement, you don't want fall-through, so you pepper break statements throughout the switch statements. But, occasionally, fall-through is just the thing you need. Take, for instance, the "Al's All Wet" song. (The classy lyrics are shown in the sidebar bearing the song's name.) Each verse of "Al's All Wet" adds new lines in addition to the lines from previous verses. This situation (accumulating lines from one verse to another) cries out for a switch statement with fall-through. Listing 5-7 demonstrates the idea.

Listing 5-7:   A switch Statement with Fall-Through

```java
import static java.lang.System.out;
import java.util.Scanner;

public class FallingForYou {

    public static void main(String args[]) {
        Scanner keyboard = new Scanner(System.in);
        out.print("Which verse? ");
        int verse = keyboard.nextInt();

        switch (verse) {
        case 3:
            out.print("Last refrain, ");
            out.println("last refrain,");
        case 2:
            out.print("He's a pain, ");
            out.println("he's a pain,");
        case 1:
            out.print("Has no brain, ");
            out.println("has no brain,");
        }

        out.println("In the rain, in the rain.");
        out.println("Ohhhhhhhh...");
        out.println();

        keyboard.close();
    }
}
```

Figure 5-10 shows several runs of the program in Listing 5-7. Because the switch has no `break` statements in it, fall-through happens all over the place. For instance, when the user selects verse 2, the computer executes the two statements in case 2:

```java
out.print("He's a pain, ");
out.println("he's a pain,");
```

Then, the computer marches right on to execute the two statements in case 1:

```java
out.print("Has no brain, ");
out.println("has no brain,");
```

That's good because the song's second verse has all these lines in it.

```
Which verse? 1
Has no brain, has no brain,
In the rain, in the rain.
Ohhhhhhhh...

Which verse? 2
He's a pain, he's a pain,
Has no brain, has no brain,
In the rain, in the rain.
Ohhhhhhhh...

Which verse? 3
Last refrain, last refrain,
He's a pain, he's a pain,
Has no brain, has no brain,
In the rain, in the rain.
Ohhhhhhhh...

Which verse? 6
In the rain, in the rain.
Ohhhhhhhh...
```

Figure 5-10:
Running
the code of
Listing 5-7
four times.

Notice what happens when the user asks for verse 6. The switch statement in Listing 5-7 has no case 6 and no default, so none of the actions inside the switch statement are executed. Even so, with statements that print In the rain, in the rain and Ohhhhhhhh... right after the switch statement, the computer displays something when the user asks for verse 6.

The new and improved switch

In Listings 5-6 and 5-7, shown earlier, the variable verse (an int value) steers the switch statement to one case or another. An int value inside a switch statement works in any version of Java, old or new. (For that matter, char values and a few other kinds of values have worked in Java's switch statements ever since Java was a brand-new language.)

But if you're using Java 7 or later, you can set it up so that the case to be executed in a switch statement depends on the value of a particular string. Listing 5-8 illustrates the use of strings in switch statements. Figure 5-11 shows a run of the code in Listing 5-8.

Listing 5-8:   A switch Statement with a String

```java
import static java.lang.System.out;
import java.util.Scanner;

public class SwitchIt7 {

    public static void main(String args[]) {
        Scanner keyboard = new Scanner(System.in);
        out.print("Which verse (one, two or three)? ");
        String verse = keyboard.next();

        switch (verse) {
        case "one":
            out.println("That's because he has no brain.");
            break;
        case "two":
            out.println("That's because he is a pain.");
            break;
        case "three":
            out.println("'Cause this is the last refrain.");
            break;
        default:
            out.println("No such verse. Please try again.");
            break;
        }

        out.println("Ohhhhhhhh. . . .");

        keyboard.close();
    }
}
```

Figure 5-11:
Running
the code of
Listing 5-8.

```
Which verse (one, two or three)? two
That's because he is a pain.
Ohhhhhhhh. . . .
```

If you use Java to create Android apps, you must use Java 5.0 or Java 6. In Java 6, or any older version of Java, you can't have a string decide the fate of a switch statement.

Chapter 6

Controlling Program Flow with Loops

In This Chapter

▶ Using basic looping

▶ Counting as you loop

▶ Repeating relentlessly (until the user gives you a clear answer)

*I*n 1966, the company that brings you Head & Shoulders shampoo made history. On the back of the bottle, the directions for using the shampoo read, "LATHER-RINSE-REPEAT." Never before had a complete set of directions (for doing anything, let alone shampooing your hair) been summarized so succinctly. People in the direction-writing business hailed this as a monumental achievement. Directions like these stood in stark contrast to others of the time. (For instance, the first sentence on a can of bug spray read, "Turn this can so that it points away from your face." Duh!)

Aside from their brevity, the thing that made the Head & Shoulders directions so cool was that, with three simple words, it managed to capture a notion that's at the heart of all instruction-giving — the notion of repetition. That last word, *REPEAT,* took an otherwise bland instructional drone and turned it into a sophisticated recipe for action.

The fundamental idea is that when you're following directions, you don't just follow one instruction after another. Instead, you take turns in the road. You make decisions ("If HAIR IS DRY, then USE CONDITIONER,") and you go into loops ("LATHER-RINSE, and then LATHER-RINSE again."). In computer programming, you use decision making and looping all the time. This chapter explores looping in Java.

Repeating Instructions Over and Over Again (Java while Statements)

Here's a guessing game for you. The computer generates a random number from 1 to 10. The computer asks you to guess the number. If you guess incorrectly, the game continues. As soon as you guess correctly, the game is over. Listing 6-1 shows the program to play the game, and Figure 6-1 shows a round of play.

Listing 6-1:   A Repeating Guessing Game

```java
import static java.lang.System.out;
import java.util.Scanner;
import java.util.Random;

public class GuessAgain {

    public static void main(String args[]) {
        Scanner keyboard = new Scanner(System.in);

        int numGuesses = 0;
        int randomNumber = new Random().nextInt(10) + 1;

        out.println("        ***********            ");
        out.println("Welcome to the Guessing Game");
        out.println("        ***********            ");
        out.println();

        out.print("Enter an int from 1 to 10: ");
        int inputNumber = keyboard.nextInt();
        numGuesses++;

        while (inputNumber != randomNumber) {
            out.println();
            out.println("Try again...");
            out.print("Enter an int from 1 to 10: ");
            inputNumber = keyboard.nextInt();
            numGuesses++;
        }

        out.print("You win after ");
        out.println(numGuesses + " guesses.");

        keyboard.close();
    }
}
```

```
    ************
Welcome to the Guessing Game
    ************

Enter an int from 1 to 10: 2

Try again...
Enter an int from 1 to 10: 5

Try again...
Enter an int from 1 to 10: 8

Try again...
Enter an int from 1 to 10: 3
You win after 4 guesses.
```

Figure 6-1:
Play until
you drop.

In Figure 6-1, the user makes four guesses. Each time around, the computer checks to see whether the guess is correct. An incorrect guess generates a request to try again. For a correct guess, the user gets a rousing You win, along with a tally of the number of guesses he or she made. The computer repeats several statements, checking each time through to see whether the user's guess is the same as a certain randomly generated number. Each time the user makes a guess, the computer adds 1 to its tally of guesses. When the user makes the correct guess, the computer displays that tally. Figure 6-2 illustrates the flow of action.

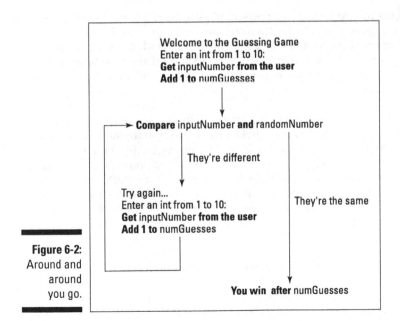

Figure 6-2:
Around and
around
you go.

When you look over Listing 6-1, you see the code that does all this work. At the core of the code is a thing called a *while statement* (also known as a *while loop*). Rephrased in English, the `while` statement says:

```
while the inputNumber is not equal to the randomNumber
keep doing all the stuff in curly braces: {



}
```

The stuff in curly braces (the stuff that repeats) is the code that prints `Try again` and `Enter an int...`, gets a value from the keyboard, and adds 1 to the count of the user's guesses.

When you're dealing with counters, like `numGuesses` in Listing 6-1, you may easily become confused and be off by 1 in either direction. You can avoid this headache by making sure that the `++` statements stay close to the statements whose events you're counting. For example, in Listing 6-1, the variable `numGuesses` starts with a value of `0`. That's because, when the program starts running, the user hasn't made any guesses. Later in the program, right after each call to `keyboard.nextInt`, is a `numGuesses++` statement. That's how you do it — you increment the counter as soon as the user enters another guess.

The statements in curly braces are repeated as long as `inputNumber != randomNumber` is true. Each repetition of the statements in the loop is called an *iteration* of the loop. In Figure 6-1, the loop undergoes three iterations. (If you don't believe that Figure 6-1 has exactly three iterations, count the number of `Try again` printings in the program's output. A `Try again` appears for each incorrect guess.)

When, at long last, the user enters the correct guess, the computer goes back to the top of the `while` statement, checks the condition in parentheses, and finds itself in double double-negative land. The not equal (`!=`) relationship between `inputNumber` and `randomNumber` no longer holds. In other words, the `while` statement's condition, `inputNumber != randomNumber`, is false. Because the `while` statement's condition is false, the computer jumps past the `while` loop and goes on to the statements just below the `while` loop. In these two statements, the computer prints `You win after 4 guesses`.

With code of the kind shown in Listing 6-1, the computer never jumps out in mid-loop. When the computer finds that `inputNumber` isn't equal to `randomNumber`, the computer marches on and executes all five statements inside the loop's curly braces. The computer performs the test again (to see whether `inputNumber` is still not equal to `randomNumber`) only after it fully executes all five statements in the loop.

Repeating a Certain Number of Times (Java for Statements)

"Write 'I will not talk in class' on the blackboard 100 times."

What your teacher really meant was,

```
Set the count to 0.
As long as the count is less than 100,
    Write 'I will not talk in class' on the blackboard,
    Add 1 to the count.
```

Fortunately, you didn't know about loops and counters at the time. If you pointed out all this stuff to your teacher, you'd have gotten into a lot more trouble than you were already in.

One way or another, life is filled with examples of counting loops. And computer programming mirrors life — or is it the other way around? When you tell a computer what to do, you're often telling the computer to print three lines, process ten accounts, dial a million phone numbers, or whatever. Because counting loops is so common in programming, the people who create programming languages have developed statements just for loops of this kind. In Java, the statement that repeats something a certain number of times is called a *for statement*. Listings 6-2 and 6-3 illustrate the use of the `for` statement. Listing 6-2 has a rock-bottom simple example, and Listing 6-3 has a more exotic example. Take your pick.

Listing 6-2: The World's Most Boring for Loop

```java
import static java.lang.System.out;

public class Yawn {

    public static void main(String args[]) {

        for (int count = 1; count <= 10; count++) {
            out.print("The value of count is ");
            out.print(count);
            out.println(".");
        }

        out.println("Done!");
    }
}
```

Figure 6-3 shows you what you get when you run the program of Listing 6-2. (You get exactly what you deserve.) The `for` statement in Listing 6-2 starts by setting the `count` variable to 1. Then the statement tests to make sure that `count` is less than or equal to 10 (which it certainly is). Then the `for` statement dives ahead and executes the printing statements between the curly braces. (At this early stage of the game, the computer prints `The value of count is 1`.) Finally, the `for` statement does that last thing inside its parentheses — it adds 1 to the value of `count`.

```
The value of count is 1.
The value of count is 2.
The value of count is 3.
The value of count is 4.
The value of count is 5.
The value of count is 6.
The value of count is 7.
The value of count is 8.
The value of count is 9.
The value of count is 10.
Done!
```

Figure 6-3:
Counting
to ten.

With `count` now equal to 2, the `for` statement checks again to make sure that `count` is less than or equal to 10. (Yes, 2 is smaller than 10.) Because the test turns out okay, the `for` statement marches back into the curly braced statements and prints `The value of count is 2` on the screen. Finally, the `for` statement does that last thing inside its parentheses — it adds 1 to the value of `count`, increasing the value of `count` to 3.

And so on. This whole thing repeats until, after 10 iterations, the value of `count` finally reaches 11. When this happens, the check for `count` being less than or equal to 10 fails, and the loop's execution ends. The computer jumps to whatever statement comes immediately after the `for` statement. In Listing 6-2, the computer prints `Done!` Figure 6-4 illustrates the whole process.

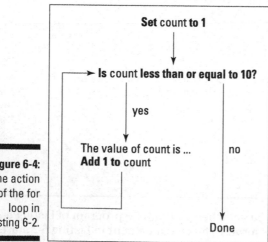

Figure 6-4:
The action
of the for
loop in
Listing 6-2.

The anatomy of a for statement

After the word *for,* you always put three things in parentheses. The first of these three things is called an *initialization,* the second is an *expression,* and the third thing is called an *update.*

```
for ( initialization ; expression ; update )
```

Each of the three items in parentheses plays its own distinct role:

- ✔ The **initialization** is executed once, when the run of your program first reaches the for statement.
- ✔ The **expression** is evaluated several times (before each iteration).
- ✔ The **update** is also evaluated several times (at the end of each iteration).

If it helps, think of the loop as if its text is shifted all around:

```
int count = 1
for count <= 10 {
    out.print("The value of count is ");
    out.print(count);
    out.println(".");
    count++
}
```

You can't write a real for statement this way. Even so, this is the order in which the parts of the statement are executed.

If you declare a variable in the initialization of a for loop, you can't use that variable outside the loop. For instance, in Listing 6-2, you get an error message if you try putting out.println(count) after the end of the loop.

Anything that can be done with a for loop can also be done with a while loop. Choosing to use a for loop is a matter of style and convenience, not necessity.

The world premiere of "Al's All Wet"

Listing 6-2 is very nice, but the program in that listing doesn't do anything interesting. For a more eye-catching example, see Listing 6-3. In Listing 6-3, I make good on a promise I made in Chapter 5. The program in Listing 6-3 prints all the lyrics of the hit single, "Al's All Wet." (You can find the lyrics in Chapter 5.)

Listing 6-3:   The Unabridged "Al's All Wet" Song

```java
import static java.lang.System.out;

public class AlsAllWet {

    public static void main(String args[]) {

        for (int verse = 1; verse <= 3; verse++) {
            out.print("Al's all wet. ");
            out.println("Oh, why is Al all wet? Oh,");
            out.print("Al's all wet 'cause ");
            out.println("he's standing in the rain.");
            out.println("Why is Al out in the rain?");

            switch (verse) {
            case 1:
                out.println("That's because he has no brain.");
                break;
            case 2:
                out.println("That's because he is a pain.");
                break;
            case 3:
                out.println("'Cause this is the last refrain.");
                break;
            }

            switch (verse) {
            case 3:
                out.println("Last refrain, last refrain,");
            case 2:
                out.println("He's a pain, he's a pain,");
            case 1:
                out.println("Has no brain, has no brain,");
            }

            out.println("In the rain, in the rain.");
            out.println("Ohhhhhhhh...");
            out.println();
        }

        out.print("Al's all wet. ");
        out.println("Oh, why is Al all wet? Oh,");
        out.print("Al's all wet 'cause ");
        out.println("he's standing in the rain.");
    }
}
```

Listing 6-3 is nice because it combines many of the ideas from Chapters 5 and 6. In Listing 6-3, two switch statements are nested inside a for loop. One of the switch statements uses break statements; the other switch statement uses fall-through. As the value of the for loop's counter variable (verse) goes from 1 to 2 and then to 3, all the cases in the switch statements are executed. When the program is near the end of its run and execution has dropped out of the for loop, the program's last four statements print the song's final verse.

When I boldly declare that a for statement is for counting, I'm stretching the truth just a bit. Java's for statement is very versatile. You can use a for statement in situations that have nothing to do with counting. For instance, a statement with no update part, such as for (i = 0; i < 10;), just keeps on going. The looping ends when some action inside the loop assigns a big number to the variable i. You can even create a for statement with nothing inside the parentheses. The loop for (; ;) runs forever, which is good if the loop controls a serious piece of machinery. Usually, when you write a for statement, you're counting how many times to repeat something. But, in truth, you can do just about any kind of repetition with a for statement.

Listing 6-3 uses break statements to jump out of a switch. But a break statement can also play a role inside a loop. To see an example, visit this book's website (www.allmycode.com/JavaForDummies).

Repeating Until You Get What You Want (Java do Statements)

"Fools rush in where angels fear to tread."

–Alexander Pope

Today, I want to be young and foolish (or, at the very least, foolish). Look back at Figure 6-2 and notice how Java's while loop works. When execution enters a while loop, the computer checks to make sure that the loop's condition is true. If the condition isn't true, the statements inside the loop are never executed — not even once. In fact, you can easily cook up a while loop whose statements are never executed (although I can't think of a reason why you would ever want to do it).

```java
int twoPlusTwo = 2 + 2;

while (twoPlusTwo == 5) {
    out.println("Are you kidding?");
    out.println("2 + 2 doesn't equal 5");
    out.print("Everyone knows that");
    out.println(" 2 + 2 equals 3");
}
```

In spite of this silly `twoPlusTwo` example, the `while` statement turns out to be the most versatile of Java's looping constructs. In particular, the `while` loop is good for situations in which you must look before you leap. For example, "While money is in my account, write a mortgage check every month." When you first encounter this statement, if your account has a zero balance, you don't want to write a mortgage check — not even one check.

But at times (not many), you want to leap before you look. Take, for instance, the situation in which you're asking the user for a response. Maybe the user's response makes sense, but maybe it doesn't. If it doesn't, you want to ask again. Maybe the user's finger slipped, or perhaps the user didn't understand the question.

Figure 6-5 shows some runs of a program to delete a file. Before deleting the file, the program asks the user whether making the deletion is okay. If the user answers *y* or *n*, the program proceeds according to the user's wishes. But if the user enters any other character (any digit, uppercase letter, punctuation symbol, or whatever), the program asks the user for another response.

Figure 6-5:
Two runs of
the code in
Listing 6-4.

```
Delete evidence? (y/n) n
Sorry, buddy. Just asking.


Delete evidence? (y/n) u
Delete evidence? (y/n) Y
Delete evidence? (y/n) L
Delete evidence? (y/n) 8
Delete evidence? (y/n) .
Delete evidence? (y/n) y
Okay, here goes...
The evidence has been deleted.
```

To write this program, you need a loop — a loop that repeatedly asks the user whether the file should be deleted. The loop keeps asking until the user gives a meaningful response. Now, the thing to notice is that the loop doesn't need to check anything before asking the user the first time. Indeed, before the user gives the first response, the loop has nothing to check. The loop doesn't start with "as long as such-and-such is true, then get a response from the user." Instead, the loop just leaps ahead, gets a response from the user, and then checks the response to see whether it makes sense.

That's why the program in Listing 6-4 has a *do* loop (also known as a *do . . . while* loop). With a `do` loop, the program jumps right in, takes action, and then checks a condition to see whether the result of the action makes sense. If the result makes sense, execution of the loop is done. If not, the program goes back to the top of the loop for another go-around.

Listing 6-4:   To Delete or Not to Delete

```java
import java.io.File;
import static java.lang.System.out;
import java.util.Scanner;

public class DeleteEvidence {

    public static void main(String args[]) {
        File evidence = new File("cookedBooks.txt");
        Scanner keyboard = new Scanner(System.in);
        char reply;

        do {
            out.print("Delete evidence? (y/n) ");
            reply =
                keyboard.findWithinHorizon(".",0).charAt(0);
        } while (reply != 'y' && reply != 'n');

        if (reply == 'y') {
            out.println("Okay, here goes...");
            evidence.delete();
            out.println("The evidence has been deleted.");
        } else {
            out.println("Sorry, buddy. Just asking.");
        }

        keyboard.close();
    }
}
```

Figure 6-5 shows two runs of the code in Listing 6-4. The program accepts lowercase letters *y* and *n*, but not the uppercase letters *Y* and *N*. To make the program accept uppercase letters, change the conditions in the code as follows:

```java
do {
    out.print("Delete evidence? (y/n) ");
    reply = keyboard.findWithinHorizon(".", 0).charAt(0);
} while (reply != 'y' && reply != 'Y' &&
         reply != 'n' && reply!='N');

if (reply == 'y' || reply == 'Y') {
```

Figure 6-6 shows the flow of control in the loop of Listing 6-4. With a do loop, the situation in the twoPlusTwo program (shown at the beginning of this section) can never happen. Because the do loop carries out its first action without testing a condition, every do loop is guaranteed to perform at least one iteration.

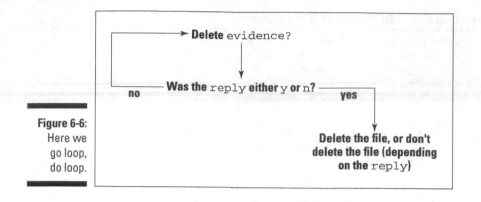

Figure 6-6:
Here we
go loop,
do loop.

The location of Listing 6-4's `cookedBooks.txt` file on your computer's hard drive depends on several things. If you create a `cookedBooks.txt` file in the wrong directory, then the code in Listing 6-4 cannot delete your file. (More precisely, if `cookedBooks.txt` is in the wrong directory on your hard drive, then the code in Listing 6-4 can't find the `cookedBooks.txt` file in preparation for deleting the file.) In most settings, you start testing Listing 6-4 by creating a project within your IDE. The new project lives in a folder on your hard drive, and the `cookedBooks.txt` file belongs directly inside that folder. For example, with the Eclipse IDE, I have a project named `Listing06-04`. That project lives on my hard drive in a folder named `c:\Users\`*my-user-name*`\workspace\Listing06-04`. Inside that folder, I have a file named `cookedBooks.txt` (until I delete the file with the code in Listing 6-4). Also in that `Listing06-04` folder I have a subfolder named `src`. My `DeleteEvidence.java` file is directly inside that `Listing06-04` folder.

For more information about files and their folders, see Chapter 8.

Reading a single character

Back in Listing 5-3 from Chapter 5, the user types a word on the keyboard. The `keyboard.next` method grabs the word and places the word into a `String` variable named *password*. Everything works nicely because a `String` variable can store many characters at once, and the `next` method can read many characters at once.

But in Listing 6-4, you're not interested in reading several characters. You expect the user to type one letter — either *y* or *n*. So you don't create a `String` variable to store the user's response. Instead, you create a `char` variable — a variable that stores just one symbol at a time.

The Java API doesn't have a `nextChar` method. So to read something suitable for storage in a `char` variable, you have to improvise. In Listing 6-4, the improvisation looks like this:

```
keyboard.findWithinHorizon(".", 0).charAt(0)
```

You can use this code exactly as it appears in Listing 6-4 whenever you want to read a single character.

A `String` variable can contain many characters or just one. But a `String` variable that contains only one character isn't the same as a `char` variable. No matter what you put in a `String` variable, `String` variables and `char` variables have to be treated differently.

File handling in Java

In Listing 6-4, the actual file-handling statements deserve some attention. These statements involve the use of classes, objects, and methods. Many of the meaty details about these things are in other chapters, like Chapters 7 and 9. Even so, I can't do any harm by touching on some highlights right here.

So, you can find a class in the Java language API named *java.io.File.* The statement

```
File evidence = new File("cookedBooks.txt");
```

creates a new object in the computer's memory. This object, formed from the `java.io.File` class, describes everything that the program needs to know about the disk file `cookedBooks.txt`. From this point on in Listing 6-4, the variable `evidence` refers to the disk file `cookedBooks.txt`.

The `evidence` object, being an instance of the `java.io.File` class, has a `delete` method. (What can I say? It's in the API documentation.) When you call `evidence.delete`, the computer gets rid of the file for you.

Of course, you can't get rid of something that doesn't already exist. When you call the constructor

```
File evidence = new File("cookedBooks.txt");
```

Java doesn't check to make sure that you have a file named `cookedBooks.txt`. To force Java to do the checking, you have a few options. The simplest is to call the `exists` method. When you call `evidence.exists()`, the method looks in the folder where Java expects to find cookedBooks.txt. The call evidence.exists() returns true if Java finds cookedBooks.txt inside that folder. Otherwise, the call evidence.exists() returns false. Here's a souped-up version of Listing 6-4, with a call to exists included in the code:

```java
import java.io.File;
import static java.lang.System.out;
import java.util.Scanner;

public class DeleteEvidence {

  public static void main(String args[]) {
    File evidence = new File("cookedBooks.txt");
    if (evidence.exists()) {
      Scanner keyboard = new Scanner(System.in);
      char reply;

      do {
        out.print("Delete evidence? (y/n) ");
        reply =
            keyboard.findWithinHorizon(".", 0).charAt(0);
      } while (reply != 'y' && reply != 'n');

      if (reply == 'y') {
        out.println("Okay, here goes...");
        evidence.delete();
        out.println("The evidence has been deleted.");
      } else {
        out.println("Sorry, buddy. Just asking.");
      }

      keyboard.close();
    }
  }
}
```

Variable declarations and blocks

A bunch of statements surrounded by curly braces forms a block. If you declare a variable inside a block, you generally can't use that variable outside the block. For instance, in Listing 6-4, you get an error message if you make the following change:

```
do {
    out.print("Delete evidence? (y/n) ");
    char reply =
        keyboard.findWithinHorizon(".", 0).charAt(0);
} while (reply != 'y' && reply != 'n');

if (reply == 'y')
```

With the declaration `char reply` inside the loop's curly braces, no use of the name `reply` makes sense anywhere outside the braces. When you try to compile this code, you get three error messages — two for the `reply` words in `while (reply != 'y' && reply != 'n')` and a third for the `if` statement's `reply`.

So in Listing 6-4, your hands are tied. The program's first real use of the `reply` variable is inside the loop. But to make that variable available after the loop, you have to declare `reply` before the loop. In this situation, you're best off declaring the `reply` variable without initializing the variable. Very interesting!

To read more about variable initializations, see Chapter 4. To find out more about blocks, see Chapter 5.

All versions of Java have the three kinds of loops described in this chapter (`while` loops, `for` loops, and `do . . . while` loops). But newer Java versions (namely, Java 5 and beyond) have yet another kind of loop called an *enhanced for loop*. For a look at Java's enhanced `for` loop, see Chapter 11.

Part III

Working with the Big Picture: Object-Oriented Programming

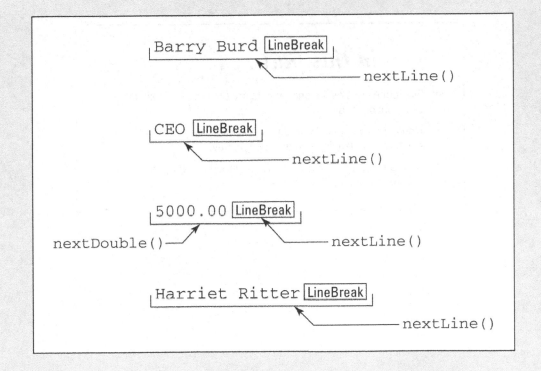

Sure, you've written a nice application, but does your code really work? There's no such thing as too much testing, and if your tests are well-organized, you're on your way to having a great app. To find out how your tests can be well organized, visit www.dummies.com/extras/java. The article on JUnit testing gives you the inside scoop.

Part III

Working with the Big Picture: Object-Oriented Programming

In this part . . .

- Find out what classes and objects are (without bending your brain out of shape).
- Find out how object-oriented programming helps you reuse existing code (saving you time and money).
- Be the emperor of your own virtual world by constructing brand-new objects.

Chapter 7

Thinking in Terms of Classes and Objects

In This Chapter

▶ Thinking like a real object-oriented programmer

▶ Passing values to and from methods

▶ Hiding details in your object-oriented code

As a computer book author, I've been told this over and over again — I shouldn't expect people to read sections and chapters in their logical order. People jump around, picking what they need and skipping what they don't feel like reading. With that in mind, I realize that you may have skipped Chapter 1. If that's the case, please don't feel guilty. You can compensate in just 60 seconds by reading the following information culled from Chapter 1:

> *Because Java is an object-oriented programming language, your primary goal is to describe classes and objects. A class is the idea behind a certain kind of thing. An object is a concrete instance of a class. The programmer defines a class, and from the class definition, the computer makes individual objects.*

Of course, you can certainly choose to skip over the 60-second summary paragraph. If that's the case, you may want to recoup some of your losses. You can do that by reading the following two-word summary of Chapter 1:

> *Classes; objects.*

Defining a Class (What It Means to Be an Account)

What distinguishes one bank account from another? If you ask a banker this question, you hear a long sales pitch. The banker describes interest rates, fees, penalties — the whole routine. Fortunately for you, I'm not interested in all that. Instead, I want to know how my account is different from your account. After all, my account is named *Barry Burd, trading as Burd Brain Consulting,* and your account is named *Jane Q. Reader, trading as Budding Java Expert.* My account has $24.02 in it. How about yours?

When you come right down to it, the differences between one account and another can be summarized as values of variables. Maybe there's a variable named *balance.* For me, the value of `balance` is `24.02`. For you, the value of `balance` is `55.63`. The question is, when writing a computer program to deal with accounts, how do I separate my `balance` variable from your `balance` variable?

The answer is to create two separate objects. Let one `balance` variable live inside one of the objects and let the other `balance` variable live inside the other object. While you're at it, put a `name` variable and an `address` variable in each of the objects. And there you have it — two objects, and each object represents an account. More precisely, each object is an instance of the `Account` class. (See Figure 7-1.)

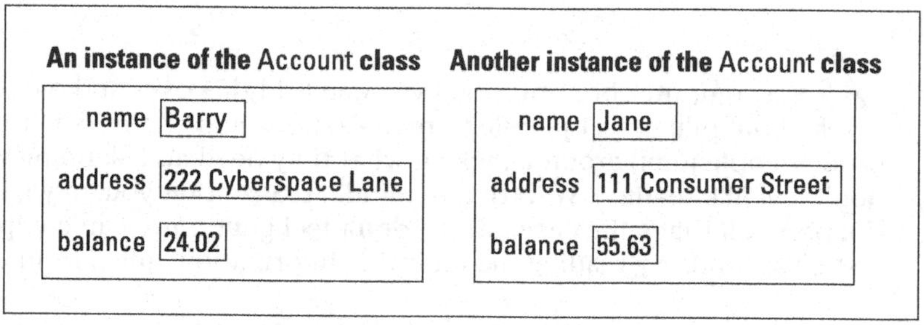

An instance of the Account class

name	Barry
address	222 Cyberspace Lane
balance	24.02

Another instance of the Account class

name	Jane
address	111 Consumer Street
balance	55.63

Figure 7-1:
Two objects.

So far, so good. However, you still haven't solved the original problem. In your computer program, how do you refer to my `balance` variable, as opposed to your `balance` variable? Well, you have two objects sitting around, so maybe you have variables to refer to these two objects. Create one variable named *myAccount* and another variable named *yourAccount.* The `myAccount` variable refers to my object (my instance of the `Account` class) with all the stuff that's inside it. To refer to my balance, write

```
myAccount.balance
```

To refer to my name, write

```
myAccount.name
```

Then `yourAccount.balance` refers to the value in your object's `balance` variable, and `yourAccount.name` refers to the value of your object's `name` variable. To tell the computer how much I have in my account, you can write

```
myAccount.balance = 24.02;
```

To display your name on the screen, you can write

```
out.println(yourAccount.name);
```

These ideas come together in Listings 7-1 and 7-2. Here's Listing 7-1:

Listing 7-1:   What It Means to Be an Account

```
public class Account {
    String name;
    String address;
    double balance;
}
```

The `Account` class in Listing 7-1 defines what it means to be an `Account`. In particular, Listing 7-1 tells you that each of the `Account` class's instances has three variables — `name`, `address`, and `balance`. This is consistent with the information in Figure 7-1. Java programmers have a special name for variables of this kind (variables that belong to instances of classes). Each of these variables — `name`, `address`, and `balance` — is called a *field*.

A variable declared inside a class but not inside any particular method is a *field*. In Listing 7-1, the variables `name`, `address`, and `balance` are fields. Another name for a field is an *instance variable*.

If you've been grappling with the material in Chapters 4 through 6, the code for class `Account` (Listing 7-1) may come as a big shock to you. Can you really define a complete Java class with only four lines of code (give or take a curly brace)? You certainly can. In fact, the `Account` class in Listing 7-1 is quite representative of what Java programmers think of when they think *class*. A class is a grouping of existing things. In the `Account` class of Listing 7-1, those existing things are two `String` values and a `double` value.

Declaring variables and creating objects

A young fellow approaches me while I'm walking down the street. He tells me to print "You'll love Java!" so I print those words. If you must know, I print them with chalk on the sidewalk. But where I print the words doesn't matter. What matters is that some guy issues instructions, and I follow the instructions.

Later that day, an elderly woman sits next to me on a park bench. She says, "An account has a name, an address, and a balance." And I say, "That's fine, but what do you want me to do about it?" In response she just stares at me, so I don't do anything about her *account* pronouncement. I just sit there, she sits there, and we both do absolutely nothing.

Listing 7-1, shown earlier, is like the elderly woman. This listing defines what it means to be an `Account`, but the listing doesn't tell me to do anything with my account, or with anyone else's account. In order to do something, I need a second piece of code. I need another class — a class that contains a `main` method. Fortunately, while the woman and I sit quietly on the park bench, a young child comes by with Listing 7-2.

Listing 7-2: Dealing with Account Objects

```
import static java.lang.System.out;

public class UseAccount {

    public static void main(String args[]) {
        Account myAccount;
        Account yourAccount;

        myAccount = new Account();
        yourAccount = new Account();

        myAccount.name = "Barry Burd";
        myAccount.address = "222 Cyberspace Lane";
        myAccount.balance = 24.02;

        yourAccount.name = "Jane Q. Public";
        yourAccount.address = "111 Consumer Street";
        yourAccount.balance = 55.63;

        out.print(myAccount.name);
        out.print(" (");
        out.print(myAccount.address);
        out.print(") has $");
        out.print(myAccount.balance);
        out.println();

        out.print(yourAccount.name);
        out.print(" (");
        out.print(yourAccount.address);
        out.print(") has $");
        out.print(yourAccount.balance);
    }
}
```

Taken together, the two classes — `Account` and `UseAccount` — form one complete program. The code in Listing 7-2 defines the `UseAccount` class, and the `UseAccount` class has a `main` method. This `main` method has variables of its own — `yourAccount` and `myAccount`.

In a way, the first two lines inside the `main` method of Listing 7-2 are misleading. Some people read `Account yourAccount` as if it's supposed to mean, "yourAccount is an `Account`," or "The variable yourAccount refers to an instance of the `Account` class." That's not really what this first line means.

Instead, the line `Account yourAccount` means, "If and when I make the variable `yourAccount` refer to something, that something will be an instance of the `Account` class." So, what's the difference?

The difference is that simply declaring `Account yourAccount` doesn't make the `yourAccount` variable refer to an object. All the declaration does is reserve the variable name *yourAccount* so that the name can eventually refer to an instance of the `Account` class. The creation of an actual object doesn't come until later in the code, when the computer executes `new Account()`.

Technically, when the computer executes `new Account()`, you're creating an object by calling the `Account` class's *constructor.* I have more to say about that in Chapter 9.

When the computer executes the assignment `yourAccount = new Account()`, the computer creates a new object (a new instance of the `Account` class) and makes the variable `yourAccount` refer to that new object. (The equal sign makes the variable refer to the new object.) Figure 7-2 illustrates the situation.

After executing
Account yourAccount;

After executing
yourAccount =
new Account ();

yourAccount [ ]

yourAccount [ ]

name [ ]

address [ ]

balance [ ]

Figure 7-2:
Before and
after a con-
structor is
called.

To test the claim that I made in the last few paragraphs, I added an extra line to the code of Listing 7-2. I tried to print `yourAccount.name` after declaring `yourAccount` but before calling `new Account()`.

```
Account myAccount;
Account yourAccount;

out.println(yourAccount.name);

myAccount = new Account();
yourAccount = new Account();
```

When I tried to compile the new code, I got this error message: `variable yourAccount might not have been initialized`. That settles it. Before you do `new Account()`, you can't print the `name` variable of an object because an object doesn't exist.

When a variable has a reference type, simply declaring the variable isn't enough. You don't get an object until you call a constructor and use the keyword `new`.

For information about reference types, see Chapter 4.

Initializing a variable

In Chapter 4, I announce that you can initialize a primitive type variable as part of the variable's declaration.

```
int weightOfAPerson = 150;
```

You can do the same thing with reference type variables, such as `myAccount` and `yourAccount` in Listing 7-2. You can combine the first four lines in the listing's `main` method into just two lines, like this:

```
Account myAccount = new Account();
Account yourAccount = new Account();
```

If you combine lines this way, you automatically avoid the `variable might not have been initialized` error that I describe in the previous section. Sometimes you find a situation in which you can't initialize a variable. But when you can initialize, it's usually a plus.

Using an object's fields

After you've bitten off and chewed the `main` method's first four lines, the rest of the code in the earlier Listing 7-2 is sensible and straightforward. You have three lines that put values in the `myAccount` object's fields, three lines that put values in the `yourAccount` object's fields, and four lines that do some printing. Figure 7-3 shows the program's output.

Figure 7-3:
Running
the code in
Listings 7-1
and 7-2.

```
Barry Burd (222 Cyberspace Lane) has $24.02
Jane Q. Public (111 Consumer Street) has $55.63
```

One program; several classes

Each program in Chapters 3 to 6 consists of a single class. That's great for a book's introductory chapters. But in real life, a typical program consists of hundreds or even thousands of classes. The program that spans Listings 7-1 and 7-2 consists of two classes. Sure, having two classes isn't like having thousands of classes, but it's a step in that direction.

In practice, most programmers put each class in a file of its own. When you create a program, such as the one in Listings 7-1 and 7-2, you create two files on your computer's hard drive. Therefore, when you download this section's example from the web, you get two separate files — Account.java and UseAccount.java.

For information about running a program consisting of more than one .java file in Eclipse, NetBeans and IntelliJ IDEA, visit this book's website (www.allmycode.com/JavaForDummies).

Public classes

The first line of Listing 7-1 is

```
public class Account {
```

The Account class is public. A public class is available for use by all other classes. For example, if you write an ATMController program in some remote corner of cyberspace, then your ATMController program can contain code, such as myAccount.balance = 24.02, making use of the Account class declared in Listing 7-1. (Of course, your code has to know where in cyberspace I've stored the code in Listing 7-1, but that's another story.)

Listing 7-2 contains the code myAccount.balance = 24.02. You might say to yourself, "The Account class has to be public because another class (the code in Listing 7-2) uses the Account class." Unfortunately, the real lowdown about public classes is a bit more complicated. In fact, when the planets align themselves correctly, one class can make use of another class's code, even though the other class isn't public. (I cover the proper aligning of planets in Chapter 14.)

The dirty secret in this chapter's code is that declaring certain classes to be public simply makes me feel good. Yes, programmers do certain things to feel good. In Listing 7-1, my esthetic sense of goodness comes from the fact that an Account class is useful to many other programmers. When I create a class that declares something useful and nameable — an Account, an Engine, a Customer, a BrainWave, a Headache, or a SevenLayerCake class — I declare the class to be public.

The UseAccount class in Listing 7-2 is also public. When a class contains a main method, Java programmers tend to make the class public without thinking too much about who uses the class. So even if no other class makes use of my main method, I declare the UseAccount class to be public. Most of the classes in this book contain main methods, so most of the classes in this book are public.

When you declare a class to be public, you must declare the class in a file whose name is exactly the same as the name of the class (but with the .java extension added). For example, if you declare public class MyImportantCode, you must put the class's code in a file named MyImportantCode.java, with uppercase letters M, I, and C and all other letters lowercase. This file-naming rule has an important consequence: If your code declares two public classes, your code must consist of at least two .java files. In other words, you can't declare two public classes in one .java file.

For more news about the word *public* and other such words, see Chapter 14.

Defining a Method within a Class (Displaying an Account)

Imagine a table containing the information about two accounts. (If you have trouble imagining such a thing, just look at Table 7-1.)

Table 7-1	Without Object-Oriented Programming	
Name	*Address*	*Balance*
Barry Burd	222 Cyberspace Lane	24.02
Jane Q. Public	111 Consumer Street	55.63

In Table 7-1, each account has three things — a name, an address, and a balance. That's how things were done before object-oriented programming came along. But object-oriented programming involved a big shift in thinking. With object-oriented programming, each account can have a name, an address, a balance, and a way of being displayed.

In object-oriented programming, each object has its own built-in functionality. An account knows how to display itself. A string can tell you whether it has the same characters inside it as another string has. A PrintStream instance, such as System.out, knows how to do println. In object-oriented programming, each object has its own methods. These methods are little subprograms that you can call to have an object do things to (or for) itself.

And why is this a good idea? It's good because you're making pieces of data take responsibility for themselves. With object-oriented programming, all the functionality that's associated with an account is collected inside the code for the Account class. Everything you have to know about a string is located in the file String.java. Anything having to do with year numbers (whether they have two or four digits, for instance) is handled right inside the Year class. Therefore, if anybody has problems with your Account class or your Year class, he or she knows just where to look for all the code. That's great!

So imagine an enhanced account table. In this new table, each object has built-in functionality. Each account knows how to display itself on the screen. Each row of the table has its own copy of a display method. Of course, you don't need much imagination to picture this table. I just happen to have a table you can look at. It's Table 7-2.

Table 7-2	The Object-Oriented Way		
Name	*Address*	*Balance*	*Display*
Barry Burd	222 Cyberspace Lane	24.02	out.print....
Jane Q. Public	111 Consumer Street	55.63	out.print....

An account that displays itself

In Table 7-2, each account object has four things — a name, an address, a balance, and a way of displaying itself on the screen. After you make the jump to object-oriented thinking, you'll never turn back. Listings 7-3 and 7-4 show programs that implement the ideas in Table 7-2.

Listing 7-3: An Account Displays Itself

```java
import static java.lang.System.out;

public class Account {
    String name;
    String address;
    double balance;

    public void display() {
        out.print(name);
        out.print(" (");
        out.print(address);
        out.print(") has $");
        out.print(balance);
    }
}
```

Listing 7-4: Using the Improved Account Class

```
public class UseAccount {

    public static void main(String args[]) {
        Account myAccount = new Account();
        Account yourAccount = new Account();

        myAccount.name = "Barry Burd";
        myAccount.address = "222 Cyberspace Lane";
        myAccount.balance = 24.02;

        yourAccount.name = "Jane Q. Public";
        yourAccount.address = "111 Consumer Street";
        yourAccount.balance = 55.63;

        myAccount.display();
        System.out.println();
        yourAccount.display();
    }
}
```

A run of the code in Listings 7-3 and 7-4 looks just like a run for Listings 7-1 and 7-2. You can see the action back in Figure 7-3.

In Listing 7-3, the Account class has four things in it — a name, an address, a balance, and a display method. These things match up with the four columns in Table 7-2. So each instance of the Account class has a name, an address, a balance, and a way of displaying itself. The way you call these things is nice and uniform. To refer to the name stored in myAccount, you write

```
myAccount.name
```

To get myAccount to display itself on the screen, you write

```
myAccount.display()
```

REMEMBER

The only difference is the parentheses.

When you call a method, you put parentheses after the method's name.

The display method's header

Look again at Listings 7-3 and 7-4. A call to the display method is inside the UseAccount class's main method, but the declaration of the display method is up in the Account class. The declaration has a header and a body. (See Chapter 3.) The header has three words and some parentheses:

✔ **The word *public* serves roughly the same purpose as the word *public* in Listing 7-1.** Roughly speaking, any code can contain a call to a public method, even if the calling code and the public method belong to two different classes. In this section's example, the decision to make the display method public is a matter of taste. Normally, when I create a method that's useful in a wide variety of applications, I declare the method to be public.

✔ **The word *void* tells the computer that when the display method is called, the display method doesn't return anything to the place that called it.** To see a method that does return something to the place that called it, see the next section.

✔ **The word *display* is the method's name.** Every method must have a name. Otherwise, you don't have a way to call the method.

✔ **The parentheses contain all the things you're going to pass to the method when you call it.** When you call a method, you can pass information to that method on the fly. The display method in Listing 7-3 looks strange because the parentheses in the method's header have nothing inside them. This nothingness indicates that no information is passed to the display method when you call it. For a meatier example, see the next section.

Listing 7-3 contains the display method's declaration, and Listing 7-4 contains a call to the display method. Although Listings 7-3 and 7-4 contain different classes, both uses of public in Listing 7-3 are optional. To find out why, check out Chapter 14.

Sending Values to and from Methods (Calculating Interest)

Think about sending someone to the supermarket to buy bread. When you do this, you say, "Go to the supermarket and buy some bread." (Try it at home. You'll have a fresh loaf of bread in no time at all!) Of course, some other time, you send that same person to the supermarket to buy bananas. You say, "Go to the supermarket and buy some bananas." And what's the point of all this? Well, you have a method, and you have some on-the-fly information that you pass to the method when you call it. The method is named *goToTheSupermarketAndBuySome*. The on-the-fly information is either *bread* or *bananas*, depending on your culinary needs. In Java, the method calls would look like this:

```
goToTheSupermarketAndBuySome(bread);
goToTheSupermarketAndBuySome(bananas);
```

The things in parentheses are called *parameters* or *parameter lists*. With parameters, your methods become much more versatile. Instead of getting the same thing each time, you can send somebody to the supermarket to buy bread one time, bananas another time, and birdseed the third time. When you call your goToTheSupermarketAndBuySome method, you decide right there what you're going to ask your pal to buy.

And what happens when your friend returns from the supermarket? "Here's the bread you asked me to buy," says your friend. By carrying out your wishes, your friend returns something to you. You make a method call, and the method returns information (or a loaf of bread).

The thing returned to you is called the method's *return value*. The general type of thing that is returned to you is called the method's *return type*. These concepts are made more concrete in Listings 7-5 and 7-6.

Listing 7-5: An Account That Calculates Its Own Interest

```
import static java.lang.System.out;

public class Account {
    String name;
    String address;
    double balance;

    public void display() {
        out.print(name);
        out.print(" (");
        out.print(address);
        out.print(") has $");
        out.print(balance);
    }

    public double getInterest(double percentageRate) {
        return balance * percentageRate / 100.00;
    }
}
```

Listing 7-6: Calculating Interest

```
import static java.lang.System.out;

public class UseAccount {

    public static void main(String args[]) {
        Account myAccount = new Account();
        Account yourAccount = new Account();

        myAccount.name = "Barry Burd";
        myAccount.address = "222 Cyberspace Lane";
        myAccount.balance = 24.02;
```

```
        yourAccount.name = "Jane Q. Public";
        yourAccount.address = "111 Consumer Street";
        yourAccount.balance = 55.63;

        myAccount.display();

        out.print(" plus $");
        out.print(myAccount.getInterest(5.00));
        out.println(" interest ");

        yourAccount.display();

        double yourInterestRate = 7.00;
        out.print(" plus $");
        double yourInterestAmount =
            yourAccount.getInterest(yourInterestRate);
        out.print(yourInterestAmount);
        out.println(" interest ");
    }
}
```

Figure 7-4 shows the output of the code in Listings 7-5 and 7-6. In Listing 7-5, the Account class has a getInterest method. This getInterest method is called twice from the main method in Listing 7-6. The actual account balances and interest rates are different each time.

Figure 7-4:
Running
the code in
Listings 7-5
and 7-6.

```
Barry Burd (222 Cyberspace Lane) has $24.02 plus $1.2009999999999998 interest
Jane Q. Public (111 Consumer Street) has $55.63 plus $3.8941000000000003 interest
```

✔ **In the first call, the balance is 24.02, and the interest rate is 5.00.** The first call, myAccount.getInterest(5.00), refers to the myAccount object and to the values stored in the myAccount object's fields. (See Figure 7-5.) When this call is made, the expression balance * percentageRate / 100.00 stands for 24.02 * 5.00 / 100.00.

✔ **In the second call, the balance is 55.63, and the interest rate is 7.00.** In the main method, just before this second call is made, the variable yourInterestRate is assigned the value 7.00. The call itself, yourAccount.getInterest(yourInterestRate), refers to the yourAccount object and to the values stored in the yourAccount object's fields. (Again, see Figure 7-5.) So, when the call is made, the expression balance * percentageRate / 100.00 stands for 55.63 * 7.00 / 100.00.

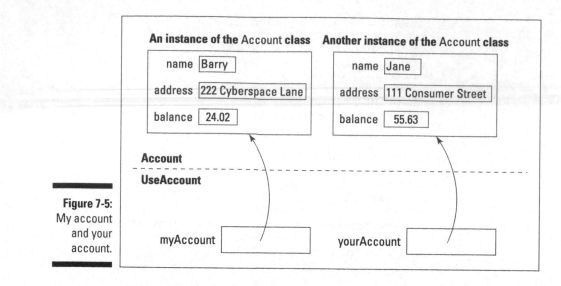

Figure 7-5:
My account
and your
account.

By the way, the `main` method in Listing 7-3 contains two calls to `getInterest`. One call has the literal `5.00` in its parameter list; the other call has the variable `yourInterestRate` in its parameter list. Why does one call use a literal and the other call use a variable? No reason. I just want to show you that you can do it either way.

Passing a value to a method

Take a look at the `getInterest` method's header. (As you read the explanation in the next few bullets, you can follow some of the ideas visually with the diagram in Figure 7-6.)

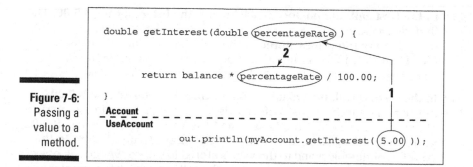

Figure 7-6:
Passing a
value to a
method.

✔ **The word *double* tells the computer that when the** `getInterest` **method is called, the** `getInterest` **method returns a** `double` **value back to the place that called it.** The statement in the `getInterest` method's body confirms this. The statement says `return balance * percentageRate / 100.00`, and the expression `balance * percentageRate / 100.00` has type `double`. (That's because all the things in the expression — `balance`, `percentageRate`, and `100.00` — have type `double`.)

When the `getInterest` method is called, the `return` statement calculates `balance * percentageRate / 100.00` and hands the calculation's result back to the code that called the method.

✔ **The word *getInterest* is the method's name.** That's the name you use to call the method when you're writing the code for the `UseAccount` class.

✔ **The parentheses contain all the things that you pass to the method when you call it.** When you call a method, you can pass information to that method on the fly. This information is the method's parameter list. The `getInterest` method's header says that the `getInterest` method takes one piece of information and that piece of information must be of type `double`.

```
public double getInterest(double   percentageRate)
```

Sure enough, if you look at the first call to `getInterest` (down in the `useAccount` class's `main` method), that call has the number `5.00` in it. And `5.00` is a `double` literal. When I call `getInterest`, I'm giving the method a value of type `double`.

If you don't remember what a literal is, see Chapter 4.

The same story holds true for the second call to `getInterest`. Down near the bottom of Listing 7-6, I call `getInterest` and feed the variable `yourInterestRate` to the method in its parameter list. Luckily for me, I declared `yourInterestRate` to be of type `double` just a few lines before that.

When you run the code in Listings 7-5 and 7-6, the flow of action isn't from top to bottom. The action goes from `main` to `getInterest`, then back to `main`, then back to `getInterest`, and finally back to `main` again. Figure 7-7 shows the whole business.

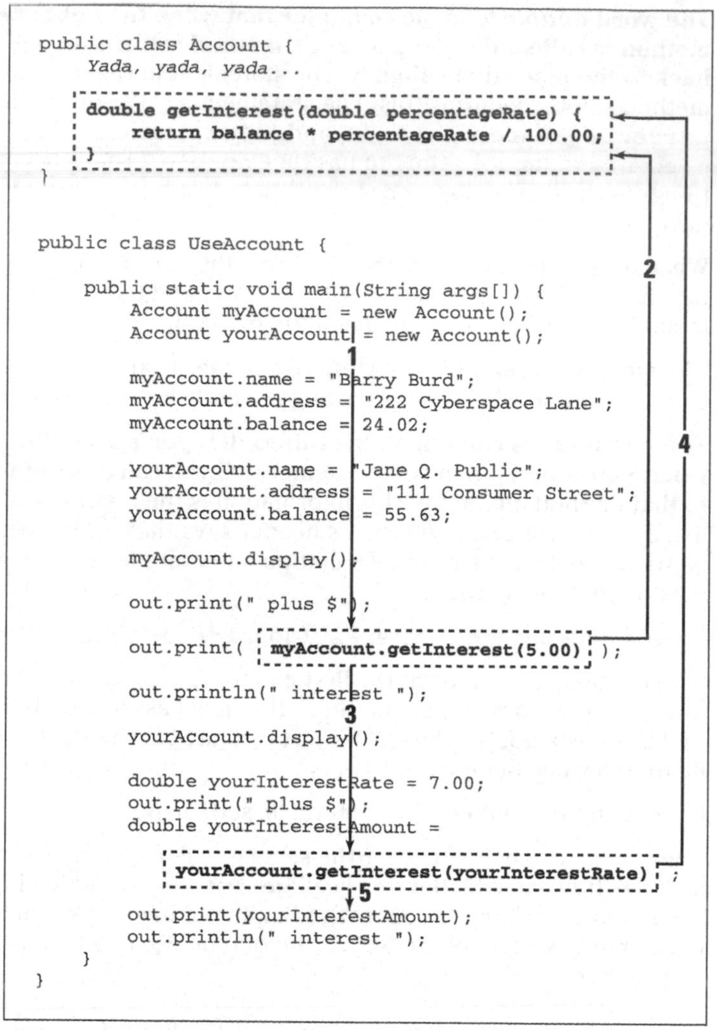

```
public class Account {
    Yada, yada, yada...

    double getInterest(double percentageRate) {
        return balance * percentageRate / 100.00;
    }
}


public class UseAccount {

    public static void main(String args[]) {
        Account myAccount = new Account();
        Account yourAccount = new Account();

        myAccount.name = "Barry Burd";
        myAccount.address = "222 Cyberspace Lane";
        myAccount.balance = 24.02;

        yourAccount.name = "Jane Q. Public";
        yourAccount.address = "111 Consumer Street";
        yourAccount.balance = 55.63;

        myAccount.display();

        out.print(" plus $");

        out.print( myAccount.getInterest(5.00) );

        out.println(" interest ");

        yourAccount.display();

        double yourInterestRate = 7.00;
        out.print(" plus $");
        double yourInterestAmount =

            yourAccount.getInterest(yourInterestRate) ;

        out.print(yourInterestAmount);
        out.println(" interest ");
    }
}
```

Figure 7-7:
The flow of
control in
Listings 7-5
and 7-6.

Returning a value from the getInterest method

When the `getInterest` method is called, the method executes the one statement that's in the method's body: a `return` statement. The `return` statement computes the value of `balance * percentageRate / 100.00`. If `balance` happens to be 24.02, and `percentageRate` is 5.00, the value of the expression is `1.201` — around $1.20. (Because the computer works exclusively with 0s and 1s, the computer gets this number wrong by an ever so tiny amount. The computer gets 1.2009999999999998. That's just something that humans have to live with.)

Anyway, after this value is calculated, the computer executes the `return`, which sends the value back to the place in `main` where `getInterest` was called. At that point in the process, the entire method call — `myAccount.getInterest(5.00)` — takes on the value 1.2009999999999998. The call itself is inside a `println`:

```
out.println(myAccount.getInterest(5.00));
```

So the `println` ends up with the following meaning:

```
out.println(1.2009999999999998);
```

The whole process, in which a value is passed back to the method call, is illustrated in Figure 7-8.

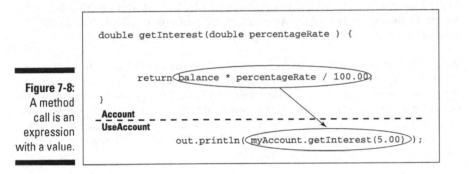

Figure 7-8: A method call is an expression with a value.

If a method returns anything, a call to the method is an expression with a value. That value can be printed, assigned to a variable, added to something else, or whatever. Anything you can do with any other kind of value, you can do with a method call.

You might use the `Account` class in Listing 7-5 to solve a real problem. You'd call the `Account` class's `display` and `getInterest` methods in the course of an actual banking application. But the `UseAccount` class in Listing 7-6 is artificial. The `UseAccount` code creates some fake account data and then calls some `Account` class methods to convince you that the `Account` class's code works correctly. (You don't seriously think that a bank has depositors named "Jane Q. Public" and "Barry Burd," do you?) The `UseAccount` class in Listing 7-6 is a *test case* — a short-lived class whose sole purpose is to test another class's code. Like the code in Listing 7-6, each test case in this book is an ordinary class — a free-form class containing its own `main` method. Free-form classes are okay, but they're not optimal. Java developers have something better — a more disciplined way of writing test cases. The "better way" is called *JUnit*, and it's described on this book's website (`www.allmycode.com/JavaForDummies`).

Making Numbers Look Good

Looking back at Figure 7-4, you may be concerned that the interest on my account is only $1.2009999999999998. Seemingly, the bank is cheating me out of two hundred-trillionths of a cent. I should go straight there and demand my fair interest. Maybe you and I should go together. We'll kick up some fur at that old bank and bust this scam right open. If my guess is correct, this is part of a big *salami scam.* In a salami scam, someone shaves little slices off millions of accounts. People don't notice their tiny little losses, but the person doing the shaving collects enough for a quick escape to Barbados (or for a whole truckload of salami).

But, wait a minute! Nothing is motivating you to come with me to the bank. Checking back at Figure 7-4, I see that you're way ahead of the game. According to my calculations, the program overpays you by three hundred-trillionths of a cent. Between the two of us, we're ahead by a hundred-trillionth of a cent. What gives?

Well, because computers use 0s (zeros) and 1s and don't have an infinite amount of space to do calculations, such inaccuracies as the ones shown in Figure 7-4 are normal. The quickest solution is to display the inaccurate numbers in a more sensible fashion. You can round the numbers and display only two digits beyond the decimal point, and some handy tools from Java's API (Application Programming Interface) can help. Listing 7-7 shows the code, and Figure 7-9 displays the pleasant result.

Listing 7-7: Making Your Numbers Look Right

```
import static java.lang.System.out;

public class UseAccount {

    public static void main(String args[]) {
        Account myAccount = new Account();
        Account yourAccount = new Account();

        myAccount.balance = 24.02;
        yourAccount.balance = 55.63;

        double myInterest = myAccount.getInterest(5.00);
        double yourInterest =
          yourAccount.getInterest(7.00);
```

```
        out.printf("$%4.2f\n", myInterest);
        out.printf("$%5.2f\n", myInterest);
        out.printf("$%.2f\n",  myInterest);
        out.printf("$%3.2f\n", myInterest);
        out.printf("$%.2f $%.2f",
                                myInterest, yourInterest);
    }
}
```

Figure 7-9:
Numbers
that look
like dollar
amounts.

```
$1.20
$ 1.20
$1.20
$1.20
$1.20 $3.89
```

The inaccurate numbers in Figure 7-4 come from the computer's use of 0s and 1s. A mythical computer whose circuits were wired to use digits 0, 1, 2, 3, 4, 5, 6, 7, 8, and 9 wouldn't suffer from the same inaccuracies. So to make things better, Java provides its own special way around the computer's inaccurate calculations. Java's API has a class named `BigDecimal` — a class that bypasses the computer's strange 0s and 1s, and uses ordinary decimal digits to perform arithmetic calculations. For more information, visit this book's website (www.allmycode.com/JavaForDummies).

Listing 7-7 uses a handy method named `printf`. When you call `printf`, you always put at least two parameters inside the call's parentheses.

> ✔ **The first parameter is a *format string*.**
>
>   The format string uses funny-looking codes to describe exactly how the other parameters are displayed.
>
> ✔ **All the other parameters (after the first) are values to be displayed.**

Look at the last `printf` call of Listing 7-7. The first parameter's format string has two placeholders for numbers. The first placeholder (`%.2f`) describes the display of `myInterest`. The second placeholder (another `%.2f`) describes the display of `yourInterest`. To find out exactly how these format strings work, see Figures 7-10 through 7-14.

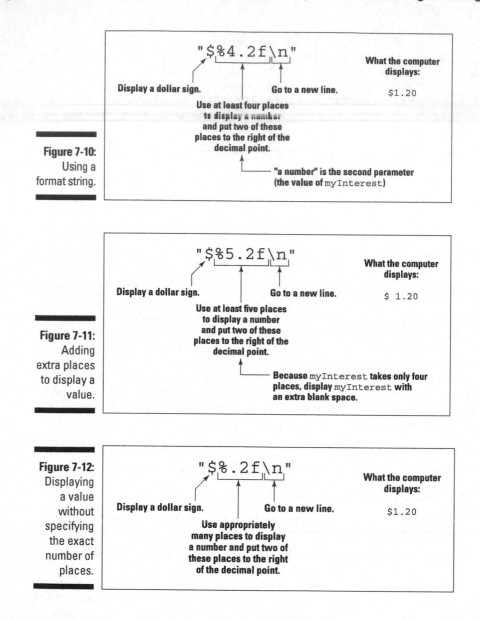

Figure 7-10:
Using a
format string.

Figure 7-11:
Adding
extra places
to display a
value.

Figure 7-12:
Displaying
a value
without
specifying
the exact
number of
places.

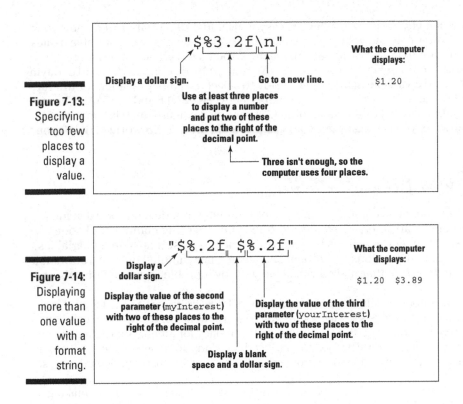

Figure 7-13: Specifying too few places to display a value.

"$%3.2f\n"

Display a dollar sign.

Go to a new line.

Use at least three places to display a number and put two of these places to the right of the decimal point.

Three isn't enough, so the computer uses four places.

What the computer displays:

$1.20

Figure 7-14: Displaying more than one value with a format string.

"$%.2f $%.2f"

Display a dollar sign.

Display the value of the second parameter (myInterest) with two of these places to the right of the decimal point.

Display the value of the third parameter (yourInterest) with two of these places to the right of the decimal point.

Display a blank space and a dollar sign.

What the computer displays:

$1.20 $3.89

For more examples using the printf method and its format strings, see Chapters 8 and 9. For a complete list of options associated with the printf method's format string, see the java.util.Formatter page of Java's API documentation.

The format string in a printf call doesn't change the way a number is stored internally for calculations. All the format string does is create a nice-looking bunch of digit characters that can be displayed on your screen.

Hiding Details with Accessor Methods

Put down this book and put on your hat. You've been such a loyal reader that I'm taking you out to lunch!

I have just one problem. I'm a bit short on cash. Would you mind if, on the way to lunch, we stopped at an automatic teller machine and picked up a few bucks? Also, we have to use your account. My account is a little low.

Fortunately, the teller machine is easy to use. Just step right up and enter your PIN. After entering your PIN, the machine asks which of several variable names you want to use for your current balance. You have a choice of `balance324`, `myBal`, `currentBalance`, `b$`, `BALANCE`, `asj999`, or `conStanTinople`. Having selected a variable name, you're ready to select a memory location for the variable's value. You can select any number between 022FFF and 0555AA. (Those numbers are in hexadecimal format.) After you configure the teller machine's software, you can easily get your cash. You did bring a screwdriver, didn't you?

Good programming

When it comes to good computer programming practice, one word stands out above all others — *simplicity*. When you're writing complicated code, the last thing you want is to deal with somebody else's misnamed variables, convoluted solutions to problems, or clever, last-minute kludges. You want a clean interface that makes you solve your own problems and no one else's.

In the automatic teller machine scenario that I describe earlier, the big problem is that the machine's design forces you to worry about other people's concerns. When you should be thinking about getting money for lunch, you're thinking instead about variables and storage locations. Sure, someone has to work out the teller machine's engineering problems, but the banking customer isn't the person.

This section is about safety, not security. Safe code keeps you from making accidental programming errors. Secure code (a completely different story) keeps malicious hackers from doing intentional damage.

So, everything connected with every aspect of a computer program has to be simple, right? Well, no. That's not right. Sometimes, to make things simple in the long run, you have to do lots of preparatory work up front. The people who built the automated teller machine worked hard to make sure that the machine is consumer-proof. The machine's interface, with its screen messages and buttons, makes the machine a very complicated, but carefully designed, device.

The point is that making things look simple takes some planning. In the case of object-oriented programming, one of the ways to make things look simple is to prevent code outside a class from directly using fields defined inside the class. Take a peek at the code in Listing 7-1. You're working at a company that has just spent $10 million for the code in the `Account` class. (That's more than a million and a half per line!) Now your job is to write the `UseAccount` class. You would like to write

```
myAccount.name = "Barry Burd";
```

but doing so would be getting you too far inside the guts of the `Account` class. After all, people who use an automatic teller machine aren't allowed to program the machine's variables. They can't use the machine's keypad to type the statement

```
balanceOnAccount29872865457 =
    balanceOnAccount29872865457 + 1000000.00;
```

Instead, they push buttons that do the job in an orderly manner. That's how a programmer achieves safety and simplicity.

So, to keep things nice and orderly, you need to change the `Account` class from Listing 7-1 by outlawing such statements as the following:

```
myAccount.name = "Barry Burd";
```

and

```
out.print(yourAccount.balance);
```

Of course, this poses a problem. You're the person who's writing the code for the `UseAccount` class. If you can't write `myAccount.name` or `yourAccount.balance`, how are you going to accomplish anything at all? The answer lies in things called *accessor methods*. Listings 7-8 and 7-9 demonstrate these methods.

Listing 7-8:   Hide Those Fields

```java
public class Account {
    private String name;
    private String address;
    private double balance;

    public void setName(String n) {
        name = n;
    }

    public String getName() {
        return name;
    }

    public void setAddress(String a) {
        address = a;
    }

    public String getAddress() {
        return address;
    }

    public void setBalance(double b) {
        balance = b;
    }

    public double getBalance() {
        return balance;
    }
}
```

Listing 7-9: Calling Accessor Methods

```java
import static java.lang.System.out;

public class UseAccount {

    public static void main(String args[]) {
        Account myAccount = new Account();
        Account yourAccount = new Account();

        myAccount.setName("Barry Burd");
        myAccount.setAddress("222 Cyberspace Lane");
        myAccount.setBalance(24.02);

        yourAccount.setName("Jane Q. Public");
        yourAccount.setAddress("111 Consumer Street");
        yourAccount.setBalance(55.63);

        out.print(myAccount.getName());
        out.print(" (");
        out.print(myAccount.getAddress());
        out.print(") has $");
        out.print(myAccount.getBalance());
        out.println();

        out.print(yourAccount.getName());
        out.print(" (");
        out.print(yourAccount.getAddress());
        out.print(") has $");
        out.print(yourAccount.getBalance());
    }
}
```

A run of the code in Listings 7-8 and 7-9 looks no different from a run of Listings 7-1 and 7-2. Either program's run is shown back in Figure 7-3. The big difference is that in Listing 7-8, the Account class enforces the carefully controlled use of its name, address, and balance fields.

Public lives and private dreams: Making a field inaccessible

Notice the addition of the word *private* in front of each of the Account class's field declarations. The word *private* is a Java keyword. When a field is declared private, no code outside of the class can make direct reference to that field. So if you put myAccount.name = "Barry Burd" in the UseAccount class of Listing 7-9, you get the error message name has private access in Account.

Instead of referencing `myAccount.name`, the `UseAccount` programmer must call method `myAccount.setName` or method `myAccount.getName`. These methods, `setName` and `getName`, are called *accessor* methods because they provide access to the `Account` class's `name` field. (Actually, the term *accessor method* isn't formally a part of the Java programming language. It's just the term that people use for methods that do this sort of thing.) To zoom in even more, `setName` is called a *setter* method, and `getName` is called a *getter* method. (I bet you won't forget that terminology!)

With many IDEs, you don't have to type your own accessor methods. First, you type a field declaration like `private String name`. Then, in your IDE's menu bar, you choose Source⇨Generate Getters and Setters, or choose Code⇨Insert Code⇨Setter or some mix of those commands. After you make all your choices, the IDE creates accessor methods and adds them to your code.

Notice that all the setter and getter methods in Listing 7-8 are declared to be public. This ensures that anyone from anywhere can call these two methods. The idea here is that manipulating the actual fields from outside the `Account` code is impossible, but you can easily reach the approved setter and getter methods for using those fields.

Think again about the automatic teller machine. Someone using the ATM can't type a command that directly changes the value in his or her account's `balance` field, but the procedure for depositing a million-dollar check is easy to follow. The people who build the teller machines know that if the check depositing procedure is complicated, plenty of customers will mess it up royally. So that's the story — make impossible anything that people shouldn't do and make sure that the tasks people should be doing are easy.

Nothing about having setter and getter methods is sacred. You don't have to write any setter and getter methods that you're not going to use. For instance, in Listing 7-8, I can omit the declaration of method `getAddress`, and everything still works. The only problem if I do this is that anyone else who wants to use my `Account` class and retrieve the address of an existing account is up a creek.

When you create a method to set the value in a `balance` field, you don't have to name your method `setBalance`. You can name it `tunaFish` or whatever you like. The trouble is that the `setFieldname` convention (with lowercase letters in `set` and an uppercase letter to start the `Fieldname` part) is an established stylistic convention in the world of Java programming. If you don't follow the convention, you confuse the kumquats out of other Java programmers. If your integrated development environment has drag-and-drop GUI design capability, you may temporarily lose that capability. (For a word about drag-and-drop GUI design, see Chapters 2 and 15.)

When you call a setter method, you feed it a value of the type that's being set. That's why, in Listing 7-9, you call yourAccount.setBalance(55.63) with a parameter of type double. In contrast, when you call a getter method, you usually don't feed any values to the method. That's why, in Listing 7-9, you call yourAccount.getBalance() with an empty parameter list. Occasionally, you may want to get and set a value with a single statement. To add a dollar to your account's existing balance, you write yourAccount.setBalance(yourAccount.getBalance() + 1.00).

Enforcing rules with accessor methods

Go back to Listing 7-8 and take a quick look at the setName method. Imagine putting the method's assignment statement inside an if statement.

```
public void setName(String n) {
    if (!n.equals("")) {
        name = n;
    }
}
```

Now, if the programmer in charge of the UseAccount class writes myAccount.setName(""), the call to setName doesn't have any effect. Furthermore, because the name field is private, the following statement is illegal in the UseAccount class:

```
myAccount.name = "";
```

Of course, a call such as myAccount.setName("Joe Schmoe") still works because "Joe Schmoe" doesn't equal the empty string "".

That's cool. With a private field and an accessor method, you can prevent someone from assigning the empty string to an account's name field. With more elaborate if statements, you can enforce any rules you want.

Chapter 8

Saving Time and Money: Reusing Existing Code

. . . .

In This Chapter

▶ Adding new life to old code

▶ Tweaking your code

▶ Making changes without spending a fortune

. . . .

*O*nce upon a time, there was a beautiful princess. When the princess turned 25 (the optimal age for strength, good looks, and fine moral character), her kind father brought her a gift in a lovely golden box. Anxious to know what was in the box, the princess ripped off the golden wrapping paper.

When the box was finally opened, the princess was thrilled. To her surprise, her father had given her what she had always wanted — a computer program that always ran correctly. The program did everything the princess wanted and did it all exactly the way she wanted it to be done. The princess was happy, and so was her kind, old father.

As time went on, the computer program never failed. For years on end, the princess changed her needs, expected more out of life, made increasing demands, expanded her career, reached for more and more fulfillment, juggled the desires of her husband and her kids, stretched the budget, and sought peace within her soul. Through all this, the program remained her steady, faithful companion.

As the princess grew old, the program became old along with her. One evening, as she sat by the fireside, she posed a daunting question to the program. "How do you do it?" she asked. "How do you manage to keep giving the right answers, time after time, year after year?"

"Clean living," replied the program. "I swim 20 apps each day, I take C++ to Word off viruses, I avoid hogarithmic algorithms, I link Java in moderation, I say GNU to bugs, I don't smoke to backup, and I never byte off more than I can queue."

Needless to say, the princess was stunned.

Defining a Class (What It Means to Be an Employee)

Wouldn't it be nice if every piece of software did just what you wanted it to do? In an ideal world, you could just buy a program, make it work right away, plug it seamlessly into new situations, and update it easily whenever your needs change. Unfortunately, software of this kind doesn't exist. (*Nothing* of this kind exists.) The truth is that no matter what you want to do, you can find software that does some of it, but not all of it.

This is one of the reasons why object-oriented programming has been so successful. For years, companies were buying prewritten code only to discover that the code didn't do what they wanted it to do. So what did the companies do about it? They started messing with the code. Their programmers dug deep into the program files, changed variable names, moved subprograms around, reworked formulas, and generally made the code worse. The reality was that if a program didn't already do what you wanted it to do (even if it did something ever so close to what you wanted), you could never improve the situation by mucking around inside the code. The best option was always to chuck the whole program (expensive as that was) and start all over again. What a sad state of affairs!

With object-oriented programming, a big change has come about. At its heart, an object-oriented program is made to be modified. With correctly written software, you can take advantage of features that are already built-in, add new features of your own, and override features that don't suit your needs. And the best part is that the changes you make are clean. No clawing and digging into other people's brittle program code. Instead, you make nice, orderly additions and modifications without touching the existing code's internal logic. It's the ideal solution.

The last word on employees

When you write an object-oriented program, you start by thinking about the data. You're writing about accounts. So what's an account? You're writing code to handle button clicks. So what's a button? You're writing a program to send payroll checks to employees. What's an employee?

In this chapter's first example, an employee is someone with a name and a job title. Sure, employees have other characteristics, but for now I stick to the basics. The code in Listing 8-1 defines what it means to be an employee.

Listing 8-1:   What Is an Employee?

```
import static java.lang.System.out;

public class Employee {
    private String name;
    private String jobTitle;

    public void setName(String nameIn) {
        name = nameIn;
    }

    public String getName() {
        return name;
    }

    public void setJobTitle(String jobTitleIn) {
        jobTitle = jobTitleIn;
    }

    public String getJobTitle() {
        return jobTitle;
    }

    public void cutCheck(double amountPaid) {
        out.printf("Pay to the order of %s ", name);
        out.printf("(%s) ***$", jobTitle);
        out.printf("%,.2f\n", amountPaid);
    }
}
```

According to Listing 8-1, each employee has seven features. Two of these features are fairly simple. Each employee has a name and a job title. (In Listing 8-1, the Employee class has a name field and a jobTitle field.)

And what else does an employee have? Each employee has four methods to handle the values of the employee's name and job title. These methods are setName, getName, setJobTitle, and getJobTitle. I explain methods like these (*accessor* methods) in Chapter 7.

On top of all that, each employee has a cutCheck method. The idea is that the method that writes payroll checks has to belong to one class or another. Because most of the information in the payroll check is customized for a particular employee, you may as well put the cutCheck method inside the Employee class.

For details about the printf calls in the cutCheck method, see the section entitled "Cutting a check," later in this chapter.

Putting your class to good use

The Employee class in Listing 8-1 has no main method, so there's no starting point for executing code. To fix this deficiency, the programmer writes a separate program with a main method and uses that program to create Employee instances. Listing 8-2 shows a class with a main method — one that puts the code in Listing 8-1 to the test.

Listing 8-2: Writing Payroll Checks

```
import java.util.Scanner;
import java.io.File;
import java.io.IOException;

public class DoPayroll {

    public static void main(String args[])
                                    throws IOException {
        Scanner diskScanner =
            new Scanner(new File("EmployeeInfo.txt"));

        for (int empNum = 1; empNum <= 3; empNum++) {
            payOneEmployee(diskScanner);
        }

        diskScanner.close();
    }

    static void payOneEmployee(Scanner aScanner) {
        Employee anEmployee = new Employee();

        anEmployee.setName(aScanner.nextLine());
        anEmployee.setJobTitle(aScanner.nextLine());
        anEmployee.cutCheck(aScanner.nextDouble());
        aScanner.nextLine();
    }
}
```

To run the code in Listing 8-2, your hard drive must contain a file named EmployeeInfo.txt. Fortunately, the stuff that you download from this book's website (www.allmycode.com/JavaForDummies) comes with an EmployeeInfo.txt file. You can import the downloaded material into any of the three most popular Java IDEs (Eclipse, NetBeans, and IntelliJ IDEA). If you import into Eclipse, you get a project named 08-02. That project typically lives on your hard drive in a folder named c:\Users*your-user-name*\workspace\08-02. Directly inside that folder, you have a file named EmployeeInfo.txt.

For more words of wisdom about files on your hard drive, see the "Working with Disk Files (A Brief Detour)" section in this chapter.

The DoPayroll class in Listing 8-2 has two methods. One of the methods, main, calls the other method, payOneEmployee, three times. Each time around, the payOneEmployee method gets stuff from the EmployeeInfo. txt file and feeds this stuff to the Employee class's methods.

Here's how the variable name *anEmployee* is reused and recycled:

- ✔ The first time that payOneEmployee is called, the statement anEmployee = new Employee() makes anEmployee refer to a new object.

- ✔ The second time that payOneEmployee is called, the computer executes the same statement again. This second execution creates a new incarnation of the anEmployee variable that refers to a brand-new object.

- ✔ The third time around, all the same stuff happens again. A new anEmployee variable ends up referring to a third object.

The whole story is pictured in Figure 8-1.

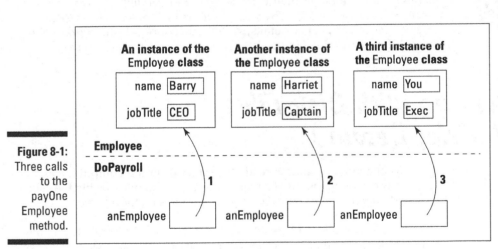

Figure 8-1:
Three calls
to the
payOne
Employee
method.

Cutting a check

Listing 8-1 has three printf calls. Each printf call has a format string (like "(%s) ***$") and a variable (like jobTitle). Each format string has a placeholder (like %s) that determines where and how the variable's value is displayed.

For example, in the second `printf` call, the format string has a `%s` placeholder. This `%s` holds a place for the `jobTitle` variable's value. According to Java's rules, the notation `%s` always holds a place for a string and, sure enough, the variable `jobTitle` is declared to be of type `String` in Listing 8-1. Parentheses and some other characters surround the `%s` placeholder, so parentheses surround each job title in the program's output. (See Figure 8-2.)

Figure 8-2:
Everybody
gets paid.

```
Pay to the order of Barry Burd (CEO) ***$5,000.00
Pay to the order of Harriet Ritter (Captain) ***$7,000.00
Pay to the order of Your Name Here (Honorary Exec of the Day) ***$10,000.00
```

Back in Listing 8-1, notice the comma inside the `%,.2f` placeholder. The comma tells the program to use *grouping separators.* That's why, in Figure 8-2, you see $5,000.00, $7,000.00, and $10,000.00 instead of $5000.00, $7000.00, and $10000.00.

Grouping separators vary from one country to another. For instance, in France, to write the number one thousand *(mille),* you write 1 000,00. Java can Frenchify your number automatically with a statement like `out.print(new java.util.Formatter().format(java.util.Locale.FRANCE, "%,.2f", 1000.00))`. For details, see the API (Application Programming Interface) documentation for Java's `Formatter` and `Locale` classes.

Working with Disk Files (A Brief Detour)

In previous chapters, programs read characters from the computer's keyboard. But the code in Listing 8-2 reads characters from a specific file. The file (named *EmployeeInfo.txt*) lives on your computer's hard drive.

This `EmployeeInfo.txt` file is like a word processing document. The file can contain letters, digits, and other characters. But unlike a word processing document, the `EmployeeInfo.txt` file contains no formatting — no italics, no bold, no font sizes, nothing of that kind.

The `EmployeeInfo.txt` file contains only ordinary characters — the kinds of keystrokes that you type while you play a guessing game from Chapters 5 or 6. Of course, getting guesses from a user's keyboard and reading employee data from a disk file aren't exactly the same. In a guessing game, the program displays prompts, such as `Enter an int from 1 to 10`. The game program conducts a back-and-forth dialogue with the person sitting at the keyboard. In contrast, Listing 8-2 has no dialogue. This DoPayroll program reads characters from a hard drive and doesn't prompt or interact with anyone.

Most of this chapter is about code reuse. But Listing 8-2 stumbles upon an important idea — an idea that's not directly related to code reuse. Unlike the examples in previous chapters, Listing 8-2 reads data from a stored disk file. So in the following sections, I take a short side trip to explore disk files.

Storing data in a file

The code in Listing 8-2 doesn't run unless you have some employee data sitting in a file. Listing 8-2 says that this file is EmployeeInfo.txt. So before running the code of Listing 8-2, I created a small EmployeeInfo.txt file. The file is shown in Figure 8-3; refer to Figure 8-2 for the resulting output.

Figure 8-3:
An
Employee
Info.txt file.

```
Barry Burd
CEO
5000.00
Harriet Ritter
Captain
7000.00
Your Name Here
Honorary Exec of the Day
10000.00
|
```

When you visit this book's web site (www.allmycode.com/JavaForDummies) and you download the book's code listings, you get a copy of the EmployeeInfo.txt file.

To keep Listing 8-2 simple I insist that, when you type the characters in Figure 8-3, you finish up by typing 10000.00 and then pressing Enter. (Look again at Figure 8-3 and notice how the cursor is at the start of a brand-new line.) If you forget to finish by pressing Enter, then the code in Listing 8-2 will crash when you try to run it.

Grouping separators vary from one country to another. The file shown in Figure 8-3 works on a computer configured in the United States where *5000.00* means "five thousand." But the file doesn't work on a computer that's configured in what I call a "comma country" — a country where *5000,00* means "five thousand." If you live in a comma country, and you use the file exactly as it's shown in Figure 8-3, you probably get an error message (an InputMismatchException) when you try to run this section's example. If so, change the number amounts in your file to match your country's number format. When you do, you should be okay.

This book's website (www.allmycode.com/JavaForDummies) has tips for readers who need to create data files. This includes instructions for Windows, Linux, and Macintosh environments.

Copying and pasting code

In almost any computer programming language, reading data from a file can be tricky. You add extra lines of code to tell the computer what to do. Sometimes you can copy and paste these lines from other peoples' code. For example, you can follow the pattern in Listing 8-2:

```java
/*
 * The pattern in Listing 8-2
 */
import java.util.Scanner;
import java.io.File;
import java.io.IOException;

class SomeClassName {

    public static void main(String args[])
                                  throws IOException {
        Scanner scannerName =
            new Scanner(new File("SomeFileName"));

        //Some code goes here

        scannerName.nextInt();
        scannerName.nextDouble();
        scannerName.next();
        scannerName.nextLine();

        //Some code goes here

        scannerName.close();
    }
}
```

You want to read data from a file. You start by imagining that you're reading from the keyboard. Put the usual `Scanner` and `next` codes into your program. Then add some extra items from the Listing 8-2 pattern:

- Add two new `import` declarations — one for `java.io.File` and another for `java.io.IOException`.

- Type **throws IOException** in your method's header.

- Type **new File(" ")** in your call to `new Scanner`.

- Take a file that's already on your hard drive. Type that filename inside the quotation marks.

✔ Take the word that you use for the name of your scanner. Reuse that word in calls to `next`, `nextInt`, `nextDouble`, and so on.

✔ Take the word that you use for the name of your scanner. Reuse that word in a call to `close`.

Occasionally, copying and pasting code can get you into trouble. Maybe you're writing a program that doesn't fit the simple Listing 8-2 pattern. You need to tweak the pattern a bit. But to tweak the pattern, you need to understand some of the ideas behind the pattern.

That's how the next section comes to your rescue. It covers some of these ideas.

Reading from a file

In previous chapters, programs read characters from the computer's keyboard. These programs use things like `Scanner`, `System.in`, and `nextDouble` — things defined in Java's API. The `DoPayroll` program in Listing 8-2 puts a new spin on this story. Instead of reading characters from the keyboard, the program reads characters from the `EmployeeInfo.txt` file. The file lives on your computer's hard drive.

To read characters from a file, you use some of the same things that help you read characters from the keyboard. You use `Scanner`, `nextDouble`, and other goodies. But in addition to these goodies, you have a few extra hurdles to jump. Here's a list:

✔ **You need a `new File` object.** To be more precise, you need a new instance of the API's `File` class. You get this new instance with code like

```
new File("EmployeeInfo.txt")
```

The stuff in quotation marks is the name of a file — a file on your computer's hard drive. The file contains characters like those shown previously in Figure 8-3.

At this point, the terminology makes mountains out of molehills. Sure, I use the phrases *new File object* and *new File instance,* but all you're doing is making `new File("EmployeeInfo.txt")` stand for a file on your hard drive. After you shove `new File("EmployeeInfo.txt")` into `new Scanner`,

```
Scanner diskScanner =
        new Scanner(new File("EmployeeInfo.txt"));
```

you can forget all about the new File business. From that point on in the code, diskScanner stands for the EmployeeInfo.txt filename on your computer's hard drive. (The name diskScanner stands for a file on your hard drive just as, in previous examples, the name keyboard stands for those buttons that you press day-in and day-out.)

Creating a new File object in Listing 8-2 is like creating a new Employee object later in the same listing. It's also like creating a new Account object in the examples of Chapter 7. The only difference is that the Employee and Account classes are defined in this book's examples. The File class is defined in Java's API.

When you connect to a disk file with new Scanner, don't forget the new File part. If you write new Scanner("EmployeeInfo.txt") without new File, the compiler won't mind. (You won't get any warnings or error messages before you run the code.) But when you run the code, you won't get anything like the results that you expect to get.

✔ **You must refer to the File class by its full name — java.io.File.** You can do this with an import declaration like the one in Listing 8-2. Alternatively, you can clutter up your code with a statement like

```
Scanner diskScanner =
    new Scanner(new java.io.File("EmployeeInfo.txt"));
```

✔ **You need a throws IOException clause.** Lots of things can go wrong when your program connects to EmployeeInfo.txt. For one thing, your hard drive may not have a file named *EmployeeInfo.txt*. For another, the file EmployeeInfo.txt may be in the wrong directory. To brace for this kind of calamity, the Java programming language takes certain precautions. The language insists that when a disk file is involved, you acknowledge the possible dangers of calling new Scanner.

You can acknowledge the hazards in several possible ways, but the simplest way is to use a throws clause. In Listing 8-2, the main method's header ends with the words *throws IOException*. By adding these two words, you appease the Java compiler. It's as if you're saying "I know that calling new Scanner can lead to problems. You don't have to remind me." And, sure enough, adding throws IOException to your main method keeps the compiler from complaining. (Without this throws clause, you get an unreported exception error message.)

For the full story on Java exceptions, read Chapter 13. In the meantime, add throws IOException to the header of any method that calls new Scanner(new File(....

✔ **You must refer to the IOException class by its full name — java. io.IOException.**

You can do this with an import declaration like the one in Listing 8-2. Alternatively, you can enlarge the main method's throws clause:

```
public static void main(String args[])
                throws java.io.IOException {
```

✔ **You must pass the file scanner's name to the** `payOneEmployee`
method.

In Listing 7-5 in Chapter 7, the `getInterest` method has a parameter
named *percentageRate*. Whenever you call the `getInterest` method,
you hand an extra, up-to-date piece of information to the method. (You
hand a number — an interest rate — to the method. Figure 7-7 illustrates
the idea.)

The same thing happens in Listing 8-2. The `payOneEmployee` method has
a parameter named *aScanner*. Whenever you call the `payOneEmployee`
method, you hand an extra, up-to-date piece of information to the method.
(You hand a scanner — a reference to a disk file — to the method.)

You may wonder why the `payOneEmployee` method needs a parameter. After
all, in Listing 8-2, the `payOneEmployee` method always reads data from the
same file. Why bother informing this method, each time you call it, that the
disk file is still the `EmployeeInfo.txt` file?

Well, there are plenty of ways to shuffle the code in Listing 8-2. Some ways
don't involve a parameter. But the way that this example has arranged things,
you have two separate methods — a `main` method and a `payOneEmployee`
method. You create a scanner once inside the `main` method and then use
the scanner three times — once inside each call to the `payOneEmployee`
method.

Anything that you define inside a method is like a private joke that's
known only to the code inside that method. So, the `diskScanner` that
you define inside the `main` method isn't automatically known inside the
`payOneEmployee` method. To make the `payOneEmployee` method aware
of the disk file, you pass `diskScanner` from the `main` method to the
`payOneEmployee` method.

To read more about things that you declare inside (and outside) of methods,
see Chapter 10.

Who moved my file?

When you download the code from this book's website, you're going to find files
named *Employee.java* and *DoPayroll.java* — the code in Listings 8-1 and 8-2.
You'll also find a file named `EmployeeInfo.txt`. That's good, because if Java
can't find the `EmployeeInfo.txt` file, the whole project doesn't run properly.
Instead, you get a `FileNotFoundException`.

In general, when you get a `FileNotFoundException`, some file that your program needs isn't available to it. This is an easy mistake to make. It can be frustrating because to you, a file such as `EmployeeInfo.txt` may look like it's available to your program. But remember — computers are stupid. If you make a tiny mistake, the computer can't read between the lines for you. So if your `EmployeeInfo.txt` file isn't in the right directory on your hard drive or the filename is spelled incorrectly, the computer chokes when it tries to run your code.

Sometimes you know darn well that an `EmployeeInfo.txt` (or *whatever. xyz*) file exists on your hard drive. But when you run your program, you still get a mean-looking `FileNotFoundException`. When this happens, the file is usually in the wrong directory on your hard drive. (Of course, it depends on your point of view. Maybe the file is in the right directory, but you've told your Java program to look for the file in the wrong directory.) When this happens, try copying the file to some other directories on your hard drive and rerunning your code. Carefully read and reread the names and locations of files on your hard drive until you figure out what's wrong.

On this book's website (`www.allmycode.com/JavaForDummies`), you can find tips on the proper location of the `EmployeeInfo.txt` file. Look for tips that apply to your operating system (Windows, Macintosh, or Linux) and to your IDE (Eclipse, NetBeans, or IntelliJ IDEA).

Adding directory names to your filenames

You can specify a file's exact location in your Java code. Code like `new File("C:\\Users\\bburd\\workspace\\Listing08-01-02\\ EmployeeInfo.txt")` looks really ugly, but it works.

In the previous paragraph, notice the double backslashes in `"C:  \\Users\\ bburd\\workspace..."`. If you're a Windows user, you'd be tempted to write `C:\Users\bburd\workspace...` with single backslashes. But in Java, the single backslash has its own special meaning. (For example, back in Listing 7-7, `\n` means to go to the next line.) So in Java, to indicate a backslash inside a quoted string, you use a double backslash instead.

Macintosh and Linux users might find comfort in the fact that their path separator, /, has no special meaning in a Java string. On a Mac, the code `new File("/Users/bburd/workspace/Listing08-01-02/EmployeeInfo. txt")` is as normal as breathing. (Well, it's almost that normal!) But Mac users and Linux wonks shouldn't claim superiority too quickly. Lines such as `new File("/Users/bburd/workspace...` work in Windows as well.

In Windows, you can use either a slash (/) or a backslash (\) as your path name separator. In the Windows Command Prompt, I can type `cd c:/users\bburd` to get to my home directory.

If you know where your Java program looks for files, you can worm your way from that place to the directory of your choice. Assume, for the moment, that the code in Listing 8-2 normally looks for the `EmployeeInfo.txt` file in a directory named `Listing08-01-03`. So, as an experiment, go to the `Listing08-01-02` directory and create a new subdirectory named *dataFiles*. Then move my `EmployeeInfo.txt` file to the new `dataFiles` directory. To read numbers and words from the file that you moved, modify Listing 8-2 with the code `new File("dataFiles\\EmployeeInfo.txt")`.

Reading a line at a time

In Listing 8-2, the `payOneEmployee` method illustrates some useful tricks for reading data. In particular, every scanner that you create has a `nextLine` method. (You might not use this `nextLine` method, but the method is available nonetheless.) When you call a scanner's `nextLine` method, the method grabs everything up to the end of the current line of text. In Listing 8-2, a call to `nextLine` can read a whole line from the `EmployeeInfo.txt` file. (In another program, a scanner's `nextLine` call may read everything the user types on the keyboard up to the pressing of the Enter key.)

Notice my careful choice of words: `nextLine` reads everything up to the end of the current line. Unfortunately, what it means to read up to the end of the current line isn't always what you think it means. Intermingling `nextInt`, `nextDouble`, and `nextLine` calls can be messy. You have to watch what you're doing and check your program's output carefully.

To understand all this, you need to be painfully aware of a data file's line breaks. Think of a line break as an extra character, stuck between one line of text and the next. Then imagine that calling `nextLine` means to read everything up to and including the next line break.

Now take a look at Figure 8-4.

- ✔ If one call to `nextLine` reads `Barry Burd[LineBreak]`, the subsequent call to `nextLine` reads `CEO[LineBreak]`.

- ✔ If one call to `nextDouble` reads the number 5000.00, the subsequent call to `nextLine` reads the `[LineBreak]` that comes immediately after the number 5000.00. (That's all the `nextLine` reads — a `[LineBreak]` and nothing more.)

- ✔ If a call to `nextLine` reads the `[LineBreak]` after the number 5000.00, the subsequent call to `nextLine` reads `Harriet Ritter[LineBreak]`.

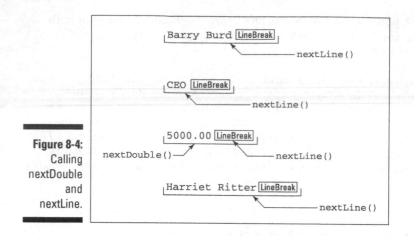

Figure 8-4:
Calling
nextDouble
and
nextLine.

So after reading the number 5000.00, you need *two* calls to `nextLine` in order to scoop up the name *Harriet Ritter*. The mistake that I usually make is to forget the first of those two calls.

Look again at the file in Figure 8-3. For this section's code to work correctly, you must have a line break after the last `10000.00`. If you don't, a final call to `nextLine` makes your program crash and burn. The error message reads `NoSuchElementException: No line found`.

I'm always surprised by the number of quirks that I find in each programming language's scanning methods. For example, the first `nextLine` that reads from the file in Figure 8-3 devours `Barry Burd[LineBreak]` from the file. But that `nextLine` call delivers `Barry Burd` (without any line break) to the running code. So `nextLine` looks for a line break, and then `nextLine` loses the line break. Yes, this is a subtle point. And no, this subtle point hardly ever causes problems for anyone.

If this business about `nextDouble` and `nextLine` confuses you, please don't put the blame on Java. Mixing input calls is delicate work in any computer programming language. And the really nasty thing is that each programming language approaches the problem a little differently. What you find out about `nextLine` in Java helps you understand the issues when you get to know C++ or Visual Basic, but it doesn't tell you all the details. Each language's details are unique to that language. (Yes, it's a big pain. But because all computer programmers become rich and famous, the pain eventually pays off.)

Closing the connection to a disk file

To the average computer user, a keyboard doesn't feel anything like a file stored on a computer's hard drive. But disk files and keyboard input have a lot in common. In fact, a basic principle of computer operating systems dictates that, for the programmer, any differences between two kinds of input be as blurry as possible. As a Java programmer, you should treat disk files and keyboard input almost the same way. That's why Listing 8-2 contains a `diskScanner.close()` call.

When you run a Java program, you normally execute the `main` method's statements, starting with the first statement in the method body and ending with the last statement in the method body. You take detours along the way, skipping past `else` parts and diving into method bodies, but basically, you finish executing statements at the end of the `main` method. That's why, in Listing 8-2, the call to `close` is at the end of the `main` method's body. When you run the code in Listing 8-2, the last thing you do is disconnect from the disk file. And, fortunately, that disconnection takes place after you've executed all the `nextLine` and `nextDouble` calls.

Defining Subclasses (What It Means to Be a Full-Time or Part-Time Employee)

This time last year, your company paid $10 million for a piece of software. That software came in the `Employee.class` file. People at Burd Brain Consulting (the company that created the software) don't want you to know about the innards of the software. (Otherwise, you may steal their ideas.) So you don't have the Java program file that the software came from. (In other words, you don't have `Employee.java`.) You can run the bytecode in the `Employee.class` file. You can also read the documentation in a web page named *Employee.html*. But you can't see the statements inside the `Employee.java` program, and you can't change any of the program's code.

Since this time last year, your company has grown. Unlike the old days, your company now has two kinds of employees: full-time and part-time. Each full-time employee is on a fixed, weekly salary. (If the employee works nights and weekends, then in return for this monumental effort, the employee receives a hearty handshake.) In contrast, each part-time employee works for an hourly wage. Your company deducts an amount from each full-time employee's paycheck to pay for the company's benefits package. Part-time employees, however, don't get benefits.

The question is whether the software that your company bought last year can keep up with the company's growth. You invested in a great program to handle employees and their payroll, but the program doesn't differentiate between your full-time and part-time employees. You have several options:

- Call your next-door neighbor, whose 12-year-old child knows more about computer programming than anyone in your company. Get this uppity little brat to take the employee software apart, rewrite it, and hand it back to you with all the changes and additions your company requires.

  On second thought, you can't do that. No matter how smart that kid is, the complexities of the employee software will probably confuse the kid. By the time you get the software back, it'll be filled with bugs and inconsistencies. Besides, you don't even have the `Employee.java` file to hand to the kid. All you have is the `Employee.class` file, which can't be read or modified with a text editor. (See Chapter 2.) Besides, your kid just beat up the neighbor's kid. You don't want to give your neighbor the satisfaction of seeing you beg for the whiz kid's help.

- Scrap the $10 million employee software. Get someone in your company to rewrite the software from scratch.

  In other words, say goodbye to your time and money.

- Write a new front end for the employee software. That is, build a piece of code that does some preliminary processing on full-time employees and then hands the preliminary results to your $10 million software. Do the same for part-time employees.

  This idea could be decent or spell disaster. Are you sure that the existing employee software has convenient *hooks* in it? (That is, does the employee software contain entry points that allow your front-end software to easily send preliminary data to the expensive employee software?) Remember, this plan treats the existing software as one big, monolithic lump, which can become cumbersome. Dividing the labor between your front-end code and the existing employee program is difficult. And if you add layer upon layer to existing black box code, you'll probably end up with a fairly inefficient system.

- Call Burd Brain Consulting, the company that sold you the employee software. Tell Dr. Burd that you want the next version of his software to differentiate between full-time and part-time employees.

  "No problem," says Dr. Burd. "It'll be ready by the start of the next fiscal quarter." That evening, Dr. Burd makes a discreet phone call to his next-door neighbor. . . .

- Create two new Java classes named *FullTimeEmployee* and *PartTime Employee*. Have each new class extend the existing functionality of the expensive `Employee` class, but have each new class define its own specialized functionality for certain kinds of employees.

  Way to go! Figure 8-5 shows the structure that you want to create.

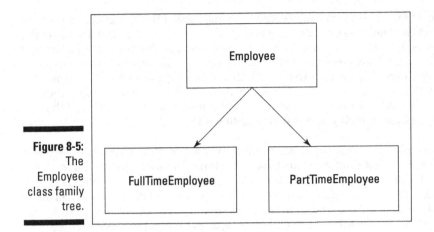

Figure 8-5:
The
Employee
class family
tree.

Creating a subclass

In Listing 8-1, I define an Employee class. I can use what I define in Listing 8-1 and extend the definition to create new, more specialized classes. So in Listing 8-3, I define a new class — a FullTimeEmployee class.

Listing 8-3:   What Is a FullTimeEmployee?

```
public class FullTimeEmployee extends Employee {
    private double weeklySalary;
    private double benefitDeduction;

    public void setWeeklySalary(double weeklySalaryIn) {
        weeklySalary = weeklySalaryIn;
    }

    public double getWeeklySalary() {
        return weeklySalary;
    }

    public void setBenefitDeduction(double benefitDedIn) {
        benefitDeduction = benefitDedIn;
    }

    public double getBenefitDeduction() {
        return benefitDeduction;
    }

    public double findPaymentAmount() {
        return weeklySalary - benefitDeduction;
    }
}
```

Looking at Listing 8-3, you can see that each instance of the FullTimeEmployee class has two fields: weeklySalary and benefitDeduction. But are those the only fields that each FullTimeEmployee instance has? No, they're not. The first line of Listing 8-3 says that the FullTimeEmployee class extends the existing Employee class. This means that in addition to having a weeklySalary and a benefitDeduction, each FullTimeEmployee instance also has two other fields: name and jobTitle. These two fields come from the definition of the Employee class, which you can find in Listing 8-1.

In Listing 8-3, the magic word is *extends*. When one class extends an existing class, the extending class automatically inherits functionality that's defined in the existing class. So, the FullTimeEmployee class *inherits* the name and jobTitle fields. The FullTimeEmployee class also inherits all the methods that are declared in the Employee class — setName, getName, setJobTitle, getJobTitle, and cutCheck. The FullTimeEmployee class is a *subclass* of the Employee class. That means the Employee class is the *superclass* of the FullTimeEmployee class. You can also talk in terms of blood relatives. The FullTimeEmployee class is the *child* of the Employee class, and the Employee class is the *parent* of the FullTimeEmployee class.

It's almost (but not quite) as if the FullTimeEmployee class was defined by the code in Listing 8-4.

Listing 8-4:   Fake (But Informative) Code

```
import static java.lang.System.out;

public class FullTimeEmployee {
    private String name;
    private String jobTitle;
    private double weeklySalary;
    private double benefitDeduction;

    public void setName(String nameIn) {
        name = nameIn;
    }

    public String getName() {
        return name;
    }

    public void setJobTitle(String jobTitleIn) {
        jobTitle = jobTitleIn;
    }

    public String getJobTitle() {
        return jobTitle;
    }
```

```
    public void setWeeklySalary(double weeklySalaryIn) {
        weeklySalary = weeklySalaryIn;
    }

    public double getWeeklySalary() {
        return weeklySalary;
    }

    public void setBenefitDeduction(double benefitDedIn) {
        benefitDeduction = benefitDedIn;
    }

    public double getBenefitDeduction() {
        return benefitDeduction;
    }

    public double findPaymentAmount() {
        return weeklySalary - benefitDeduction;
    }

    public void cutCheck(double amountPaid) {
        out.printf("Pay to the order of %s ", name);
        out.printf("(%s) ***$", jobTitle);
        out.printf("%,.2f\n", amountPaid);
    }
}
```

Why does the title for Listing 8-4 call that code fake? (Should the code feel insulted?) Well, the main difference between Listing 8-4 and the inheritance situation in Listings 8-1 and 8-3 is this: A child class can't directly reference the private fields of its parent class. To do anything with the parent class's private fields, the child class has to call the parent class's accessor methods. Back in Listing 8-3, calling `setName("Rufus")` would be legal, but the code `name="Rufus"` wouldn't be. If you believe everything you read in Listing 8-4, you'd think that code in the `FullTimeEmployee` class can do `name="Rufus"`. Well, it can't. (My, what a subtle point this is!)

You don't need the `Employee.java` file on your hard drive to write code that extends the `Employee` class. All you need is the file `Employee.class`.

Creating subclasses is habit-forming

After you're accustomed to extending classes, you can get extend-happy. If you created a `FullTimeEmployee` class, you might as well create a `PartTimeEmployee` class, as shown in Listing 8-5.

Listing 8-5:   What Is a PartTimeEmployee?

```
public class PartTimeEmployee extends Employee {
    private double hourlyRate;

    public void setHourlyRate(double rateIn) {
        hourlyRate = rateIn;
    }

    public double getHourlyRate() {
        return hourlyRate;
    }

    public double findPaymentAmount(int hours) {
        return hourlyRate * hours;
    }
}
```

Unlike the `FullTimeEmployee` class, `PartTimeEmployee` has no salary or deduction. Instead `PartTimeEmployee` has an `hourlyRate` field. (Adding a `numberOfHoursWorked` field would also be a possibility. I chose not to do this, figuring that the number of hours a part-time employee works will change drastically from week to week.)

Using Subclasses

The previous section tells a story about creating subclasses. It's a good story, but it's incomplete. Creating subclasses is fine, but you gain nothing from these subclasses unless you write code to use them. So in this section, you explore code that uses subclasses.

Now the time has come for you to classify yourself as either a type-F person, a type-P person, or a type-T person. (I'm this book's author so I get to make up some personality types. I can even point to someone in public and say, "Look! He's a type-T person!")

- ✔ **A type-F person** wants to see the fundamentals. (The letter *F* stands for *fundamentals.*) "Show me a program that lays out the principles in their barest, most basic form," says the type-F person. A type-F person isn't worried about bells and whistles. The bells come later, and the whistles may never come at all. If you're a type-F person, you want to see a program that uses the `FullTimeEmployee` and `PartTimeEmployee` subclasses and then moves out of your way so you can get some work done.

- ✔ **A type-P person** wants practical applications. (The letter *P* stands for *practical.*) Type-P people need to see ideas in context; otherwise, the ideas float away too quickly. "Show me a program that demonstrates the usefulness of the FullTimeEmployee and PartTimeEmployee subclasses," says the type-P person. "I have no use for your stinking abstractions. I want real-life examples, and I want them now!"

✔ **A type-T person** is inspired by something that I write about briefly in Chapter 7. The T person wants to *test* the code in the FullTimeEmployee and PartTimeEmployee subclasses. Testing the code means putting the code through its paces — checking the output's accuracy when the input is ordinary, when the input is unexpected, and even when the input is completely unrealistic. What's more, the type-T person wants to use a standard, easily recognizable outline for the testing code so that other programmers can quickly understand the test results. The type-T person creates *JUnit* tests that use the FullTimeEmployee and PartTimeEmployee subclasses.

Listing 8-6, which is for the type-F crowd, is lean and simple and makes good bedtime reading.

If you're a type-P or type-T person, please visit this book's website (www.all mycode.com/JavaForDummies). The site contains examples to satisfy type-P and type-T readers.

Listing 8-6 shows you a bare-bones program that uses the subclasses FullTimeEmployee and PartTimeEmployee. Figure 8-6 shows the program's output.

Listing 8-6:   Putting Subclasses to Good Use

```
public class DoPayrollTypeF {

  public static void main(String args[]) {

    FullTimeEmployee ftEmployee = new FullTimeEmployee();

    ftEmployee.setName("Barry Burd");
    ftEmployee.setJobTitle("CEO");
    ftEmployee.setWeeklySalary(5000.00);
    ftEmployee.setBenefitDeduction(500.00);
    ftEmployee.cutCheck(ftEmployee.findPaymentAmount());
    System.out.println();

    PartTimeEmployee ptEmployee = new PartTimeEmployee();

    ptEmployee.setName("Steve Surace");
    ptEmployee.setJobTitle("Driver");
    ptEmployee.setHourlyRate(7.53);
    ptEmployee.cutCheck
                 (ptEmployee.findPaymentAmount(10));
  }
}
```

Figure 8-6:
The output
of the
program in
Listing 8-6.

```
Pay to the order of Barry Burd (CEO) ***$4,500.00

Pay to the order of Steve Surace (Driver) ***$75.30
```

To understand Listing 8-6, you need to keep an eye on three classes: `Employee`, `FullTimeEmployee`, and `PartTimeEmployee`. (For a look at the code that defines these classes, see Listings 8-1, 8-3, and 8-5.)

The first half of Listing 8-6 deals with a full-time employee. Notice how so many methods are available for use with the `ftEmployee` variable. For instance, you can call `ftEmployee.setWeeklySalary` because `ftEmployee` has type `FullTimeEmployee`. You can also call `ftEmployee.setName` because the `FullTimeEmployee` class extends the `Employee` class.

Because `cutCheck` is declared in the `Employee` class, you can call `ftEmployee.cutCheck`. But you can also call `ftEmployee.findPaymentAmount` because a `findPaymentAmount` method is in the `FullTimeEmployee` class.

Making types match

Look again at the first half of Listing 8-6. Take special notice of that last statement — the one in which the full-time employee is actually cut a check. The statement forms a nice, long chain of values and their types. You can see this by reading the statement from the inside out.

✔ Method `ftEmployee.findPaymentAmount` is called with an empty parameter list (Listing 8-6). That's good because the `findPaymentAmount` method takes no parameters (Listing 8-3).

✔ The `findPaymentAmount` method returns a value of type `double` (again, Listing 8-3).

✔ The `double` value that `ftEmployee.findPaymentAmount` returns is passed to method `ftEmployee.cutCheck` (Listing 8-6). That's good because the `cutCheck` method takes one parameter of type `double` (Listing 8-1).

For a fanciful graphic illustration, see Figure 8-7.

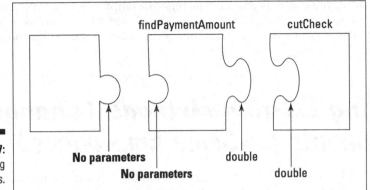

Figure 8-7:
Matching
parameters.

Always feed a method the value types that it wants in its parameter list.

The second half of the story

In the second half of Listing 8-6, the code creates an object of type `PartTime Employee`. A variable of type `PartTimeEmployee` can do some of the same things a `FullTimeEmployee` variable can do. But the `PartTimeEmployee` class doesn't have the `setWeeklySalary` and `setBenefitDeduction` methods. Instead, the `PartTimeEmployee` class has the `setHourlyRate` method. (See Listing 8-5.) So, in Listing 8-6, the next-to-last line is a call to the `setHourlyRate` method.

The last line of Listing 8-6 is by far the most interesting. On that line, the code hands the number 10 (the number of hours worked) to the `findPaymentAmount` method. Compare this with the earlier call to `findPaymentAmount` — the call for the full-time employee in the first half of Listing 8-6. Between the two subclasses, `FullTimeEmployee` and `PartTimeEmployee`, are two different `findPaymentAmount` methods. The two methods have two different kinds of parameter lists:

✔ The `FullTimeEmployee` class's `findPaymentAmount` method takes no parameters (Listing 8-3).

✔ The `PartTimeEmployee` class's `findPaymentAmount` method takes one `int` parameter (Listing 8-5).

This is par for the course. Finding the payment amount for a part-time employee isn't the same as finding the payment amount for a full-time employee. A part-time employee's pay changes each week, depending on the number of hours the employee works in a week. The full-time employee's pay stays the same each week. So the `FullTimeEmployee` and `PartTimeEmployee` classes both have `findPaymentAmount` methods, but each class's method works quite differently.

Overriding Existing Methods (Changing the Payments for Some Employees)

Wouldn't you know it! Some knucklehead in the human resources department offered double pay for overtime to one of your part-time employees. Now word is getting around, and some of the other part-timers want double pay for their overtime work. If this keeps up, you'll end up in the poorhouse, so you need to send out a memo to all the part-time employees, explaining why earning more money is not to their benefit.

In the meantime, you have two kinds of part-time employees — the ones who receive double pay for overtime hours and the ones who don't — so you need to modify your payroll software. What are your options?

✔ Well, you can dig right into the `PartTimeEmployee` class code, make a few changes, and hope for the best. (Not a good idea!)

✔ You can follow the previous section's advice and create a subclass of the existing `PartTimeEmployee` class. "But wait," you say. "The existing `PartTimeEmployee` class already has a `findPaymentAmount` method. Do I need some tricky way of bypassing this existing `findPaymentAmount` method for each double-pay-for-overtime employee?"

At this point, you can thank your lucky stars that you're doing object-oriented programming in Java. With object-oriented programming, you can create a subclass that overrides the functionality of its parent class. Listing 8-7 has just such a subclass.

Listing 8-7:   Yet Another Subclass

```
public class PartTimeWithOver extends PartTimeEmployee {

    @Override
    public double findPaymentAmount(int hours) {

        if(hours <= 40) {
            return getHourlyRate() * hours;
        } else {
            return getHourlyRate() * 40 +
                    getHourlyRate() * 2 * (hours - 40);
        }
    }
}
```

Figure 8-8 shows the relationship between the code in Listing 8-7 and other pieces of code in this chapter. In particular, PartTimeWithOver is a subclass of a subclass. In object-oriented programming, a chain of this kind is not the least bit unusual. In fact, as subclasses go, this chain is rather short.

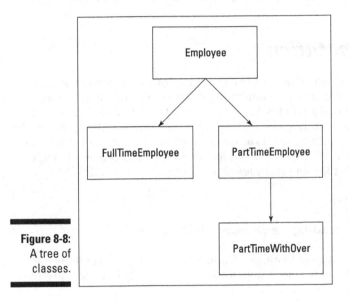

Figure 8-8:
A tree of classes.

The PartTimeWithOver class extends the PartTimeEmployee class, but PartTimeWithOver picks and chooses what it wants to inherit from the PartTimeEmployee class. Because PartTimeWithOver has its own declaration for the findPaymentAmount method, the PartTimeWithOver class doesn't inherit a findPaymentAmount method from its parent. (See Figure 8-9.)

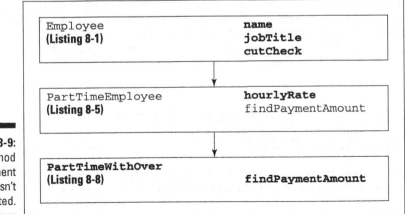

Figure 8-9:
Method findPayment Amount isn't inherited.

According to the official terminology, the PartTimeWithOver class *overrides* its parent class's findPaymentAmount method. If you create an object from the PartTimeWithOver class, that object has the name, jobTitle, hourlyRate, and cutCheck of the PartTimeEmployee class, but the object has the findPaymentAmount method that's defined in Listing 8-7.

A Java annotation

The word @Override in Listing 8-7 is an example of an *annotation*. A Java annotation tells your computer something about your code. In particular, the @Override annotation in Listing 8-7 tells the Java compiler to be on the lookout for a common coding error. The annotation says, "Make sure that the method immediately following this annotation has the same stuff (the same name, the same parameters, and so on) as one of the methods in the superclass. If not, then display an error message."

So if I accidentally type

```
public double findPaymentAmount(double hours) {
```

instead of int hours as in Listings 8-5 and 8-7, the compiler reminds me that my new findPaymentAmount method doesn't really override anything that's in Listing 8-5.

Java has other kinds of annotations (such as @Deprecated and @Suppress Warnings). You can read a bit about the @SuppressWarnings annotation in Chapter 9.

Java's annotations are optional. If you remove the word @Override from Listing 8-7, then your code still runs correctly. But the @Override annotation gives your code some added safety. With @Override, the compiler checks to make sure that you're doing something that you intend to do (namely, overriding one of the superclass's methods). And with apologies to George Orwell, some types of annotations are less optional than others. You can omit certain annotations from your code only if you're willing to replace the annotation with lots and lots of unannotated Java code.

Using methods from classes and subclasses

If you need clarification on this notion of overriding a method, look at the code in Listing 8-8. A run of that code is shown in Figure 8-10.

Listing 8-8:   Testing the Code from Listing 8-7

```
public class DoPayrollTypeF {

    public static void main(String args[]) {

        FullTimeEmployee ftEmployee = new FullTimeEmployee();

        ftEmployee.setName("Barry Burd");
        ftEmployee.setJobTitle("CEO");
        ftEmployee.setWeeklySalary(5000.00);
        ftEmployee.setBenefitDeduction(500.00);
        ftEmployee.cutCheck(ftEmployee.findPaymentAmount());

        PartTimeEmployee ptEmployee = new PartTimeEmployee();

        ptEmployee.setName("Chris Apelian");
        ptEmployee.setJobTitle("Computer Book Author");
        ptEmployee.setHourlyRate(7.53);
        ptEmployee.cutCheck
                        (ptEmployee.findPaymentAmount(50));

        PartTimeWithOver ptoEmployee =
                            new PartTimeWithOver();

        ptoEmployee.setName("Steve Surace");
        ptoEmployee.setJobTitle("Driver");
        ptoEmployee.setHourlyRate(7.53);
        ptoEmployee.cutCheck
                        (ptoEmployee.findPaymentAmount(50));
    }
}
```

Figure 8-10:
Running
the code of
Listing 8-8.

```
Pay to the order of Barry Burd (CEO) ***$4,500.00
Pay to the order of Chris Apelian (Computer Book Author) ***$376.50
Pay to the order of Steve Surace (Driver) ***$451.80
```

The code in Listing 8-8 writes checks to three employees. The first employee is a full-timer. The second is a part-time employee who hasn't yet gotten wind of the overtime payment scheme. The third employee knows about the overtime payment scheme and demands a fair wage.

With the subclasses, all three of these employees coexist in Listing 8-8. Sure, one subclass comes from the old `PartTimeEmployee` class, but that doesn't mean you can't create an object from the `PartTimeEmployee` class. In fact, Java is very smart about this. Listing 8-8 has three calls to the `findPaymentAmount` method, and each call reaches out to a different version of the method.

✔ In the first call, `ftEmployee.findPaymentAmount`, the `ftEmployee` variable is an instance of the `FullTimeEmployee` class. So the method that's called is the one in Listing 8-3.

✔ In the second call, `ptEmployee.findPaymentAmount`, the `ptEmployee` variable is an instance of the `PartTimeEmployee` class. So the method that's called is the one in Listing 8-5.

✔ In the third call, `ptoEmployee.findPaymentAmount`, the `ptoEmployee` variable is an instance of the `PartTimeWithOver` class. So the method that's called is the one in Listing 8-7.

This code is fantastic. It's clean, elegant, and efficient. With all the money that you save on software, you can afford to pay everyone double for overtime hours. (Whether you do that or keep the money for yourself is another story.)

Chapter 9

Constructing New Objects

- -

In This Chapter

▶ Defining constructors

▶ Using constructors in subclasses

▶ Using Java's default constructor features

▶ Constructing a simple GUI

- -

Ms. Jennie Burd
121 Schoolhouse Lane
Anywhere, Kansas

Dear Ms. Burd,

In response to your letter of June 21, I believe I can say with complete assurance that objects are not created spontaneously from nothing. Although I've never actually seen an object being created (and no one else in this office can claim to have seen an object in its moment of creation), I have every confidence that some process or other is responsible for the building of these interesting and useful thingamajigs. We here at ClassesAndObjects.com support the unanimous opinions of both the scientific community and the private sector on matters of this nature. Furthermore, we agree with the recent finding of a Blue Ribbon Presidential Panel, which concludes beyond any doubt that spontaneous object creation would impede the present economic outlook.

Please be assured that I have taken all steps necessary to ensure the safety and well-being of you, our loyal customer. If you have any further questions, please do not hesitate to contact our complaint department. The department's manager is Mr. Blake Wholl. You can contact him by visiting our company's website.

Once again, let me thank you for your concern, and I hope you continue to patronize ClassesAndObjects.com.

Yours truly,

Mr. Scott Brickenchicker
The one who couldn't get on the elevator in Chapter 4

Defining Constructors (What It Means to Be a Temperature)

Here's a statement that creates an object:

```
Account myAccount = new Account();
```

I know this works — I got it from one of my own examples in Chapter 7. Anyway, in Chapter 7, I say, "when the computer executes `new Account()`, you're creating an object by calling the `Account` class's constructor." What does this mean?

Well, when you ask the computer to create a new object, the computer responds by performing certain actions. For starters, the computer finds a place in its memory to store information about the new object. If the object has fields, the fields should eventually have meaningful values.

To find out about fields, see Chapter 7.

So one question is, when you ask the computer to create a new object, can you control what's placed in the object's fields? And what if you're interested in doing more than filling fields? Perhaps, when the computer creates a new object, you have a whole list of jobs for the computer to carry out. For instance, when the computer creates a new window object, you want the computer to realign the sizes of all the buttons in that window.

Creating a new object can involve all kinds of tasks, so in this chapter, you create constructors. A constructor tells the computer to perform a new object's startup tasks.

What is a temperature?

"Good morning, and welcome to Object News. The local temperature in your area is a pleasant 73 degrees Fahrenheit."

Each temperature consists of two things: a number and a temperature scale. A number is just a `double` value, such as 32.0 or 70.52. But what's a temperature scale? Is it a string of characters, like `"Fahrenheit"` or `"Celsius"`? Not really, because some strings aren't temperature scales. There's no `"Quelploof"` temperature scale, and a program that can display the temperature "73 degrees Quelploof" is a bad program. So how can you limit the temperature scales to the small number of scales that people use? One way to do it is with Java's `enum` type.

What is a temperature scale?
(Java's enum type)

Java provides lots of ways for you to group things together. In Chapter 11, you group things together to form an array. And in Chapter 12, you group things together to form a collection. In this chapter, you group things into an enum type. (Of course, you can't group anything unless you can pronounce enum. The word *enum* is pronounced *ee-noom,* like the first two syllables of the word *enumeration.*)

Creating a complicated enum type isn't easy, but to create a simple enum type, just write a bunch of words inside a pair of curly braces. Listing 9-1 defines an enum type. The name of the enum type is TempScale.

Listing 9-1:   The TempScale enum Type

```
public enum TempScale {
    CELSIUS, FAHRENHEIT, KELVIN, RANKINE,
    NEWTON, DELISLE, RÉAUMUR, RØMER, LEIDEN
};
```

When you define an enum type, two important things happen:

- ✔ **You create values.**

  Just as 13 and 151 are int values, CELSIUS and FAHRENHEIT are TempScale values.

- ✔ **You can create variables to refer to those values.**

  In Listing 9-2, I declare the fields number and scale. Just as double number declares a number variable is of type double, TempScale scale declares variable scale to be of type TempScale.

  Being of type TempScale means that you can have values CELSIUS, FAHRENHEIT, KELVIN, and so on. So in Listing 9-2, I can give the scale variable the value FAHRENHEIT (or TempScale.FAHRENHEIT, to be more precise).

An enum type is a Java class in disguise. That's why Listing 9-1 contains an entire file devoted to one thing; namely, the declaration of the TempScale enum type. Like the declaration of a class, an enum type declaration belongs in a file all its own. The code in Listing 9-1 belongs in a file named TempScale.java.

Okay, so then what is a temperature?

Each temperature consists of two things: a number and a temperature scale. The code in Listing 9-2 makes this fact abundantly clear.

Listing 9-2:   The Temperature Class

```java
public class Temperature {
    private double number;

    private TempScale scale;

    public Temperature() {
        number = 0.0;
        scale = TempScale.FAHRENHEIT;
    }

    public Temperature(double number) {
        this.number = number;
        scale = TempScale.FAHRENHEIT;
    }

    public Temperature(TempScale scale) {
        number = 0.0;
        this.scale = scale;
    }

    public Temperature(double number, TempScale scale) {
        this.number = number;
        this.scale = scale;
    }

    public void setNumber(double number) {
        this.number = number;
    }

    public double getNumber() {
        return number;
    }

    public void setScale(TempScale scale) {
        this.scale = scale;
    }

    public TempScale getScale() {
        return scale;
    }
}
```

The code in Listing 9-2 has the usual setter and getter methods (accessor methods for the number and scale fields).

For some good reading on setter and getter methods (also known as accessor methods), see Chapter 7.

On top of all that, Listing 9-2 has four other method-like looking things. Each of these method-like things has the name *Temperature,* which happens to be the same as the name of the class. None of these Temperature method-like things has a return type of any kind — not even void, which is the cop-out return type.

Each of these method-like things is called a *constructor.* A constructor is like a method, except that a constructor has a very special purpose — creating new objects.

Whenever the computer creates a new object, the computer executes the statements inside a constructor.

You can omit the word public in the first lines of Listings 9-1 and 9-2. If you omit public, other Java programs might not be able to use the features defined in your TempScale enum and in your Temperature class. (Don't worry about the programs in this chapter. With or without the word public, all the programs in this chapter can use the code in Listings 9-1 and 9-2. To find out which Java programs can and cannot use non-public classes, see Chapter 14.) If you *do* use the word public in the first line of Listing 9-1, Listing 9-1 *must* be in a file named TempScale.java, starting with a capital letter T. And if you *do* use the word public in the first line of Listing 9-2, Listing 9-2 *must* be in a file named Temperature.java, starting with a capital letter T. (For an introduction to public classes, see Chapter 7.)

What you can do with a temperature

Listing 9-3 gives form to some of the ideas that I describe in the preceding section. In Listing 9-3, you call the constructors that are declared back in Listing 9-2. Figure 9-1 shows what happens when you run all this code.

Figure 9-1:
Running the
code from
Listing 9-3.

```
70.00 degrees FAHRENHEIT
32.00 degrees FAHRENHEIT
 0.00 degrees CELSIUS
 2.73 degrees KELVIN
```

Listing 9-3:   Using the Temperature Class

```java
import static java.lang.System.out;

public class UseTemperature {

    public static void main(String args[]) {
        final String format = "%5.2f degrees %s\n";

        Temperature temp = new Temperature();
        temp.setNumber(70.0);
        temp.setScale(TempScale.FAHRENHEIT);
        out.printf(format, temp.getNumber(),
                           temp.getScale());

        temp = new Temperature(32.0);
        out.printf(format, temp.getNumber(),
                           temp.getScale());

        temp = new Temperature(TempScale.CELSIUS);
        out.printf(format, temp.getNumber(),
                           temp.getScale());

        temp = new Temperature(2.73, TempScale.KELVIN);
        out.printf(format, temp.getNumber(),
                           temp.getScale());
    }
}
```

The examples in the printed book are mostly text-based, but you can find fancier versions of most examples on this book's website (www.allmycode.com/JavaForDummies). These fancier versions have windows, buttons, text fields, and other elements of a typical *graphical user interface* (GUI).

In Listing 9-3, each statement of the kind

```java
temp = new Temperature(blah,blah,blah);
```

calls one of the constructors from Listing 9-2. So, by the time the code in Listing 9-3 is done running, it creates four instances of the Temperature class. Each instance is created by calling a different constructor from Listing 9-2.

In Listing 9-3, the last of the four constructor calls has two parameters — 2.73 and TempScale.KELVIN. This isn't particular to constructor calls. A method call or a constructor call can have a bunch of parameters. You separate one parameter from another with a comma. Another name for "a bunch of parameters" is a *parameter list*.

How to cheat: enum types and switch statements

Listings 9-2 and 9-3 contain long-winded names such as `TempScale.FAHRENHEIT` and `TempScale.CELSIUS`. Names such as `FAHRENHEIT` and `CELSIUS` belong to my `TempScale` enum type (the type defined in Listing 9-1). These names have no meaning outside of my `TempScale` context. (If you think I'm being egotistical with this "no meaning outside of my context" remark, try deleting the `TempScale.` part of `TempScale.FAHRENHEIT` in Listing 9-2. Suddenly, Java tells you that your code contains an error.)

Java is normally very fussy about type names and dots. But when they created enum types, the makers of Java decided that enums and `switch` statements deserved special treatment. You can use an enum value to decide which `case` to execute in a `switch` statement. When you do this, you don't use the enum type name in the `case` expressions. For example, the following Java code is correct:

```
TempScale scale = TempScale.
    RANKINE;
char letter;
```

```
switch (scale) {
case CELSIUS:
    letter = 'C';
    break;
case KELVIN:
    letter = 'K';
    break;
case RANKINE:
case RÉAUMUR:
case RØMER:
    letter = 'R';
    break;
default:
    letter = 'X';
    break;
}
```

In the first line of code, I write `TempScale.RANKINE` because this first line isn't inside a `switch` statement. But in the next several lines of code, I write `case CELSIUS`, `case KELVIN`, and `case RANKINE` without the word `TempScale`. In fact, if I create a `case` clause by writing `case TempScale.RANKINE`, then Java complains with a loud, obnoxious error message.

The only rule you must follow is to match the parameters in the call with the parameters in the declaration. For example, in Listing 9-3, the fourth and last constructor call

```
new Temperature(2.73, TempScale.KELVIN)
```

has two parameters — the first of type `double`, and the second of type `TempScale`. Java approves of this constructor call because Listing 9-2 contains a matching declaration. That is, the header

```
public Temperature(double number, TempScale scale)
```

has two parameters — the first of type `double`, and the second of type `TempScale`. If a Temperature constructor call in Listing 9-3 had no matching declaration in Listing 9-2, then Listing 9-3 would crash and burn. (To state things more politely, Java would display errors when you tried to compile the code in Listing 9-3.)

By the way, this business about multiple parameters isn't new. Back in Chapter 6, I write `keyboard.findWithinHorizon(".",0).charAt(0)`. In that line, the method call `findWithinHorizon(".",0)` has two parameters — a string and an `int` value. Lucky for me, the Java API has a method declaration for `findWithinHorizon` — a declaration whose first parameter is a string, and whose second parameter is an `int` value.

Calling new Temperature (32.0): A case study

When the computer executes one of the `new Temperature` statements in Listing 9-3, the computer has to decide which of the constructors in Listing 9-2 to use. The computer decides by looking at the parameter list — the stuff in parentheses after the words `new Temperature`. For instance, when the computer executes

```
temp = new Temperature(32.0);
```

from Listing 9-3, the computer says to itself, "The number 32.0 in parentheses is a `double` value. One of the `Temperature` constructors in Listing 9-2 has just one parameter with type `double`. The constructor's header looks like this:

```
public Temperature(double number)
```

"So, I guess I'll execute the statements inside that particular constructor." The computer goes on to execute the following statements:

```
this.number = number;
scale = TempScale.FAHRENHEIT;
```

As a result, you get a brand-new object whose `number` field has the value `32.0` and whose `scale` field has the value `TempScale.FAHRENHEIT`.

In the two lines of code, you have two statements that set values for the fields `number` and `scale`. Take a look at the second of these statements, which is a bit easier to understand. The second statement sets the new object's `scale` field to `TempScale.FAHRENHEIT`. You see, the constructor's parameter list is `(double number)`, and that list doesn't include a `scale` value. So whoever programmed this code had to make a decision about what value to use for the `scale` field. The programmer could have chosen FAHRENHEIT or CELSIUS, but she could also have chosen KELVIN, RANKINE, or any of the other obscure scales named in Listing 9-1. (This programmer happens to live in New Jersey, in the United States, where people commonly use the old Fahrenheit temperature scale.)

Marching back to the first of the two statements, this first statement assigns a value to the new object's `number` field. The statement uses a cute trick that you can see in many constructors (and in other methods that assign values to objects' fields). To understand the trick, take a look at Listing 9-4. The listing shows you two ways that I could have written the same constructor code.

Listing 9-4:   Two Ways to Accomplish the Same Thing

```
//Use this constructor . . .

        public Temperature(double whatever) {
            number = whatever;
            scale = TempScale.FAHRENHEIT;
        }

//. . . or use this constructor . . .

        public Temperature(double number) {
            this.number = number;
            scale = TempScale.FAHRENHEIT;
        }

//. . . but don't put both constructors in your code.
```

Listing 9-4 has two constructors in it. In the first constructor, I use two different names — number and whatever. In the second constructor, I don't need two names. Instead of making up a new name for the constructor's parameter, I reuse an existing name by writing this.number.

So here's what's going on in Listing 9-2:

✔ In the statement this.number = number, the name *this.number* refers to the new object's number field — the field that's declared near the very top of Listing 9-2. (See Figure 9-2.)

✔ In the statement this.number = number, *number* (on its own, without this) refers to the constructor's parameter. (Again, see Figure 9-2.)

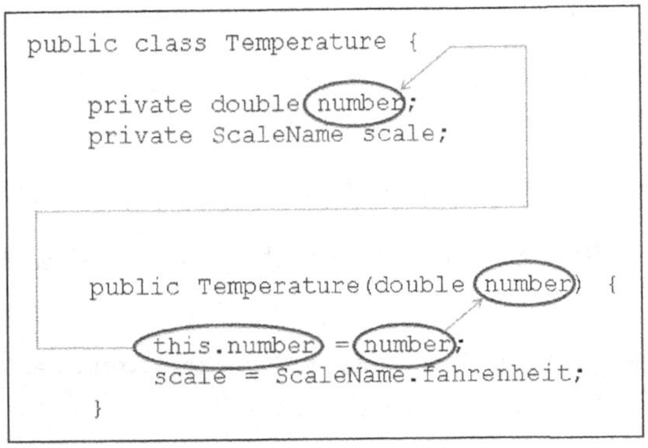

Figure 9-2:
What this.
number and
number
mean.

```
public class Temperature {

    private double number;
    private ScaleName scale;



    public Temperature(double number) {
        this.number = number;
        scale = ScaleName.fahrenheit;
    }
```

What's this all about?

Suppose your code contains a constructor — the first of the two constructors in Listing 9-4. The whatever parameter is passed a number like 32.0, for instance. Then the first statement in the constructor's body assigns that value, 32.0, to the new object's number field. The code works. But in writing this code, you had to make up a new name for a parameter — the name *whatever*. And the only purpose for this new name is to hand a value to the object's number field. What a waste! To distinguish between the parameter and the number field, you gave a name to something that was just momentary storage for the number value.

Making up names is an art, not a science. I've gone through plenty of naming phases. Years ago, whenever I needed a new name for a parameter, I picked a confusing misspelling of the original variable name. (I'd name the parameter something like numbr or nuhmber.) I've also tried changing a variable name's capitalization to come up with a parameter name. (I'd use parameter names like Number or nUMBER.) In Chapter 8, I name all my parameters by adding the suffix *In* to their corresponding variable names. (The jobTitle variable matched up with the jobTitleIn parameter.) None of these naming schemes works very well. I can never remember the quirky new names that I've created. The good news is that this parameter-naming effort isn't necessary. You can give the parameter the same name as the variable. To distinguish between the two, you use the Java keyword this.

In general, this.*someName* refers to a field belonging to the object that contains the code. In contrast, plain old *someName* refers to the closest place where *someName* happens to be declared. In the statement this.number = number (Listing 9-2), that closest place happens to be the Temperature constructor's parameter list.

Some things never change

Chapter 7 introduces the printf method and explains that each printf call starts with a format string. The format string describes the way the other parameters are to be displayed.

In previous examples, this format string is always a quoted literal. For instance, the first printf call in Listing 7-7 is

```
out.printf("$%4.2f\n", myInterest);
```

In Listing 9-3, I break with tradition and begin the printf call with a variable that I name *format*.

```
out.printf(format, temp.getNumber(), temp.getScale());
```

That's okay as long as my `format` variable is of type `String`. And indeed, in Listing 9-3, the first variable declaration is

```
final String format = "%5.2f degrees %s\n";
```

In this declaration of the `format` variable, take special note of the word *final*. This Java keyword indicates that the value of `format` can't be changed. If I add another assignment statement to Listing 9-3

```
format = "%6.2f (%s)\n";
```

then the compiler barks back at me with a `cannot assign a value to final variable` message.

When I write the code in Listing 9-3, the use of the `final` keyword isn't absolutely necessary. But the `final` keyword provides some extra protection. When I initialize `format` to `"%5.2f degrees %s\n"`, I intend to use this same `format` just as it is, over and over again. I know darn well that I don't intend to change the `format` variable's value. Of course, in a 10,000-line program, I can become confused and try to assign a new value to `format` somewhere deep down in the code. So to prevent me from accidentally changing the format string, I declare the `format` variable to be final. It's just good, safe programming practice.

More Subclasses (Doing Something about the Weather)

In Chapter 8, I make a big fuss over the notion of subclasses. That's the right thing to do. Subclasses make code reusable, and reusable code is good code. With that in mind, it's time to create a subclass of the `Temperature` class (which I develop in this chapter's first section).

Building better temperatures

After perusing the code in Listing 9-3, you decide that the responsibility for displaying temperatures has been seriously misplaced. Listing 9-3 has several tedious repetitions of the lines to print temperature values. A 1970s programmer would tell you to collect those lines into one place and turn them into a method. (The 1970s programmer wouldn't have used the word *method,* but that's not important right now.) Collecting lines into methods is fine, but with today's object-oriented programming methodology, you think in broader terms. Why not get each `temperature` object to take responsibility for displaying itself? After all, if you develop a display method, you probably want to share the method with other people who use temperatures. So put the method right inside the declaration of a temperature object. That way, anyone who uses the code for temperatures has easy access to your display method.

Now replay the tape from Chapter 8. "Blah, blah, blah . . . don't want to modify existing code . . . blah, blah, blah . . . too costly to start again from scratch . . . blah, blah, blah . . . extend existing functionality." It all adds up to one thing:

> Don't abuse it. Instead, reuse it.

So you decide to create a subclass of the Temperature class — the class defined in Listing 9-2. Your new subclass complements the Temperature class's functionality by having methods to display values in a nice, uniform fashion. The new class, TemperatureNice, is shown in Listing 9-5.

Listing 9-5: The TemperatureNice Class

```java
import static java.lang.System.out;

public class TemperatureNice extends Temperature {

    public TemperatureNice() {
        super();
    }

    public TemperatureNice(double number) {
        super(number);
    }

    public TemperatureNice(TempScale scale) {
        super(scale);
    }

    public TemperatureNice(double number, TempScale scale)
    {
        super(number, scale);
    }

    public void display() {
        out.printf("%5.2f degrees %s\n",
                            getNumber(), getScale());
    }
}
```

In the `display` method of Listing 9-5, notice the calls to the `Temperature` class's `getNumber` and `getScale` methods. Why do I do this? Well, inside the `TemperatureNice` class's code, any direct references to the `number` and `scale` fields would generate error messages. It's true that every `TemperatureNice` object has its own `number` and `scale` fields. (After all, `TemperatureNice` is a subclass of the `Temperature` class, and the code for the `Temperature` class defines the `number` and `scale` fields.) But because `number` and `scale` are declared to be private inside the `Temperature` class, only code that's right inside the `Temperature` class can directly use these fields.

Don't put additional declarations of the `number` and `scale` fields inside the `TemperatureNice` class's code. If you do, you inadvertently create four different variables (two called *number,* and another two called *scale*). You'll assign values to one pair of variables. Then you'll be shocked that, when you display the other pair of variables, those values seem to have disappeared.

When an object's code contains a call to one of the object's own methods, you don't need to preface the call with a dot. For instance, in the last statement of Listing 9-5, the object calls its own methods with `getNumber()` and `getScale()`, not with *someObject*`.getNumber()` and *somethingOrOther*`.getScale()`. If going dotless makes you queasy, you can compensate by taking advantage of yet another use for the `this` keyword. Just write `this.getNumber()` and `this.getScale()` in the last line of Listing 9-5.

Constructors for subclasses

By far, the biggest news in Listing 9-5 is the way the code declares constructors. The `TemperatureNice` class has four of its own constructors. If you've gotten in gear thinking about subclass inheritance, you may wonder why these constructor declarations are necessary. Doesn't `TemperatureNice` inherit the parent `Temperature` class's constructors? No, subclasses don't inherit constructors.

Subclasses don't inherit constructors.

That's right. Subclasses don't inherit constructors. In one oddball case, a constructor may look like it's being inherited, but that oddball situation is a fluke, not the norm. In general, when you define a subclass, you declare new constructors to go with the subclass.

I describe the oddball case (in which a constructor looks like it's being inherited) later in this chapter, in the section "The default constructor."

So the code in Listing 9-5 has four constructors. Each constructor has the name *TemperatureNice*, and each constructor has its own uniquely identifiable parameter list. That's the boring part. The interesting part is that each constructor makes a call to something named *super*, which is a Java keyword.

In Listing 9-5, `super` stands for a constructor in the parent class.

✔ The statement `super()` in Listing 9-5 calls the parameterless `Temperature()` constructor that's in Listing 9-2. That parameterless constructor assigns `0.0` to the `number` field and `TempScale.FAHRENHEIT` to the `scale` field.

✔ The statement `super(number, scale)` in Listing 9-5 calls the constructor `Temperature(double number, TempScale scale)` that's in Listing 9-2. In turn, the constructor assigns values to the `number` and `scale` fields.

✔ In a similar way, the statements `super(number)` and `super(scale)` in Listing 9-5 call constructors from Listing 9-2.

The computer decides which of the `Temperature` class's constructors is being called by looking at the parameter list after the word *super*. For instance, when the computer executes

```
super(number, scale);
```

from Listing 9-5, the computer says to itself, "The `number` and `scale` fields in parentheses have types `double` and `TempScale`. But only one of the `Temperature` constructors in Listing 9-2 has two parameters with types `double` and `TempScale`. The constructor's header looks like this:

```
public Temperature(double number, TempScale scale)
```

"So, I guess I'll execute the statements inside that particular constructor."

Using all this stuff

In Listing 9-5, I define what it means to be in the `TemperatureNice` class. Now it's time to put this `TemperatureNice` class to good use. Listing 9-6 has code that uses `TemperatureNice`.

Listing 9-6:   Using the TemperatureNice Class

```
public class UseTemperatureNice {

    public static void main(String args[]) {

        TemperatureNice temp = new TemperatureNice();
        temp.setNumber(70.0);
        temp.setScale(TempScale.FAHRENHEIT);
        temp.display();

        temp = new TemperatureNice(32.0);
        temp.display();

        temp = new TemperatureNice(TempScale.CELSIUS);
        temp.display();

        temp = new TemperatureNice(2.73,
                                   TempScale.KELVIN);
        temp.display();
    }
}
```

The code in Listing 9-6 is very much like its cousin code in Listing 9-3. The big differences are as follows:

✔ Listing 9-6 creates instances of the TemperatureNice class. That is, Listing 9-6 calls constructors from the TemperatureNice class, not the Temperature class.

✔ Listing 9-6 takes advantage of the display method in the TemperatureNice class. So the code in Listing 9-6 is much tidier than its counterpart in Listing 9-3.

A run of Listing 9-6 looks exactly like a run of the code in Listing 9-3 — it just gets to the finish line in far more elegant fashion. (The run is shown previously in Figure 9-1.)

The default constructor

The main message in the previous section is that subclasses don't inherit constructors. So what gives with all the listings back in Chapter 8? In Listing 8-6, a statement says

```
FullTimeEmployee ftEmployee = new FullTimeEmployee();
```

But, here's the problem: The code defining FullTimeEmployee (Listing 8-3) doesn't seem to have any constructors declared inside it. So, in Listing 8-6, how can you possibly call the FullTimeEmployee constructor?

Here's what's going on. When you create a subclass and don't put any explicit constructor declarations in your code, Java creates one constructor for you. It's called a *default constructor*. If you're creating the public FullTimeEmployee subclass, the default constructor looks like the one in Listing 9-7.

Listing 9-7: A Default Constructor

```
public FullTimeEmployee() {
    super();
}
```

The constructor in Listing 9-7 takes no parameters, and its one statement calls the constructor of whatever class you're extending. (Woe be to you if the class that you're extending doesn't have a parameterless constructor.)

You've just read about default constructors, but watch out! Notice one thing that this talk about default constructors *doesn't* say: It doesn't say that you always get a default constructor. In particular, if you create a subclass and define any constructors yourself, Java doesn't add a default constructor for the subclass (and the subclass doesn't inherit any constructors, either).

So how can this trip you up? Listing 9-8 has a copy of the code from Listing 8-3, but with one constructor added to it. Take a look at this modified version of the FullTimeEmployee code.

Listing 9-8: Look, I Have a Constructor!

```
public class FullTimeEmployee extends Employee {
    private double weeklySalary;
    private double benefitDeduction;

    public FullTimeEmployee(double weeklySalary) {
        this.weeklySalary = weeklySalary;
    }

    public void setWeeklySalary(double weeklySalaryIn) {
        weeklySalary = weeklySalaryIn;
    }

    public double getWeeklySalary() {
        return weeklySalary;
    }
```

```
    public void setBenefitDeduction(double benefitDedIn) {
        benefitDeduction = benefitDedIn;
    }

    public double getBenefitDeduction() {
        return benefitDeduction;
    }

    public double findPaymentAmount() {
        return weeklySalary - benefitDeduction;
    }
}
```

If you use the `FullTimeEmployee` code in Listing 9-8, a line like the following doesn't work:

```
FullTimeEmployee ftEmployee = new FullTimeEmployee();
```

It doesn't work because, having declared a `FullTimeEmployee` constructor that takes one `double` parameter, you no longer get a default parameterless constructor for free.

So what do you do about this? If you declare any constructors, declare all the constructors that you're possibly going to need. Take the constructor in Listing 9-7 and add it to the code in Listing 9-8. Then the call `new FullTimeEmployee()` starts working again.

Under certain circumstances, Java automatically adds an invisible call to a parent class's constructor at the top of a constructor body. This automatic addition of a `super` call is a tricky bit of business that doesn't appear often, so when it does appear, it may seem quite mysterious. For more information, see this book's website (`www.allmycode.com/JavaForDummies`).

A Constructor That Does More

Here's a quote from someplace near the start of this chapter: "And what if you're interested in doing more than filling fields? Perhaps, when the computer creates a new object, you have a whole list of jobs for the computer to carry out." Okay, what if?

This section's example has a constructor that does more than just assign values to fields. The example is in Listings 9-9 and 9-10. The result of running the example's code is shown in Figure 9-3.

Listing 9-9: Defining a Frame

```java
import java.awt.FlowLayout;
import javax.swing.JFrame;
import javax.swing.JButton;

@SuppressWarnings("serial")
public class SimpleFrame extends JFrame {

    public SimpleFrame() {
        setTitle("Don't click the button!");
        setLayout(new FlowLayout());
        setDefaultCloseOperation(EXIT_ON_CLOSE);
        add(new JButton("Panic"));
        setSize(300, 100);
        setVisible(true);
    }
}
```

Listing 9-10: Displaying a Frame

```java
public class ShowAFrame {

    public static void main(String args[]) {
        new SimpleFrame();
    }
}
```

Figure 9-3:
Don't panic.

The code in Listing 9-9 is made up mostly of calls to Java API (Application Programming Interface) methods. What this means to you is that the code contains lots of names that are probably unfamiliar to you. When I was first becoming acquainted with Java, I foolishly believed that knowing Java meant knowing all these names. Quite the contrary: These names are just carry-on baggage. The real Java is the way the language implements object-oriented concepts.

Anyway, Listing 9-10's main method has only one statement: a call to the constructor in the SimpleFrame class. Notice how the object that this call creates isn't even assigned to a variable. That's okay because the code doesn't need to refer to the object anywhere else.

Up in the SimpleFrame class is only one constructor declaration. Far from just setting variables' values, this constructor calls method after method from the Java API.

Packages and import declarations

Java has a feature that lets you lump classes into groups of classes. Each lump of classes is called a *package.* In the Java world, programmers customarily give these packages long, dot-filled names. For instance, because I've registered the domain name *allmycode.com,* I may name a package `com.allmycode.utils.textUtils`. The Java API is actually a big collection of packages. The API has packages with names like `java.lang`, `java.util`, `java.awt`, `javax.swing`, and so on.

With this information about packages, I can clear up some of the confusion about `import` declarations. Any `import` declaration that doesn't use the word `static` must start with the name of a package and must end with either of the following:

✔ The name of a class within that package

✔ An asterisk (indicating all classes within that package)

For example, the declaration

```
import java.util.Scanner;
```

is valid because `java.util` is the name of a package in the Java API, and `Scanner` is the name of a class in the `java.util` package. The dotted name `java.util.Scanner` is the *fully qualified name* of the `Scanner` class. A class's fully qualified name includes the name of the package in which the class is defined. (You can find out all this stuff about `java.util` and `Scanner` by reading Java's API documentation. For tips on reading the documentation, see Chapter 3 and this book's website.)

Here's another example. The declaration

```
import javax.swing.*;
```

is valid because `javax.swing` is the name of a package in the Java API, and the asterisk refers to all classes in the `javax.swing` package. With this `import` declaration at the top of your Java code, you can use abbreviated names for classes in the `javax.swing` package — names like `JFrame`, `JButton`, `JMenuBar`, `JCheckBox`, and many others.

Here's one more example. A line like

```
import javax.*;   //Bad!!
```

is *not* a valid `import` declaration. The Java API has no package with the one-word name `javax`. You may think that this line allows you to abbreviate all names beginning with `javax` (names like `javax.swing.JFrame` and `javax.sound.midi`), but that's not the way the `import` declaration works. Because `javax` isn't the name of a package, the line `import javax.*` just angers the Java compiler.

All the methods called in the `SimpleFrame` class's constructor come from the parent class, `JFrame`. The `JFrame` class lives in the `javax.swing` package. This package and another package, `java.awt`, have classes that help you put windows, images, drawings, and other gizmos on a computer screen. (In the `java.awt` package, the letters *awt* stand for *abstract windowing toolkit.*)

For a little gossip about the notion of a Java package, see the sidebar entitled "Packages and import declarations." For lots of gossip about the notion of a Java package, see Chapter 14.

In the Java API, what people normally call a *window* is an instance of the `javax.swing.JFrame` class.

Classes and methods from the Java API

Looking at Figure 9-3, you can probably tell that an instance of the `Simple Frame` class doesn't do much. The frame has only one button, and when you click the button, nothing happens. I made the frame this way to keep the example from becoming too complicated. Even so, the code in Listing 9-9 uses several API classes and methods. The `setTitle`, `setLayout`, `setDefaultCloseOperation`, `add`, `setSize`, and `setVisible` methods all belong to the `javax.swing.JFrame` class. Here's a list of names used in the code:

- ✔ `setTitle`: Calling `setTitle` puts words in the frame's title bar. (The new `SimpleFrame` object is calling its own `setTitle` method.)

- ✔ `FlowLayout`: An instance of the `FlowLayout` class positions objects on the frame in centered, typewriter fashion. Because the frame in Figure 9-3 has only one button on it, that button is centered near the top of the frame. If the frame had eight buttons, five of them may be lined up in a row across the top of the frame and the remaining three would be centered along a second row.

- ✔ `setLayout`: Calling `setLayout` puts the new `FlowLayout` object in charge of arranging components, such as buttons, on the frame. (The new `SimpleFrame` object is calling its own `setLayout` method.)

- ✔ `setDefaultCloseOperation`: Calling `setDefaultCloseOperation` tells Java what to do when you click the little × in the frame's upper-right corner. Without this method call, the frame itself disappears, but the Java Virtual Machine (JVM) keeps running. If you use Eclipse, you have to halt the JVM by clicking the red square near the top of the Console view. (See Figure 9-4.)

  Calling `setDefaultCloseOperation(EXIT_ON_CLOSE)` tells Java to shut itself down when you click the × in the frame's upper-right corner. The alternatives to `EXIT_ON_CLOSE` are `HIDE_ON_CLOSE`, `DISPOSE_ON_CLOSE`, and my personal favorite, `DO_NOTHING_ON_CLOSE`.

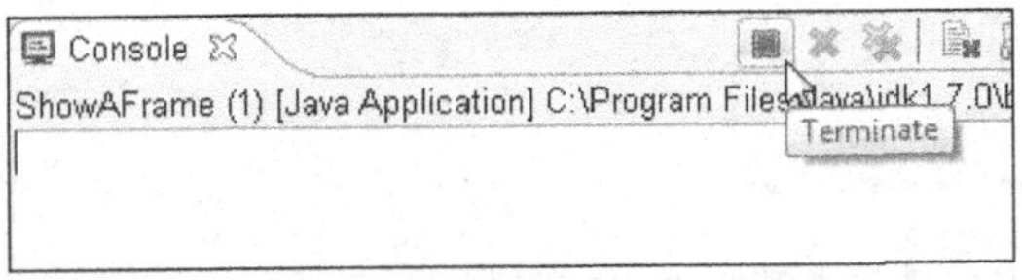

Figure 9-4:
Telling
Eclipse to
terminate
the run
of a Java
program.

Figure 9-4:
Telling Eclipse to terminate the run of a Java program.

✔ JButton: The JButton class lives in the javax.swing package. One of the class's constructors takes a String instance (such as "Panic") for its parameter. Calling this constructor makes that String instance into the label on the face of the new button.

✔ add: The new SimpleFrame object calls its add method. Calling the add method places the button on the object's surface (in this case, the surface of the frame).

✔ setSize: The frame becomes 300 pixels wide and 100 pixels tall. (In the javax.swing package, whenever you specify two dimension numbers, the width number always comes before the height number.)

✔ setVisible: When it's first created, a new frame is invisible. But when the new frame calls setVisible(true), the frame appears on your computer screen.

The SuppressWarnings annotation

Chapter 8 introduces the annotation — extra code that provides useful information about the nature of your program. In particular, Chapter 8 describes the Override annotation.

In this chapter, Listing 9-9 introduces another type of annotation: the SuppressWarnings annotation. When you use a SuppressWarnings annotation, you tell Java not to remind you that your program contains certain questionable code. In Listing 9-9, the line @SuppressWarnings("serial") tells Java not to remind you that you've omitted something called a serial VersionUID field. In other words, the SuppressWarnings annotation tells Java not to display a warning like the one in Figure 9-5.

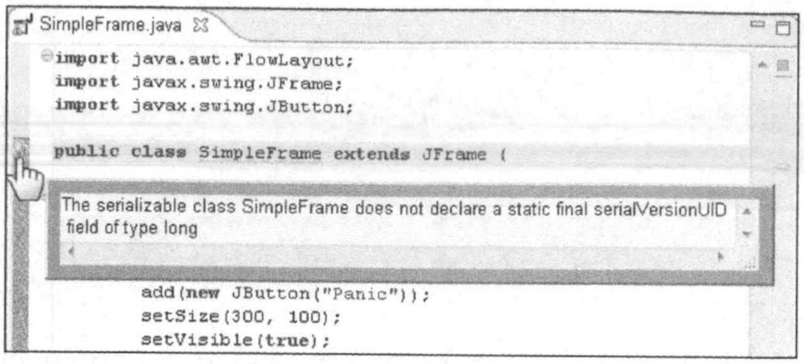

Figure 9-5:
Without a
Suppress
Warnings
annotation,
Java warns
you about
a missing
serial
VersionUID
field.

"And what," you ask, "is a serialVersionUID field?" It's something having to do with extending the JFrame class — something that you don't care about. Not having a serialVersionUID field generates a warning, not an error. So live dangerously! Just suppress the warning (with the annotation in Listing 9-9) and don't worry about serialVersionUID fields.

Part IV
Savvy Java Techniques

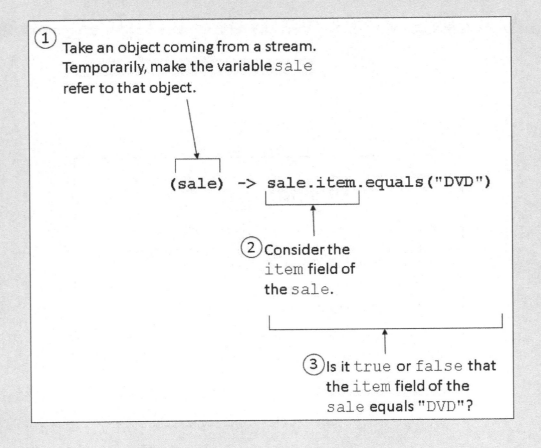

① Take an object coming from a stream. Temporarily, make the variable `sale` refer to that object.

`(sale) -> sale.item.equals("DVD")`

② Consider the `item` field of the `sale`.

③ Is it `true` or `false` that the `item` field of the `sale` equals `"DVD"`?

Read what I have to say about your studies, your career, and your life! It's free advice, and it's all online at www.dummies.com/extras/java.

In this part . . .

✔ Decide where declarations belong in your Java program.

✔ Deal with bunches of things (bunches of rooms, bunches of sales, and even bunches of bunches).

✔ Create a windowed app and respond to mouse clicks.

✔ Talk to your favorite database.

Chapter 10

Putting Variables and Methods Where They Belong

In This Chapter

▶ Making something belong to an entire class

▶ Putting variables inside and outside methods

▶ Improving your batting average

H ello, again. You're listening to radio station WWW, and I'm your host, Sam Burd. It's the start again of the big baseball season, and today station WWW brought you live coverage of the Hankees versus Socks game. At this moment, I'm awaiting news of the game's final score.

If you remember from earlier this afternoon, the Socks looked like they were going to take those Hankees to the cleaners. Then, the Hankees were belting ball after ball, giving the Socks a run for their money. Those Socks! I'm glad I wasn't in their shoes.

Anyway, as the game went on, the Socks pulled themselves up. Now the Socks are nose to nose with the Hankees. We'll get the final score in a minute, but first, a few reminders. Stay tuned after this broadcast for the big Jersey's game. And don't forget to tune in next week when the Cleveland Gowns play the Bermuda Shorts.

Okay, here's the final score. Which team has the upper hand? Which team will come out a head? And the winner is . . . oh, no! It's a tie!

Defining a Class (What It Means to Be a Baseball Player)

As far as I'm concerned, a baseball player has a name and a batting average. Listing 10-1 puts my feeling about this into Java program form.

Listing 10-1: The Player Class

```java
import java.text.DecimalFormat;

public class Player {
    private String name;
    private double average;

    public Player(String name, double average) {
        this.name=name;
        this.average=average;
    }

    public String getName() {
        return name;
    }

    public double getAverage() {
        return average;
    }

    public String getAverageString() {
        DecimalFormat decFormat = new DecimalFormat();
        decFormat.setMaximumIntegerDigits(0);
        decFormat.setMaximumFractionDigits(3);
        decFormat.setMinimumFractionDigits(3);
        return decFormat.format(average);
    }
}
```

So here I go, picking apart the code in Listing 10-1. Luckily, earlier chapters cover lots of stuff in this code. The code defines what it means to be an instance of the Player class. Here's what's in the code:

- **Declarations of the fields name and average:** For bedtime reading about field declarations, see Chapter 7.

- **A constructor to make new instances of the Player class:** For the lowdown on constructors, see Chapter 9.

- **Getter methods for the fields name and average:** For chitchat about accessor methods (that is, setter and getter methods), see Chapter 7.

- **A method that returns the player's batting average in String form:** For the good word about methods, see Chapter 7. (I put a lot of good stuff in Chapter 7, didn't I?)

Another way to beautify your numbers

The getAverageString method in Listing 10-1 takes the value from the average field (a player's batting average), converts that value (normally of type double) into a String, and then sends that String value right back to the method caller. The use of DecimalFormat, which comes right from the Java API (Application Programming Interface), makes sure that the String value looks like a baseball player's batting average. According to the decFormat.setMaximum... and decFormat.setMinimum... method calls, the String value has no digits to the left of the decimal point and has exactly three digits to the right of the decimal point.

Java's DecimalFormat class can be quite handy. For example, to display the values 345 and –345 with an accounting-friendly format, you can use the following code:

```
DecimalFormat decFormat = new DecimalFormat();
decFormat.setMinimumFractionDigits(2);
decFormat.setNegativePrefix("(");
decFormat.setNegativeSuffix(")");
System.out.println(decFormat.format(345));
System.out.println(decFormat.format(-345));
```

In this little example's format string, everything before the semicolon dictates the way positive numbers are displayed, and everything after the semicolon determines the way negative numbers are displayed. So with this format, the numbers 345 and –345 appear as follows:

```
345.00
(345.00)
```

To discover some other tricks with numbers, visit the DecimalFormat page of Java's API documentation.

Using the Player class

Listings 10-2 and 10-3 have code that uses the Player class — the class that's defined back in Listing 10-1.

Listing 10-2: Using the Player Class

```
import java.util.Scanner;
import java.io.File;
import java.io.IOException;
import javax.swing.JFrame;
import javax.swing.JLabel;
import java.awt.GridLayout;

@SuppressWarnings("serial")
public class TeamFrame extends JFrame {

    public TeamFrame() throws IOException {
        Player player;
        Scanner hankeesData =
                    new Scanner(new File("Hankees.txt"));

        for (int num = 1; num <= 9; num++) {
            player = new Player(hankeesData.nextLine(),
                                hankeesData.nextDouble());
            hankeesData.nextLine();

            addPlayerInfo(player);
        }

        setTitle("The Hankees");
        setLayout(new GridLayout(9, 2, 20, 3));
        setDefaultCloseOperation(EXIT_ON_CLOSE);
        pack();
        setVisible(true);

        hankeesData.close();
    }

    void addPlayerInfo(Player player) {
        add(new JLabel("  " + player.getName()));
        add(new JLabel(player.getAverageString()));
    }
}
```

Listing 10-3: Displaying a Frame

```
import java.io.IOException;

public class ShowTeamFrame {

    public static void main(String args[])
                                throws IOException {
        new TeamFrame();
    }
}
```

For a run of the code in Listings 10-1, 10-2, and 10-3, see Figure 10-1.

The Hankees	
Barry Burd	.101
Harriet Ritter	.200
Weelie J. Katz	.030
Harry "The Crazyman" Spoonswagler	.124
Felicia "Fishy" Katz	.075
Mia, Just "Mia"	.111
Jeremy Flooflong Jones	.102
I. M. D'Arthur	.001
Hugh R. DaReader	.212

Figure 10-1:
Would you
bet money
on these
people?

To run this program yourself, you need the `Hankees.txt` file. This file contains data on your favorite baseball players. (See Figure 10-2.)

```
Barry Burd
.101
Harriet Ritter
.200
Weelie J. Katz
.030
Harry "The Crazyman" Spoonswagler
.124
Felicia "Fishy" Katz
.075
Mia, Just "Mia"
.111
Jeremy Flooflong Jones
.102
I. M. D'Arthur
.001
Hugh R. DaReader
.212
```

Figure 10-2:
What a
team!

You don't have to create your own `Hankees.txt` file. The stuff that you download from this book's website comes with a `Hankees.txt` file as shown in Figure 10-2. (Visit `www.allmycode.com/JavaForDummies`.)

You must have the `Hankees.txt` file in a certain place on your hard drive. If you're using Eclipse, that "certain place" is a project directory within your Eclipse workspace. On the other hand, if you're running Java from the command line, that "place" may be the directory that contains the Listing 10-3 code. One way or another, you can't get away without having the `Hankees.txt` file in the right place on your hard drive. If you don't have `Hankees.txt` in the right place, then when you try to run this section's example, you'll get an unpleasant `FileNotFoundException` message.

When you download stuff from this book's website, you get instructions for importing the download into your favorite IDE (Eclipse, NetBeans, or IntelliJ IDEA). The import process puts the `Hankees.txt` file exactly where it needs to be. You don't have to worry about putting the file where it belongs.

If you create this section's example from scratch, you have to think about the correct location of the Hankees.txt file. In that case, deciding where to put the Hankees.txt file depends on your computer. To read about all these things, visit this book's website (www.allmycode.com/JavaForDummies).

For this section's code to work correctly, you must have a line break after the last .212 in Figure 10-2. For details about line breaks, see Chapter 8.

Nine, count 'em, nine

The code in Listing 10-2 calls the Player constructor nine times. This means that the code creates nine instances of the Player class. The first time through the loop, the code creates an instance with the name Barry Burd. The second time through the loop, the code abandons the Barry Burd instance and creates another instance with name Harriet Ritter. The third time through, the code abandons poor Harriet Ritter and creates an instance for Weelie J. Katz. The code has only one instance at a time but, all in all, the code creates nine instances.

Each Player instance has its own name and average fields. Each instance also has its own Player constructor and its own getName, getAverage, and getAverageString methods. Look at Figure 10-3 and think of the Player class with its nine incarnations.

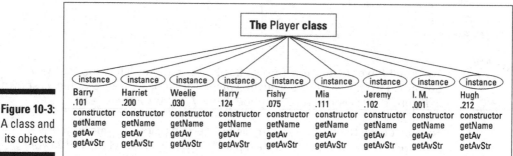

Figure 10-3: A class and its objects.

Don't get all GUI on me

The code in Listing 10-2 uses several names from the Java API. Some of these names are explained in Chapter 9. Others are explained right here:

✔ JLabel: A JLabel is an object with some text in it. One of the ways to display text inside the frame is to add an instance of the JLabel class to the frame.

In Listing 10-2, the addPlayerInfo method is called nine times, once for each player on the team. Each time addPlayerInfo is called, the method adds two new JLabel objects to the frame. The text for each JLabel object comes from a player object's getter method.

✔ GridLayout: A GridLayout arranges things in evenly spaced rows and columns. This constructor for the GridLayout class takes two parameters: the number of rows and the number of columns.

In Listing 10-2, the call to the GridLayout constructor takes parameters (9, 2, 20, 3). So in Figure 10-1, the display has nine rows (one for each player) and two columns (one for a name and another for an average). The horizontal gap between the two columns is 20 pixels wide, and the vertical gap between any two rows is 3 pixels tall.

✔ pack: When you pack a frame, you set the frame's size. That's the size the frame has when it appears on your computer screen. Packing a frame shrink-wraps the frame around whatever objects you've added inside the frame.

In Listing 10-2, by the time you've reached the call to pack, you've already called addPlayerInfo nine times and added 18 labels to the frame. In executing the pack method, the computer picks a nice size for each label, given whatever text you've put inside the label. Then, the computer picks a nice size for the whole frame, given that the frame has these 18 labels inside it.

When you plop stuff onto frames, you have quite a bit of leeway with the order in which you do things. For instance, you can set the layout before or after you've added labels and other stuff to the frame. If you call setLayout and then add labels, the labels appear in nice, orderly positions on the frame. If you reverse this order (add labels and then call setLayout), the calling of setLayout rearranges the labels in a nice, orderly fashion. It works fine either way.

In setting up a frame, the one thing that you shouldn't do is violate the following sequence:

```
Add things to the frame, then
pack();
setVisible(true);
```

If you call pack and then add more things to the frame, the pack method doesn't take the more recent things that you've added into consideration. If you call setVisible before you add things or call pack, the user sees the frame as it's being constructed. Finally, if you forget to set the frame's size (by calling pack or some other sizing method), the frame that you see looks like the one in Figure 10-4. (Normally, I wouldn't show you an anomalous run like the one in Figure 10-4, but I've made the mistake so many times that I feel as if this puny frame is an old friend of mine.)

Figure 10-4:
An under-
nourished
frame.

The H...

Tossing an exception from method to method

Chapter 8 introduces input from a disk file, and along with that topic comes the notion of an exception. When you tinker with a disk file, you need to acknowledge the possibility of raising an IOException. That's the lesson from Chapter 8, and that's why the constructor in Listing 10-2 has a throws IOException clause.

But what about the main method in Listing 10-3? With no apparent reference to disk files in this main method, why does the method need its own throws IOException clause? Well, an exception is a hot potato. If you have one, you either have to eat it (as you can see in Chapter 13) or use a throws clause to toss it to someone else. If you toss an exception with a throws clause, some-one else is stuck with the exception just the way you were.

The constructor in Listing 10-2 throws an IOException, but to whom is this exception thrown? Who in this chain of code becomes the bearer of respon-sibility for the problematic IOException? Well, who called the constructor in Listing 10-2? It was the main method in Listing 10-3 — that's who called the TeamFrame constructor. Because the TeamFrame constructor throws its hot potato to the main method in Listing 10-3, the main method has to deal with it. As shown in Listing 10-3, the main method deals with it by tossing the IOException again (by having a throws IOException clause of its own). That's how the throws clause works in Java programs.

If a method calls another method and the called method has a throws clause, the calling method must contain code that deals with the exception. To find out more about dealing with exceptions, read Chapter 13.

At this point in the book, the astute *For Dummies* reader may pose a follow-up question or two. "When a main method has a throws clause, someone else has to deal with the exception in that throws clause. But who called the main method? Who deals with the IOException in the throws clause of Listing 10-3?" The answer is that the Java Virtual Machine (or JVM, the thing that runs all your Java code) called the main method. So the JVM takes care of the IOException in Listing 10-3. If the program has any trouble reading the Hankees.txt file, the responsibility ultimately falls on the JVM. The JVM takes care of things by displaying an error message and then ending the run of your program. How convenient!

Making Static (Finding the Team Average)

Thinking about the code in Listings 10-1 through 10-3, you decide that you'd like to find the team's overall batting average. Not a bad idea! The Hankees in Figure 10-1 have an average of about .106, so the team needs some intensive training. While the players are out practicing on the ball field, you have a philosophical hurdle to overcome.

In Listings 10-1 through 10-3, you have three classes: a Player class and two other classes that help display data from the Player class. So in this class morass, where do the variables storing your overall, team-average tally go?

✔ It makes no sense to put tally variables in either of the displaying classes (TeamFrame and ShowTeamFrame). After all, the tally has something or other to do with players, teams, and baseball. The displaying classes are about creating windows, not about playing baseball.

✔ You're uncomfortable putting an overall team average in an instance of the Player class because an instance of the Player class represents just one player on the team. What business does a single player have storing overall team data? Sure, you could make the code work, but it wouldn't be an elegant solution to the problem.

Finally, you discover the keyword static. Anything that's declared to be static belongs to the whole class, not to any particular instance of the class. When you create the static field, totalOfAverages, you create just one copy of the field. This copy stays with the entire Players class. No matter how many instances of the Player class you create — one, nine, or none — you have just one totalOfAverages field. And, while you're at it, you create other static fields (playerCount and decFormat) and static methods (findTeamAverage and findTeamAverageString). To see what I mean, look at Figure 10-5.

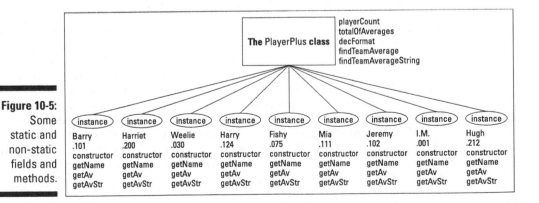

Figure 10-5: Some static and non-static fields and methods.

Going along with your passion for subclasses, you put code for team-wide tallies in a subclass of the `Player` class. The code is shown in Listing 10-4.

Listing 10-4:   Creating a Team Batting Average

```java
import java.text.DecimalFormat;

public class PlayerPlus extends Player {
    private static int playerCount = 0;
    private static double totalOfAverages = .000;
    private static DecimalFormat decFormat =
                                    new DecimalFormat();

    static {
        decFormat.setMaximumIntegerDigits(0);
        decFormat.setMaximumFractionDigits(3);
        decFormat.setMinimumFractionDigits(3);
    }

    public PlayerPlus(String name, double average) {
        super(name, average);
        playerCount++;
        totalOfAverages += average;
    }

    public static double findTeamAverage() {
        return totalOfAverages / playerCount;
    }

    public static String findTeamAverageString() {
        return decFormat.format
                    (totalOfAverages / playerCount);
    }
}
```

Why is there so much static?

Maybe you've noticed — the code in Listing 10-4 is overflowing with the word *static*. That's because nearly everything in this code belongs to the entire `PlayerPlus` class and not to individual instances of the class. That's good because something like `playerCount` (the number of players on the team) shouldn't belong to individual players, and having each `PlayerPlus` object keep track of its own count would be silly. ("I know how many players I am. I'm just one player!") If you had nine individual `playerCount` fields, either each field would store the number 1 (which is useless) or you would have nine different copies of the count, which is wasteful and prone to error. So by making `playerCount` static, you're keeping the `playerCount` in just one place, where it belongs.

The same kind of reasoning holds for the `totalOfAverages`. Eventually, the `totalOfAverages` field will store the sum of the players' batting averages. For all nine members of the Hankees, this adds up to .956. It's not until someone calls the `findTeamAverage` or `findTeamAverageString` method that the computer actually finds the overall Hankee team batting average.

You also want the methods `findTeamAverage` and `findTeamAverage String` to be static. Without the word *static*, there would be nine `find TeamAverage` methods — one for each instance of the `PlayerPlus` class. This wouldn't make much sense. Each instance would have the code to calculate `totalOfAverages/playerCount` on its own, and each of the nine calculations would yield the very same answer.

In general, any task that all the instances have in common (and that yields the same result for each instance) should be coded as a `static` method.

Constructors are never static.

Meet the static initializer

In Listing 10-4, the `decFormat` field is static. This makes sense, because `decFormat` makes `totalOfAverages / playerCount` look nice, and both fields in the expression `totalOfAverages / playerCount` are static. Thinking more directly, the code needs only one thing for formatting numbers. If you have several numbers to format, the same `decFormat` thing that belongs to the entire class can format each number. Creating a `decFormat` for each player is not only inelegant, but also wasteful.

But declaring `decFormat` to be static presents a little problem. To set up the formatting, you have to call methods like `decFormat.setMaximum IntegerDigits(0)`. You can't just plop these method calls anywhere in the `PlayerPlus` class. For example, the following code is bad, invalid, illegal, and otherwise un-Java-like:

```
// THIS IS BAD CODE:
public class PlayerPlus extends Player {
    private static DecimalFormat decFormat =
                                new DecimalFormat();

    decFormat.setMaximumIntegerDigits(0);    // Bad!
    decFormat.setMaximumFractionDigits(3);   // Bad!
    decFormat.setMinimumFractionDigits(3);   // Bad!
```

Look at the examples from previous chapters. In those examples, I never let a method call just dangle on its own, the way I do in the bad, bad code. In this chapter, in Listing 10-1, I don't call `setMaximumIntegerDigits` without putting the method call inside the `getAverageString` method's body. This no-dangling-method-calls business isn't an accident. Java's rules restrict the places in the code where you can issue calls to methods, and putting a lonely method call on its own immediately inside a class definition is a big no-no.

So in Listing 10-4, where can you put the necessary `setMax` and `setMin` calls? You can put them inside the body of the `findTeamAverageString` method, much the way I put them inside the `getAverageString` method in Listing 10-1. But putting those method calls inside the `findTeamAverageString` method's body might defeat the purpose of having `decFormat` be static. After all, a programmer might call `findTeamAverageString` several times, calling `decFormat.setMaximumIntegerDigits(0)` each time. But that would be very wasteful. The entire `PlayerPlus` class has only one `decFormat` field, and that `decFormat` field's `MaximumIntegerDigits` value is always 0. So don't keep setting `MaximumIntegerDigits(0)` over and over again.

The best alternative is to take the bad lines in this section's bad code and put them inside a *static initializer*. Then they become good lines inside good code. (See Listing 10-4.) A static initializer is a block that's preceded by the word `static`. Java executes the static initializer's statements once for the entire class. That's exactly what you want for something called "static."

Displaying the overall team average

You may be noticing a pattern. When you create code for a class, you generally write two pieces of code. One piece of code defines the class, and the other piece of code uses the class. (The ways to use a class include calling the class's constructor, referencing the class's non-private fields, calling the class's methods, and so on.) Listing 10-4, shown previously, contains code that defines the `PlayerPlus` class, and Listing 10-5 contains code that uses this `PlayerPlus` class.

Listing 10-5:   Using the Code from Listing 10-4

```
import java.util.Scanner;
import java.io.File;
import java.io.IOException;
import javax.swing.JFrame;
import javax.swing.JLabel;
import java.awt.GridLayout;

@SuppressWarnings("serial")
public class TeamFrame extends JFrame {
```

```
public TeamFrame() throws IOException {
    PlayerPlus player;
    Scanner hankeesData =
                new Scanner(new File("Hankees.txt"));

    for (int num = 1; num <= 9; num++) {
        player =
            new PlayerPlus(hankeesData.nextLine(),
                            hankeesData.nextDouble());
        hankeesData.nextLine();

        addPlayerInfo(player);
    }

    add(new JLabel());
    add(new JLabel("  ------"));
    add(new JLabel("Team Batting Average:"));
    add(new
        JLabel(PlayerPlus.findTeamAverageString()));

    setTitle("The Hankees");
    setLayout(new GridLayout(11, 2, 20, 3));
    setDefaultCloseOperation(EXIT_ON_CLOSE);
    pack();
    setVisible(true);

    hankeesData.close();
}

void addPlayerInfo(PlayerPlus player) {
    add(new JLabel("  " + player.getName()));
    add(new JLabel(player.getAverageString()));
}
}
```

To run the code in Listing 10-5, you need a class with a `main` method. The `ShowTeamFrame` class in Listing 10-3 works just fine.

Figure 10-6 shows a run of the code from Listing 10-5. This run depends on the availability of the `Hankees.txt` file from Figure 10-2. The code in Listing 10-5 is almost an exact copy of the code from Listing 10-2. (So close is the copy that if I could afford it, I'd sue myself for theft of intellectual property.) The only thing new in Listing 10-5 is the stuff shown in bold.

The Hankees	
Barry Burd	.101
Harriet Ritter	.200
Weelie J. Katz	.030
Harry "The Crazyman" Spoonswagler	.124
Felicia "Fishy" Katz	.075
Mia, Just "Mia"	.111
Jeremy Flooflong Jones	.102
I. M. D'Arthur	.001
Hugh R. DaReader	.212

Team Batting Average:	.106

Figure 10-6:
A run of
the code in
Listing 10-5.

In Listing 10-5, the `GridLayout` has two extra rows: one row for spacing and another row for the Hankee team's average. Each of these rows has two `Label` objects in it.

- ✔ **The spacing row has a blank label and a label with a dashed line.** The blank label is a placeholder. When you add components to a `GridLayout`, the components are added row by row, starting at the left end of a row and working toward the right end. Without this blank label, the dashed line label would appear at the left end of the row, under Hugh R. DaReader's name.

- ✔ **The other row has a label displaying the words *Team Batting Average,* and another label displaying the number *.106*.** The method call that gets the number .106 is interesting. The call looks like this:

```
PlayerPlus.findTeamAverageString()
```

Take a look at that method call. That call has the following form:

```
ClassName.methodName()
```

That's new and different. In earlier chapters, I say that you normally preface a method call with an object's name, not a class's name. So why do I use a class name here? The answer: When you call a `static` method, you preface the method's name with the name of the class that contains the method. The same holds true whenever you reference another class's `static` field. This makes sense. Remember, the whole class that defines a `static` field or method owns that field or method. So, to refer to a `static` field or method, you preface the field or method's name with the class's name.

When you're referring to a `static` field or method, you can cheat and use an object's name in place of the class name. For instance, in Listing 10-5, with judicious rearranging of some other statements, you can use the expression `player.findTeamAverageString()`.

Static is old hat

This section makes a big noise about `static` fields and methods, but `static` things have been part of the picture since early in this book. For example, Chapter 3 introduces `System.out.println`. The name *System* refers to a class, and *out* is a `static` field in that class. That's why, in Chapter 4 and beyond, I use the `static` keyword to import the `out` field:

```
import static java.lang.System.out;
```

In Java, `static` fields and methods show up all over the place. When they're declared in someone else's code, and you're making use of them in your code, you hardly ever have to worry about them. But when you're declaring your own fields and methods and must decide whether to make them static, you have to think a little harder.

In this book, my first serious use of the word *static* is way back in Listing 3-1. I use the `static` keyword as part of every `main` method (and lots of `main` methods are in this book's listings). So why does `main` have to be static? Well, remember that non-static things belong to objects, not classes. If the `main` method isn't static, you can't have a `main` method until you create an object. But, when you start up a Java program, no objects have been created yet. The statements that are executed in the `main` method start creating objects. So, if the `main` method isn't static, you have a big chicken-and-egg problem.

Could cause static; handle with care

When I first started writing Java, I had recurring dreams about getting a certain error message. The message was `non-static variable or method cannot be referenced from a static context`. So often did I see this message, so thoroughly was I perplexed, that the memory of this message became burned into my subconscious existence.

These days, I know why I got that error message so often. I can even make the message occur if I want. But I still feel a little shiver whenever I see this message on my screen.

Before you can understand why the message occurs and how to fix the problem, you need to get some terminology under your belt. If a field or method isn't static, it's called *non-static*. (Real surprising, hey?) Given that terminology, there are at least two ways to make the dreaded message appear:

- Put `Class.nonstaticThing` somewhere in your program.
- Put `nonstaticThing` somewhere inside a `static` method.

In either case, you're getting yourself into trouble. You're taking something that belongs to an object (the non-static thing) and putting it in a place where no objects are in sight.

Take, for instance, the first of the two situations I just described. To see this calamity in action, go back to Listing 10-5. Toward the end of the listing, change `player.getName()` to `Player.getName()`. That does the trick. What could `Player.getName` possibly mean? If anything, the expression `Player.getName` means "call the `getName` method that belongs to the entire `Player` class." But look back at Listing 10-1. The `getName` method isn't static. Each instance of the `Player` (or `PlayerPlus`) class has a `getName` method. None of the `getName` methods belong to the entire class. So the call `Player.getName` doesn't make any sense. (Maybe the computer is pulling punches when it displays the inoffensive `cannot be referenced ...` message. Perhaps a harsh `nonsensical expression` message would be more fitting.)

For a taste of the second situation (in the bullet list that I give earlier in this section), go back to Listing 10-4. While no one's looking, quietly remove the word *static* from the declaration of the `decFormat` field (near the top of the listing). This removal turns `decFormat` into a non-static field. Suddenly, each player on the team has a separate `decFormat` field.

Well, things are just hunky-dory until the computer reaches the `findTeamAverageString` method. That `static` method has four `decFormat.SuchAndSuch` statements in it. Once again, you're forced to ask what a statement of this kind could possibly mean. Method `findTeamAverageString` belongs to no instance in particular. (The method is `static`, so the entire `PlayerPlus` class has one `findTeamAverageString` method.) But with the way you've just butchered the code, plain old `decFormat` without reference to a particular object has no meaning. So again, you're referencing the non-static field, `decFormat`, from inside a `static` method's context. For shame, for shame, for shame!

Experiments with Variables

One summer during my college days, I was sitting on the front porch, loafing around, talking with someone I'd just met. I think her name was Janine. "Where are you from?" I asked. "Mars," she answered. She paused to see whether I'd ask a follow-up question.

As it turned out, Janine was from Mars, Pennsylvania, a small town about 20 miles north of Pittsburgh. Okay, so what's my point? The point is that the meaning of a name depends on the context. If you're just north of Pittsburgh and ask, "How do I get to Mars from here?" you may get a sensible, nonchalant answer. But if you ask the same question standing on a street corner in Manhattan, you'll probably arouse some suspicion. (Okay, knowing Manhattan, people would probably just ignore you.)

Of course, the people who live in Mars, Pennsylvania, are very much aware that their town has an oddball name. Fond memories of teenage years at Mars High School don't prevent a person from knowing about the big red planet. On a clear evening in August, you can still have the following conversation with one of the local residents:

> *You:* How do I get to Mars?
>
> *Local resident:* You're in Mars, pal. What particular part of Mars are you looking for?
>
> *You:* No, I don't mean Mars, Pennsylvania. I mean the planet Mars.
>
> *Local resident:* Oh, the planet! Well, then, catch the 8:19 train leaving for Cape Canaveral . . . No, wait, that's the local train. That'd take you through West Virginia. . . .

So the meaning of a name depends on where you're using the name. Although most English-speaking people think of Mars as a place with a carbon dioxide atmosphere, some folks in Pennsylvania think about all the shopping they can do in Mars. And those folks in Pennsylvania really have two meanings for the name *Mars*. In Java, those names may look like this: Mars and planets.Mars.

Putting a variable in its place

Your first experiment is shown in Listings 10-6 and 10-7. The listings' code highlights the difference between variables that are declared inside and outside methods.

Listing 10-6: Two Meanings for Mars

```java
import static java.lang.System.out;

class EnglishSpeakingWorld {
    String mars = "    red planet";

    void visitPennsylvania() {
        out.println("visitPA is running:");

        String mars = "    Janine's home town";

        out.println(mars);
        out.println(this.mars);
    }
}
```

Listing 10-7: Calling the Code of Listing 10-6

```
import static java.lang.System.out;

public class GetGoing {

    public static void main(String args[]) {

        out.println("main is running:");

        EnglishSpeakingWorld e =
                        new EnglishSpeakingWorld();

        //out.println(mars);    cannot resolve symbol
        out.println(e.mars);
        e.visitPennsylvania();
    }
}
```

Figure 10-7 shows a run of the code in Listings 10-6 and 10-7. Figure 10-8 shows a diagram of the code's structure. In the `GetGoing` class, the `main` method creates an instance of the `EnglishSpeakingWorld` class. The variable `e` refers to the new instance. The new instance is an object with a variable named *mars* inside it. That `mars` variable has the value `"red planet"`. The `"red planet"` `mars` variable is a field.

Figure 10-7:
A run of
the code in
Listings 10-6
and 10-7.

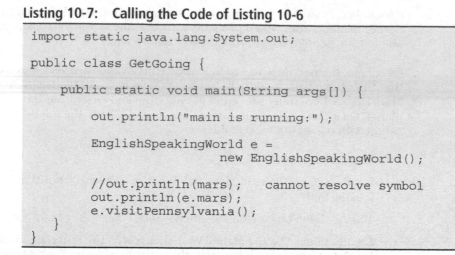

```
main is running:
    red planet
visitPA is running:
    Janine's home town
    red planet
```

Another way to describe that `mars` field is to call it an *instance variable,* because that `mars` variable (the variable whose value is `"red planet"`) belongs to an *instance* of the `EnglishSpeakingWorld` class. In contrast, you can refer to static fields (like the `playerCount`, `totalOfAverages`, and `decFormat` fields in Listing 10-4) as *class variables.* For example, `playerCount` in Listing 10-4 is a class variable because one copy of `playerCount` belongs to the entire `PlayerPlus` class.

Now look at the `main` method in Listing 10-7. Inside the `GetGoing` class's `main` method, you aren't permitted to write `out.println(mars)`. In other words, a bare-faced reference to any `mars` variable is a definite no-no. The `mars` variable that I mention in the previous paragraph belongs to the `EnglishSpeakingWorld` object, not the `GetGoing` class.

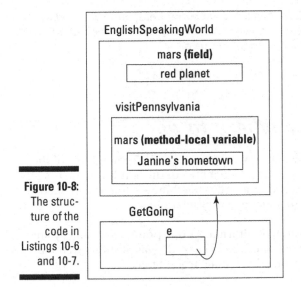

Figure 10-8:
The struc-
ture of the
code in
Listings 10-6
and 10-7.

However, inside the GetGoing class's main method, you can certainly write e.mars because the e variable refers to your EnglishSpeakingWorld object. That's nice.

Near the bottom of the code, the visitPennsylvania method is called. When you're inside visitPennsylvania, you have another declaration of a mars variable, whose value is "Janine's home town". This particular mars variable is called a *method-local variable* because it belongs to just one method — the visitPennsylvania method.

So now you have two variables, both with the name *mars*. One mars variable, a field, has the value "red planet". The other mars variable, a method-local variable, has the value "Janine's home town". In the code, when you use the word *mars,* to which of the two variables are you referring?

The answer is, when you're visiting Pennsylvania, the variable with value "Janine's home town" wins. When in Pennsylvania, think the way the Pennsylvanians think. When you're executing code inside the visitPennsylvania method, resolve any variable name conflicts by going with method-local variables — variables declared right inside the visitPennsylvania method.

So what if you're in Pennsylvania and need to refer to that two-mooned celestial object? More precisely, how does code inside the visitPennsylvania method refer to the field with value "red planet"? The answer is, use this.mars. The word *this* points to whatever object contains all this code (and not to any methods inside the code). That object, an instance of the

EnglishSpeakingWorld class, has a big, fat `mars` field, and that field's value is `"red planet"`. So that's how you can force code to see outside the method it's in — you use the Java keyword `this`.

For more information on the keyword `this`, see Chapter 9.

Telling a variable where to go

Years ago, when I lived in Milwaukee, Wisconsin, I made frequent use of the local bank's automatic teller machines. Machines of this kind were just beginning to become standardized. The local teller machine system was named *TYME,* which stood for *Take Your Money Everywhere.*

I remember traveling by car out to California. At one point, I got hungry and stopped for a meal, but I was out of cash. So I asked a gas station attendant, "Do you know where there's a TYME machine around here?"

So you see, a name that works well in one place could work terribly, or not at all, in another place. In Listings 10-8 and 10-9, I illustrate this point (with more than just an anecdote about teller machines).

Listing 10-8:   Tale of Atomic City

```
import static java.lang.System.out;

class EnglishSpeakingWorld2 {
    String mars;

    void visitIdaho() {
        out.println("visitID is running:");

        mars = "   red planet";
        String atomicCity = "   Population: 25";

        out.println(mars);
        out.println(atomicCity);
    }

    void visitNewJersey() {
        out.println("visitNJ is running:");

        out.println(mars);
        //out.println(atomicCity);
        //   cannot resolve symbol
    }
}
```

Listing 10-9: Calling the Code of Listing 10-8

```
public class GetGoing2 {

    public static void main(String args[]) {
        EnglishSpeakingWorld2 e =
                        new EnglishSpeakingWorld2();

        e.visitIdaho();
        e.visitNewJersey();
    }
}
```

Figure 10-9 shows a run of the code in Listings 10-8 and 10-9. Figure 10-10 shows a diagram of the code's structure. The code for EnglishSpeakingWorld2 has two variables. The mars variable, which isn't declared inside a method, is a field. The other variable, atomicCity, is a method-local variable and is declared inside the visitIdaho method.

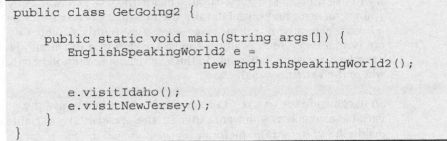

```
visitID is running:
    red planet
    Population: 25
visitNJ is running:
    red planet
```

EnglishSpeakingWorld2

mars (field)

red planet

visitIdaho

atomicCity
(method-local variable)

Population: 25

visitNewJersey

In Listing 10-8, notice where each variable can and can't be used. When you try to use the `atomicCity` variable inside the `visitNewJersey` method, you get an error message. Literally, the message says `cannot resolve symbol`. Figuratively, the message says, "Hey, buddy, Atomic City is in Idaho, not New Jersey." Technically, the message says that the method-local variable `atomicCity` is available only in the `visitIdaho` method because that's where the variable was declared.

So back inside the `visitIdaho` method, you're free to use the `atomicCity` variable as much as you want. After all, the `atomicCity` variable is declared inside the `visitIdaho` method.

And what about Mars? Have you forgotten about your old friend, that lovely 80-degrees-below-zero planet? Well, both the `visitIdaho` and `visitNew Jersey` methods can access the `mars` variable. That's because the `mars` variable is a field. That is, the `mars` variable is declared in the code for the `EnglishSpeakingWorld2` class but not inside any particular method. (In my stories about the names for things, remember that people who live in both states, Idaho and New Jersey, have heard of the planet Mars.)

The lifecycle of the `mars` field has three separate steps:

✔ When the `EnglishSpeakingWorld2` class first flashes into existence, the computer sees `String mars` and creates space for the `mars` field.

✔ When the `visitIdaho` method is executed, the method assigns the value `"red planet"` to the `mars` field. (The `visitIdaho` method also prints the value of the `mars` field.)

✔ When the `visitNewJersey` method is executed, the method prints the `mars` value once again.

In this way, the `mars` field's value is passed from one method to another.

Passing Parameters

A method can communicate with another part of your Java program in several ways. One of the ways is through the method's parameter list. Using a parameter list, you pass on-the-fly information to a method as the method is being called.

So imagine that the information you pass to the method is stored in one of your program's variables. What, if anything, does the method actually do with that variable? The following sections present a few interesting case studies.

Pass by value

According to my web research, the town of Smackover, Arkansas, has 2,232 people in it. But my research isn't current. Just yesterday, Dora Kermongoos celebrated a joyous occasion over at Smackover General Hospital — the birth of her healthy, blue-eyed baby girl. (The girl weighs 7 pounds, 4 ounces, and is 21 inches tall.) Now the town's population has risen to 2,233.

Listing 10-10 has a very bad program in it. The program is supposed to add 1 to a variable that stores Smackover's population, but the program doesn't work. Take a look at Listing 10-10 and see why.

Listing 10-10:   This Program Doesn't Work

```
public class TrackPopulation {

    public static void main(String args[]) {
        int smackoverARpop = 2232;

        birth(smackoverARpop);
        System.out.println(smackoverARpop);
    }

    static void birth(int cityPop) {
        cityPop++;
    }
}
```

When you run the program in Listing 10-10, the program displays the number 2,232 onscreen. After nine months of planning and anticipation and Dora's whopping seven hours in labor, the Kermongoos family's baby girl wasn't registered in the system. What a shame!

The improper use of parameter passing caused the problem. In Java, when you pass a parameter that has one of the eight primitive types to a method, that parameter is *passed by value*.

For a review of Java's eight primitive types, see Chapter 4.

Here's what this means in plain English: Any changes that the method makes to the value of its parameter don't affect the values of variables back in the calling code. In Listing 10-10, the birth method can apply the ++ operator to cityPop all it wants — the application of ++ to the cityPop parameter has absolutely no effect on the value of the smackoverARpop variable back in the main method.

Technically, what's happening is the copying of a value. (See Figure 10-11.) When the `main` method calls the `birth` method, the value stored in `smackoverARpop` is copied to another memory location — a location reserved for the `cityPop` parameter's value. During the `birth` method's -execution, 1 is added to the `cityPop` parameter. But the place where the original `2232` value was stored — the memory location for the `smackoverARpop` variable — remains unaffected.

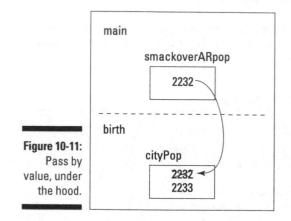

Figure 10-11:
Pass by value, under the hood.

When you do parameter passing with any of the eight primitive types, the computer uses *pass by value*. The value stored in the calling code's variable remains unchanged. This happens even if the calling code's variable and the called method's parameter happen to have the exact same name.

Returning a result

You must fix the problem that the code in Listing 10-10 poses. After all, a young baby Kermongoos can't go through life untracked. To record this baby's existence, you have to add 1 to the value of the `smackoverARpop` variable. You can do this in plenty of ways, and the way presented in Listing 10-11 isn't the simplest. Even so, the way shown in Listing 10-11 illustrates a point: Returning a value from a method call can be an acceptable alternative to parameter passing. Look at Listing 10-11 to see what I mean.

After running the code in Listing 10-11, the number you see on your computer screen is the correct number, 2,233.

The code in Listing 10-11 has no new features in it (unless you call *working correctly* a new feature). The most important idea in Listing 10-11 is the `return` statement, which also appears in Chapter 7. Even so, Listing 10-11 presents a nice contrast to the approach in Listing 10-10, which had to be discarded.

Listing 10-11:   This Program Works

```
public class TrackPopulation2 {

    public static void main(String args[]) {
        int smackoverARpop = 2232;

        smackoverARpop = birth(smackoverARpop);
        System.out.println(smackoverARpop);
    }

    static int birth(int cityPop) {
        return cityPop + 1;
    }
}
```

Pass by reference

In the previous section or two, I take great pains to emphasize a certain
point — that when a parameter has one of the eight primitive types, the
parameter is passed by value. If you read this, you probably missed the
emphasis on the parameter's having one of the eight primitive types.
The emphasis is needed because passing objects (reference types)
doesn't quite work the same way.

When you pass an object to a method, the object is *passed by reference*. What
this means to you is that statements in the called method *can* change any
values that are stored in the object's variables. Those changes *do* affect the
values that are seen by whatever code called the method. Listings 10-12 and
10-13 illustrate the point.

Listing 10-12:   What Is a City?

```
class City {
    int population;
}
```

Listing 10-13:   Passing an Object to a Method

```
public class TrackPopulation3 {

    public static void main(String args[]) {
        City smackoverAR = new City();
        smackoverAR.population = 2232;
        birth(smackoverAR);
        System.out.println(smackoverAR.population);
    }
```

(continued)

Listing 10-13 *(continued)*

```
static void birth(City aCity) {
    aCity.population++;
    }
}
```

When you run the code in Listings 10-12 and 10-13, the output that you get is the number 2,233. That's good because the code has things like ++ and the word *birth* in it. The deal is, adding 1 to aCity.population inside the birth method actually changes the value of smackoverAR.population as it's known in the main method.

To see how the birth method changes the value of smackoverAR.population, look at Figure 10-12. When you pass an object to a method, the computer doesn't make a copy of the entire object. Instead, the computer makes a copy of a reference to that object. (Think of it the way it's shown in Figure 10-12. The computer makes a copy of an arrow that points to the object.)

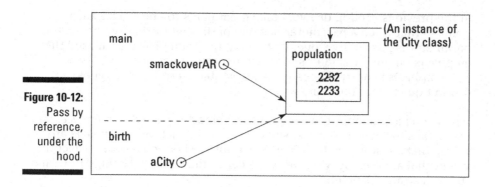

Figure 10-12:
Pass by
reference,
under the
hood.

In Figure 10-12, you see just one instance of the City class, with a population variable inside it. Now keep your eye on that object as you read the following steps:

1. Just before the birth method is called, the smackoverAR variable refers to that object — the instance of the City class.

2. When the birth method is called and smackoverAR is passed to the birth method's aCity parameter, the computer copies the reference from smackoverAR to aCity. Now aCity refers to that same object — the instance of the City class.

3. When the statement aCity.population++ is executed inside the birth method, the computer adds 1 to the object's population field. Now the program's one and only City instance has 2233 stored in its population field.

4. The flow of execution goes back to the main method. The value of smackoverAR.population is printed. But smackoverAR refers to that one instance of the City class. So smackoverAR.population has the value 2233. The Kermongoos family is so proud.

Returning an object from a method

Believe it or not, the previous sections on parameter passing left one nook and cranny of Java methods unexplored. When you call a method, the method can return something right back to the calling code. In previous chapters and sections, I return primitive values, such as int values, or nothing (otherwise known as *void*). In this section, I return a whole object. It's an object of type City from Listing 10-12. The code that makes this happen is in Listing 10-14.

Listing 10-14:   Here, Have a City

```
public class TrackPopulation4 {

    public static void main(String args[]) {
        City smackoverAR = new City();
        smackoverAR.population = 2232;
        smackoverAR = doBirth(smackoverAR);
        System.out.println(smackoverAR.population);
    }

    static City doBirth(City aCity) {
        City myCity = new City();
        myCity.population = aCity.population + 1;
        return myCity;
    }
}
```

If you run the code in Listing 10-14, you get the number 2,233. That's good. The code works by telling the doBirth method to create another City instance. In the new instance, the value of population is 2333. (See Figure 10-13.)

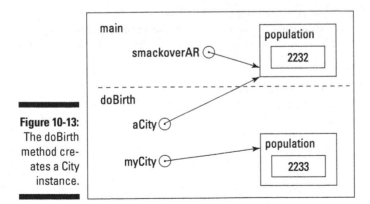

Figure 10-13:
The doBirth method creates a City instance.

After the `doBirth` method is executed, that `City` instance is returned to the `main` method. Then, back in the `main` method, that instance (the one that `doBirth` returns) is assigned to the `smackoverAR` variable. (See Figure 10-14.) Now `smackoverAR` refers to a brand-new `City` instance — an instance whose population is 2,233.

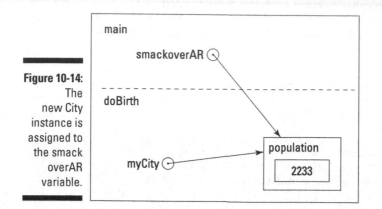

Figure 10-14:
The new City instance is assigned to the smack overAR variable.

In Listing 10-14, notice the type consistency in the calling and returning of the `doBirth` method:

- ✔ The `smackoverAR` variable has type `City`. The `smackoverAR` variable is passed to the `aCity` parameter, which is also of type `City`.

- ✔ The `myCity` variable is of type `City`. The `myCity` variable is sent back in the `doBirth` method's return statement. That's consistent, because the `doBirth` method's header begins with `static City doBirth(blah, blah, blah...` — a promise to return an object of type `City`.

- ✔ The `doBirth` method returns an object of type `City`. Back in the `main` method, the object that the call to `doBirth` returns is assigned to the `smackoverAR` variable, and (you guessed it) the `smackoverAR` variable is of type `City`.

Aside from being very harmonious, all this type agreement is absolutely necessary. If you write a program in which your types don't agree with one another, the compiler spits out an unsympathetic `incompatible types` message.

Epilogue

Dora Kermongoos and her newborn baby daughter are safe, healthy, and resting happily in their Smackover, Arkansas, home.

Chapter 11

Using Arrays to Juggle Values

In This Chapter

▶ Dealing with several values at once

▶ Searching for things

▶ Creating values as you get a program running

*W*elcome to the Java Motel! No haughty bellhops, no overpriced room service, none of the usual silly puns. Just a clean double room that's a darn good value!

Getting Your Ducks All in a Row

The Java Motel, with its ten comfortable rooms, sits in a quiet place off the main highway. Aside from a small, separate office, the motel is just one long row of ground floor rooms. Each room is easily accessible from the spacious front parking lot.

Oddly enough, the motel's rooms are numbered 0 through 9. I could say that the numbering is a fluke — something to do with the builder's original design plan. But the truth is that starting with 0 makes the examples in this chapter easier to write.

Anyway, you're trying to keep track of the number of guests in each room. Because you have ten rooms, you may think about declaring ten variables:

```
int guestsInRoomNum0, guestsInRoomNum1, guestsInRoomNum2,
    guestsInRoomNum3, guestsInRoomNum4, guestsInRoomNum5,
    guestsInRoomNum6, guestsInRoomNum7, guestsInRoomNum8,
    guestsInRoomNum9;
```

Doing it this way may seem a bit inefficient — but inefficiency isn't the only thing wrong with this code. Even more problematic is the fact that you can't loop through these variables. To read a value for each variable, you have to copy the `nextInt` method ten times.

```
guestsInRoomNum0 = diskScanner.nextInt();
guestsInRoomNum1 = diskScanner.nextInt();
guestsInRoomNum2 = diskScanner.nextInt();
... and so on.
```

Surely a better way exists.

That better way involves an array. An *array* is a row of values, like the row of rooms in a one-floor motel. To picture the array, just picture the Java Motel:

- ✔ First, picture the rooms, lined up next to one another.

- ✔ Next, picture the same rooms with their front walls missing. Inside each room you can see a certain number of guests.

- ✔ If you can, forget that the two guests in Room 9 are putting piles of bills into a big briefcase. Ignore the fact that the guests in Room 6 haven't moved away from the TV set in a day and a half. Instead of all these details, just see numbers. In each room, see a number representing the count of guests in that room. (If free-form visualization isn't your strong point, look at Figure 11-1.)

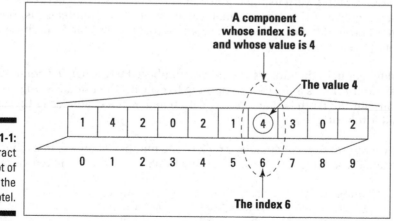

Figure 11-1: An abstract snapshot of rooms in the Java Motel.

In the lingo of this chapter, the entire row of rooms is called an *array*. Each room in the array is called a *component* of the array (also known as an array *element*). Each component has two numbers associated with it:

> ✔ The room number (a number from 0 to 9), which is called an *index* of the array
> ✔ A number of guests, which is a *value* stored in a component of the array

Using an array saves you from all the repetitive nonsense in the sample code shown at the beginning of this section. For instance, to declare an array with ten values in it, you can write one fairly short statement:

```
int guests[] = new int[10];
```

If you're especially verbose, you can expand this statement so that it becomes two separate statements:

```
int guests[];
guests = new int[10];
```

In either of these code snippets, notice the use of the number 10. This number tells the computer to make the guests array have ten components. Each component of the array has a name of its own. The starting component is named *guests[0]*, the next is named *guests[1]*, and so on. The last of the ten components is named *guests[9]*.

In creating an array, you always specify the number of components. The array's indices start with 0 and end with the number that's one less than the total number of components.

The snippets that I show you give you two ways to create an array. The first way uses one line. The second way uses two lines. If you take the single line route, you can put that line inside or outside a method. The choice is yours. On the other hand, if you use two separate lines, the second line, `guests = new int[10]`, should be inside a method.

In an array declaration, you can put the square brackets before or after the variable name. In other words, you can write **int guests[]** or **int[] guests**. The computer creates the same guests variable no matter which form you use.

Creating an array in two easy steps

Look once again at the two lines that you can use to create an array:

```
int guests[];
guests = new int[10];
```

Each line serves its own distinct purpose:

✔ int guests[]: This first line is a declaration. The declaration reserves the array name (a name like *guests*) for use in the rest of the program. In the Java Motel metaphor, this line says, "I plan to build a motel here and put a certain number of guests in each room." (See Figure 11-2.)

Never mind what the declaration int guests[] actually does. It's more important to notice what the declaration int guests[] *doesn't* do. The declaration doesn't reserve ten memory locations. Indeed, a declaration like int guests[] doesn't really create an array. All the declaration does is set up the guests variable. At that point in the code, the guests variable still doesn't refer to a real array. (In other words, the motel has a name, but the motel hasn't been built yet.)

✔ guests = new int[10]: This second line is an assignment statement. The assignment statement reserves space in the computer's memory for ten int values. In terms of real estate, this line says, "I've finally built the motel. Go ahead and put guests in each room." (Again, see Figure 11-2.)

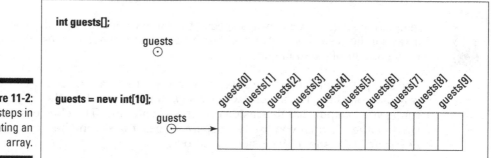

Figure 11-2:
Two steps in creating an array.

Storing values

After you've created an array, you can put values into the array's components. For instance, you would like to store the fact that Room 6 contains 4 guests. To put the value 4 in the component with index 6, you write **guests[6] = 4**.

Now business starts to pick up. A big bus pulls up to the motel. On the side of the bus is a sign that says "Noah's Ark." Out of the bus come 25 couples, each walking, stomping, flying, hopping, or slithering to the motel's small office. Only 10 of the couples can stay at the Java Motel, but that's okay because you can send the other 15 couples down the road to the old C-Side Resort and Motor Lodge.

Anyway, to register 10 couples into the Java Motel, you put a couple (2 guests) in each of your 10 rooms. Having created an array, you can take advantage of the array's indexing and write a `for` loop, like this:

```
for (int roomNum = 0; roomNum < 10; roomNum++) {
    guests[roomNum] = 2;
}
```

This loop takes the place of ten assignment statements. Notice how the loop's counter goes from 0 to 9. Compare this with Figure 11-2 and remember that the indices of an array go from 0 to one less than the number of components in the array.

However, given the way the world works, your guests won't always arrive in neat pairs, and you'll have to fill each room with a different number of guests. You probably store information about rooms and guests in a database. If you do, you can still loop through an array, gathering numbers of guests as you go. The code to perform such a task may look like this:

```
resultset =
    statement.executeQuery("select GUESTS from RoomData");
for (int roomNum = 0; roomNum < 10; roomNum++) {
    resultset.next();
    guests[roomNum] = resultset.getInt("GUESTS");
}
```

But because this book doesn't cover databases until Chapter 17 you may be better off reading numbers of guests from a plain text file. A sample file named `GuestList.txt` is shown in Figure 11-3.

Figure 11-3:
The
GuestList.txt
file.

```
1 4 2 0 2 1 4 3 0 2
```

After you've made a file, you can call on the `Scanner` class to get values from the file. The code is shown in Listing 11-1, and the resulting output is in Figure 11-4.

This book's website (`www.allmycode.com/JavaForDummies`) has tips for readers who need to create data files. This includes instructions for Windows, Linux, and Macintosh environments.

Listing 11-1:   Filling an Array with Values

```java
import static java.lang.System.out;
import java.util.Scanner;
import java.io.File;
import java.io.IOException;

public class ShowGuests {

    public static void main(String args[])
                                        throws IOException {
        int guests[] = new int[10];
        Scanner diskScanner =
                new Scanner(new File("GuestList.txt"));

        for(int roomNum = 0; roomNum < 10; roomNum++) {
            guests[roomNum] = diskScanner.nextInt();
        }

        out.println("Room\tGuests");

        for(int roomNum = 0; roomNum < 10; roomNum++) {
            out.print(roomNum);
            out.print("\t");
            out.println(guests[roomNum]);
        }
        diskScanner.close();
    }
}
```

```
Room    Guests
  0        1
  1        4
  2        2
  3        0
  4        2
  5        1
  6        4
  7        3
  8        0
  9        2
```

Figure 11-4:
Running the
code from
Listing 11-1.

The code in Listing 11-1 has two `for` loops. The first loop reads numbers of guests, and the second loop writes numbers of guests.

Every array has a built-in length field. An array's *length* is the number of components in the array. So, in Listing 11-1, if you print the value of `guests.length`, you get 10.

Tab stops and other special things

In Listing 11-1, some calls to `print` and `println` use the `\t` escape sequence. It's called an *escape sequence* because you escape from displaying the letter t on the screen. Instead, the characters `\t` stand for a tab. The computer moves forward to the next tab stop before printing any more characters. Java has a few of these handy escape sequences. Some of them are shown in Table 11-1.

Table 11-1	Escape Sequences
Sequence	*Meaning*
`\b`	backspace
`\t`	horizontal tab
`\n`	line feed
`\f`	form feed
`\r`	carriage return
`\"`	double quote "
`\'`	single quote '
`\\`	backslash \

Using an array initializer

Besides what you see in Listing 11-1, you have another way to fill an array in Java — with an *array initializer*. When you use an array initializer, you don't even have to tell the computer how many components the array has. The computer figures this out for you.

Listing 11-2 shows a new version of the code to fill an array. The program's output is the same as the output of Listing 11-1. (It's the stuff shown in Figure 11-4.) The only difference between Listings 11-1 and 11-2 is the bold text in Listing 11-2. That bold doodad is an array initializer.

Listing 11-2: Using an Array Initializer

```
import static java.lang.System.out;

public class ShowGuests {

    public static void main(String args[]) {
```

(continued)

Listing 11-2 *(continued)*

```
        int guests[] = {1, 4, 2, 0, 2, 1, 4, 3, 0, 2};

        out.println("Room\tGuests");

        for (int roomNum = 0; roomNum < 10; roomNum++) {
            out.print(roomNum);
            out.print("\t");
            out.println(guests[roomNum]);
        }
    }
}
```

 An array initializer can contain expressions as well as literals. In plain English, this means that you can put all kinds of things between the commas in the initializer. For instance, an initializer like {1 + 3, keyboard.nextInt(), 2, 0, 2, 1, 4, 3, 0, 2} works just fine.

Stepping through an array with the enhanced for loop

Java has an enhanced `for` loop — a `for` loop that doesn't use counters or indices. Listing 11-3 shows you how to do it.

 The material in this section applies to Java 5.0 and later Java versions. But this section's material doesn't work with older versions of Java — versions such as 1.3, 1.4, and so on. For a bit more about Java's version numbers, see Chapter 2.

Listing 11-3: Get a Load o' That for Loop!

```
import static java.lang.System.out;

public class ShowGuests {

    public static void main(String args[]) {
        int guests[] = {1, 4, 2, 0, 2, 1, 4, 3, 0, 2};
        int roomNum = 0;

        out.println("Room\tGuests");
        for (int numGuests : guests) {
            out.print(roomNum++);
            out.print("\t");
            out.println(numGuests);
        }
    }
}
```

Listings 11-1 and 11-3 have the same output. It's in Figure 11-4.

If you look at the loop in Listing 11-3, you see the same old pattern. Just like the loops in Listing 6-5, this example's loop has three parts:

```
for (variable-type variable-name : range-of-values)
```

The first two parts are *variable-type* and *variable-name*. The loop in Listing 11-3 defines a variable named numGuests, and numGuests has type int. During each loop iteration, the variable numGuests takes on a new value. Look at Figure 11-4 to see these values. The initial value is 1. The next value is 4. After that comes 2. And so on.

Where is the loop finding all these numbers? The answer lies in the loop's *range-of-values*. In Listing 11-3, the loop's *range-of-values* is guests. So, during the initial loop iteration, the value of numGuests is guests[0] (which is 1). During the next iteration, the value of numGuests is guests[1] (which is 4). After that comes guests[2] (which is 2). And so on.

Java's enhanced for loop requires a word of caution. Each time through the loop, the variable that steps through the range of values stores a *copy* of the value in the original range. The variable does *not* point to the range itself.

So for example, if you add an assignment statement that changes the value of numGuests in Listing 11-3, this statement has no effect on any of the values stored in the guests array. To drive this point home, imagine that business is bad and I've filled my hotel's guests array with zeros. Then I execute the following code:

```
for (int numGuests : guests) {
    numGuests += 1;
    out.print(numGuests + " ");
}

out.println();

for (int numGuests : guests) {
    out.print(numGuests + " ");
}
```

The numGuests variable takes on values stored in the guests array. But the numGuests += 1 statement doesn't change the values stored in this guests array. The code's output looks like this:

```
1 1 1 1 1 1 1 1 1 1
0 0 0 0 0 0 0 0 0 0
```

Searching

You're sitting behind the desk at the Java Motel. Look! Here comes a party of five. These people want a room, so you need software that checks whether a room is vacant. If one is, the software modifies the GuestList.txt file (refer to Figure 11-3) by replacing the number 0 with the number 5. As luck would have it, the software is right on your hard drive. The software is shown in Listing 11-4.

Listing 11-4: Do You Have a Room?

```
import static java.lang.System.out;
import java.util.Scanner;
import java.io.File;
import java.io.IOException;
import java.io.PrintStream;

public class FindVacancy {

    public static void main(String args[])
                                throws IOException {
        int guests[] = new int[10];
        int roomNum;

        Scanner diskScanner =
            new Scanner(new File("GuestList.txt"));
        for (roomNum = 0; roomNum < 10; roomNum++) {
            guests[roomNum] = diskScanner.nextInt();
        }
        diskScanner.close();

        roomNum = 0;
        while (roomNum < 10 && guests[roomNum] != 0) {
            roomNum++;
        }

        if (roomNum == 10) {
            out.println("Sorry, no vacancy");
        } else {
            out.print("How many people for room ");
            out.print(roomNum);
            out.print("? ");

            Scanner keyboard = new Scanner(System.in);
            guests[roomNum] = keyboard.nextInt();
            keyboard.close();

            PrintStream listOut =
                new PrintStream("GuestList.txt");
            for (roomNum = 0; roomNum < 10; roomNum++) {
                listOut.print(guests[roomNum]);
```

```
                      listOut.print(" ");
              }
              listOut.close();
          }
       }
    }
```

Figures 11-5 through 11-7 show the running of the code in Listing 11-4. Back in Figure 11-3, the motel starts with two vacant rooms — Rooms 3 and 8. (Remember, the rooms start with Room 0.) The first time that you run the code in Listing 11-4, the program tells you that Room 3 is vacant and puts five people into the room. The second time you run the code, the program finds the remaining vacant room (Room 8) and puts a party of ten in the room. (What a party!) The third time you run the code, you don't have any more vacant rooms. When the program discovers this, it displays the message Sorry, no vacancy, omitting at least one letter in the tradition of all motel neon signs.

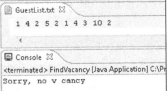

Figure 11-5: Filling a vacancy.

Figure 11-6: Filling the last vacant room.

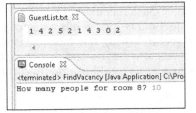

Figure 11-7: Sorry, Bud. No rooms.

A run of the code in Listing 11-4 writes a brand-new GuestList.txt file. This can be confusing because each Java IDE has its own way of displaying the GuestList.txt file's content. Some IDEs don't automatically display the newest GuestList.txt file, so after running the code from Listing 11-4, you may not immediately see a change. (For example, in Figure 11-5, Room 3 is empty. But after a run of the code, Figure 11-6 shows Room 3 having five guests.) Even if you don't see a change, consecutive runs of Listing 11-4 change the GuestList.txt file. Poke around within your favorite IDE to find out how to make the IDE refresh the GuestList.txt file's display.

In Listing 11-4, the condition roomNum < 10 && guests[roomNum] != 0 can be really tricky. If you move things around and write **guests[roomNum] != 0 && roomNum < 10**, you can get yourself into lots of trouble. For details, see this book's website (www.allmycode.com/JavaForDummies).

Writing to a file

The code in Listing 11-4 uses tricks from other chapters and sections of this book. The code's only brand-new feature is the use of PrintStream to write to a disk file. Think about any example in this book that calls System.out.print, out.println, or their variants. What's really going on when you call one of these methods?

The thing called System.out is an object. The object is defined in the Java API. In fact, System.out is an instance of a class named java.io.PrintStream (or just PrintStream to its close friends). Now each object created from the PrintStream class has methods named print and println. Just as each Account object in Listing 7-3 has a display method, and just as the DecimalFormat object in Listing 10-1 has a format method, so the PrintStream object named out has print and println methods. When you call System.out.println, you're calling a method that belongs to a PrintStream instance.

Okay, so what of it? Well, System.out always stands for some text area on your computer screen. If you create your own PrintStream object and you make that object refer to a disk file, that PrintStream object refers to the disk file. When you call that object's print method, you write text to a file on your hard drive.

So in Listing 11-4, when you say

```
PrintStream listOut =
                new PrintStream("GuestList.txt");

listOut.print(guests[roomNum]);
listOut.print(" ");
```

you're telling Java to write text to a file on your hard drive — the GuestList.txt file.

That's how you update the count of guests staying in the hotel. When you call listOut.print for the number of guests in Room 3, you may print the number 5. So, between Figures 11-5 and 11-6, a number in the GuestList.txt file changes from 0 to 5. Then in Figure 11-6, you run the program a second time. When the program gets data from the newly written GuestList.txt file, Room 3 is no longer vacant. So this time, the program suggests Room 8.

This is more an observation than a tip. Say that you want to *read* data from a file named Employees.txt. To do this, you make a scanner. You call new Scanner(new File("Employees.txt")). If you accidentally call new Scanner("Employees.txt") without the new File part, the call doesn't connect to your Employees.txt file. But notice how you prepare to *write* data to a file. You make a PrintStream instance by calling new PrintStream("GuestList.txt"). You don't use new File anywhere in the call. If you goof and accidentally include new File, the Java compiler becomes angry, jumps out, and bites you.

When to close a file

Notice the placement of new Scanner calls, new PrintStream calls, and close calls in Listing 11-4. As in all the examples, each new Scanner call has a corresponding close call. And in Listing 11-4, the new PrintStream call has its own close call (the listOut.close() call). But in Listing 11-4, I'm careful to place these calls tightly around their corresponding nextInt and print calls. For example, I don't set up diskScanner at the very start of the program, and I don't wait until the very end of the program to close diskScanner. Instead, I perform all my diskScanner tasks one after the other in quick succession:

```
Scanner diskScanner =
    new Scanner(new File("GuestList.txt"));    //construct
for (roomNum = 0; roomNum < 10; roomNum++) {
    guests[roomNum] = diskScanner.nextInt();   //read
}
diskScanner.close();                           //close
```

I do the same kind of thing with the keyboard and listOut objects.

I do this quick dance with input and output because my program uses GuestList.txt twice — once for reading numbers and a second time for writing numbers. If I'm not careful, the two uses of GuestList.txt might conflict with one another. Consider the following program:

```java
// THIS IS BAD CODE
import java.io.File;
import java.io.IOException;
import java.io.PrintStream;
import java.util.Scanner;

public class BadCode {

    public static void main(String args[])
                                        throws IOException {
        int guests[] = new int[10];

        Scanner diskScanner =
            new Scanner(new File("GuestList.txt"));
        PrintStream listOut =
            new PrintStream("GuestList.txt");

        guests[0] = diskScanner.nextInt();
        listOut.print(5);

        diskScanner.close();
        listOut.close();
    }
}
```

Like many methods and constructors of its kind, the PrintStream constructor doesn't pussyfoot around with files. If it can't find a GuestList.txt file, the constructor creates a GuestList.txt file and prepares to write values into it. But, if a GuestList.txt file already exists, the PrintStream constructor deletes the existing file and prepares to write to a new, empty GuestList.txt file. So, in the BadCode class, the new PrintStream constructor call deletes whatever GuestList.txt file already exists. This deletion comes *before* the call to diskScanner.nextInt(). So diskScanner.nextInt() can't read whatever was originally in the GuestList.txt file. That's bad!

To avoid this disaster, I carefully separate the two uses of the GuestList.txt file in Listing 11-4. Near the top of the listing, I construct diskScanner, then read from the original GuestList.txt file, and then close diskScanner. Later, toward the end of the listing, I construct listOut, then write to a new GuestList.txt file, and then close listOut. With writing separated completely from reading, everything works correctly.

The keyboard variable in Listing 11-4 doesn't refer to GuestList.txt, so keyboard doesn't conflict with the other input or output variables. No harm would come from following my regular routine — putting keyboard = new

Scanner(System.in) at the start of the program and putting keyboard.close() at the end of the program. But to make Listing 11-4 as readable and as uniform as possible, I place the keyboard constructor and the close call very tightly around the keyboard.nextInt call.

Arrays of Objects

The Java Motel is open for business, now with improved guest registration software! The people who brought you this chapter's first section are always scratching their heads, looking for the best ways to improve their services. Now, with some ideas from object-oriented programming, they've started thinking in terms of a Room class.

"And what," you ask, "would a Room instance look like?" That's easy. A Room instance has three properties — the number of guests in the room, the room rate, and a smoking/nonsmoking stamp. Figure 11-8 illustrates the situation.

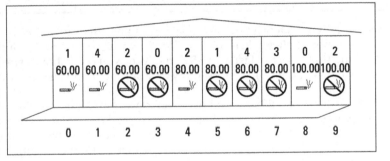

Figure 11-8: Another abstract snapshot of rooms in the Java Motel.

Listing 11-5 shows the code that describes the Room class. As promised, each instance of the Room class has three fields: the guests, rate, and smoking fields. (A false value for the boolean field, smoking, indicates a non-smoking room.) In addition, the entire Room class has a static field named currency. This currency object makes room rates look like dollar amounts.

To find out what static means, see Chapter 10.

Listing 11-5:   So This Is What a Room Looks Like!

```
import static java.lang.System.out;
import java.util.Scanner;
import java.text.NumberFormat;
```

(continued)

Listing 11-5 *(continued)*

```java
public class Room {
    private int guests;
    private double rate;
    private boolean smoking;
    private static NumberFormat currency =
        NumberFormat.getCurrencyInstance();

    public void readRoom(Scanner diskScanner) {
        guests = diskScanner.nextInt();
        rate = diskScanner.nextDouble();
        smoking = diskScanner.nextBoolean();
    }

    public void writeRoom() {
        out.print(guests);
        out.print("\t");
        out.print(currency.format(rate));
        out.print("\t");
        out.println(smoking ? "yes" : "no");
    }
}
```

Listing 11-5 has a few interesting quirks, but I'd rather not describe them until after you see all the code in action. That's why, at this point, I move right on to the code that calls the Listing 11-5 code. After you read about arrays of rooms (shown in Listing 11-6), check out my description of the Listing 11-5 quirks.

This warning is a deliberate repeat of an idea from Chapter 4, Chapter 7, and from who-knows-what-other chapter: You should be very careful when you use type `double` or type `float` to store money values. Calculations with `double` or `float` can be inaccurate. For more information (and more finger wagging) see Chapters 4 and 7.

This tip has absolutely nothing to do with Java. If you're the kind of person who prefers a smoking room (with boolean field `smoking = true` in Listing 11-5), find someone you like — someone who can take three consecutive days off work. Have that person sit with you and comfort you for 72 straight hours while you refrain from smoking. You might become temporarily insane while the nicotine leaves your body, but eventually you'll be okay. And your friend will feel like a real hero.

Using the Room class

So now you need an array of rooms. The code to create such a thing is in Listing 11-6. The code reads data from the `RoomList.txt` file. (Figure 11-9 shows the contents of the `RoomList.txt` file.)

Figure 11-10 shows a run of the code in Listing 11-6.

Listing 11-6:   Would You Like to See a Room?

```java
import static java.lang.System.out;
import java.util.Scanner;
import java.io.File;
import java.io.IOException;

public class ShowRooms {

    public static void main(String args[])
                                throws IOException {
        Room rooms[];
        rooms = new Room[10];

        Scanner diskScanner =
            new Scanner(new File("RoomList.txt"));

        for (int roomNum = 0; roomNum < 10; roomNum++) {
            rooms[roomNum] = new Room();
            rooms[roomNum].readRoom(diskScanner);
        }

        out.println("Room\tGuests\tRate\tSmoking?");
        for (int roomNum = 0; roomNum < 10; roomNum++) {
            out.print(roomNum);
            out.print("\t");
            rooms[roomNum].writeRoom();
        }
        diskScanner.close();
    }
}
```

Say what you want about the code in Listing 11-6. As far as I'm concerned, only one issue in the whole listing should concern you. And what, you ask, is that issue? Well, to create an array of *objects* — as opposed to an array made up of primitive values — you have to do three things: make the array variable, make the array itself, and then construct each individual object in the array. This is different from creating an array of int values or an array containing any other primitive type values. When you create an array of primitive type values, you do only the first two of these three things.

To help make sense of all this, follow along in Listing 11-6 and Figure 11-11 as you read the following points:

✔ Room rooms[];: This declaration creates a rooms variable. This variable is destined to refer to an array (but doesn't yet refer to anything at all).

```
1
60.00
true
4
60.00
true
2
60.00
false
0
60.00
false
2
80.00
true
1
80.00
false
4
80.00
false
3
80.00
false
0
100.00
true
2
100.00
false
```

Figure 11-9:
A file of
Room data.

```
Room    Guests    Rate        Smoking?
0       1         $60.00      yes
1       4         $60.00      yes
2       2         $60.00      no
3       0         $60.00      no
4       2         $80.00      yes
5       1         $80.00      no
6       4         $80.00      no
7       3         $80.00      no
8       0         $100.00     yes
9       2         $100.00     no
```

Figure 11-10:
A run of the
code in
Listing 11-6.

✔ `rooms = new Room[10];`: This statement reserves ten slots of storage in the computer's memory. The statement also makes the `rooms` variable refer to the group of storage slots. Each slot is destined to refer to an object (but doesn't yet refer to anything at all).

✔ `rooms[roomNum] = new Room();`: This statement is inside a `for` loop. The statement is executed once for each of the ten room numbers. For example, the first time through the loop, this statement says `rooms[0] = new Room()`. That first time around, the statement makes the slot `rooms[0]` refer to an actual object (an instance of the `Room` class).

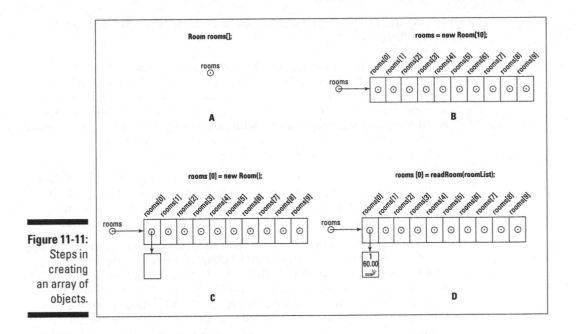

Figure 11-11:
Steps in creating an array of objects.

Although it's technically not considered a step in array making, you still have to fill each object's fields with values. For instance, the first time through the loop, the `readRoom` call says `rooms[1].readRoom(diskScanner)`, which means, "Read data from the `RoomList.txt` file into the `rooms[1]` object's fields (the `guests`, `rate`, and `smoking` fields)." Each time through the loop, the program creates a new object and reads data into that new object's fields.

You can squeeze the steps together just as you do when creating arrays of primitive values. For instance, you can do the first two steps in one fell swoop, like this:

```
Room rooms[] = new Room[10];
```

You can also use an array initializer. (For an introduction to array initializers, see the section "Using an array initializer," earlier in this chapter.)

Yet another way to beautify your numbers

You can make numbers look nice in plenty of ways. If you take a peek at some earlier chapters, for example, you can see that Listing 7-7 uses `printf`, and Listing 10-1 uses a `DecimalFormat`. But in Listing 11-5, I display a currency amount. I use the `NumberFormat` class with its `getCurrencyInstance` method.

If you compare the formatting statements in Listings 10-1 and 11-5, you don't see much difference.

- **One listing uses a constructor; the other listing calls `getCurrencyInstance`.** The `getCurrencyInstance` method is a good example of what's called a *factory method*. A factory method is a convenient tool for creating commonly used objects. People always need code that displays dollar amounts. So the `getCurrencyInstance` method creates a dollar format without forcing you to write `new DecimalFormat ("$###0.00;($###0.00)")`.

  Like a constructor, a factory method returns a brand-new object. But unlike a constructor, a factory method has no special status. When you create a factory method, you can name it anything you want. When you call a factory method, you don't use the keyword `new`.

- **One listing uses `DecimalFormat`; the other listing uses `NumberFormat`.** A decimal number is a certain kind of number. (In fact, a decimal number is a number written in the base-10 system.) Accordingly, the `DecimalFormat` class is a subclass of the `NumberFormat` class. The `DecimalFormat` methods are more specific, so for most purposes, I use `DecimalFormat`. But it's harder to use the `DecimalFormat` class's `getCurrencyInstance` method. So for programs that involve money, I tend to use `NumberFormat`.

- **Both listings use `format` methods.** In the end, you just write something like `currency.format(rate)` or `decFormat.format(average)`. After that, Java does the work for you.

From Chapter 4 onward, I issue gentle warnings against using types such as `double` and `float` for storing currency values. For the most accurate currency calculations, use `int`, `long`, or best of all, `BigDecimal`.

You can read more about the dangers of `double` types, `float` types, and currency values in Chapter 5.

The conditional operator

Listing 11-5 uses an interesting doodad called the *conditional operator*. This conditional operator takes three expressions and returns the value of just one of them. It's like a mini `if` statement. When you use the conditional operator, it looks something like this:

```
conditionToBeTested ? expression1 : expression2
```

The computer evaluates the *conditionToBeTested* condition. If the condition is true, the computer returns the value of *expression1*. But, if the condition is false, the computer returns the value of *expression2*.

So, in the code

```
smoking ? "yes" : "no"
```

the computer checks whether smoking has the value true. If so, the whole three-part expression stands for the first string, "yes". If not, the whole expression stands for the second string, "no".

In Listing 11-5, the call to out.println causes either "yes" or "no" to display. Which string gets displayed depends on whether smoking has the value true or false.

Command Line Arguments

*O*nce upon a time, most programmers used a text-based development interface. To run the Displayer example in Chapter 3, they didn't select Run from a menu in a fancy integrated development environment. Instead they typed a command in a plain-looking window, usually with white text on a black background. Figure 11-12 illustrates the point. In Figure 11-12, I type the words java Displayer, and the computer responds with my Java program's output (the words You'll love Java!).

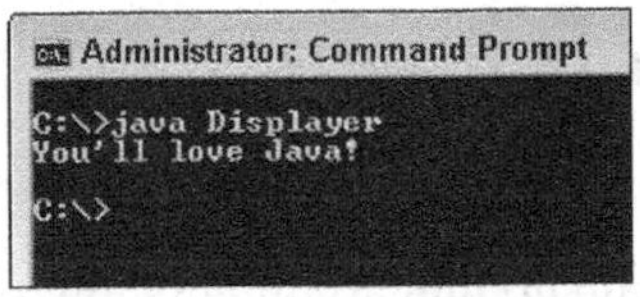

Figure 11-12: How dull!

```
Administrator: Command Prompt
C:\>java Displayer
You'll love Java!

C:\>
```

The plain-looking window goes by the various names, depending on the kind of operating system that you use. In Windows, a text window of this kind is a *command prompt window*. On a Macintosh and in Linux, this window is the *terminal*. Some versions of Linux and UNIX call this window a *shell*.

Anyway, back in ancient times, you could write a program that sucked up extra information when you typed the command to launch the program. Figure 11-13 shows you how this worked.

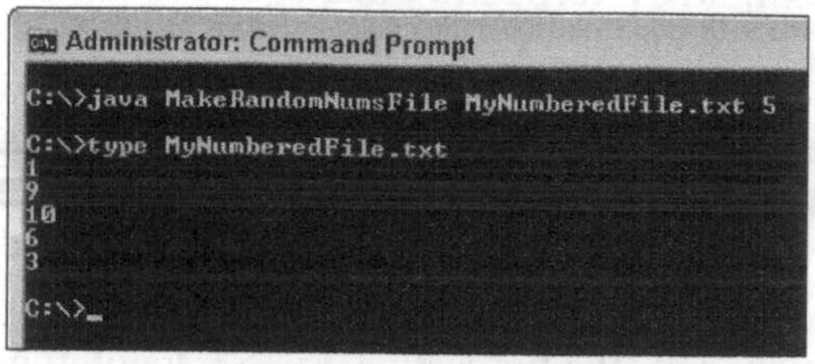

Figure 11-13:
When you launch Make-Random-NumsFile, you type some extra information.

In Figure 11-13, the programmer types `java MakeRandomNumsFile` to run the `MakeRandomNumsFile` program. But the programmer follows `java MakeRandomNumsFile` with two extra pieces of information; namely, `MyNumberedFile.txt` and `5`. When the `MakeRandomNumsFile` program runs, the program sucks up two extra pieces of information and uses them to do whatever the program has to do. In Figure 11-13, the program sucks up `MyNumberedFile.txt 5`, but on another occasion the programmer might type `SomeStuff 28` or `BunchONumbers 2000`. The extra information can be different each time you run the program.

So the next question is, "How does a Java program know that it's supposed to snarf up extra information each time it runs?" Since you first started working with Java, you've been seeing this `String args[]` business in the header of every `main` method. Well, it's high time you found out what that's all about. The parameter `args[]` is an array of `String` values. These `String` values are called *command line arguments*.

Using command line arguments in a Java program

Listing 11-7 shows you how to use command line arguments in your code.

Listing 11-7:   Generate a File of Numbers

```java
import java.util.Random;
import java.io.PrintStream;
import java.io.IOException;

public class MakeRandomNumsFile {

    public static void main(String args[])
                                    throws IOException {
```

```
Random generator = new Random();

if (args.length < 2) {
    System.out.println
        ("Usage: MakeRandomNumsFile filename number");
    System.exit(1);
}

PrintStream printOut = new PrintStream(args[0]);
int numLines = Integer.parseInt(args[1]);

for (int count = 1; count <= numLines; count++) {
    printOut.println(generator.nextInt(10) + 1);
}

printOut.close();
}
}
```

If a particular program expects some command line arguments, you can't start the program running the same way you'd start most of the other programs in this book. The way you feed command line arguments to a program depends on the IDE that you're using — Eclipse, NetBeans, or whatever. That's why this book's website (www.allmycode.com/JavaForDummies) has instructions for feeding arguments to programs using various IDEs.

When the code in Listing 11-7 begins running, the args array gets its values. In the main method of Listing 11-7, the array component args[0] automatically takes on the value "MyNumberedFile.txt", and args[1] automatically becomes "5". So the program's assignment statements end up having the following meaning:

```
PrintStream printOut = new
        PrintStream("MyNumberedFile.txt");
int numLines = Integer.parseInt("5");
```

The program creates a file named MyNumberedFile.txt and sets numLines to 5. So later in the code, the program randomly generates five values and puts those values into MyNumberedFile.txt. One run of the program gives me the file shown in Figure 11-14.

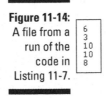

Figure 11-14:
A file from a run of the code in Listing 11-7.

```
6
3
10
10
8
```

After running the code in Listing 11-7, where can you find the new file (My NumberedFile.txt) on your hard drive? The answer depends on a lot of different things, so I don't want to commit to one particular answer. If you use an IDE with programs divided into projects, then the new file is somewhere in the project's folder. One way or another, you can change Listing 11-7 to specify a full path name — a name like "c:\\MyNumberedFile.txt".

In Windows, file path names contain backslash characters. And in Java, when you want to indicate a backslash inside a double-quoted String literal, you use a double backslash instead. That's why "c:\\MyNumberedFile. txt" contains two backslashes. In contrast, file paths in the Linux and Macintosh operating systems contain forward slashes. To indicate a forward slash in a Java String, use one forward slash. To refer to a file in your Macintosh Documents directory, you might write "/Users/*YourUserName*/ Documents/MyNumberedFile.txt".

Notice how each command line argument in Listing 11-7 is a String value. When you look at args[1], you don't see the number 5 — you see the string "5" with a digit character in it. Unfortunately, you can't use that "5" to do any counting. To get an int value from "5", you have to apply the parseInt method. (Again, see Listing 11-7.)

The parseInt method lives inside a class named *Integer*. So, to call parseInt, you preface the name *parseInt* with the word *Integer*. The Integer class has all kinds of handy methods for doing things with int values.

In Java, *Integer* is the name of a class, and *int* is the name of a primitive (simple) type. The two things are related, but they're not the same. The Integer class has methods and other tools for dealing with int values.

Checking for the right number of command line arguments

What happens if the user makes a mistake? What if the user forgets to type the number 5 on the first line in Figure 11-13?

Then the computer assigns "MyNumberedFile.txt" to args[0], but it doesn't assign anything to args[1]. This is bad. If the computer ever reaches the statement

```
int numLines = Integer.parseInt(args[1]);
```

the program crashes with an unfriendly ArrayIndexOutOfBoundsException.

So, what do you do about this? In Listing 11-7, you check the length of the `args` array. You compare `args.length` with 2. If the `args` array has fewer than two components, you display a message on the screen and exit from the program. Figure 11-15 shows the resulting output.

Figure 11-15:
The code in
Listing 11-7
tells you
how to run it.

```
Usage: MakeRandomNumsFile filename number
```

Despite the checking of `args.length` in Listing 11-7, the code still isn't crash-proof. If the user types **five** instead of **5**, the program takes a nosedive with a `NumberFormatException`. The second command line argument can't be a word. The argument has to be a number (and a whole number at that). I can add statements to Listing 11-7 to make the code more bulletproof, but checking for the `NumberFormatException` is better done in Chapter 13.

When you're working with command line arguments, you can enter a `String` value with a blank space in it. Just enclose the value in double quote marks. For instance, you can run the code of Listing 11-7 with arguments `"My Big Fat File.txt"` 7.

The sun is about to set on this book's discussion of arrays. The next section deals with something slightly different. But before you leave the subject of arrays, think about this: An array is a row of things, and not every kind of thing fits into just one row. Take the first few examples in this chapter involving the motel. The motel rooms, numbered 0 through 9, are in one big line. But what if you move up in the world? You buy a big hotel with 50 floors and with 100 rooms on each floor. Then the data is square shaped. We have 50 rows, and each row contains 100 items. Sure, you can think of the rooms as if they're all in one big row, but why should you have to do that? How about having a two-dimensional array? It's a square-shaped array in which each component has two indices — a row number and a column number. Alas, I have no space in this book to show you a two-dimensional array (and I can't afford a big hotel's prices anyway). But if you visit this book's website (`www.allmycode.com/JavaForDummies`), you can read all about it.

Chapter 12

Using Collections and Streams (When Arrays Aren't Good Enough)

In This Chapter

▶ Facing the limitations of arrays

▶ Dealing with a bunch of objects at once

▶ Using Java's cool functional programming features

▶ Developing code for multicore processors

Chapter 11 is about arrays. With an array, you can manage a bunch of things all at once. In a hotel-management program, you can keep track of all the rooms. You can quickly find the number of people in a room or find one of the vacant rooms.

However, arrays don't always fit the bill. In this chapter, you find out where arrays fall short and how collections can save the day.

Understanding the Limitations of Arrays

Arrays are nice, but they have some serious limitations. Imagine that you store customer names in some predetermined order. Your code contains an array, and the array has space for 100 names.

```
String name[] = new String[100];
for (int i = 0; i < 100; i++) {
    name[i] = new String();
}
```

All is well until, one day, customer number 101 shows up. As your program runs, you enter data for customer 101, hoping desperately that the array with 100 components can expand to fit your growing needs.

No such luck. Arrays don't expand. Your program crashes with an `Array IndexOutOfBoundsException`.

"In my next life, I'll create arrays of length 1,000," you say to yourself. And when your next life rolls around, you do just that.

```
String name[] = new String[1000];
for (int i = 0; i < 1000; i++) {
    name[i] = new String();
}
```

But during your next life, an economic recession occurs. Instead of having 101 customers, you have only 3 customers. Now you're wasting space for 1,000 names when space for 3 names would do.

And what if no economic recession occurs? You're sailing along with your array of size 1,000, using a tidy 825 spaces in the array. The components with indices 0 through 824 are being used, and the components with indices 825 through 999 are waiting quietly to be filled.

One day, a brand-new customer shows up. Because your customers are stored in order (alphabetically by last name, numerically by Social Security number, whatever), you want to squeeze this customer into the correct component of your array. The trouble is that this customer belongs very early on in the array, at the component with index 7. What happens then?

You take the name in component number 824 and move it to component 825. Then you take the name in component 823 and move it to component 824. Take the name in component 822 and move it to component 823. You keep doing this until you've moved the name in component 7. Then you put the new customer's name into component 7. What a pain! Sure, the computer doesn't complain. (If the computer has feelings, it probably likes this kind of busy work.) But as you move around all these names, you waste processing time, you waste power, and you waste all kinds of resources.

"In my next life, I'll leave three empty components between every two names." And of course, your business expands. Eventually you find that three aren't enough.

Collection Classes to the Rescue

The issues in the previous section aren't new. Computer scientists have been working on these issues for a long time. They haven't discovered any magic one-size-fits-all solution, but they've discovered some clever tricks.

The Java API has a bunch of classes known as *collection* classes. Each collection class has methods for storing bunches of values, and each collection class's methods use some clever tricks. For you, the bottom line is as follows:

Certain collection classes deal as efficiently as possible with the issues raised in the previous section. If you have to deal with such issues when writing code, you can use these collection classes and call the classes' methods. Instead of fretting about a customer whose name belongs in position 7, you can just call a class's add method. The method inserts the name at a position of your choice and deals reasonably with whatever ripple effects have to take place. In the best circumstances, the insertion is very efficient. In the worst circumstances, you can rest assured that the code does everything the best way it can.

Using an ArrayList

One of the most versatile of Java's collection classes is the ArrayList. Listing 12-1 shows you how it works.

Listing 12-1:   Working with a Java Collection

```java
import static java.lang.System.out;
import java.util.Scanner;
import java.io.File;
import java.io.IOException;
import java.util.ArrayList;

public class ShowNames {

    public static void main(String args[])
                              throws IOException {
        ArrayList<String> people =
                          new ArrayList<String>();
        Scanner diskScanner =
            new Scanner(new File("names.txt"));

        while (diskScanner.hasNext()) {
            people.add(diskScanner.nextLine());
        }

        people.remove(0);
        people.add(2, "Jim Newton");

        for (String name : people) {
            out.println(name);
        }

        diskScanner.close();
    }
}
```

Figure 12-1 shows you a sample names.txt file. The code in Listing 12-1 reads that names.txt file and prints the stuff in Figure 12-2.

Figure 12-1:
Several
names in
a file.

```
Barry Burd
Harriet Ritter
Weelie J. Katz
Harry "The Crazyman" Spoonswagler
Felicia "Fishy" Katz
Mia, Just "Mia"
Jeremy Flooflong Jones
I. M. D'Arthur
Hugh R. DaReader
```

Figure 12-2:
The code in
Listing 12-1
changes
some of the
names.

```
Harriet Ritter
Weelie J. Katz
Jim Newton
Harry "The Crazyman" Spoonswagler
Felicia "Fishy" Katz
Mia, Just "Mia"
Jeremy Flooflong Jones
I. M. D'Arthur
Hugh R. DaReader
```

All the interesting things happen when you execute the remove and add methods. The variable named people refers to an ArrayList object. When you call that object's remove method,

```
people.remove(0);
```

you eliminate a value from the list. In this case, you eliminate whatever value is in the list's initial position (the position numbered 0). So in Listing 12-1, the call to remove takes the name Barry Burd out of the list.

That leaves only eight names in the list, but then the next statement,

```
people.add(2, "Jim Newton");
```

inserts a name into position number 2. (After Barry is removed, position number 2 is the position occupied by Harry Spoonswagler, so Harry moves to position 3, and Jim Newton becomes the number 2 man.)

Notice that an ArrayList object has two different add methods. The method that adds Jim Newton has two parameters: a position number and a value to be added. Another add method

```
people.add(diskScanner.nextLine());
```

takes only one parameter. This statement takes whatever name it finds on a line of the input file and appends that name to the end of the list. (The add method with only one parameter always appends its value to what's currently the end of the ArrayList object.)

The last few lines of Listing 12-1 contain an enhanced for loop. Like the loop in Listing 11-3, the enhanced loop in Listing 12-1 has the following form:

```
for (variable-type variable-name : range-of-values)
```

In Listing 12-1, the *variable-type* is String, the *variable-name* is name, and the *range-of-values* includes the things stored in the people collection. During an iteration of the loop, name refers to one of the String values stored in people. (So if the people collection contains nine values, then the for loop goes through nine iterations.) During each iteration, the statement inside the loop displays a name on the screen.

Using generics

Look again at Listing 12-1, shown earlier, and notice the funky ArrayList declaration:

```
ArrayList<String> people = new ArrayList<String>();
```

Starting with Java 5.0, each collection class is *generified.* That ugly-sounding word means that every collection declaration should contain some angle-bracketed stuff, such as <String>. The thing that's sandwiched between < and > tells Java what kinds of values the new collection may contain. For example, in Listing 12-1, the words ArrayList<String> people tell Java that people is a bunch of strings. That is, the people list contains String objects (not Room objects, not Account objects, not Employee objects, nothing other than String objects).

Most of this section's material applies only to Java 5.0 and later. You can't use generics in any version of Java before Java 5.0. For more about generics, see the sidebar. And for more about Java's version numbers, see Chapter 2.

In Listing 12-1 the words ArrayList<String> people say that the people variable can refer only to a collection of String values. So from that point on, any reference to an item from the people collection is treated exclusively as a String. If you write

```
people.add(new Room());
```

then the compiler coughs up your code and spits it out because a Room (created in Chapter 11) isn't the same as a String. (This coughing and spitting happens even if the compiler has access to the Room class's code — the code in Chapter 11.) But the statement

```
people.add("George Gow");
```

is just fine. Because "George Gow" has type String, the compiler smiles happily.

Java 7 and later versions have a cool feature allowing you to abbreviate generic declarations. In Listing 12-1, you can write ArrayList <String> people = new ArrayList<>() without repeating the word String a second time in the declaration. The <> symbol without any words inside it is called a *diamond operator.* The diamond operator saves you from having to rewrite stuff like <String> over and over.

All about generics

One of the original design goals for Java was to keep the language as simple as possible. The language's developer took some unnecessarily complicated features of C++ and tossed them out the window. The result was a language that was elegant and sleek. Some people said the language was too sleek. So after several years of discussion and squabbling, Java became a bit more complicated. By the year 2004, Java had enum types, enhanced for loops, static import, and some other interesting new features. But the most talked-about new feature was the introduction of generics.

```
ArrayList<String> people = new ArrayList<String>();
```

The use of anything like <String> was new in Java 5.0. In old-style Java, you'd write

```
ArrayList people = new ArrayList();
```

In those days, an ArrayList could store almost anything you wanted to put in it — a number, an Account, a Room, a String . . . anything. The ArrayList class was very versatile, but with this versatility came some headaches. If you could put anything into an ArrayList, you couldn't easily predict what you would get out of an ArrayList. In particular, you couldn't easily write code that assumed you had stored certain types of values in the ArrayList. Here's an example:

```
ArrayList things = new ArrayList();
things.add(new Account());
Account myAccount = things.get(0);
//DON'T USE THIS. IT'S BAD CODE.
```

In the third line, the call to get(0) grabs the earliest value in the things collection. The call to get(0) is okay, but then the compiler chokes on the attempted assignment to myAccount. You get a message on the third line saying that whatever you get from the things list can't be stuffed into the myAccount variable. You get this message because by the time the compiler reaches the third line, it has forgotten that the item added on the second line was of type Account!

The introduction of generics fixes this problem:

```
ArrayList<Account> things = new ArrayList<Account>();
things.add(new Account());
Account myAccount = things.get(0);
//USE THIS CODE INSTEAD. IT'S GOOD CODE.
```

Adding <Account> in two places tells the compiler that things stores Account instances — nothing else. So, in the third line in the preceding code, you get a value from the things collection. Then, because things stores only Account objects, you can make myAccount refer to that new value.

Java 5.0 added generics to Java. But soon after the birth of Java 5.0, programmers noticed how clumsy the code for generics can be. After all, you can create generics within generics. An ArrayList can contain a bunch of arrays, each of which can be an ArrayList. So you can write

```
ArrayList<ArrayList<String>[]> mess =
                new ArrayList<ArrayList<String>[]>();
```

All the repetition in that `mess` declaration gives me a headache! To avoid this ugliness, Java 7 and later versions have a *diamond operator,* `<>`. The diamond operator tells Java to reuse whatever insanely complicated stuff you put in the previous part of the generic declaration. In this example, the `<>` tells Java to reuse `<ArrayList<String>[]>`, even though you write `<ArrayList<String>[]>` only once. Here's how the streamlined Java 7 code looks:

```
ArrayList<ArrayList<String>[]> mess =
                    new ArrayList<>();
```

In Java 7 and later, you can write either of these `mess` declarations — the original, nasty declaration with two occurrences of `ArrayList<String>[]`, or the streamlined (only mildly nasty) declaration with the diamond operator and only one `ArrayList<String>[]` occurrence.

Yes, the streamlined code is still complicated. But without all the `ArrayList<String>[]` repetition, the streamlined code is less cumbersome. The Java 7 diamond operator takes away one chance for you to copy something incorrectly and have a big error in your code.

Testing for the presence of more data

Here's a pleasant surprise. When you write a program like the one shown previously in Listing 12-1, you don't have to know how many names are in the input file. Having to know the number of names may defeat the purpose of using the easily expandable `ArrayList` class. Instead of looping until you read exactly nine names, you can loop until you run out of data.

The `Scanner` class has several nice methods such as `hasNextInt`, `hasNext Double`, and plain old `hasNext`. Each of these methods checks for more input data. If there's more data, the method returns `true`. Otherwise, the method returns `false`.

Listing 12-1 uses the general-purpose `hasNext` method. This `hasNext` method returns `true` as long as there's anything more to read from the program's input. So after the program scoops up that last `Hugh R. DaReader` line in Figure 12-1, the subsequent `hasNext` call returns `false`. This `false` condition ends execution of the `while` loop and plummets the computer toward the remainder of the Listing 12-1 code.

The `hasNext` method is very handy. In fact, `hasNext` is so handy that it's part of a bigger concept known as an *iterator,* and iterators are baked into all of Java's collection classes.

Using an iterator

An iterator spits out a collection's values, one after another. To obtain a value from the collection, you call the iterator's next method. To find out whether the collection has any more values in it, you call the iterator's hasNext method. Listing 12-2 uses an iterator to display people's names.

Listing 12-2:   Iterating through a Collection

```
import static java.lang.System.out;

import java.util.Iterator;
import java.util.Scanner;
import java.io.File;
import java.io.IOException;
import java.util.ArrayList;

public class ShowNames {

    public static void main(String args[])
                              throws IOException {
        ArrayList<String> people =
                     new ArrayList<String>();
        Scanner diskScanner =
            new Scanner(new File("names.txt"));

        while (diskScanner.hasNext()) {
            people.add(diskScanner.nextLine());
        }

        people.remove(0);
        people.add(2, "Jim Newton");

        Iterator<String> iterator = people.iterator();
        while (iterator.hasNext()) {
            out.println(iterator.next());
        }

        diskScanner.close();
    }
}
```

You can replace the enhanced for loop at the end of Listing 12-1 with the boldface code in Listing 12-2. When you do, you get the get the same output as before. (You get the output in Figure 12-2.) In Listing 12-2, the first bold-face line of code creates an iterator from the people collection. The second and third lines call the iterator's `hasNext` and `next` methods to grab all the objects stored in the `people` collection — one for each iteration of the loop. These lines display each of the `people` collection's values.

Which is better? An enhanced `for` loop or an iterator? Java programmers prefer the enhanced `for` loop because the `for` loop involves less baggage — no `iterator` object to carry from one line of code to the next. But as you see later in this chapter, the most programming-enhanced feature can be upgraded, streamlined, tweaked, and otherwise reconstituted. There's no end to the way you can improve upon your code.

Java's many collection classes

The `ArrayList` class that I use in many of this chapter's examples is only the tip of the Java collections iceberg. The Java library contains many collections classes, each with its own advantages. Table 12-1 contains an abbreviated list.

Table 12-1	Some Collection Classes
Class Name	**Characteristic**
`ArrayList`	A resizable array.
`LinkedList`	A list of values, each having a field that points to the next one in the list.
`Stack`	A structure that grows from bottom to top. The structure is optimized for access to the topmost value. You can easily add a value to the top or remove the value from the top.
`Queue`	A structure that grows at one end. The structure is optimized for adding values to one end (the rear) and removing values from the other end (the front).
`PriorityQueue`	A structure, like a queue, that lets certain (higher-priority) values move toward the front.
`HashSet`	A collection containing no duplicate values.
`HashMap`	A collection of key/value pairs.

Each collection class has its own set of methods (in addition to the methods that it inherits from `AbstractCollection`, the ancestor of all collection classes).

To find out which collection classes best meet your needs, visit the Java API documentation pages at `http://docs.oracle.com/javase/8/docs/api`.

New in Java 8: Functional Programming

From 1953 to 1957, John Backus and others developed the FORTRAN programming language, which contained the basic framework for thousands of 20th century programming languages. The framework has come to be known as *imperative programming* because of its "do this, then do that" nature.

A few years after the rise of FORTRAN, John McCarthy created another language named *Lisp*. Unlike FORTRAN, the underlying framework for Lisp is *functional programming*. In a purely functional program, you avoid writing "do this, then do that." Instead, you write things like "here's how you'll be transforming this into that when you get around to doing the transformation."

For one reason or another, imperative programming became the dominant mode. As a result, Java is fundamentally an imperative programming language. But recently, functional programming has emerged as a powerful and useful way of thinking about code.

I've read lots of articles and attended dozens of presentations describing functional programming. Frankly, most of these descriptions aren't very helpful. Some of them feed you a bunch of rigorous definitions and expect you to form your own intuitions. Others describe the intuitive ideas without giving you any concrete examples to work with.

So instead of describing functional programming in detail, I start this section with an analogy. Then, in the rest of this chapter, I present some Java 8 examples.

The analogy that I use to describe functional programming is very rough. A friend of mine called this analogy a stretch because it applies to many different programming frameworks, not only to functional programming. One way or another, I think the analogy is helpful.

Here's the analogy: Imagine a programming problem as a cube, and imagine an imperative programming solution as a way of slicing up the cube into manageable pieces. (See Figure 12-3.)

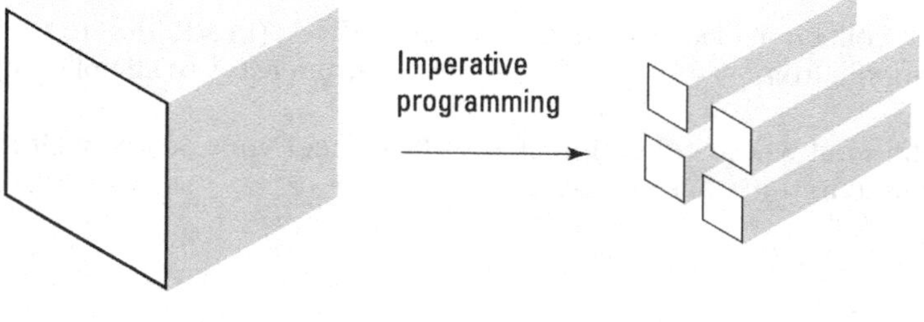

Figure 12-3: Imperative programming slices up a problem.

Imperative programming

All was well until 2007 when, for the first time, computers sold to consumers had multicore processors. A multicore processor can perform more than one instruction at a time. Figure 12-4 shows what happens when you try to squeeze an imperative program into a multicore processor.

It doesn't fit easily, so...   ...squeeze it all into one core.

Figure 12-4:
An
imperative
program's
pieces
don't fit
neatly into
a multicore
chip.

To get the most out of a four-core processor, you divide your code into four pieces — one piece for each core. But with imperative programming, your program's pieces don't fit neatly into your processor's cores.

In imperative programming, your code's pieces interact with one another. All the pieces might be updating the current price of Oracle stock shares (ticker symbol ORCL). The simultaneous updates become tangled. It's like several high-school boys asking the same girl to the senior prom. Nothing good ever comes of it. You've experienced the same phenomenon if you've ever clicked a website's Purchase button only to learn that the item you're trying to purchase is out of stock. Someone else completed a purchase while you were filling in your credit card information. Too many customers were grabbing for the same goods at the same time.

Figure 12-3 suggests that, with imperative programming, you divide your code into several pieces. Functional programming also divides code into pieces, but it does so along different lines. (See Figure 12-5.) And here's the good news: With functional programming, the pieces of the code fit neatly into the processor's cores. (See Figure 12-6.)

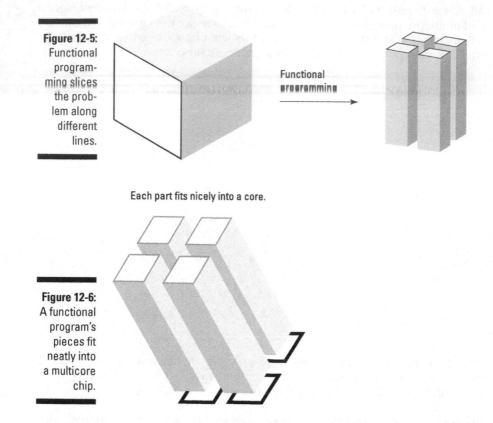

Figure 12-5: Functional programming slices the problem along different lines.

Functional programming

Each part fits nicely into a core.

Figure 12-6: A functional program's pieces fit neatly into a multicore chip.

Solving a problem the old-fashioned way

In Chapter 11, you used arrays to manage the Java Motel. But that venture is behind you now. You've given up the hotel business. (You tell people that you decided to move on. But in all honesty, the hotel was losing a lot of money. According to the United States bankruptcy court, the old Java Motel is currently in Chapter 11.)

Since leaving the hotel business, you've transitioned into online sales. Nowadays, you run a website that sells books, DVDs, and other content-related items. (Barry Burd's *Java For Dummies,* 6th Edition is currently your best seller, but that's beside the point.)

In your world, the sale of a single item looks something like the stuff in Listing 12-3. Each sale has an item and a price.

Listing 12-3:   The Sale Class

```
public class Sale {
    String item;
    double price;

    public Sale(String item, double price) {
        this.item = item;
        this.price = price;
    }
}
```

To make use of the Sale class, you create a small program. The program totals up the sales on DVDs. The program is shown in Listing 12-4.

Listing 12-4:   Using the Sale Class

```
import java.text.NumberFormat;
import java.util.ArrayList;

public class TallySales {

    public static void main(String[] args) {
        ArrayList<Sale> sales = new ArrayList<Sale>();
        NumberFormat currency =
            NumberFormat.getCurrencyInstance();

        fillTheList(sales);

        double total = 0;
        for (Sale sale : sales) {
            if (sale.item.equals("DVD")) {
                total += sale.price;
            }
        }

        System.out.println(currency.format(total));
    }

    static void fillTheList(ArrayList<Sale> sales) {
        sales.add(new Sale("DVD", 15.00));
        sales.add(new Sale("Book", 12.00));
        sales.add(new Sale("DVD", 21.00));
        sales.add(new Sale("CD", 5.25));
    }
}
```

In Chapter 11, you step through an array by using an enhanced `for` statement. Listing 12-4 has its own enhanced `for` statement. But in Listing 12-4, the enhanced `for` statement steps through the values in a collection. Each such value is a sale. The loop repeatedly checks a sale to find out whether the item sold is a DVD. If so, the code adds the sale's price to the running total. The program's output is $36.00 — the running total displayed as a currency amount.

The scenario in Listing 12-4 isn't unusual. You have a collection of things (such as sales). You step through the things in the collection, finding the things that meet certain criteria (being the sale of a DVD, for example). You grab a certain value (such as the sale price) of each thing that meets your criteria. Then you do something useful with the values that you've grabbed (for example, adding the values together).

Here are some other examples:

- Step through your list of employees. Find each employee whose performance evaluation has score 3 or above. Give each such employee a $100 bonus and then determine the total amount of money you'll pay in bonuses.

- Step through your list of customers. For each customer who has shown interest in buying a smartphone, send the customer an e-mail about this month's discount plans.

- Step through the list of planets that have been discovered. For each M-class planet, find the probability of finding intelligent life on that planet. Then find the average of all such probabilities.

This scenario is so common that it's worth finding better and better ways to deal with the scenario. One way to deal with it is to use some of the new functional programming features in Java 8.

Streams

The "Using an iterator" section introduces iterators. You use an iterator's `next` method to spit out a collection's values. Java 8 takes this concept one step further with the notion of a stream. A *stream* is like an iterator except that, with a stream, you don't have to call a `next` method. After being created, a stream spits out a collection's values automatically. To get values from a stream, you don't call a stream's `next` method. In fact, a typical stream has no `next` method.

How does this work as part of a Java program? How do you create a stream that spits out values? How does the stream know when to start spitting, and where does the stream aim when it spits? For answers to these and other questions, read the next several sections.

Lambda expressions

In the 1930s, mathematician Alonzo Church used the Greek letter lambda (λ) to represent a certain mathematical construct that's created on-the-fly.[*] Over the next several decades, the idea survived quietly in mathematics and computer science journals. These days, in Java 8, the term *lambda expression* represents a short piece of code that serves as both a method declaration and a method call, all created on-the-fly.

A dirt-simple lambda expression

Here's an example of a lambda expression:

```
(sale) -> sale.price
```

Figure 12-7 describes the lambda expression's meaning.

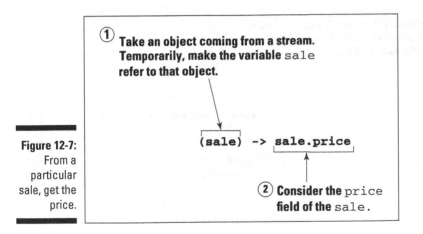

Figure 12-7:
From a
particular
sale, get the
price.

(1) **Take an object coming from a stream. Temporarily, make the variable** `sale` **refer to that object.**

`(sale) -> sale.price`

(2) **Consider the** `price` **field of the** `sale`.

---

[*] I attended a lecture given by Alonzo Church many years ago at the University of Illinois. He was the world's most meticulous presenter. Every detail of his lecture was carefully planned and scrupulously executed. He handed out paper copies of his notes, and I spent half the lecture staring at the notes, trying to decide whether the notes were hand-written or typed.

A lambda expression is a concise way of defining a method and calling the method without even giving the method a name. The lambda expression in Figure 12-7 does (roughly) what the following code does:

```
double getPrice(Sale sale) {
    return sale.price;
}

getPrice(sale);
```

(Remember, the `Sale` class in Listing 12-3 has no `getPrice` method of its own.) The lambda expression in Figure 12-7 takes objects from a stream and calls a method resembling `getPrice` on each object. The result is a new stream — a stream of `double` values.

A more interesting example

Here's another lambda expression:

```
(sale) -> sale.item.equals("DVD")
```

Figure 12-8 describes the lambda expression's meaning.

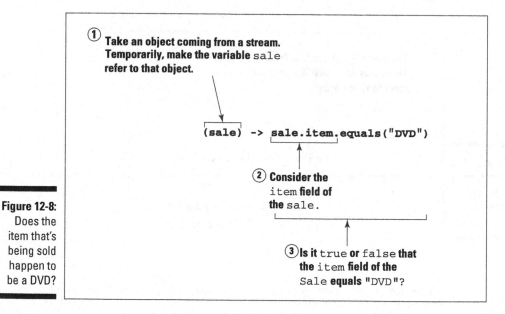

The lambda expression in Figure 12-8 does (roughly) what the following code does:

```
boolean itemIsDVD(Sale sale) {
    if sale.item.equals("DVD") {
        return true;
    } else {
        return false;
    }
}

itemIsDVD(sale);
```

The lambda expression in Figure 12-8 takes objects from a stream and calls a method resembling `itemIsDVD` on each object. The result is a bunch of `boolean` values — `true` for each sale of a DVD and `false` for a sale of something other than a DVD.

With or without lambda expressions, you can rewrite the `itemIsDVD` method with a one-line body:

```
boolean itemIsDVD(Sale sale) {
    return sale.item.equals("DVD");
}
```

A lambda expression with two parameters

Consider the following lambda expression:

```
(price1, price2) -> price1 + price2
```

Figure 12-9 describes the new lambda expression's meaning.

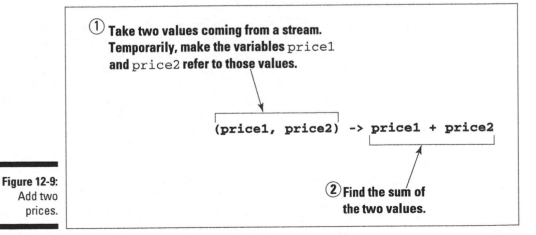

Figure 12-9:
Add two
prices.

① **Take two values coming from a stream.
Temporarily, make the variables** price1
and price2 **refer to those values.**

(price1, price2) -> price1 + price2

② **Find the sum of
the two values.**

The lambda expression in Figure 12-9 does (roughly) what the following code does:

```
double sum(double price1, double price2) {
    return price1 + price2;
}

sum(price1, price2);
```

The lambda expression in Figure 12-9 takes values from a stream and calls a method resembling sum to combine the values. The result is the total of all prices.

The black sheep of lambda expressions

Here's an interesting lambda expression:

```
(sale) -> System.out.println(sale.price)
```

This lambda expression does (roughly) what the following code does:

```
void display(Sale sale) {
    System.out.println(sale.price);
}

display(sale);
```

The lambda expression takes objects from a stream and calls a method resembling display on each object. In the display method's header, the word void indicates that the method doesn't return a value. When you call the display method (or you use the equivalent lambda expression), you don't expect to get back a value. Instead, you expect the code to do something in response to the call (something like displaying text on the computer's screen).

To draw a sharp distinction between returning a value and "doing something," functional programmers have a name for "doing something without returning a value." They call that something a *side effect*. In functional programming, a side effect is considered a second-class citizen, a last resort, a tactic that you use when you can't simply return a result. Unfortunately, displaying information on a screen (something that so many computer programs do) is a side effect. Any program that displays output (on a screen, on paper, or as tea leaves in a cup) isn't a purely functional program.

A taxonomy of lambda expressions

Java 8 divides lambda expressions into about 45 different categories. Table 12-2 lists a few of the categories.

Table 12-2	A Few Kinds of Lambda Expressions	
Name	*Description*	*Example*
Function	Accepts one parameter; produces a result of any type	`(sale) -> sale.price`
Predicate	Accepts one parameter; produces a `boolean` valued result	`(sale) -> sale.item.equals("DVD")`
BinaryOperator	Accepts two parameters of the same type; produces a result of the same type	`(price1, price2) -> price1 + price2`
Consumer	Accepts one parameter; produces no result	`(sale) -> System.out.println(sale.price)`

The categories in Table 12-2 aren't mutually exclusive. For example, every `Predicate` is a `Function`. (Every `Predicate` accepts one parameter and returns a result. The result happens to be `boolean`.)

Using streams and lambda expressions

Java 8 has fancy methods that make optimal use of streams and lambda expressions. With streams and lambda expressions, you can create an assembly line that elegantly solves this chapter's sales problem. Unlike the code in Listing 12-4, the new assembly line solution uses concepts from functional programming.

The assembly line consists of several methods. Each method takes the data, transforms the data in some way or other, and hands its results to the next method in line. Figure 12-10 illustrates the assembly line for this chapter's sales problem.

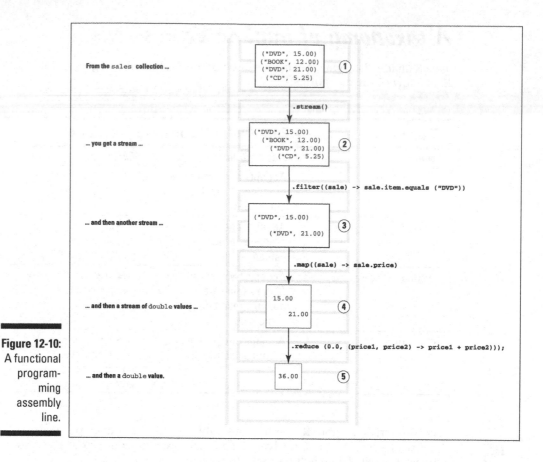

From the `sales` collection ...

```
("DVD", 15.00)
("BOOK", 12.00)
("DVD", 21.00)
("CD", 5.25)
```
①

`.stream()`

... you get a stream ...

```
("DVD", 15.00)
("BOOK", 12.00)
("DVD", 21.00)
("CD", 5.25)
```
②

`.filter((sale) -> sale.item.equals ("DVD"))`

... and then another stream ...

```
("DVD", 15.00)

("DVD", 21.00)
```
③

`.map((sale) -> sale.price)`

... and then a stream of `double` values ...

```
15.00

21.00
```
④

`.reduce (0.0, (price1, price2) -> price1 + price2)));`

... and then a `double` value.

```
36.00
```
⑤

Figure 12-10:
A functional
program-
ming
assembly
line.

In Figure 12-10, each box represents a bunch of raw materials as they're transformed along an assembly line. Each arrow represents a method (or metaphorically, a worker on the assembly line).

For example, in the transition from the second box to the third box, a worker method (the `filter` method) sifts out sales of items that aren't DVDs. Imagine Lucy Ricardo standing between the second and third boxes, removing each book or CD from the assembly line and tossing it carelessly onto the floor.

The parameter to Java's `filter` method is a `Predicate` — a lambda expression whose result is `boolean`. (See Tables 12-2 and 12-3.) The `filter` method in Figure 12-10 sifts out items that don't pass the lambda expression's `true`/`false` test.

For some help understanding the words in the third column of Table 12-3 (`Predicate`, `Function` and `BinaryOperator`), see the preceding section, "A taxonomy of lambda expressions."

Table 12-3	Some Functional Programming Methods			
Method Name	*Member Of*	*Parameter(s)*	*Result Type*	*Result Value*
`stream`	`Collection` (for example, an `ArrayList` object)	(none)	`Stream`	A stream that spits out elements of the collection
`filter`	`Stream`	`Predicate`	`Stream`	A new stream containing values for which the lambda expression returns `true`
`map`	`Stream`	`Function`	`Stream`	A new stream containing the results of applying the lambda expression to the incoming stream
`reduce`	`Stream`	`Binary Operator`	The type used by the `Binary Operator`	The result of combining all the values in the incoming stream

In Figure 12-10, in the transition from the third box to the fourth box, a worker method (the `map` method) pulls the `price` out of each `sale`. From that worker's place onward, the assembly line contains only `price` values.

To be more precise, Java's `map` method takes a `Function` such as

```
(sale) -> sale.price
```

and applies the `Function` to each value in a stream. (See Tables 12-2 and 12-3.) So the `map` method in Figure 12-10 takes an incoming stream of `sale` objects and creates an outgoing stream of `price` values.

In Figure 12-10, in the transition from the fourth box to the fifth box, a worker method (the `reduce` method) adds up the prices of DVD sales. Java's `reduce` method takes two parameters:

✔ The first parameter is an initial value.

In Figure 12-10, the initial value is `0.0`.

✔ The second parameter is a `BinaryOperator`. (See Tables 12-2 and 12-3.)
In Figure 12-10, the `reduce` method's `BinaryOperator` is

```
(price1, price2) -> price1 + price2
```

The `reduce` method uses its `BinaryOperator` to combine the values from the incoming stream. The initial value serves as the starting point for all the combining. So, in Figure 12-10, the `reduce` method does two additions. (See Figure 12-11.)

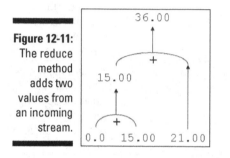

Figure 12-11: The reduce method adds two values from an incoming stream.

For comparison, imagine calling the method

```
reduce(10.0, (value1, value2) -> value1 * value2)
```

with the stream whose values include 3.0, 2.0, and 5.0. The resulting action is shown in Figure 12-12.

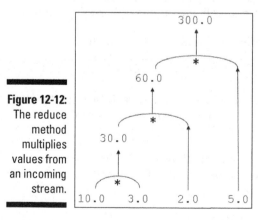

Figure 12-12: The reduce method multiplies values from an incoming stream.

You might have heard of Google's MapReduce programming model. The similarity between the programming model's name and the Java method names `map` and `reduce` is not a coincidence.

Taken as a whole, the entire assembly line shown in Figure 12-10 adds up the prices of DVDs sold. Listing 12-5 contains a complete program using the streams and lambda expressions of Figure 12-10.

Listing 12-5:   Living the Functional Way of Life

```
import java.text.NumberFormat;
import java.util.ArrayList;

public class TallySales {

    public static void main(String[] args) {
        ArrayList<Sale> sales = new ArrayList<Sale>();
        NumberFormat currency =
            NumberFormat.getCurrencyInstance();

        fillTheList(sales);
        System.out.println(currency.format(
        sales.stream()
            .filter((sale) -> sale.item.equals("DVD"))
            .map((sale) -> sale.price)
            .reduce
            (0.0, (price1, price2) -> price1 + price2)));
    }

    static void fillTheList(ArrayList<Sale> sales) {
        sales.add(new Sale("DVD", 15.00));
        sales.add(new Sale("Book", 12.00));
        sales.add(new Sale("DVD", 21.00));
        sales.add(new Sale("CD", 5.25));
    }
}
```

The boldface code in Listing 12-5 is one big Java statement. The statement is a sequence of method calls. Each method call returns an object, and each such object is the thing before the dot in the next method call. That's how you form the assembly line.

For example, at the start of the boldface code, the name `sales` refers to an `ArrayList` object. Each `ArrayList` object has a `stream` method. So in Listing 12-5, `sales.stream()` is a call to that `ArrayList` object's `stream` method.

The `stream` method returns an instance of Java's `Stream` class. (What a surprise!) So `sales.stream()` refers to a `Stream` object. (See Figure 12-13.)

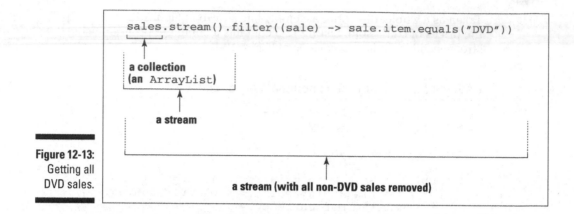

Figure 12-13: Getting all DVD sales.

Every `Stream` object has a `filter` method. So `sales.stream().filter ((sale) -> sale.item.equals("DVD"))` is a call to the `Stream` object's `filter` method. (Refer to Figure 12-13.)

The pattern continues. The `Stream` object's `map` method returns yet another `Stream` object — a `Stream` object containing prices. (See Figure 12-14.) To that `Stream` of prices you apply the `reduce` method, which yields one `double` value — the total of the DVD prices. (See Figure 12-15.)

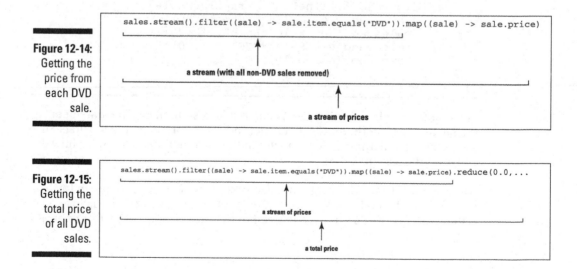

Figure 12-14: Getting the price from each DVD sale.

Figure 12-15: Getting the total price of all DVD sales.

Why bother?

The chain of method calls in Listing 12-5 accomplishes everything that the loop in Listing 12-4 accomplishes. But the code in Figure 12-15 uses concepts from functional programming. So what's the big deal? Are you better off with Listing 12-5 than with Listing 12-4?

You are. For the past several years, the big trend in chip design has been multicore processors. With several cores, a processor can execute several statements at once, speeding up a program's execution by a factor of 2, or 4 or 8, or even more. Programs run much faster if you divide the work among several cores. But how do you divide the work?

You can modify the imperative code in Listing 12-4. For example, with some fancy features, you can hand different loop iterations to different cores. But the resulting code is very messy. For the code to work properly, you have to micromanage the loop iterations, checking carefully to make sure that the final `total` is correct.

In contrast, the functional code is easy to modify. To take advantage of multi-core processors, you change *only one word* in Listing 12-5!

```
sales.parallelStream()
   .filter((sale) -> sale.item.equals("DVD"))
   .map((sale) -> sale.price)
   .reduce
      (0.0, (price1, price2) -> price1 + price2)
```

A *parallel stream* is like an ordinary stream except that a parallel stream's objects aren't processed in any particular order. A parallel stream's values don't depend on one another, so you can process several of the values at the same time. If your processor has more than one core (and most processors do these days) you can divide the stream's values among the available cores. Each core works independently of the others, and each core dumps its result into a final `reduce` method. The `reduce` method combines the cores' results into a final tally, and your answer is computed in lightning-fast time. It's a win for everyone.

Method references

Take a critical look at the last lambda expression in Listing 12-5:

```
(price1, price2) -> price1 + price2
```

No variables? No problem!

Consider the problems posed at the start of the "New in Java 8: Functional Programming" section. Several clients try to update Oracle's stock price at the same time, or two visitors try to buy the same item on a website. The source of the problem is *shared data.* How many clients share access to Oracle's stock price? How many customers share access to a web page's Purchase button? How many of your processor's cores can modify the same variable's value? If you get rid of data sharing, your multicore processing problems go away.

In imperative programming, a variable is a place where statements share their values with one another. Can you avoid using variables in your code?

Compare the loop in Listing 12-4 with the functional programming code in Listing 12-5. In Listing 12-4, the `total` variable is shared among all loop iterations. Because each iteration can potentially change the value of `total`, you can't assign each iteration to a different processor core. If you did, you'd risk having two cores updating the total at once. (Chances are good that, because of the simultaneous updating, neither core would do its update correctly!) But the functional programming code in Listing 12-5 has no `total` variable. A running total plays no role in the functional version of the code. Instead, in Listing 12-5, the `reduce` method applies the sum operation to values coming from a stream. This incoming stream pops out of the previous method call (the `map` method), so the incoming stream has no name. That's nice. You don't even need a variable to store a stream of values.

In imperative programming, a variable is a place where statements share their values with one another. But functional programming shuns variables. So, when you do functional programming, you don't have a lot of data sharing. Many of the difficulties associated with multicore processors vanish into thin air. Your code can take advantage of many cores at once. When you write the code, you don't worry about data being shared among the cores. It's an elegant solution to an important computing problem.

This expression does roughly the same work as a `sum` method. (In fact, you can find a `sum` method's declaration in the earlier "Lambda expressions" section.) If your choice is between typing a three-line `sum` method and typing a one-line lambda expression, you'll probably choose the lambda expression. But what if you have a third alternative? Instead of typing your own `sum` method, you can refer to an existing `sum` method. Using an existing method is the quickest and safest thing to do.

As luck would have it, Java 8 has a class named `Double`. The `Double` class contains a static `sum` method. You don't have to create your own `sum` method. If you run the following code:

```
double i = 5.0, j = 7.0;
System.out.println(Double.sum(i, j));
```

the computer displays `12.0`. So, instead of typing the `price1 + price2` lambda expression in Listing 12-5, you can create a *method reference* — an expression that refers to an existing method.

```
sales.stream()
    .filter((sale) -> sale.item.equals("DVD"))
    .map((sale) -> sale.price)
    .reduce(0.0, Double::sum)
```

The expression Double::sum refers to the sum method belonging to Java's Double class. When you use this Double::sum method reference, you do the same thing that the last lambda expression does in Listing 12-5. Everybody is happy.

For information about static methods, see Chapter 10.

Java's Double class is a lot like the Integer class that I describe in Chapter 11. The Double class has methods and other tools for dealing with double values.

Chapter 13

Looking Good When Things Take Unexpected Turns

*S*eptember 9, 1945: A moth flies into one of the relays of the Harvard Mark II computer and gums up the works. This becomes the first recorded case of a real computer bug.

April 19, 1957: Herbert Bright, manager of the data processing center at Westinghouse in Pittsburgh, receives an unmarked deck of computer punch cards in the mail (which is like getting an unlabeled CD-ROM in the mail today). Mr. Bright guesses that this deck comes from the development team for FORTRAN — the first computer programming language. He's been waiting a few years for this software. (No web downloads were available at the time.)

Armed with nothing but this good guess, Bright writes a small FORTRAN program and tries to compile it on his IBM 704. (The IBM 704 lives in its own specially built, 2,000-square-foot room. With vacuum tubes instead of transistors, the machine has a whopping 32K of RAM. The operating system has to be loaded from tape before the running of each program, and a typical program takes between two and four hours to run.) After the usual waiting time, Bright's attempt to compile a FORTRAN program comes back with a single error — a missing comma in one of the statements. Bright corrects the error, and the program runs like a charm.

July 22, 1962: Mariner I, the first U.S. spacecraft aimed at another planet, is destroyed when it behaves badly four minutes after launch. The bad behavior is attributed to a missing bar (like a hyphen) in the formula for the rocket's velocity.

Around the same time, orbit computation software at NASA is found to contain the incorrect statement `DO 10 I=1.10` (instead of the correct `DO 10 I=1,10`). In modern notation, this is like writing `do10i = 1.10` in place of `for (int i=1; i<=10; i++)`. The change from a comma to a period turns a loop into an assignment statement.

January 1, 2000: The Year 2000 Problem wreaks havoc on the modern world.

Any historically accurate facts in these notes were borrowed from the following sources: the Computer Folklore newsgroup (`https://groups.google.com/d/forum/alt.folklore.computers`), the Free On-line Dictionary of Computing (`http://foldoc.org`), the "Looking Back" column in *Computer Now* (`http://www.computer.org/portal/web/computingnow/computer`), and the web pages of the IEEE (`www.computer.org`).

Handling Exceptions

You're taking inventory. This means counting item after item, box after box, and marking the numbers of such things on log sheets, in little handheld gizmos, and into forms on computer keyboards. A particular part of the project involves entering the number of boxes that you find on the Big Dusty Boxes That Haven't Been Opened Since Year One shelf. Rather than break the company's decades-old habit, you decide not to open any of these boxes. You arbitrarily assign the value $3.25 to each box.

Listing 13-1 shows the software to handle this bit of inventory. The software has a flaw, which is revealed in Figure 13-1. When the user enters a whole number value, things are okay. But when the user enters something else (like the number 3.5), the program comes crashing to the ground. Surely something can be done about this. Computers are stupid, but they're not so stupid that they should fail royally when a user enters an improper value.

Listing 13-1: Counting Boxes

```
import static java.lang.System.out;
import java.util.Scanner;
import java.text.NumberFormat;

public class InventoryA {

    public static void main(String args[]) {
        final double boxPrice = 3.25;
        Scanner keyboard = new Scanner(System.in);
```

```
NumberFormat currency =
    NumberFormat.getCurrencyInstance();

out.print("How many boxes do we have? ");
String numBoxesIn = keyboard.next();
int numBoxes = Integer.parseInt(numBoxesIn);

out.print("The value is ");
out.println(currency.format(numBoxes * boxPrice));
keyboard.close();
    }
}
```

```
How many boxes do we have? 3
The value is $9.75

How many boxes do we have? 3.5
Exception in thread "main" java.lang.NumberFormatException: For input string: "3.5"
        at java.lang.NumberFormatException.forInputString(Unknown Source)
        at java.lang.Integer.parseInt(Unknown Source)
        at java.lang.Integer.parseInt(Unknown Source)
        at InventoryA.main(InventoryA.java:15)

How many boxes do we have? three
Exception in thread "main" java.lang.NumberFormatException: For input string: "three"
        at java.lang.NumberFormatException.forInputString(Unknown Source)
        at java.lang.Integer.parseInt(Unknown Source)
        at java.lang.Integer.parseInt(Unknown Source)
        at InventoryA.main(InventoryA.java:15)
```

Figure 13-1:
Three sepa-
rate runs of
the code in
Listing 13-1.

The key to fixing a program bug is examining the message that appears when the program crashes. The inventory program's message says `java.lang.NumberFormatException`. That means a class named *NumberFormatException* is in the `java.lang` API package. Somehow, the call to `Integer.parseInt` brought this `NumberFormatException` class out of hiding.

For a brief explanation of the `Integer.parseInt` method, see Chapter 11.

Well, here's what's going on. The Java programming language has a mechanism called *exception handling*. With exception handling, a program can detect that things are about to go wrong and respond by creating a brand-new object. In the official terminology, the program is said to be *throwing* an exception. That new object, an instance of the `Exception` class, is passed like a hot potato from one piece of code to another until some piece of code decides to *catch* the exception. When the exception is caught, the program executes some recovery code, buries the exception, and moves on to the next normal statement as if nothing had ever happened. The process is illustrated in Figure 13-2.

The whole thing is done with the aid of several Java keywords. These keywords are as follows:

- ✔ throw: Creates a new exception object.

- ✔ throws: Passes the buck from a method up to whatever code called the method.

- ✔ try: Encloses code that has the potential to create a new exception object. In the usual scenario, the code inside a try clause contains calls to methods whose code can create one or more exceptions.

- ✔ catch: Deals with the exception, buries it, and then moves on.

So, the truth is out. Through some chain of events like the one shown in Figure 13-2, the method Integer.parseInt can throw a NumberFormat Exception. When you call Integer.parseInt, this NumberFormat Exception is passed on to you.

The Java API (Application Programming Interface) documentation for the parseInt method says, "Throws: NumberFormatException — if the string does not contain a parsable integer." Once in a while, reading the documentation actually pays.

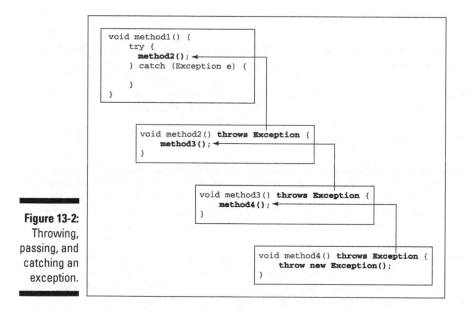

Figure 13-2:
Throwing, passing, and catching an exception.

```
void method1() {
    try {
        method2();  ◀
    } catch (Exception e) {

    }
}
```

```
void method2() throws Exception {
    method3();  ◀
}
```

```
void method3() throws Exception {
    method4();  ◀
}
```

```
void method4() throws Exception {
    throw new Exception();
}
```

If you call yourself a hero, you'd better catch the exception so that all the other code can get on with its regular business. Listing 13-2 shows the catching of an exception.

Listing 13-2:   A Hero Counts Boxes

```java
import static java.lang.System.out;
import java.util.Scanner;
import java.text.NumberFormat;

public class InventoryB {

    public static void main(String args[]) {
        final double boxPrice = 3.25;
        Scanner keyboard = new Scanner(System.in);
        NumberFormat currency =
            NumberFormat.getCurrencyInstance();

        out.print("How many boxes do we have? ");
        String numBoxesIn = keyboard.next();

        try {
            int numBoxes = Integer.parseInt(numBoxesIn);
            out.print("The value is ");
            out.println(
                currency.format(numBoxes * boxPrice));
        } catch (NumberFormatException e) {
            out.println("That's not a number.");
        }

        keyboard.close();
    }
}
```

Figure 13-3 shows three runs of the code from Listing 13-2. When a misguided user types **three** instead of **3**, the program maintains its cool by displaying That's not a number. The trick is to enclose the call to Integer.parse Int inside a try clause. If you do this, the computer watches for exceptions when any statement inside the try clause is executed. If an exception is thrown, the computer jumps from inside the try clause to a catch clause below it. In Listing 13-2, the computer jumps directly to the catch (Number FormatException e) clause. The computer executes the println statement inside the clause and then marches on with normal processing. (If there were statements in Listing 13-2 after the end of the catch clause, the computer would go on and execute them.)

Figure 13-3:
Three
runs of
the code in
Listing 13-2.

```
How many boxes do we have? 3
The value is $9.75

How many boxes do we have? three
That's not a number.

How many boxes do we have? -25
The value is ($81.25)
```

An entire `try-catch` assembly — complete with a `try` clause, `catch` clause, and what have you — is called a *try statement*. Sometimes, for emphasis, I call it a *try-catch statement*.

The parameter in a catch clause

Take a look at the `catch` clause in Listing 13-2 and pay particular attention to the words `(NumberFormatException e)`. This looks a lot like a method's parameter list, doesn't it? In fact, every `catch` clause is like a little mini-method with its own parameter list. The parameter list always has an exception type name and then a parameter.

In Listing 13-2, I don't do anything with the `catch` clause's e parameter, but I certainly could if I wanted to. Remember, the exception that's thrown is an object — an instance of the `NumberFormatException` class. When an exception is caught, the computer makes the `catch` clause's parameter refer to that exception object. In other words, the name *e* stores a bunch of information about the exception. To take advantage of this, you can call some of the exception object's methods.

```
} catch (NumberFormatException e) {
    out.println("Message: ***" + e.getMessage() + "***");
    e.printStackTrace();
}
```

With this new `catch` clause, a run of the `inventory` program may look like the run shown in Figure 13-4. When you call `getMessage`, you fetch some detail about the exception. (In Figure 13-4, the detail is `Message: ***For input string: "three"***`.) When you call `printStackTrace`, you get some additional information; namely, a display showing the methods that were running at the moment when the exception was thrown. (In Figure 13-4, the display includes `Integer.parseInt` and the `main` method.) Both `getMessage` and `printStackTrace` present information to help you find the source of the program's difficulties.

Figure 13-4:
Calling an exception object's methods.

```
How many boxes do we have? three
Message: ***For input string: "three"***
java.lang.NumberFormatException: For input string: "three"
        at java.lang.NumberFormatException.forInputString(Unknown Source)
        at java.lang.Integer.parseInt(Unknown Source)
        at java.lang.Integer.parseInt(Unknown Source)
        at InventoryB.main(InventoryB.java:17)
```

When you mix `System.out.println` calls with `printStackTrace` calls, the order in which Java displays the information is not predictable. For example, in Figure 13-4, the text `Message: ***For input string: "three"***` may appear before or after the stack trace. If the ordering of this output matters to you, change `out.println("Message: ***"` to `System.err.println("Message: ***"`.

Exception types

So what else can go wrong today? Are there other kinds of exceptions — things that don't come from the `NumberFormatException` class? Sure, plenty of different exception types are out there. You can even create one of your own. You wanna try? If so, look at Listings 13-3 and 13-4.

Listing 13-3: Making Your Own Kind of Exception

```
@SuppressWarnings("serial")
class OutOfRangeException extends Exception {
}
```

Listing 13-4: Using Your Custom Made Exception

```
import static java.lang.System.out;
import java.util.Scanner;
import java.text.NumberFormat;

public class InventoryC {

    public static void main(String args[]) {
        final double boxPrice = 3.25;
        Scanner keyboard = new Scanner(System.in);
        NumberFormat currency =
            NumberFormat.getCurrencyInstance();

        out.print("How many boxes do we have? ");
        String numBoxesIn = keyboard.next();

        try {
            int numBoxes = Integer.parseInt(numBoxesIn);

            if (numBoxes < 0) {
                throw new OutOfRangeException();
            }

            out.print("The value is ");
            out.println(
                currency.format(numBoxes * boxPrice));
        } catch (NumberFormatException e) {
```

(continued)

Listing 13-4 *(continued)*

```
      out.println("That's not a number.");
   } catch (OutOfRangeException e) {
      out.print(numBoxesIn);
      out.println("? That's impossible!");
   }

   keyboard.close();
}
}
```

Listings 13-3 and 13-4 remedy a problem that cropped up in Figure 13-3. Look at the last of the three runs in Figure 13-3. The user reports that the shelves have –25 boxes, and the computer takes this value without blinking an eye. The truth is that you would need a black hole (or some other exotic space-time warping phenomenon) to have a negative number of boxes on any shelf in your warehouse. So the program should get upset if the user enters a negative number of boxes, which is what the code in Listing 13-4 does. To see the upset code, look at Figure 13-5.

Figure 13-5:
Three
runs of the
code from
Listings 13-3
and 13-4.

```
How many boxes do we have? 3
The value is $9.75

How many boxes do we have? three
That's not a number.

How many boxes do we have? -25
-25? That's impossible!
```

The code in Listing 13-3 declares a new kind of exception class — OutOf RangeException. In many situations, typing a negative number would be just fine, so OutOfRangeException isn't built in to the Java API. However, in the inventory program, a negative number should be flagged as an anomaly.

The OutOfRangeException class in Listing 13-3 wins the award for the shortest self-contained piece of code in the book. The class's code is just a declaration line and an empty pair of braces. The code's operative phrase is extends Exception. Being a subclass of the Java API Exception class allows any instance of the OutOfRangeException class to be thrown.

Back in Listing 13-4, a new OutOfRangeException instance is thrown. When this happens, the catch clause (OutOfRangeException e) catches the instance. The clause echoes the user's input and displays the message That's impossible!

The text @SuppressWarnings("serial") in Listing 13-3 is a Java annotation. For an introduction to annotations, see Chapter 8. For a few words about the SuppressWarnings annotation, see Chapter 9.

If you use Eclipse, you might see a yellow warning marker next to the throw new OutOfRangeException() line in Listing 13-4. When you hover your pointer over the warning marker, Eclipse says, "Resource leak: 'keyboard' is not closed at this location." Eclipse is being very fussy to make sure that your code eventually executes the keyboard.close() statement. (Yes, under certain circumstances, throwing your OutOfRangeException can cause the program to skip the keyboard.close() statement. But no, that can't happen when you run the code in Listing 13-4.) In my opinion, you can safely ignore this warning.

Who's going to catch the exception?

Take one more look at Listing 13-4. Notice that more than one catch clause can accompany a single try clause. When an exception is thrown inside a try clause, the computer starts going down the accompanying list of catch clauses. The computer starts at whatever catch clause comes immediately after the try clause and works its way down the program's text.

For each catch clause, the computer asks itself, "Is the exception that was just thrown an instance of the class in this clause's parameter list?"

- ✔ If not, the computer skips this catch clause and moves on to the next catch clause in line.

- ✔ If so, the computer executes this catch clause and then skips past all the other catch clauses that come with this try clause. The computer goes on and executes whatever statements come after the whole try-catch statement.

For some concrete examples, see Listings 13-5 and 13-6.

Listing 13-5:   Yet Another Exception

```
@SuppressWarnings("serial")
class NumberTooLargeException
                    extends OutOfRangeException {
}
```

Listing 13-6:   Where Does the Buck Stop?

```java
import static java.lang.System.out;
import java.util.Scanner;
import java.text.NumberFormat;

public class InventoryD {

    public static void main(String args[]) {
        final double boxPrice = 3.25;
        Scanner keyboard = new Scanner(System.in);
        NumberFormat currency =
            NumberFormat.getCurrencyInstance();

        out.print("How many boxes do we have? ");
        String numBoxesIn = keyboard.next();

        try {
            int numBoxes = Integer.parseInt(numBoxesIn);

            if (numBoxes < 0) {
                throw new OutOfRangeException();
            }

            if (numBoxes > 1000) {
                throw new NumberTooLargeException();
            }

            out.print("The value is ");
            out.println(
                currency.format(numBoxes * boxPrice));
        }

        catch (NumberFormatException e) {
            out.println("That's not a number.");
        }

        catch (OutOfRangeException e) {
            out.print(numBoxesIn);
            out.println("? That's impossible!");
        }

        catch (Exception e) {
            out.print("Something went wrong, ");
            out.print("but I'm clueless about what ");
            out.println("it actually was.");
        }

        out.println("That's that.");

        keyboard.close();
    }
}
```

To run the code in Listings 13-5 and 13-6, you need one additional Java program file. You need the `OutOfRangeException` class in Listing 13-3.

Listing 13-6 addresses the scenario in which you have limited shelf space. You don't have room for more than 1,000 boxes, but once in a while the program asks how many boxes you have, and somebody enters the number _100000_ by accident. In cases like this, Listing 13-6 does a quick reality check. Any number of boxes over 1,000 is tossed out as being unrealistic.

Listing 13-6 watches for a `NumberTooLargeException`, but to make life more interesting, Listing 13-6 doesn't have a `catch` clause for the `Number TooLargeException`. In spite of this, everything still works out just fine. It's fine because `NumberTooLargeException` is declared to be a subclass of `OutOfRangeException`, and Listing 13-6 has a `catch` clause for the `OutOfRangeException`.

You see, because `NumberTooLargeException` is a subclass of `OutOfRange Exception`, any instance of `NumberTooLargeException` is just a special kind of `OutOfRangeException`. So in Listing 13-6, the computer may start looking for a clause to catch a `NumberTooLargeException`. When the computer stumbles upon the `OutOfRangeException` catch clause, the computer says, "Okay, I've found a match. I'll execute the statements in this `catch` clause."

To keep from having to write this whole story over and over again, I introduce some new terminology. I say that the `catch` clause with parameter `OutOfRangeException` _matches_ the `NumberTooLargeException` that's been thrown. I call this `catch` clause a _matching catch clause._

The following bullets describe different things that the user may do and how the computer responds. As you read through the bullets, you can follow along by looking at the runs shown in Figure 13-6.

Figure 13-6:
Four runs
of the
code from
Listing 13-6.

```
How many boxes do we have? 3
The value is $9.75
That's that.

How many boxes do we have? fish
That's not a number.
That's that.

How many boxes do we have? -25
-25? That's impossible!
That's that.

How many boxes do we have? 1001
1001? That's impossible!
That's that.
```

✔ **The user enters an ordinary whole number, like the number _3_.** All the statements in the `try` clause are executed. Then the computer skips past all the `catch` clauses and executes the code that comes immediately after all the `catch` clauses. (See Figure 13-7.)

✔ **The user enters something that's not a whole number, like the word** *fish.* The code throws a `NumberFormatException`. The computer skips past the remaining statements in the `try` clause. The computer executes the statements inside the first `catch` clause — the clause whose parameter is of type `NumberFormatException`. Then the computer skips past the second and third `catch` clauses and executes the code that comes immediately after all the `catch` clauses. (See Figure 13-8.)

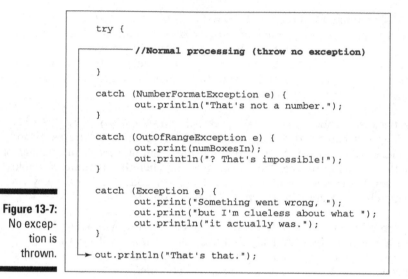

```
try {

        //Normal processing (throw no exception)

    }

    catch (NumberFormatException e) {
        out.println("That's not a number.");
    }

    catch (OutOfRangeException e) {
        out.print(numBoxesIn);
        out.println("? That's impossible!");
    }

    catch (Exception e) {
        out.print("Something went wrong, ");
        out.print("but I'm clueless about what ");
        out.println("it actually was.");
    }

    out.println("That's that.");
```

Figure 13-7:
No exception is thrown.

```
try {

        throw new NumberFormatException ();

    }

    catch (NumberFormatException e) {
        out.println("That's not a number.");
    }

    catch (OutOfRangeException e) {
        out.print(numBoxesIn);
        out.println("? That's impossible!");
    }

    catch (Exception e) {
        out.print("Something went wrong, ");
        out.print("but I'm clueless about what ");
        out.println("it actually was.");
    }

    out.println("That's that.");
```

Figure 13-8:
A Number Format Exception is thrown.

✔ **The user enters a negative number, like the number –25.** The code throws an `OutOfRangeException`. The computer skips past the remaining statements in the `try` clause. The computer even skips past the statements in the first `catch` clause. (After all, an `OutOfRangeException` isn't any kind of a `NumberFormatException`. The `catch` clause with parameter `NumberFormatException` isn't a match for this `OutOfRangeException`.) The computer executes the statements inside the second `catch` clause — the clause whose parameter is of type `OutOfRangeException`. Then the computer skips past the third `catch` clause and executes the code that comes immediately after all the `catch` clauses. (See Figure 13-9.)

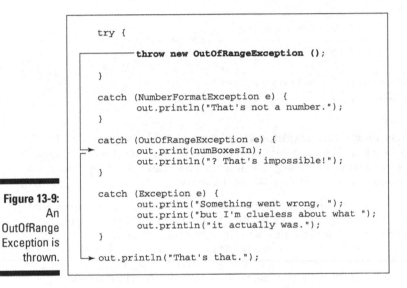

```
      try {

                   throw new OutOfRangeException ();

      }

      catch (NumberFormatException e) {
             out.println("That's not a number.");
      }

      catch (OutOfRangeException e) {
             out.print(numBoxesIn);
             out.println("? That's impossible!");
      }

      catch (Exception e) {
             out.print("Something went wrong, ");
             out.print("but I'm clueless about what ");
             out.println("it actually was.");
      }

      out.println("That's that.");
```

Figure 13-9:
An
OutOfRange
Exception is
thrown.

✔ **The user enters an unrealistically large number, like the number 1001.** The code throws a `NumberTooLargeException`. The computer skips past the remaining statements in the `try` clause. The computer even skips past the statements in the first `catch` clause. (After all, a `NumberTooLargeException` isn't any kind of `NumberFormat Exception`.)

But, according to the code in Listing 13-5, `NumberTooLargeException` is a subclass of `OutOfRangeException`. When the computer reaches the second `catch` clause, the computer says, "Hmm! A `NumberToo LargeException` is a kind of `OutOfRangeException`. I'll execute the statements in this `catch` clause — the clause with parameter of type `OutOfRangeException`." In other words, it's a match.

So, the computer executes the statements inside the second `catch` clause. Then the computer skips the third `catch` clause and executes the code that comes immediately after all the `catch` clauses. (See Figure 13-10.)

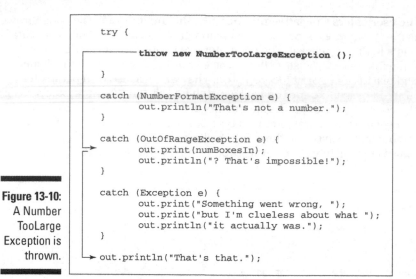

Figure 13-10:
A Number
TooLarge
Exception is
thrown.

```
    try {

            throw new NumberTooLargeException ();

    }

    catch (NumberFormatException e) {
            out.println("That's not a number.");
    }

    catch (OutOfRangeException e) {
            out.print(numBoxesIn);
            out.println("? That's impossible!");
    }

    catch (Exception e) {
            out.print("Something went wrong, ");
            out.print("but I'm clueless about what ");
            out.println("it actually was.");
    }

    out.println("That's that.");
```

✔ **Something else, something very unpredictable, happens. (I don't know what.)** With my unending urge to experiment, I reached into the `try` clause of Listing 13-6 and added a statement that throws an `IOException`. No reason — I just wanted to see what would happen.

When the code threw an `IOException`, the computer skipped past the remaining statements in the `try` clause. Then the computer skipped past the statements in the first and second `catch` clauses. When the computer reached the third `catch` clause, I could hear the computer say, "Hmm! An `IOException` is a kind of `Exception`. I've found a matching `catch` clause — a clause with a parameter of type `Exception`. I'll execute the statements in this `catch` clause."

So, the computer executed the statements inside the third `catch` clause. Then the computer executed the code that comes immediately after all the `catch` clauses. (See Figure 13-11.)

When the computer looks for a matching `catch` clause, the computer latches on to the topmost clause that fits one of the following descriptions:

✔ The clause's parameter type is the same as the type of the exception that was thrown.

✔ The clause's parameter type is a superclass of the exception's type.

```
    try {

┌───────throw new IOException ();

│       }

│       catch (NumberFormatException e) {
│           out.println("That's not a number.");
│       }

│       catch (OutOfRangeException e) {
│           out.print(numBoxesIn);
│           out.println("? That's impossible!");
│       }

│       catch (Exception e) {
│           out.print("Something went wrong, ");
│       ┌─  out.print("but I'm clueless about what ");
│       │   out.println("it actually was.");
│       │ }
└───────┼► out.println("That's that.");
```

Figure 13-11:
An
IOException
is thrown.

If a better match appears farther down the list of catch clauses, that's just too bad. For instance, imagine that you added a catch clause with a parameter of type NumberTooLargeException to the code in Listing 13-6. Imagine, also, that you put this new catch clause *after* the catch clause with parameter of type OutOfRangeException. Then, because NumberTooLargeException is a subclass of the OutOfRangeException class, the code in your new NumberTooLargeException clause would never be executed. That's just the way the cookie crumbles.

The multi-catch clause

Starting with Java 7, you can catch more than one kind of exception in a single catch clause. For example, in a particular inventory program, you might not want to distinguish between the throwing of a NumberFormatException and your own OutOfRangeException. In that case, you can rewrite part of Listing 13-6 as follows:

```
try {
    int numBoxes = Integer.parseInt(numBoxesIn);

    if (numBoxes < 0) {
        throw new OutOfRangeException();
    }

    if (numBoxes > 1000) {
        throw new NumberTooLargeException();
    }
```

```
    out.print("The value is ");
    out.println(
        currency.format(numBoxes * boxPrice));
}

catch (NumberFormatException | OutOfRangeException e) {
    out.print(numBoxesIn);
    out.println("? That's impossible!");
}

catch (Exception e) {
    out.print("Something went wrong, ");
    out.print("but I'm clueless about what ");
    out.println("it actually was.");
}
```

The pipe symbol, |, tells Java to catch either a NumberFormatException or an
OutOfRangeException. If you throw an exception of either type, the program
displays the value of numBoxesIn followed by the text ? That's impossible!
If you throw an exception that is neither a NumberFormatException nor an
OutOfRangeException, the program jumps to the last catch clause and
displays Something went wrong, but I'm clueless...

Throwing caution to the wind

Are you one of those obsessive-compulsive types? Do you like to catch every
possible exception before the exception can possibly crash your program?
Well, watch out. Java doesn't let you become paranoid. You can't catch an
exception if the exception has no chance of being thrown.

Consider the following code. The code has a very innocent i++ statement
inside a try clause. That's fair enough. But then the code's catch clause is
pretending to catch an IOException.

```
// Bad code!
try {
    i++;
} catch (IOException e) {
    e.printStackTrace();
}
```

Who is this catch clause trying to impress? A statement like i++ doesn't do
any input or output. The code inside the try clause can't possibly throw an
IOException. So the compiler comes back and says, "Hey, catch clause. Get
real. Get off your high horse." Well, to be a bit more precise, the compiler's
reprimand reads as follows:

```
exception java.io.IOException is never thrown in body of
            corresponding try statement
```

Doing useful things

So far, each example in this chapter catches an exception, prints a "bad input" message, and then closes up shop. Wouldn't it be nice to see a program that actually carries on after an exception has been caught? Well, it's time for something nice. Listing 13-7 has a `try-catch` statement inside a loop. The loop keeps running until the user types something sensible.

Listing 13-7:   Keep Pluggin' Along

```java
import static java.lang.System.out;
import java.util.Scanner;
import java.text.NumberFormat;

public class InventoryLoop {

    public static void main(String args[]) {
        final double boxPrice = 3.25;
        boolean gotGoodInput = false;
        Scanner keyboard = new Scanner(System.in);
        NumberFormat currency =
            NumberFormat.getCurrencyInstance();

        do {
            out.print("How many boxes do we have? ");
            String numBoxesIn = keyboard.next();

            try {
                int numBoxes = Integer.parseInt(numBoxesIn);
                out.print("The value is ");
                out.println
                    (currency.format(numBoxes * boxPrice));
                gotGoodInput = true;
            } catch (NumberFormatException e) {
                out.println();
                out.println("That's not a number.");
            }
        } while (!gotGoodInput);

        out.println("That's that.");

        keyboard.close();
    }
}
```

Figure 13-12 shows a run of the code from Listing 13-7. In the first three attempts, the user types just about everything except a valid whole number. At last, the fourth attempt is a success. The user types **3**, and the computer leaves the loop.

Figure 13-12:
A run of the
code in
Listing 13-7.

```
How many boxes do we have? 3.5

That's not a number.
How many boxes do we have? three

That's not a number.
How many boxes do we have? fish

That's not a number.
How many boxes do we have? 3
The value is $9.75
That's that.
```

Our friends, the good exceptions

A rumor is going around that Java exceptions always come from unwanted, erroneous situations. Although there's some truth to this rumor, the rumor isn't entirely accurate. Occasionally, an exception arises from a normal, expected occurrence. Take, for instance, the detection of the end of a file. The following code makes a copy of a file:

```
try {
    while (true) {
        dataOut.writeByte(dataIn.readByte());
    }
} catch (EOFException e) {
    numFilesCopied = 1;
}
```

To copy bytes from `dataIn` to `dataOut`, you just go into a `while` loop. With its `true` condition, the `while` loop is seemingly endless. But eventually, you reach the end of the `dataIn` file. When this happens, the `readByte` method throws an `EOFException` (an end-of-file exception). The throwing of this exception sends the computer out of the `try` clause and out of the `while` loop. From there, you do whatever you want to do in the `catch` clause and then proceed with normal processing.

Handle an Exception or Pass the Buck

So you're getting to know Java, hey? What? You say you're all the way up to Chapter 13? I'm impressed. You must be a hard worker. But remember, all work and no play. . . .

So, how about taking a break? A little nap could do you a world of good. Is ten seconds okay? Or is that too long? Better make it five seconds.

Listing 13-8 has a program that's supposed to pause its execution for five seconds. The problem is that the program in Listing 13-8 is incorrect. Take a look at Listing 13-8 for a minute, and then I'll tell you what's wrong with it.

Listing 13-8: An Incorrect Program

```
/*
 * This code does not compile.
 */

import static java.lang.System.out;

public class NoSleepForTheWeary {

    public static void main(String args[]) {
        out.print("Excuse me while I nap ");
        out.println("for just five seconds...");

        takeANap();

        out.println("Ah, that was refreshing.");
    }

    static void takeANap() {
        Thread.sleep(5000);
    }
}
```

The strategy in Listing 13-8 isn't bad. The idea is to call the `sleep` method, which is defined in the Java API. This `sleep` method belongs to the API `Thread` class. When you call the `sleep` method, the number that you feed it is a number of milliseconds. So, `Thread.sleep(5000)` means pause for five seconds.

The problem is that the code inside the `sleep` method can throw an exception. This kind of exception is an instance of the `InterruptedException` class. When you try to compile the code in Listing 13-8, you get a message such as

```
unreported exception java.lang.InterruptedException;
must be caught or declared to be thrown
```

Maybe the message reads

```
Unhandled exception type InterruptedException
```

One way or another, the message is unwelcome.

For the purpose of understanding exceptions in general, you don't need to know exactly what an `InterruptedException` is. All you really have to know is that a call to `Thread.sleep` can throw one of these `InterruptedException` objects. But if you're really curious, an `InterruptedException` is thrown when some code interrupts some other code's sleep. Imagine that you have two pieces of code running at the same time. One piece of code calls the `Thread.sleep` method. At the same time, another piece of code calls the `interrupt` method. By calling the `interrupt` method, the second piece of code brings the first code's `Thread.sleep` method to a screeching halt. The `Thread.sleep` method responds by spitting out an `InterruptedException`.

Now, the Java programming language has two kinds of exceptions. They're called *checked* and *unchecked* exceptions:

✔ The potential throwing of a checked exception must be acknowledged in the code.

✔ The potential throwing of an unchecked exception doesn't need to be acknowledged in the code.

An `InterruptedException` is one of Java's checked exception types. When you call a method that has the potential to throw an `InterruptedException`, you need to acknowledge that exception in the code.

Now, when I say that an exception is *acknowledged in the code,* what do I really mean?

```
// The author wishes to thank that InterruptedException,
// without which this code could not have been written.
```

No, that's not what it means to be acknowledged in the code. Acknowledging an exception in the code means one of two things:

✔ The statements (including method calls) that can throw the exception are inside a `try` clause. That `try` clause has a `catch` clause with a matching exception type in its parameter list.

✔ The statements (including method calls) that can throw the exception are inside a method that has a `throws` clause in its header. The `throws` clause contains a matching exception type.

If you're confused by the wording of these two bullets, don't worry. The next two listings illustrate the points made in the bullets.

In Listing 13-9, the method call that can throw an `InterruptedException` is inside a `try` clause. That `try` clause has a `catch` clause with exception type `InterruptedException`.

Listing 13-9:   Acknowledging with a try-catch Statement

```java
import static java.lang.System.out;

public class GoodNightsSleepA {

    public static void main(String args[]) {
        out.print("Excuse me while I nap ");
        out.println("for just five seconds...");

        takeANap();

        out.println("Ah, that was refreshing.");
    }

    static void takeANap() {
        try {
            Thread.sleep(5000);
        } catch (InterruptedException e) {
            out.println("Hey, who woke me up?");
        }
    }
}
```

It's my custom, at this point in a section, to remind you that a run of Listing Such-and-Such is shown in Figure So-and-So. But the problem here is that Figure 13-13 doesn't do justice to the code in Listing 13-9. When you run the program in Listing 13-9, the computer displays Excuse me while I nap for just five seconds, pauses for five seconds, and then displays Ah, that was refreshing. The code works because the call to the sleep method, which can throw an InterruptedException, is inside a try clause. That try clause has a catch clause whose exception is of type InterruptedException.

Figure 13-13:
There's a
five-second
pause
before the
"Ah" line.

```
Excuse me while I nap for just five seconds...
Ah, that was refreshing.
```

So much for acknowledging an exception with a try-catch statement. You can acknowledge an exception another way, shown in Listing 13-10.

Listing 13-10:   Acknowledging with throws

```java
import static java.lang.System.out;

public class GoodNightsSleepB {

    public static void main(String args[]) {
        out.print("Excuse me while I nap ");
        out.println("for just five seconds...");

        try {
            takeANap();
        } catch (InterruptedException e) {
            out.println("Hey, who woke me up?");
        }

        out.println("Ah, that was refreshing.");
    }

    static void takeANap() throws InterruptedException {
        Thread.sleep(5000);
    }
}
```

To see a run of the code in Listing 13-10, refer to Figure 13-13. Once again, Figure 13-13 fails to capture the true essence of the run, but that's okay. Just remember that in Figure 13-13, the computer pauses for five seconds before it displays Ah, that was refreshing.

The important part of Listing 13-10 is in the takeANap method's header. That header ends with throws InterruptedException. By announcing that it throws an InterruptedException, method takeANap passes the buck. What this throws clause really says is, "I realize that a statement inside this method has the potential to throw an InterruptedException, but I'm not acknowledging the exception in a try-catch statement. Java compiler, please don't bug me about this. Instead of having a try-catch statement, I'm passing the responsibility for acknowledging the exception to the main method (the method that called the takeANap method)."

Indeed, in the main method, the call to takeANap is inside a try clause. That try clause has a catch clause with a parameter of type Interrupted Exception. So everything is okay. Method takeANap passes the responsibility to the main method, and the main method accepts the responsibility with an appropriate try-catch statement. Everybody's happy. Even the Java compiler is happy.

To better understand the `throws` clause, imagine a volleyball game in which the volleyball is an exception. When a player on the other team serves, that player is throwing the exception. The ball crosses the net and comes right to you. If you pound the ball back across the net, you're catching the exception. But if you pass the ball to another player, you're using the `throws` clause. In essence, you're saying, "Here, other player. You deal with this exception."

A statement in a method can throw an exception that's not matched by a `catch` clause. This includes situations in which the statement throwing the exception isn't even inside a `try` block. When this happens, execution of the program jumps out of the method that contains the offending statement. Execution jumps back to whatever code called the method in the first place.

A method can name more than one exception type in its `throws` clause. Just use commas to separate the names of the exception types, as in the following example:

```
throws InterruptedException, IOException,
                            ArithmeticException
```

The Java API has hundreds of exception types. Several of them are subclasses of the `RuntimeException` class. Anything that's a subclass of `RuntimeException` (or a sub-subclass, sub-sub-subclass, and so on) is unchecked. Any exception that's not a descendent of `RuntimeException` is checked. The unchecked exceptions include things that would be hard for the computer to predict. Such things include the `NumberFormatException` (of Listings 13-2, 13-4, and others), the `ArithmeticException`, the `IndexOutOfBoundsException`, the infamous `NullPointerException`, and many others. When you write Java code, much of your code is susceptible to these exceptions, but enclosing the code in `try` clauses (or passing the buck with `throws` clauses) is completely optional.

The Java API also has its share of checked exceptions. The computer can readily detect exceptions of this kind. So Java insists that, for an exception of this kind, any potential exception-throwing statement is acknowledged with either a `try` statement or a `throws` clause. Java's checked exceptions include the `InterruptedException` (Listings 13-9 and 13-10), the `IOException`, the `SQLException`, and a gang of other interesting exceptions.

Finishing the Job with a finally Clause

Once upon a time, I was a young fellow, living with my parents in Philadelphia, just starting to drive a car. I was heading toward a friend's house and thinking about who knows what when another car came from nowhere and bashed my car's passenger door. This kind of thing is called a *RunARedLightException*.

Anyway, both cars were still drivable, and we were right in the middle of a busy intersection. To avoid causing a traffic jam, we both pulled over to the nearest curb. I fumbled for my driver's license (which had a very young picture of me on it) and opened the door to get out of my car.

And that's when the second accident happened. As I was getting out of my car, a city bus was coming by. The bus hit me and rolled me against my car a few times. This kind of thing is called a *DealWithLawyersException*.

The truth is that everything came out just fine. I was bruised but not battered. My parents paid for the damage to the car, so I never suffered any financial consequences. (I managed to pass on the financial burden by putting the `Run ARedLightException` into my `throws` clause.)

This incident helps to explain why I think the way I do about exception handling. In particular, I wonder, "What happens if, while the computer is recovering from one exception, a second exception is thrown?" After all, the statements inside a `catch` clause aren't immune to calamities.

Well, the answer to this question is anything but simple. For starters, you can put a `try` statement inside a `catch` clause. This protects you against unexpected, potentially embarrassing incidents that can crop up during the execution of the `catch` clause. But when you start worrying about cascading exceptions, you open up a very slimy can of worms. The number of scenarios is large, and things can become complicated very quickly.

One not-too-complicated thing that you can do is to create a `finally` clause. Like a `catch` clause, a `finally` clause comes after a `try` clause. The big difference is that the statements in a `finally` clause are executed whether or not an exception is thrown. The idea is, "No matter what happens, good or bad, execute the statements inside this `finally` clause." Listing 13-11 has an example.

Listing 13-11:   Jumping Around

```java
import static java.lang.System.out;

public class DemoFinally {

    public static void main(String args[]) {
        try {
            doSomething();
        } catch (Exception e) {
            out.println("Exception caught in main.");
        }
    }

    static void doSomething() {
        try {
            out.println(0 / 0);
        } catch (Exception e) {
            out.println(
                "Exception caught in doSomething.");
            out.println(0 / 0);
        } finally {
            out.println("I'll get printed.");
        }

        out.println("I won't get printed.");
    }
}
```

Normally, when I think about a `try` statement, I think about the computer recovering from an unpleasant situation. The recovery takes place inside a `catch` clause, and then the computer marches on to whatever statements come after the `try` statement. Well, if something goes wrong during execution of a `catch` clause, this picture can start looking different.

Listing 13-11 gets a workout in Figure 13-14. First, the `main` method calls `do Something`. Then, the stupid `doSomething` method goes out of its way to cause trouble. The `doSomething` method divides 0 by 0, which is illegal and undoable in anyone's programming language. This foolish action by the `doSomething` method throws an `ArithmeticException`, which is caught by the `try` statement's one and only `catch` clause.

Figure 13-14:
Running the
code from
Listing 13-11.

```
Exception caught in doSomething.
I'll get printed.
Exception caught in main.
```

Inside the `catch` clause, that lowlife `doSomething` method divides 0 by 0 again. This time, the statement that does the division isn't inside a protective `try` clause. That's okay, because an `ArithmeticException` isn't checked. (It's one of those `RuntimeException` subclasses. It's an exception that doesn't have to be acknowledged in a `try` or a `throws` clause. For details, see the previous section.)

Well, checked or not, the throwing of another `ArithmeticException` causes control to jump out of the `doSomething` method. But, before leaving the `doSomething` method, the computer executes the `try` statement's last will and testament — namely, the statements inside the `finally` clause. That's why in Figure 13-14 you see the words `I'll get printed`.

Interestingly enough, you don't see the words `I won't get printed` in Figure 13-14. Because the `catch` clause's execution throws its own uncaught exception, the computer never makes it down past the `try-catch-finally` statement.

So, the computer goes back to where it left off in the `main` method. Back in the `main` method, word of the `doSomething` method's `ArithmeticException` mishaps causes execution to jump into a `catch` clause. The computer prints `Exception caught in main`, and then this terrible nightmare of a run is finished.

A try Statement with Resources

Imagine a program that gets input from two different files or from a `Scanner` and a disk file. To make sure that you clean up properly, you put `close` method calls in a `finally` clause. (See Listing 13-12.)

Listing 13-12:   Using Two Files

```java
import java.io.File;
import java.io.IOException;
import java.util.Scanner;

public class Main {

    public static void main(String args[]) {
        Scanner scan1 = null;
        Scanner scan2 = null;
        try {
            scan1 = new Scanner(new File("File1.txt"));
            scan2 = new Scanner(new File("File2.txt"));
            // Do useful stuff
        } catch (IOException e) {
            // Oops!
        } finally {
            scan1.close();
            scan2.close();
            System.out.println("Done!");
        }
    }
}
```

In theory, the computer always executes `scan1.close()` and `scan2.close()` no matter what goes wrong during execution of the `try` clause. But that's theory. In reality, another programmer (not you, of course) might modify the code by closing `scan1` in the middle of the `try` clause:

```java
try {
    scan1 = new Scanner(new File("File1.txt"));
    scan2 = new Scanner(new File("File2.txt"));
    // Do useful stuff but also ...
    scan1.close();
    scan1 = null;
} catch (IOException e) {
    // Oops!
} finally {
    scan1.close();
    scan2.close();
    System.out.println("Done!");
}
```

Now you have a real predicament. Inside the `finally` clause, the value of `scan1` is null. The call to `scan1.close()` fails, so the program throws a `NullPointerException` and stops running before reaching the call to `scan2.close()`. In the worst of circumstances, `scan2` isn't closed, and your program has `File2.txt` locked up so that no other program can use the file.

When a program uses several resources (many files, a database and a file, or whatever) the buildup of `try` statements becomes very complicated. You can make `try` statements within `catch` clauses and all kinds of crazy combinations. But Java has a better way to solve the problem. In Java 7 (and later versions of Java), you can create a *try-with-resources statement*. Listing 13-13 shows you how.

Listing 13-13: Making Sure to Close Resources

```
import java.io.File;
import java.io.IOException;
import java.util.Scanner;

public class NewMain {

    public static void main(String args[]) {
        try (Scanner scan1 =
                new Scanner(new File("File1.txt"));
            Scanner scan2 =
                new Scanner(new File("File2.txt"))) {
            // Do useful stuff
        } catch (IOException e) {
            // Oops!
        }
        System.out.println("Done!");
    }
}
```

In Listing 13-13, the declarations of `scan1` and `scan2` are in parentheses after the word `try`. The parenthesized declarations tell Java to close `scan1` and `scan2` automatically after execution of the statements in the `try` clause. You can declare several resources inside one `try` statement's parentheses. When you do, Java closes all the resources automatically after execution of the `try` clause's statements. You can add `catch` clauses and a `finally` clause if you want. You can access all kinds of resources (files, databases, connections to servers, and others) and have peace of mind knowing that Java will sever the connections automatically.

Life is good.

Chapter 14

Sharing Names among the Parts of a Java Program

· ·

· ·

peaking of private fields and methods (and I do speak about these things in this chapter). . . .

I'm eating lunch with some friends at work. "They can read your e-mail," says one fellow. Another chimes in, "They know every single website that you visit. They know what products you buy, what you eat for dinner, what you wear, what you think. They even know your deepest, darkest secrets. Why, I wouldn't be surprised if they know when you're going to die."

A third voice enters the fray. "It's getting to the point where you can't blow your nose without someone taking a record of it. I visited a website a few weeks ago, and the page wished me a Happy Birthday. How did they know it was me, and how did they remember that it was my birthday?"

"Yeah," says the first guy. "I have a tag on my car that lets me sail through toll booths. It senses that I'm going through and puts the charge on my credit card automatically. So every month, I get a list from the company showing where I've been and when I was there. I'm amazed it doesn't say who I was visiting and what I did when I got there."

I think quietly to myself. I think about saying, "That's just a bunch of baloney. Personally, I'd be flattered if my employer, the government, or some big company thought so much of me that they tracked my every move. I have enough trouble getting people's attention when I really want it. And most agencies that keep logs of all my purchasing and viewing habits can't even spell my name right when they send me junk mail. 'Hello, this is a courtesy call for Larry Burg. Is Mr. Burg at home?' Spying on people is really boring. I can just see the headline on the front page of *The Times:* 'Author of *Java For Dummies* Wears His Undershirt Inside Out!' Big deal!"

So I think for a few seconds, and then I say, "They're out to get us. TV cameras! That's the next big thing — TV cameras everywhere."

Access Modifiers

If you've read this far into *Java For Dummies,* 6th Edition, you probably know one thing: Object-oriented programming is big on hiding details. Programmers who write one piece of code shouldn't tinker with the details inside another programmer's code. It's not a matter of security and secrecy. It's a matter of modularity. When you hide details, you keep the intricacies inside one piece of code from being twisted and broken by another piece of code. Your code comes in nice, discrete, manageable lumps. You keep complexity to a minimum. You make fewer mistakes. You save money. You help promote world peace.

Other chapters have plenty of examples of the use of private fields. When a field is declared private, it's hidden from all outside meddling. This hiding enhances modularity, minimizes complexity, and so on.

Elsewhere in the annals of *Java For Dummies,* 6th Edition, are examples of things that are declared public. Just like a public celebrity, a field that's declared public is left wide open. Plenty of people probably know what kind of toothpaste Elvis used, and any programmer can reference a public field, even a field that's not named *Elvis.*

In Java, the words *public* and *private* are called *access modifiers.* No doubt you've seen fields and methods without access modifiers in their declarations. A method or field of this kind is said to have *default access.* Many examples in this book use default access without making a big fuss about it. That's okay in some chapters, but not in this chapter. In this chapter, I describe the nitty-gritty details about default access.

And you can find out about yet another access modifier that isn't used in any example before this chapter. (At least, I don't remember using it in any earlier examples.) It's the `protected` access modifier. Yes, this chapter covers some of the slimy, grimy facts about protected access.

Classes, Access, and Multipart Programs

With this topic, you can become all tangled up in terminology, so you need to get some basics out of the way. (Most of the terminology that you need comes from Chapter 10, but it's worth reviewing at the start of this chapter.) Here's a fake piece of Java code:

```
class MyClass {
    int myField;              //a field
                              // (a member)

    void myMethod() {         //a method (another member)

        int myOtherField;     //a method-local variable
                              // (NOT a member)
    }
}
```

The comments on the right side of the code tell the whole story. Two kinds of variables exist here — fields and method-local variables. This chapter isn't about method-local variables. It's about methods and fields.

Believe me, carrying around the phrase "methods and fields" wherever you go isn't easy. It's much better to give these things one name and be done with it. That's why both methods and fields are called *members* of a class.

Members versus classes

At this point, you make an important distinction. Think about Java's `public` keyword. As you may already know from earlier chapters, you can put `public` in front of a member. For example, you can write

```
public static void main(String args[]) {
```

or

```
public amountInAccount = 50.22;
```

These uses of the `public` keyword come as no big surprise. What you may not already know is that you can put the `public` keyword in front of a class. For example, you can write

```
public class Drawing {

    // Your code goes here

}
```

In Java, the `public` keyword has two slightly different meanings — one meaning for members and another meaning for classes. Most of this chapter deals with the meaning of `public` (and other such keywords) for members. The last part of this chapter (appropriately titled "Access Modifiers for Java Classes") deals with the meaning for classes.

Access modifiers for members

Sure, this section is about members. But that doesn't mean that you can ignore Java classes. Members or not, the Java class is still where all the action takes place. Each field is declared in a particular class, belongs to that class, and is a member of that class. The same is true of methods. Each method is declared in a particular class, belongs to that class, and is a member of that class. Can you use a certain member name in a particular place in your code? To begin answering the question, check whether that place is inside or outside of the member's class:

✔ If the member is private, only code that's inside the member's class can refer directly to that member's name.

```
class SomeClass {
    private int myField = 10;
}


class SomeOtherClass {

    public static void main(String args[]) {
        SomeClass someObject = new SomeClass();

        //This doesn't work:
        System.out.println(someObject.myField);
    }
}
```

✔ If the member is public, any code can refer directly to that member's name.

```
class SomeClass {
    public int myField = 10;
}


class SomeOtherClass {

    public static void main(String args[]) {
        SomeClass someObject = new SomeClass();

        //This works:
        System.out.println(someObject.myField);
    }
}
```

Figures 14-1 through 14-3 illustrate the ideas in a slightly different way.

class1	classA	classX
class2 extends class1	classB extends classA	classY extends classX
class3 extends class2	classC extends classB	classZ extends classY

Figure 14-1:
Several
classes
and their
subclasses.

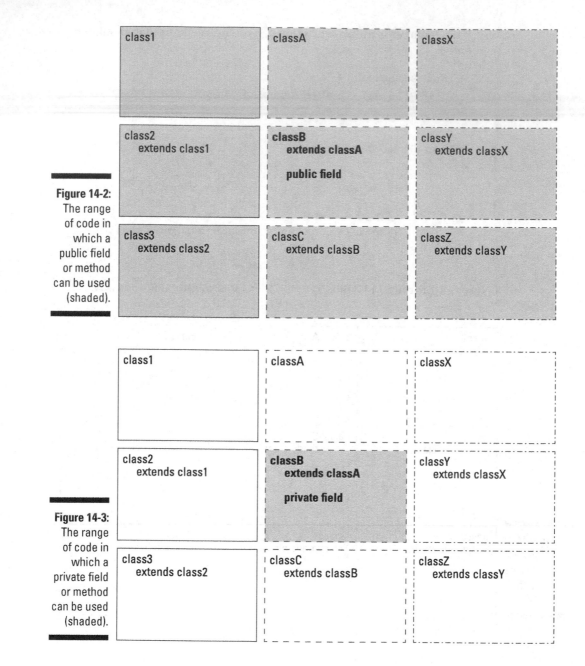

Figure 14-2:
The range of code in which a public field or method can be used (shaded).

Figure 14-3:
The range of code in which a private field or method can be used (shaded).

Putting a drawing on a frame

To make this business about access modifiers clear, you need an example or two. In this chapter's first example, almost everything is public. With public access, you don't have to worry about who can use what.

The code for this first example comes in several parts. The first part, which is in Listing 14-1, displays an ArtFrame. On the face of the ArtFrame is a Drawing. If all the right pieces are in place, running the code of Listing 14-1 displays a window like the one shown in Figure 14-4.

Listing 14-1:   Displaying a Frame

```java
import com.burdbrain.drawings.Drawing;
import com.burdbrain.frames.ArtFrame;

class ShowFrame {

    public static void main(String args[]) {
        ArtFrame artFrame = new ArtFrame(new Drawing());

        artFrame.setSize(200, 100);
        artFrame.setVisible(true);
    }
}
```

Figure 14-4:
An
ArtFrame.

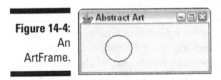

The code in Listing 14-1 creates a new ArtFrame instance. You may suspect that ArtFrame is a subclass of a Java frame class, and that's certainly the case. Chapter 9 says that Java frames are, by default, invisible. So, in Listing 14-1, to make the ArtFrame instance visible, you call the setVisible method.

Now notice that Listing 14-1 starts with two import declarations. The first import declaration allows you to abbreviate the name Drawing from the com.burdbrain.drawings package. The second import declaration allows you to abbreviate the name *ArtFrame* from com.burdbrain.frames.

For a review of import declarations, see Chapter 4.

The detective in you may be thinking, "He must have written more code (code that I don't see here) and put that code in packages that he named *com.burdbrain.drawings* and *com.burdbrain.frames*." And, indeed, you are correct. To make Listing 14-1 work, I create something called a *Drawing,* and I'm putting all my drawings in the `com.burdbrain.drawings` package. I also need an `ArtFrame` class, and I'm putting all such classes in my `com.burdbrain.frames` package.

So, really, what's a `Drawing`? Well, if you're so anxious to know, look at Listing 14-2.

Listing 14-2: The Drawing Class

```java
package com.burdbrain.drawings;

import java.awt.Graphics;

public class Drawing {
    public int x = 40, y = 40, width = 40, height = 40;

    public void paint(Graphics g) {
        g.drawOval(x, y, width, height);
    }
}
```

The code for the `Drawing` class is pretty slim. It contains a few `int` fields and a `paint` method. That's all. Well, when I create my classes, I try to keep 'em lean. Anyway, here are some notes about my `Drawing` class:

✔ **At the top of the code is a *package declaration.*** Lo and behold! I've made my `Drawing` class belong to a package — the `com.burdbrain.drawings` package. I didn't pull this package name out of the air. The convention (handed down by the people who created Java) says that you start a package name by reversing the parts of your domain name, so I reversed `burdbrain.com`. Then, you add one or more descriptive names, separated by dots. I added the name *drawings* because I intend to put all my drawing goodies in this package.

✔ **The `Drawing` class is *public.*** A public class is vulnerable to intrusion from the outside. So in general, I avoid plastering the `public` keyword in front of any old class. But in Listing 14-2, I have to declare my `Drawing` class to be public. If I don't, classes that aren't in the `com.burdbrain.drawings` package can't use the goodies in Listing 14-2. In particular, the line

```java
ArtFrame artFrame = new ArtFrame(new Drawing());
```

in Listing 14-1 is illegal unless the `Drawing` class is public.

For more information on public and nonpublic classes, see the section entitled "Access Modifiers for Java Classes," later in this chapter.

✔ **The code has a `paint` method.** This `paint` method uses a standard Java trick for making things appear onscreen. The parameter g in Listing 14-2 is called a *graphics buffer.* To make things appear, all you do is draw on this graphics buffer, and the buffer is eventually rendered on the computer screen.

Here's a little more detail: In Listing 14-2, the `paint` method takes a g parameter. This g parameter refers to an instance of the `java.awt.Graphics` class. Because a `Graphics` instance is a buffer, the things that you put onto this buffer are eventually displayed on the screen. Like all instances of the `java.awt.Graphics` class, this buffer has several drawing methods — one of them being `drawOval`. When you call `drawOval`, you specify a starting position (*x* pixels from the left edge of the frame and *y* pixels from the top of the frame). You also specify an oval size by putting numbers of pixels in the `width` and `height` parameters. Calling the `drawOval` method puts a little round thing into the `Graphics` buffer. That `Graphics` buffer, round thing and all, is displayed onscreen.

Directory structure

The code in Listing 14-2 belongs to the `com.burdbrain.drawings` package. When you put a class into a package, you have to create a directory structure that mirrors the name of the package.

To house code that's in the `com.burdbrain.drawings` package, you have to have three directories: a `com` directory, a subdirectory of `com` named `burdbrain`, and a subdirectory of `burdbrain` named `drawings`. The overall directory structure is shown in Figure 14-5.

If you don't have your code in the appropriate directories, you get a repulsive and disgusting `NoClassDefFoundError`. Believe me, this error is never fun to get. When you see this error, you don't have any clues to help you figure out where the missing class is or where the compiler expects to find it. If you stay calm, you can figure out all this stuff on your own. If you panic, you'll be poking around for hours. As a seasoned Java programmer, I can remember plenty of scraped knuckles that came from this heinous `NoClassDefFoundError`.

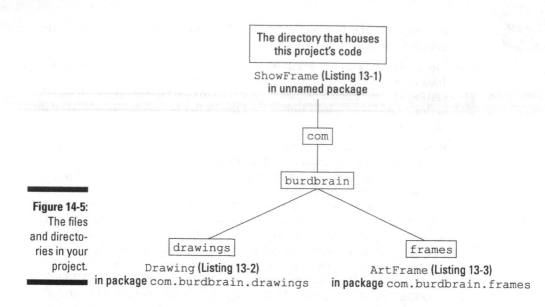

Figure 14-5:
The files
and directo-
ries in your
project.

Looking for files in all the right places

You try to compile the program in Listing 14-1. The Java compiler pokes through the code and stumbles upon some missing pieces. First there's this thing called an `ArtFrame`. Then you have this `Drawing` business. Listing 14-1 defines a class named `ShowFrame`, not `ArtFrame` or `Drawing`. So where does the compiler go for information about the `ArtFrame` and `Drawing` classes?

If you stop to think about it, the problem can be daunting. Should the compiler go searching all over your hard drive for files named `ArtFrame.java` or `Drawing.class`? How large is your new hard drive? 500GB? 750GB? 6,000,000GB? And what about references to files on network drives? The search space is potentially unlimited. What if the compiler eventually resolves all these issues? Then you try to run your code, and the Java Virtual Machine (JVM) starts searching all over again. (For info on the Java Virtual Machine, see Chapter 2.)

To tame this problem, Java defines something called a *CLASSPATH*. The *CLASSPATH* is a list of places where the compiler and the JVM look for code. There are several ways to set a CLASSPATH. Some programmers create a new CLASSPATH each time they run a Java program. Others create a system-wide `CLASSPATH` variable. (If you're familiar with the `PATH` variable on Windows and UNIX computers, you may already know how this stuff works.) One way or another, the compiler and the JVM need a list of places to look for code. Without such a list, these Java tools don't look anywhere. They don't find classes like `ArtFrame` or `Drawing`. You get a `cannot find symbol` message or a `NoClassDefFoundError` message, and you're very unhappy.

Making a frame

This chapter's first three listings develop one multipart example. This section has the last of three pieces in that example. This last piece isn't crucial for the understanding of access modifiers, which is the main topic of this chapter. So, if you want to skip past the explanation of Listing 14-3, you can do so without losing the chapter's thread. On the other hand, if you want to know more about the Java Swing classes, read on.

Listing 14-3:   The ArtFrame Class

```
package com.burdbrain.frames;

import java.awt.Graphics;

import javax.swing.JFrame;

import com.burdbrain.drawings.Drawing;

public class ArtFrame extends JFrame {
    private static final long serialVersionUID = 1L;

    Drawing drawing;

    public ArtFrame(Drawing drawing) {
        this.drawing = drawing;
        setTitle("Abstract Art");
        setDefaultCloseOperation(EXIT_ON_CLOSE);
    }

    public void paint(Graphics g) {
        drawing.paint(g);
    }
}
```

Listing 14-3 has all the gadgetry that you need for putting a drawing on a Java frame. The code uses several names from the Java API (Application Programming Interface). I explain most of these names in Chapters 9 and 10.

The only new name in Listing 14-3 is the word paint. The paint method in Listing 14-3 defers to another paint method — the paint method belonging to a Drawing object. The ArtFrame object creates a floating window on your computer screen. What's drawn in that floating window depends on whatever Drawing object was passed to the ArtFrame constructor.

If you trace the flow of Listings 14-1 through 14-3, you may notice something peculiar. The `paint` method in Listing 14-3 never seems to be called. Well, for many of Java's window-making components, you just declare a `paint` method and let the method sit there quietly in the code. When the program runs, the computer calls the `paint` method automatically.

That's what happens with `javax.swing.JFrame` objects. In Listing 14-3, the frame's `paint` method is called from behind the scenes. Then, the frame's `paint` method calls the `Drawing` object's `paint` method, which in turn, draws an oval on the frame. That's how you get the stuff you see in Figure 14-4.

Sneaking Away from the Original Code

Your preferred software vendor, Burd Brain Consulting, has sold you two files — `Drawing.class` and `ArtFrame.class`. As a customer, you can't see the code inside the files `Drawing.java` and `ArtFrame.java`. So, you have to live with whatever happens to be inside these two files. (If only you'd purchased a copy of *Java For Dummies*, 6th Edition, which has the code for these files in Listings 14-2 and 14-3!) Anyway, you want to tweak the way the oval looks in Figure 14-4 so that it's a bit wider. To do this, you create a subclass of the `Drawing` class — DrawingWide — and put it in Listing 14-4.

Listing 14-4:   A Subclass of the Drawing Class

```java
import java.awt.Graphics;

import com.burdbrain.drawings.Drawing;

public class DrawingWide extends Drawing {
    int width = 100, height = 30;

    public void paint(Graphics g) {
        g.drawOval(x, y, width, height);
    }
}
```

To make use of the code in Listing 14-4, you remember to change one of the lines in Listing 14-1. You change the line to

```java
ArtFrame artFrame = new ArtFrame(new DrawingWide());
```

In Listing 14-1 you can also remove the `com.burdbrain.drawings.Drawing` import declaration because you no longer need it.

Listing 14-4 defines a subclass of the original `Drawing` class. In that subclass, you override the original class's width and height fields and the original class's `paint` method. The frame that you get is shown in Figure 14-6.

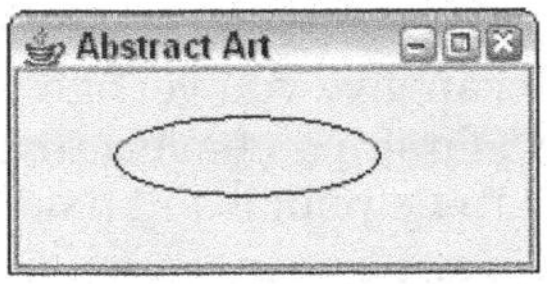

Figure 14-6:
Another art
frame.

Figure 14-6:
Another art
frame.

In passing, you may notice that the code in Listing 14-4 doesn't start with a package declaration. This means that your whole collection of files comes from the following three packages:

- **The `com.burdbrain.drawings` package:** The original `Drawing` class from Listing 14-2 is in this package.

- **The `com.burdbrain.frames` package:** The `ArtFrame` class from Listing 14-3 is in this package.

- **An ever-present, unnamed package:** In Java, when you don't start a file with a package declaration, all the code in that file goes into one big, unnamed package. Listings 14-1 and 14-4 are in the same unnamed package. In fact, most of the listings from the first 13 chapters of this book are in Java's unnamed package.

At this point, your project has two drawing classes — the original `Drawing` class and your new `DrawingWide` class. Similar as these classes may be, they live in two separate packages. That's not surprising. The `Drawing` class, developed by your friends at Burd Brain Consulting, lives in a package whose name starts with *com.burdbrain*. But you developed `DrawingWide` on your own, so you shouldn't put it in a `com.burdbrain` package.

The most sensible thing to do is to put it in one of your own packages, such as `com.myhomedomain.drawings`; but putting your class in the unnamed package will do for now.

One way or another, your `DrawingWide` subclass compiles and runs as planned. You go home, beaming with the confidence of having written useful, working code.

Default access

If you're reading these paragraphs in order, you know that the last example ends very happily. The code in Listing 14-4 runs like a charm. Everyone, including my wonderful editor, Brian Walls, is happy.

But, wait! Do you ever wonder what life would be like if you hadn't chosen that particular career, dated that certain someone, or read that certain *For Dummies* book? In this section, I roll back the clock a bit to show you what would have happened if one word had been omitted from the code in Listing 14-2.

Dealing with different versions of a program can give you vertigo, so I start this discussion by describing what you have. First, you have a Drawing class. In this class, the fields aren't declared to be public and have the default access. The Drawing class lives in the com.burdbrain.drawings package. (See Listing 14-5.)

Listing 14-5:   Fields with Default Access

```
package com.burdbrain.drawings;

import java.awt.Graphics;

public class Drawing {
    int x = 40, y = 40, width = 40, height = 40;

    public void paint(Graphics g) {
        g.drawOval(x, y, width, height);
    }
}
```

Next, you have a DrawingWide subclass (copied, for your convenience, in Listing 14-6). The DrawingWide class is in Java's unnamed package.

Listing 14-6:   A Failed Attempt to Create a Subclass

```
import com.burdbrain.drawings.*;
import java.awt.Graphics;

public class DrawingWide extends Drawing {
    int width = 100, height = 30;

    public void paint(Graphics g) {
        g.drawOval(x, y, width, height);
    }
}
```

The trouble is that the whole thing falls apart at the seams. The code in Listing 14-6 doesn't compile. Instead, you get the following error messages:

```
x is not public in com.burdbrain.drawings.Drawing;
cannot be accessed from outside package
y is not public in com.burdbrain.drawings.Drawing;
cannot be accessed from outside package
```

The code doesn't compile, because a field that has default access can't be directly referenced outside its package — not even by a subclass of the class containing the field. The same holds true for any methods that have default access.

A class's fields and methods are called *members* of the class. The rules for access — default and otherwise — apply to all members of classes.

The access rules that I describe in this chapter don't apply to method-local variables. A method-local variable can be accessed only within its own method.

For the rundown on method-local variables, see Chapter 10.

In Java, the default access for a member of a class is package-wide access. A member declared without the word *public, private,* or *protected* in front of it is accessible in the package in which its class resides. Figures 14-7 and 14-8 illustrate the point.

The names of packages, with all their dots and subparts, can be slightly misleading. For instance, when you write a program that responds to button clicks, you normally import classes from two separate packages. On one line, you may have `import java.awt.*;`. On another line, you may have `import java.awt.event.*;`. Importing all classes from the `java.awt` package doesn't automatically import classes from the `java.awt.event` package.

class1	classA	classX	Legend:
			A package
class2 extends class1	classB extends classA	classY extends classX	Another package
class3 extends class2	classC extends classB	classZ extends classY	Yet another package

Figure 14-7: Packages cut across subclass hierarchies.

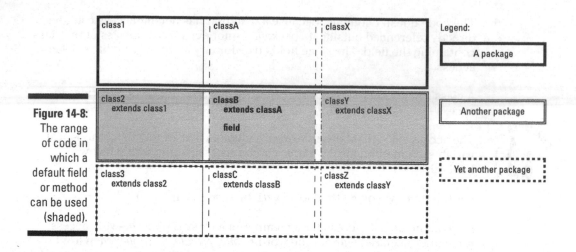

Figure 14-8:
The range
of code in
which a
default field
or method
can be used
(shaded).

Crawling back into the package

I love getting things in the mail. At worst, it's junk mail that I can throw right into the trash. At best, it's something I can use, a new toy, or something somebody sent especially for me.

Well, today is my lucky day. Somebody from Burd Brain Consulting sent a subclass of the Drawing class. It's essentially the same as the code in Listing 14-6. The only difference is that this new DrawingWideBB class lives inside the com.burdbrain.drawings package. The code is shown in Listing 14-7. To run this code, I have to modify Listing 14-1 with the line

```
ArtFrame artFrame = new ArtFrame(new DrawingWideBB());
```

Listing 14-7:   Yes, Virginia, This Is a Subclass

```
package com.burdbrain.drawings;

import java.awt.Graphics;

public class DrawingWideBB extends Drawing {
    int width = 100, height = 30;

    public void paint(Graphics g) {
        g.drawOval(x, y, width, height);
    }
}
```

When you run Listing 14-7 alongside the Drawing class in Listing 14-5, everything works just fine. The reason? It's because Drawing and DrawingWideBB are in the same package. Look back at Figure 14-8 and notice the shaded region that spans across an entire package. The code in the DrawingWideBB class has every right to use the x and y fields, which are defined with default access in the Drawing class because Drawing and DrawingWideBB are in the same package.

To use the DrawingWideBB class in Listing 14-7, you make two changes in the original Listing 14-1. Change the first import declaration to

```
import com.burdbrain.drawings.DrawingWideBB;
```

Also, change the ArtFrame object's constructor call to new ArtFrame (new DrawingWideBB()).

Protected Access

When I was first getting to know Java, I thought the word *protected* meant *nice and secure,* or something like that. "Wow, that field is protected. It must be hard to get at." Well, this notion turned out to be wrong. In Java, a member that's protected is less hidden, less secure, and easier to use than one that has default access. The concept is rather strange.

Think of protected access this way. You start with a field that has default access (a field without the word *public, private,* or *protected* in its declaration). That field can be accessed only inside the package in which it lives. Now add the word *protected* to the front of the field's declaration. Suddenly, classes outside that field's package have some access to the field. You can now reference the field from a subclass (of the class in which the field is declared). You can also reference the field from a sub-subclass, a sub-sub-subclass, and so on. Any descendent class will do. For an example, see Listings 14-8 and 14-9.

Listing 14-8: Protected Fields

```
package com.burdbrain.drawings;

import java.awt.Graphics;

public class Drawing {
    protected int x = 40, y = 40, width = 40, height = 40;

    public void paint(Graphics g) {
        g.drawOval(x, y, width, height);
    }
}
```

Listing 14-9:   The Subclass from the Blue Lagoon, Part II

```
import java.awt.Graphics;

import com.burdbrain.drawings.Drawing;

public class DrawingWide extends Drawing {
    int width = 100, height = 30;

    public void paint(Graphics g) {
        g.drawOval(x, y, width, height);
    }
}
```

Listing 14-8 defines the Drawing class. Listing 14-9 defines DrawingWide, which is a subclass of the Drawing class.

In the Drawing class, the x, y, width, and height fields are protected. The DrawingWide class has its own width and height fields, but DrawingWide references the x and y fields that are defined in the parent Drawing class. That's okay even though DrawingWide isn't in the same package as its parent Drawing class. (The Drawing class is in the com.burdbrain. drawings package; the DrawingWide class is in Java's great, unnamed package.) It's okay because the x and y fields are protected in the Drawing class.

Compare Figures 14-8 and 14-9. Notice the extra bit of shading in Figure 14-9. A subclass can access a protected member of a class, even if that subclass belongs to some other package.

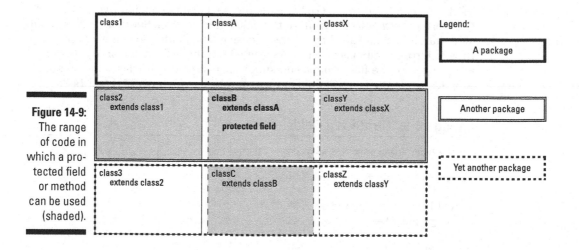

Figure 14-9: The range of code in which a protected field or method can be used (shaded).

Do you work with a team of programmers? Do people from outside your team use their own team's package names? If so, when they use your code, they may make subclasses of the classes that you've defined. This is where protected access comes in handy. Use protected access when you want people from outside your team to make direct references to your code's fields or methods.

Putting non-subclasses in the same package

Those people from Burd Brain Consulting are sending you one piece of software after another. This time, they've sent an alternative to the ShowFrame class — the class in Listing 14-1. This new ShowFrameWideBB class displays a wider oval (how exciting!), but it does this without creating a subclass of the old Drawing class. Instead, the new ShowFrameWideBB code creates a Drawing instance and then changes the value of the instance's width and height fields. The code is shown in Listing 14-10.

Listing 14-10: Drawing a Wider Oval

```
package com.burdbrain.drawings;

import com.burdbrain.frames.ArtFrame;

class ShowFrameWideBB {

    public static void main(String args[]) {
        Drawing drawing = new Drawing();
        drawing.width = 100;
        drawing.height = 30;

        ArtFrame artFrame = new ArtFrame(drawing);
        artFrame.setSize(200, 100);
        artFrame.setVisible(true);
    }
}
```

So, here's the story. This ShowFrameWideBB class in Listing 14-10 is in the same package as the Drawing class (the com.burdbrain.drawings package). But ShowFrameWideBB isn't a subclass of the Drawing class.

Now imagine compiling ShowFrameWideBB with the Drawing class that's shown in Listing 14-8 — the class with all those protected fields. What happens? Well, everything goes smoothly because a protected member is available in two (somewhat unrelated) places. Look again at Figure 14-9. A protected member is available to subclasses outside the package, but the member is also available to code (subclasses or not) within the member's package.

Listing 14-10 has a `main` method, which is inside a class, which is in turn inside the `com.burdbrain.drawings` package. With most Integrated Development Environments (IDEs), you don't think twice about running a `main` method that's in a named package. But if you run programs from the command line, you may need to type a fully qualified class name. For example, to run the code in Listing 14-10, you type `java com.burdbrain.drawings.ShowFrameWideBB`.

The real story about protected access is one step more complicated than the story that I describe in this section. The Java Language Specification mentions a hair-splitting point about code being responsible for an object's implementation. When you're first figuring out how to program in Java, don't worry about this point. Wait until you've written many Java programs. Then, when you stumble upon a `variable has protected access` error message, you can start worrying. Better yet, skip the worrying and take a careful look at the protected access section in the Java Language Specification.

For info about the Java Language Specification, visit Chapter 3.

Access Modifiers for Java Classes

Maybe the things that you read about access modifiers for members make you a tad dizzy. After all, member access in Java is a very complicated subject with lots of plot twists and cliffhangers. Well, the dizziness is over. Compared with the saga for fields and methods, the access story for classes is rather simple.

A class can be either public or nonpublic. If you see something like

```
public class Drawing
```

you're looking at the declaration of a public class. But, if you see plain old

```
class ShowFrame
```

the class that's being declared isn't public.

Public classes

If a class is public, you can refer to the class from anywhere in your code. Of course, some restrictions apply. You must obey all the rules in this chapter's "Directory structure" section. You must also refer to a packaged class properly. For example, in Listing 14-1, you can write

```
import com.burdbrain.drawings.Drawing;
import com.burdbrain.frames.ArtFrame;
...
ArtFrame artFrame = new ArtFrame(new Drawing());
```

or you can do without the import declarations and write

```
com.burdbrain.frames.ArtFrame artFrame =
    new com.burdbrain.frames.ArtFrame
        (new com.burdbrain.drawings.Drawing());
```

One way or another, your code must acknowledge that the ArtFrame and Drawing classes are in named packages.

Nonpublic classes

If a class isn't public, you can refer to the class only from code within the class's package.

I tried it. First, I went back to Listing 14-2 and deleted the word *public*. I turned public class Drawing into plain old class Drawing, like this:

```
package com.burdbrain.drawings;

import java.awt.Graphics;

class Drawing {
    public int x = 40, y = 40, width = 40, height = 40;

    public void paint(Graphics g) {
        g.drawOval(x, y, width, height);
    }
}
```

Then I compiled the code in Listing 14-7. Everything was peachy because Listing 14-7 contains the following lines:

```
package com.burdbrain.drawings;

public class DrawingWideBB extends Drawing
```

Because both pieces of code are in the same `com.burdbrain.drawings` package, access from `DrawingWideBB` back to the nonpublic `Drawing` class was no problem at all.

But then I tried to compile the code in Listing 14-3. The code in Listing 14-3 begins with

```
package com.burdbrain.frames;
```

That code isn't in the `com.burdbrain.drawings` package. So when the computer reached the line

```
Drawing drawing;
```

from Listing 14-3, the computer went *poof!* To be more precise, the computer displayed this message:

```
com.burdbrain.drawings.Drawing is not public
in com.burdbrain.drawings;
cannot be accessed from outside package
```

Well, I guess I got what was coming to me.

Things are never as simple as they seem. The rules that I describe in this section apply to almost every class in this book. But Java has fancy things called *inner classes,* and inner classes follow a different set of rules. Fortunately, a typical novice programmer has little contact with inner classes. The only inner classes in this book are in Chapter 15 (and a few inner classes disguised as `enum` types). So for now, you can live very happily with the rules that I describe in this section.

Chapter 15

Responding to Keystrokes and Mouse Clicks

In This Chapter
▶ Creating code to handle mouse clicks (and other such events)
▶ Writing and using a Java interface

*I*n the late 1980s, I bought my first mouse. I paid $100 and, because I didn't really need a mouse, I checked with my wife before buying it. (At the time, my computer ran a hybrid text/windowed environment. Anything that I could do with a mouse, I could just as easily do with the Alt key.)

Now it's the 21st century. The last ten mice that I got were free. Ordinary ones just fall into my lap somehow. A few exotic mice were on sale at the local computer superstore. One cost $10 and came with a $10 rebate.

As I write this chapter, I'm using the most recent addition to my collection — an official *For Dummies* mouse. This yellow and white beauty has a little compartment filled with water. Instead of a snowy Atlantic City scene, the water surrounds a tiny Dummies Man charm. It's so cute. It was a present from the folks at Wiley Publishing.

Go On . . . Click That Button

In previous chapters, I create windows that don't do much. A typical window displays some information but doesn't have any interactive elements. Well, the time has come to change all that. This chapter's first example is a window with a button on it. When the user clicks the button, darn it, something happens. The code is shown in Listing 15-1, and the main method that calls the code in Listing 15-1 is in Listing 15-2.

Listing 15-1:   A Guessing Game

```java
import java.awt.FlowLayout;
import java.awt.event.ActionEvent;
import java.awt.event.ActionListener;
import java.util.Random;

import javax.swing.JButton;
import javax.swing.JFrame;
import javax.swing.JLabel;
import javax.swing.JTextField;

class GameFrame extends JFrame implements ActionListener {
    private static final long serialVersionUID = 1L;

    int randomNumber = new Random().nextInt(10) + 1;
    int numGuesses = 0;

    JTextField textField = new JTextField(5);
    JButton button = new JButton("Guess");
    JLabel label = new JLabel(numGuesses + " guesses");

    public GameFrame() {
        setDefaultCloseOperation(JFrame.EXIT_ON_CLOSE);
        setLayout(new FlowLayout());
        add(textField);
        add(button);
        add(label);
        button.addActionListener(this);
        pack();
        setVisible(true);
    }

    @Override
    public void actionPerformed(ActionEvent e) {
        String textFieldText = textField.getText();

        if (Integer.parseInt(textFieldText)==randomNumber) {
            button.setEnabled(false);
            textField.setText(textField.getText() + " Yes!");
            textField.setEnabled(false);
        } else {
            textField.setText("");
            textField.requestFocus();
        }

        numGuesses++;
        String guessWord =
            (numGuesses == 1) ? " guess" : " guesses";
        label.setText(numGuesses + guessWord);
    }
}
```

Listing 15-2:   Starting the Guessing Game

```
public class ShowGameFrame {

    public static void main(String args[]) {
        new GameFrame();
    }
}
```

Some snapshots from a run of this section's code are shown in Figures 15-1 and 15-2. In a window, the user plays a guessing game. Behind the scenes, the program chooses a secret number (a number from 1 to 10). Then the program displays a text field and a button. The user types a number in the text field and clicks the button. One of two things happens next:

✔ **If the number that the user types in isn't the same as the secret number,** the computer posts the number of guesses made so far. The user gets to make another guess.

✔ **If the number that the user types in is the same as the secret number,** the text field displays Yes!. Meanwhile, the game is over, so both the text field and the button become disabled. Both components have that gray, washed-out look, and neither component responds to keystrokes or mouse clicks.

Figure 15-1:
An incorrect guess.

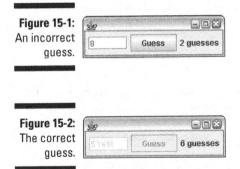

Figure 15-2:
The correct guess.

In Listing 15-1, the code to create the frame, the button, and the text field isn't earth-shattering. I did similar things in Chapters 9 and 10. The JTextField class is new in this chapter, but a text field isn't much different from a button or a label. Like so many other components, the JTextField class is defined in the javax.swing package. When you create a new JTextField instance, you can specify a number of columns. In Listing 15-1, I create a text field that's five columns wide.

Listing 15-1 uses a fancy operator to decide between the singular *guess* and the plural *guesses*. If you're not familiar with this use of the question mark and colon, see Chapter 11.

Events and event handling

The big news in Listing 15-1, shown in the preceding section, is the handling of the user's button click. When you're working in a graphical user interface (GUI), anything the user does (like pressing a key, moving the mouse, clicking the mouse, or whatever) is called an *event*. The code that responds to the user's press, movement, or click is called *event-handling code.*

Listing 15-1 deals with the button-click event with three parts of its code:

- ✔ The top of the `GameFrame` class declaration says that this class `implements ActionListener`.
- ✔ The constructor for the `GameFrame` class adds `this` to the button's list of action listeners.
- ✔ The code for the `GameFrame` class has an `actionPerformed` method.

Taken together, all three of these tricks make the `GameFrame` class handle button clicks. To understand how it works, you have to know about something called an *interface,* which I discuss in the following section.

The Java interface

You may have noticed that, in Java, you never get a class to extend more than one parent class. In other words, you never say

```
class DontDoThis extends FirstClass, SecondClass
```

A class can have only one parent class, and that's fine when you want your new class to be like a frame. But what if you want your new class to be like a frame and a button-click-listening thing? Can your new class be like both things?

Yes, it can be. Java has this thing called an *interface.* An interface is like a class, but it's different. (So, what else is new? A cow is like a planet, but it's quite a bit different. Cows moo; planets hang in space.) Anyway, when you hear the word *interface,* you can start by thinking of a class. Then, in your head, note the following things:

✔ **A class can extend only one parent class, but a class can implement more than one interface.**

For instance, if you want GameFrame to listen for keystrokes as well as button clicks, you can say

```
class GameFrame extends JFrame
    implements ActionListener, ItemListener
```

✔ **An interface's methods have no bodies of their own.**

Here's a copy of the API code for the ActionListener interface:

```
package java.awt.event;

import java.util.EventListener;

public interface ActionListener
                            extends EventListener {

    public void actionPerformed(ActionEvent e);

}
```

I've removed the code's comments, but I've avoided messing with the API code in any significant ways. In this code, the actionPerformed method has no body — no curly braces and no statements to execute. In place of a body, there's just a semicolon.

A method with no body, like the method defined in the ActionListener interface, is called an *abstract* method.

✔ **When you implement an interface, you provide bodies for all the interface's methods.**

That's why an actionPerformed method appears in Listing 15-1. By announcing that it will implement the ActionListener interface, the code in Listing 15-1 agrees that it will give meaning to the interface's actionPerformed method. In this situation, *giving meaning* means declaring an actionPerformed method with curly braces, a body, and maybe some statements to execute.

When you announce that you're going to implement an interface, the Java compiler takes this announcement seriously. Later on in the code, if you fail to give meaning to any of the interface's methods, the compiler yells at you.

If you're really lazy, you can quickly find out what methods need to be declared in your interface-implementing code. Try to compile the code, and the compiler lists all the methods that you should have declared but didn't.

Chapter 8 introduces the use of @Override — a Java annotation. Normally, you use @Override to signal the replacement of a method that's already been declared in a superclass. But from Java 6 onward, you can also use @Override to signal an interface method's implementation. That's what I do in Listing 15-1.

Threads of execution

Here's a well-kept secret: Java programs are *multithreaded,* which means that several things are going on at once whenever you run a Java program. Sure, the computer is executing the code that you've written, but it's executing other code as well (code that you didn't write and don't see). All this code is being executed at the same time. While the computer executes your `main` method's statements, one after another, the computer takes time out, sneaks away briefly, and executes statements from some other, unseen methods. For most simple Java programs, these other methods are ones that are defined as part of the Java Virtual Machine (JVM).

For instance, Java has an event-handling thread. While your code runs, the event-handling thread's code runs in the background. The event-handling thread's code listens for mouse clicks and takes appropriate action whenever a user clicks the mouse. Figure 15-3 illustrates how this works.

Your code's thread	The event handling thread
setLayout(new FlowLayout()); add(textField); add(button); add(label);	Did the user click the mouse? . Did the user click the mouse?
button.addActionListener(this); pack(); setVisible(true);	. Did the user click the mouse? Yes? Okay, then. I'll call the actionPerformed method.

Figure 15-3: Two Java threads.

When the user clicks the button, the event-handling thread says, "Okay, the button was clicked. So, what should I do about that?" And the answer is, "Call some `actionPerformed` methods." It's as if the event-handling thread has code that looks like this:

```
if (buttonJustGotClicked()) {
    object1.actionPerformed(infoAboutTheClick);
    object2.actionPerformed(infoAboutTheClick);
    object3.actionPerformed(infoAboutTheClick);
}
```

Of course, behind every answer is yet another question. In this situation, the follow-up question is, "Where does the event-handling thread find `actionPerformed` methods to call?" And there's another question: "What if you don't want the event-handling thread to call certain `actionPerformed` methods that are lurking in your code?"

Well, that's why you call the `addActionListener` method. In Listing 15-1, the call

```
button.addActionListener(this);
```

tells the event-handling thread, "Put this code's `actionPerformed` method on your list of methods to be called. Call this code's `actionPerformed` method whenever the button is clicked."

So, that's how it works. To have the computer call an `actionPerformed` method, you register the method with Java's event-handling thread. You do this registration by calling `addActionListener`. The `addActionListener` method belongs to the object whose clicks (and other events) you're waiting for. In Listing 15-1, you're waiting for the button object to be clicked, and the `addActionListener` method belongs to that button object.

The keyword this

In Chapters 9 and 10, the keyword `this` gives you access to instance variables from the code inside a method. So, what does the `this` keyword really mean? Well, compare it with the English phrase "state your name."

> I, (state your name), do solemnly swear, to uphold the constitution of the *Philadelphia Central High School Photography Society*. . . .

The phrase "state your name" is a placeholder. It's a space in which each person puts his or her own name.

> I, Bob, do solemnly swear. . . .

> I, Fred, do solemnly swear. . . .

Think of the pledge ("I . . . do solemnly swear . . .") as a piece of code in a Java class. In that piece of code is the placeholder phrase, "state your name." Whenever an instance of the class (a person) executes the code (that is, takes the pledge), the instance fills in its own name in place of the phrase "state your name."

The `this` keyword works the same way. It sits inside the code that defines the `GameFrame` class. Whenever an instance of `GameFrame` is constructed, the instance calls `addActionListener(this)`. In that call, the `this` keyword stands for the instance itself.

```
button.addActionListener(thisGameFrameInstance);
```

By calling `button.addActionListener(this)`, the `GameFrame` instance is saying, "Add my `actionPerformed` method to the list of methods that are called whenever the button is clicked." And indeed, the `GameFrame` instance has an `actionPerformed` method. The `GameFrame` has to have an `actionPerformed` method because the `GameFrame` class implements the `ActionListener` interface. It's funny how that all fits together.

Inside the actionPerformed method

The `actionPerformed` method in Listing 15-1 uses a bunch of tricks from the Java API. Here's a brief list of those tricks:

- Every instance of `JTextField` (and of `JLabel`) has its own getter and setter methods, including `getText` and `setText`. Calling `getText` fetches whatever string of characters is in the component. Calling `setText` changes the characters that are in the component. In Listing 15-1, judicious use of `getText` and `setText` pulls a number out of the text field and replaces the number with either nothing (the empty string `" "`) or the number, followed by the word *Yes!*

- Every component in the `javax.swing` package (`JTextField`, `JButton`, or whatever) has a `setEnabled` method. When you call `setEnabled(false)`, the component gets that limp, gray, washed-out look and can no longer receive button clicks or keystrokes.

- Every component in the `javax.swing` package has a `requestFocus` method. When you call `requestFocus`, the component gets the privilege of receiving the user's next input. For example, in Listing 15-1, the call `textField.requestFocus()` says "even though the user may have just clicked the button, put a cursor in the text field. That way, the user can type another guess in the text field without clicking the text field first."

 You can perform a test to make sure that the object referred to by the button variable is really the thing that was clicked. Just write `if (e.getSource() == button)`. If your code has two buttons, `button1` and `button2`, you can test to find out which button was clicked. You can write `if (e.getSource() == button1)` and `if (e.getSource() == button2)`.

The serialVersionUID

Chapter 9 introduces the SuppressWarnings annotation to avoid dealing with something called a serialVersionUID. A serialVersionUID is a number that helps Java avoid version conflicts when you send an object from one place to another. For example, you can send the state of your JFrame object to another computer's screen. Then the other computer can check the frame's version number to make sure that no funny business is taking place.

In Chapter 9, I side-step the serialVersionUID issue by telling Java to ignore any warnings about missing serial version numbers. But in Listing 15-1, I take a bolder approach. I give my JFrame object a real serialVersionUID. This is my first version of GameFrame, so I give this GameFrame the version number 1. (Actually, I give this GameFrame the number 1L, meaning the long value 1. See Chapter 4.)

So when would you bother to change a class's serialVersionUID number? If version number 1 is nice, is version number 2 even better? The answer is complicated, but the bottom line is, don't change the serialVersionUID number unless you make incompatible changes to the class's code. By "incompatible changes," I mean changes that make it impossible for the receiving computer's existing code to handle your newly created objects.

For more details about the serialVersionUID and what constitutes an incompatible code change, check out this site:

```
http://download.oracle.com/javase/7/docs/platform/
           serialization/spec/version.html#6678
```

Java has some visual tools to help you design a GUI interface. If you visit www.eclipse.org/windowbuilder, you can read about WindowBuilder for Eclipse. With WindowBuilder, you drag components from a palette onto a frame. (The components include buttons, text fields, and other goodies.) Using your mouse, you can move and resize each component. As you design the frame visually, Eclipse creates the frame's code automatically. Each component on the frame has a little spreadsheet showing the component's properties. For example, you can change the text on a button's face by changing the *text* entry in the button's spreadsheet. When you right-click or control-click the picture of a component, you get the option of jumping to the component's actionPerformed method. In the actionPerformed method, you add Java code, such as button.setText("You clicked me!"). A tool like WindowBuilder makes the design of GUI interfaces quicker, more natural, and more intuitive.

This chapter describes features of Java's Swing framework. Since 1998, Swing has been Java's primary framework for developing GUI applications. But late in 2011, Oracle added a newer framework — JavaFX — to Java's core. JavaFX provides a richer set of components than Swing. But for simple applications, JavaFX is more difficult to use. If you're interested in reading more about JavaFX, visit this book's website (www.allmycode.com/JavaForDummies). At the website, you can download GUI versions of many examples in this book. Some of the downloadable GUI versions use JavaFX.

Responding to Things Other Than Button Clicks

When you know how to respond to one kind of event, responding to other kinds of events is easy. Listings 15-3 and 15-4 display a window that converts between U.S. and U.K. currencies. The code in these listings responds to many kinds of events. Figures 15-4, 15-5, and 15-6 show some pictures of the code in action.

Listing 15-3:   Displaying the Local Currency

```java
import java.awt.Color;
import java.awt.FlowLayout;
import java.awt.event.ItemEvent;
import java.awt.event.ItemListener;
import java.awt.event.KeyEvent;
import java.awt.event.KeyListener;
import java.awt.event.MouseEvent;
import java.awt.event.MouseListener;
import java.text.NumberFormat;
import java.util.Locale;

import javax.swing.JComboBox;
import javax.swing.JFrame;
import javax.swing.JLabel;
import javax.swing.JTextField;

class MoneyFrame extends JFrame implements
            KeyListener, ItemListener, MouseListener {
    private static final long serialVersionUID = 1L;

    JLabel fromCurrencyLabel = new JLabel(" ");
    JTextField textField = new JTextField(5);
    JLabel label = new JLabel("            ");
    JComboBox<String> combo = new JComboBox<String>();
```

```java
NumberFormat currencyUS =
    NumberFormat.getCurrencyInstance();
NumberFormat currencyUK =
    NumberFormat.getCurrencyInstance(Locale.UK);

public MoneyFrame() {
    setLayout(new FlowLayout());

    add(fromCurrencyLabel);
    add(textField);
    combo.addItem("US to UK");
    combo.addItem("UK to US");
    add(label);
    add(combo);

    textField.addKeyListener(this);
    combo.addItemListener(this);
    label.addMouseListener(this);
    setDefaultCloseOperation(JFrame.EXIT_ON_CLOSE);

    setSize(300, 100);
    setVisible(true);
}

void setTextOnLabel() {
    String amountString = "";
    String fromCurrency = "";

    try {
        double amount =
            Double.parseDouble(textField.getText());

        if(combo.getSelectedItem().equals("US to UK"))
        {
            amountString = " = " +
                currencyUK.format(amount * 0.61214);
            fromCurrency = "$";
        }
        if(combo.getSelectedItem().equals("UK to US"))
        {
            amountString = " = " +
                currencyUS.format(amount * 1.63361);
            fromCurrency = "\u00A3";
        }
    } catch (NumberFormatException e) {
    }

    label.setText(amountString);
    fromCurrencyLabel.setText(fromCurrency);
}
```

(continued)

Listing 15-3 *(continued)*

```
    @Override
    public void keyReleased(KeyEvent k) {
        setTextOnLabel();
    }

    @Override
    public void keyPressed(KeyEvent k) {
    }

    @Override
    public void keyTyped(KeyEvent k) {
    }

    @Override
    public void itemStateChanged(ItemEvent i) {
        setTextOnLabel();
    }

    @Override
    public void mouseEntered(MouseEvent m) {
        label.setForeground(Color.red);
    }

    @Override
    public void mouseExited(MouseEvent m) {
        label.setForeground(Color.black);
    }

    @Override
    public void mouseClicked(MouseEvent m) {
    }

    @Override
    public void mousePressed(MouseEvent m) {
    }

    @Override
    public void mouseReleased(MouseEvent m) {
    }
}
```

Listing 15-4:   Calling the Code in Listing 15-3

```
public class ShowMoneyFrame {

    public static void main(String args[]) {
        new MoneyFrame();
    }
}
```

Figure 15-4:
U.S. to U.K.
currency.

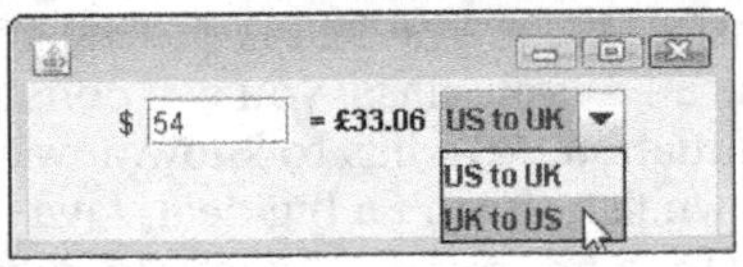

Figure 15-5:
Using the
combo box.

Figure 15-6:
U.K. to U.S.
currency.

Okay, so Listing 15-3 is a little long. Even so, the outline of the code in Listing 15-3 isn't too bad. Here's what the outline looks like:

```
class MoneyFrame extends JFrame implements
            KeyListener, ItemListener, MouseListener {

    variable declarations

    constructor for the MoneyFrame class

    declaration of a method named setTextOnLabel

    all the methods that are required because the class
        implements three interfaces
}
```

The constructor in Listing 15-3 adds the following four components to the new MoneyFrame window:

✔ **A label:** In Figure 15-4, the label displays a dollar sign.

✔ **A text field:** In Figure 15-4, the user types **54** in the text field.

✔ **Another label:** In Figure 15-4, the label displays £33.06.

✔ **A combo box:** In Figure 15-4, the combo box displays *US to UK*. In Figure 15-5, the user selects an item in the box. In Figure 15-6, the selected item is *UK to US*.

In Java, a JComboBox (commonly called a *drop-down list*) can display items of any kind. In Listing 15-3, the generic new JComboBox<String>() code constructs a JComboBox whose entries have type String. That seems sensible, but if your application has a Person class, you can construct new JComboBox<Person>(). In that situation, Java has to know how to display each Person object in the drop-down list. (It isn't a big deal. Java finds out how to display a person by looking for a toString() method inside the Person class.)

The MoneyFrame implements three interfaces — the KeyListener, ItemListener, and MouseListener interfaces. Because it implements three interfaces, the code can listen for three kinds of events. I discuss the interfaces and events in the following list:

✔ KeyListener: A class that implements the KeyListener interface must have three methods named keyReleased, keyPressed, and keyTyped. When you lift your finger off a key, the event-handling thread calls keyReleased.

In Listing 15-3, the keyReleased method calls setTextOnLabel. My setTextOnLabel method checks to see what's currently selected in the combo box. If the user selects the US to UK option, the setTextOnLabel method converts dollars to pounds. If the user selects the UK to US option, the setTextOnLabel method converts pounds to dollars.

In the setTextOnLabel method, I use the string "\u00A3". The funny-looking \u00A3 code is Java's UK pound sign. (The u in \u00A3 stands for *Unicode* — an international standard for representing characters in the world's alphabets.) If my operating system's settings defaulted to UK currency, in the runs of Java programs, the pound sign would appear on its own. For information about all this, check out the Locale class in Java's API documentation.

By the way, if you're thinking in terms of real currency conversion, forget about it. This program uses rates that may or may not have been accurate at one time. Sure, a program can reach out on the Internet for the most up-to-date currency rates, but at the moment, you have other Javafish to fry.

✔ ItemListener: A class that implements the ItemListener interface
must have an itemStateChanged method. When you select an item in
a combo box, the event-handling thread calls itemStateChanged.

In Listing 15-3, when the user selects US to UK or UK to US in the combo
box, the event-handling thread calls the itemStateChanged method.
In turn, the itemStateChanged method calls setTextOnLabel,
and so on.

✔ MouseListener: A class that implements the MouseListener interface must have mouseEntered, mouseExited, mouseClicked,
mousePressed, and mouseReleased methods. Implementing
MouseListener is different from implementing ActionListener.
When you implement ActionListener, as in Listing 15-1, the
event-handling thread responds only to mouse clicks. But with
MouseListener, the thread responds to the user pressing the
mouse, releasing the mouse, and more.

In Listing 15-3, the mouseEntered and mouseExited methods are
called whenever you move over or away from the label. How do you
know that the label is involved? Just look at the code in the MoneyFrame
constructor. The label variable's addMouseListener method is the
one that's called.

Look at the mouseEntered and mouseExited methods in Listing 15-3.
When mouseEntered or mouseExited is called, the computer forges
ahead and calls setForeground. This setForeground method
changes the color of the label's text.

Isn't modern life wonderful? The Java API even has a Color class with
names like Color.red and Color.black.

Listing 15-3 has several methods that aren't really used. For instance,
when you implement MouseListener, your code has to have its own
mouseReleased method. You need the mouseReleased method not
because you're going to do anything special when the user releases the
mouse button, but because you made a promise to the Java compiler and
have to keep that promise.

Creating Inner Classes

Here's big news! You can define a class inside of another class! For the user,
Listing 15-5 behaves the same way as Listing 15-1. But in Listing 15-5, the
GameFrame class contains a class named MyActionListener.

Listing 15-5:   A Class within a Class

```java
import java.awt.FlowLayout;
import java.awt.event.ActionEvent;
import java.awt.event.ActionListener;
import java.util.Random;

import javax.swing.JButton;
import javax.swing.JFrame;
import javax.swing.JLabel;
import javax.swing.JTextField;

class GameFrame extends JFrame {
    private static final long serialVersionUID = 1L;

    int randomNumber = new Random().nextInt(10) + 1;
    int numGuesses = 0;

    JTextField textField = new JTextField(5);
    JButton button = new JButton("Guess");
    JLabel label = new JLabel(numGuesses + " guesses");

    public GameFrame() {
        setDefaultCloseOperation(JFrame.EXIT_ON_CLOSE);
        setLayout(new FlowLayout());
        add(textField);
        add(button);
        add(label);
        button.addActionListener(new MyActionListener());
        pack();
        setVisible(true);
    }

    class MyActionListener implements ActionListener {

        @Override
        public void actionPerformed(ActionEvent e) {
            String textFieldText = textField.getText();

            if (Integer.parseInt
                    (textFieldText) == randomNumber) {
                button.setEnabled(false);
                textField.setText
                    (textField.getText() + " Yes!");
                textField.setEnabled(false);
            } else {
                textField.setText("");
                textField.requestFocus();
            }
```

```
            numGuesses++;
            String guessWord =
                (numGuesses == 1) ? " guess" : " guesses";
            label.setText(numGuesses + guessWord);
        }
    }
}
```

The `MyActionListener` class in Listing 15-5 is an *inner class*. An inner class is a lot like any other class. But within an inner class's code, you can refer to the enclosing class's fields. For example, several statements inside `MyActionListener` use the name `textField`, and `textField` is defined in the enclosing `GameFrame` class.

Notice that the code in Listing 15-5 uses the `MyActionListener` class only once. (The only use is in a call to `button.addActionListener`.) So I ask, do you really need a name for something that's used only once? No, you don't. You can substitute the entire definition of the inner class inside the call to `button.addActionListener`. When you do this, you have an *anonymous inner class*. Listing 15-6 shows you how it works.

Listing 15-6:   A Class with No Name (Inside a Class with a Name)

```java
import java.awt.FlowLayout;
import java.awt.event.ActionEvent;
import java.awt.event.ActionListener;
import java.util.Random;

import javax.swing.JButton;
import javax.swing.JFrame;
import javax.swing.JLabel;
import javax.swing.JTextField;

class GameFrame extends JFrame {
    private static final long serialVersionUID = 1L;

    int randomNumber = new Random().nextInt(10) + 1;
    int numGuesses = 0;

    JTextField textField = new JTextField(5);
    JButton button = new JButton("Guess");
    JLabel label = new JLabel(numGuesses + " guesses");

    public GameFrame() {
        setDefaultCloseOperation(JFrame.EXIT_ON_CLOSE);
        setLayout(new FlowLayout());
        add(textField);
        add(button);
        add(label);
```

(continued)

Listing 15-6 *(continued)*

```java
        button.addActionListener(new ActionListener() {

            @Override
            public void actionPerformed(ActionEvent e) {
                String textFieldText = textField.getText();

                if (Integer.parseInt
                        (textFieldText) == randomNumber) {
                    button.setEnabled(false);
                    textField.setText
                        (textField.getText() + " Yes!");
                    textField.setEnabled(false);
                } else {
                    textField.setText("");
                    textField.requestFocus();
                }

                numGuesses++;
                String guessWord =
                    (numGuesses == 1) ? " guess" : " guesses";
                label.setText(numGuesses + guessWord);
            }
        });
        pack();
        setVisible(true);
    }
}
```

Inner classes are good for things like event handlers, such as the `action Performed` method in this chapter's examples. The most difficult thing about an *anonymous* inner class is keeping track of the parentheses, the curly braces, and the indentation. So my humble advice is, start by writing code without any inner classes, as in the code from Listing 15-1. Later, when you become bored with ordinary Java classes, experiment by changing some of your ordinary classes into inner classes.

Chapter 16

Writing Java Applets

● ●

In This Chapter

▶ Creating a simple applet

▶ Building applet animation

▶ Putting buttons (and other such things) on an applet

● ●

*W*ith Java's first big burst onto the scene in 1995, the thing that made the language so popular was the notion of an applet. An *applet* is a Java program that sits inside a web browser window. The applet has its own rectangular area on a web page. The applet can display a drawing, show an image, make a figure move, respond to information from the user, and do all kinds of interesting things. When you put a real, live computer program on a web page, you open up a world of possibilities.

Applets 101

Listings 16-1 and 16-2 show you a very simple Java applet. The applet displays the words *Java For Dummies* inside a rectangular box. (See Figure 16-1.)

Listing 16-1:   An Applet

```
import javax.swing.JApplet;

public class SimpleApplet extends JApplet {
    private static final long serialVersionUID = 1L;

    public void init() {
        setContentPane(new DummiesPanel());
    }
}
```

Listing 16-2:   Some Helper Code for the Applet

```java
import javax.swing.JPanel;
import java.awt.Font;
import java.awt.Graphics;

class DummiesPanel extends JPanel {
    private static final long serialVersionUID = 1L;

    public void paint(Graphics myGraphics) {

        myGraphics.drawRect(50, 60, 220, 75);
        myGraphics.setFont
                    (new Font("Dialog", Font.BOLD, 24));
        myGraphics.drawString("Java For Dummies", 55, 100);
    }
}
```

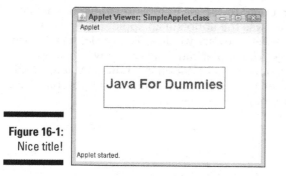

Figure 16-1:
Nice title!

When you run the code in Listings 16-1 and 16-2, you don't execute a `main` method. Instead, you run a web browser, and the web browser visits an HTML file. The HTML file includes a reference to the applet's Java code, and the applet appears on your web page. Listing 16-3 shows a bare minimum HTML file.

Listing 16-3:   A One-Line Web Page

```html
<applet code=SimpleApplet width=350 height=200></applet>
```

These days, most web browsers make it difficult to run Java applets. So in Figure 16-1, I don't run Firefox, Internet Explorer, or any other commonly used web browser. Instead, I run Java's own *Applet Viewer* — a small browser-like application made specifically for testing Java applets.

If you use an IDE such as Eclipse, NetBeans, or IntelliJ IDEA to launch this section's example, the IDE probably opens the Java AppletViewer automatically. If you don't use an IDE (or if the IDE doesn't open the AppletViewer), you can launch the AppletViewer manually. The command to launch the AppletViewer is

```
appletviewer name-of-the-file-containing-Listing-16-3
```

Waiting to be called

When you look at the code in Listings 16-1 and 16-2, you may notice one thing — an applet doesn't have a `main` method. That's because an applet isn't a complete program. An applet is a class that contains methods, and your web browser calls those methods (directly or indirectly). Do you see the `init` method in Listing 16-1? The browser calls this `init` method. Then the `init` method's call to `setContentPane` drags in the code from Listing 16-2.

Now, take a look at the `paint` method in Listing 16-2. The browser calls this `paint` method automatically, and the `paint` method tells the browser how to draw your applet on the screen.

For a list of applet methods that your web browser calls, see the section entitled "The methods in an applet," later in this chapter.

A public class

Notice that the `SimpleApplet` in Listing 16-1 is a public class. If you create an applet and you don't make the class public, you get an `Applet not inited` or a `Loading Java Applet Failed` error. To state things very plainly, any class that extends `JApplet` must be public. If the class isn't public, your web browser can't call the class's methods.

To state things a little less plainly, a class can have either `default` access or `public` access. The only code that can reference a `default` access class is code that's in the *same package* as the `default` access class. Now remember that your web browser tries to call methods that are buried inside your applet class. Because the web browser isn't likely to be in the same package as your applet (believe me, it's not), the applet must be public. If the applet isn't public, your web browser's code (code that's not in the same package as the applet) can't call any of your applet's methods.

For more information on `public` and `default` access, see Chapter 14.

The Java API (again)

The code in Listing 16-2 uses a few interesting Java API tricks. Here are some tricks that don't appear in any earlier chapters:

✔ `drawRect`: Draws an unfilled rectangle.

Look at the call to `drawRect` in Listing 16-2. According to that call, the rectangle's upper-left corner is 50 pixels across and 60 pixels down from the upper-left corner of the panel. The rectangle's lower-right corner is 220 pixels across and 75 pixels down from the upper-left corner of the panel.

I wanted the rectangle to surround the words *Java For Dummies*. To come up with numbers for the `drawRect` call, I used trial and error. However, you can make the program figure out how many pixels the words *Java For Dummies* take up. To do this, you need the `FontMetrics` class. (For information on `FontMetrics`, see the Java API documentation.)

✔ The `Font` class: Describes the features of a character font.

Listing 16-2 creates a bold, 24-point font with the Dialog typeface style. Other typeface styles include DialogInput, Monospaced, Serif, and SansSerif.

✔ `drawString`: Draws a string of characters.

Listing 16-2 draws the string `"Java For Dummies"` on the face of the panel. The string's lower-left corner is 55 pixels across and 100 pixels down from the upper-left corner of the panel.

Making Things Move

This section's applet is cool because it's animated — you can see an odometer change on the screen. When you look at the code for this applet, you may think the code is quite complicated. Well, in a way, it is. A lot is going on when you use Java to create animation. On the other hand, the code for this applet is mostly boilerplate. To create your own animation, you can borrow most of this section's code. To see what I'm talking about, look at Listings 16-4 and 16-5.

Listing 16-4:   An Odometer Applet

```
import javax.swing.JApplet;
import javax.swing.Timer;
import java.awt.Color;
import java.awt.event.ActionListener;
import java.awt.event.ActionEvent;

public class Odometer extends JApplet
                                implements ActionListener {
    private static final long serialVersionUID = 1L;

    Timer timer;

    public void init() {
        OdometerPanel panel = new OdometerPanel();

        panel.setBackground(Color.white);
        setContentPane(panel);
    }
```

```java
    public void start() {

        if (timer == null) {
            timer = new Timer(100, this);
            timer.start();
        } else {
            timer.restart();
        }
    }

    public void stop() {

        if (timer != null) {
            timer.stop();
            timer = null;
        }
    }

    public void actionPerformed(ActionEvent e) {

        repaint();
    }
}
```

Listing 16-5: The Odometer Panel

```java
import javax.swing.JPanel;
import java.awt.Font;
import java.awt.Graphics;

class OdometerPanel extends JPanel {
    private static final long serialVersionUID = 1L;

    long hitCount = 239472938472L;

    public void paint(Graphics myGraphics) {

        myGraphics.setFont
            (new Font("Monospaced", Font.PLAIN, 24));
        myGraphics.drawString
            ("You are visitor number " +
                Long.toString(hitCount++), 50, 50);
    }
}
```

A complete web page to display the applet in Listings 16-4 and 16-5 might consist of only one line, such as

```
<applet code=Odometer width=600 height=200></applet>
```

For a snapshot of the odometer applet in action, see Figure 16-2. Notice the number in the figure. It's not the same as the starting value of the `hitCount` variable. That's because every 100 milliseconds the applet adds 1 to the value of `hitCount` and displays the new value. The odometer isn't reporting an honest hit count, but it's still really cute.

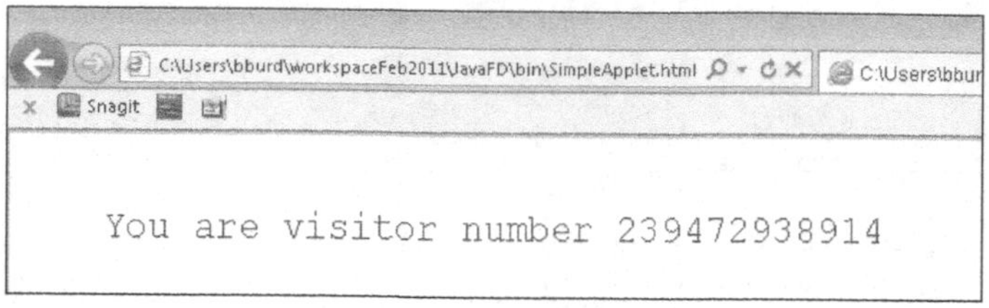

Figure 16-2: A popular website.

> ← → | C:\Users\bburd\workspaceFeb2011\JavaFD\bin\SimpleApplet.html | 🔍 ▾ ⓒ ✕ | 🌐 C:\Users\bbur
> ✕ | 📷 Snagit 🖼 🖼
>
>   You are visitor number 239472938914

The methods in an applet

Most of the method names in Listings 16-4 and 16-5 are standard for an applet. The Java API `JApplet` and `JPanel` classes have default declarations for these methods, so you don't really have to declare these methods yourself. The only methods that you have to put in your code are the methods that you want to customize.

Here's a list of `JApplet` and `JPanel` methods that your web browser automatically calls:

- ✔ `init`: The browser calls `init` when you first visit the page containing the applet. Imagine that you close the web browser. Later, you start the browser running again and revisit the page containing the applet. Then the browser calls the applet's `init` method again.

- ✔ `start`: The browser calls `start` right after it calls `init`. If your applet performs any continuous work, you can begin that work's code in the applet's `start` method. For instance, if your applet has any animation, the code to begin running that animation is in your `start` method.

- ✔ `paint`: The browser calls the `paint` method in Listing 16-5 right after it calls `start`. (Yes, the `start` method and the `paint` method are in different classes, but the browser figures things out because of the call to `setContentPane` in Listing 16-4.) The `paint` method has instructions for drawing your applet on the screen. For an explanation, see Chapter 14.

  The browser can call `paint` several times. For instance, imagine that you cover part of the browser with another window. Or maybe you shrink the browser so that only part of the applet is showing. Later, when you uncover the applet or enlarge the browser window again, the browser calls the panel's `paint` method.

✔ stop: When the applet's work should cease, the browser calls the stop method. Say, for instance, that you click a link that takes you away from the page with the applet on it. Then the browser calls the applet's stop method. Later, when you revisit the page with the applet on it, the browser calls the applet's start method again.

What to put into all these methods

The code in Listings 16-4 and 16-5 uses a standard formula for creating animation inside an applet. Here's a *very brief* explanation:

✔ The applet implements the ActionListener interface.

✔ The start method creates a new timer with the following code:

```
new Timer(100, this)
```

Every 100 milliseconds (every tenth of a second), the timer in Listing 16-4 rings its alarm.

When it "rings its alarm," the timer actually gets Java to call an action Performed method. And whose actionPerformed method does Java call? Once again, the keyword this answers the question. In Listing 16-4, the word this refers to this very same code — this instance of the Odometer object that contains the new Timer(100, this) call. So every tenth of a second, when the timer rings its alarm, Java calls the actionPerformed method in Listing 16-4. How nice and tidy it is!

✔ The actionPerformed method calls the repaint method. Under the hood, a call to repaint always calls somebody's paint method. In this example, that somebody is the code in Listing 16-5. This paint method draws the words You are visitor number *whatever* on the screen.

✔ At some point, the day is done, and your browser calls the stop method. When this happens, the stop method tosses the timer into the dumpster.

If it weren't such standard code, I'd feel guilty for explaining this stuff so briefly. But, really, to achieve motion in your own applet, just copy Listings 16-4 and 16-5. Then replace the listing's init and paint methods with your own code.

So, what do you put in your init and paint methods?

✔ **If you declare an init method, the method should contain setup code for the applet — stuff that happens once, the first time the applet is loaded.**

In Listing 16-4, the setup code fiddles with a panel:

• It creates a panel by calling the OdometerPanel constructor.

- It makes the panel's background white. (This ensures that the rectangle housing the applet blends nicely with the rest of the web page.)

- It forges a rock-solid connection between the panel and the applet. It does this by calling the setContentPane method.

✔ **The paint method describes a single snapshot of the applet's motion.**

In Listing 16-5, the paint method sets the graphics buffer's font, writes the hitCount value on the screen, and then adds 1 to the hitCount. (Who needs real visitors when you can increment your own hitCount variable?)

The value of the hitCount variable starts high and becomes even higher. To store such big numbers, I give hitCount the type long. I use the Long class's toString method to turn hitCount into a string of characters. This toString method is like the Integer class's parseInt method.

I introduce the parseInt method in Chapter 11.

To debug an applet, you can put calls to System.out.println in the applet's code. If you use Eclipse, the println output appears in Eclipse's Console view.

Responding to Events in an Applet

This section has an applet with interactive thingamajigs on it. This applet is just like the examples in Chapter 15. In fact, to create Listing 16-7, I started with the code in Listing 15-1. I didn't do this out of laziness (although, heaven knows, I can certainly be lazy). I did it because applets are so much like Java frames. If you take the code for a frame and trim it down, you can usually create a decent applet. This section's applet lives in Listings 16-6 and 16-7.

Listing 16-6: A Guessing Game Applet

```
import javax.swing.JApplet;

public class GameApplet extends JApplet {
    private static final long serialVersionUID = 1L;

    public void init() {
        setContentPane(new GamePanel());
    }
}
```

Listing 16-7:   The Guessing Game Panel

```java
import java.awt.Color;
import java.awt.event.ActionEvent;
import java.awt.event.ActionListener;
import java.util.Random;

import javax.swing.JButton;
import javax.swing.JLabel;
import javax.swing.JPanel;
import javax.swing.JTextField;

class GamePanel extends JPanel implements ActionListener {
    private static final long serialVersionUID = 1L;

    int randomNumber = new Random().nextInt(10) + 1;
    int numGuesses = 0;

    JTextField textField = new JTextField(5);
    JButton button = new JButton("Guess");
    JLabel label = new JLabel(numGuesses + " guesses");

    GamePanel() {
        setBackground(Color.WHITE);
        add(textField);
        add(button);
        add(label);
        button.addActionListener(this);
    }

    public void actionPerformed(ActionEvent e) {
        String textFieldText = textField.getText();

        if (Integer.parseInt(textFieldText)
                                    == randomNumber) {
            button.setEnabled(false);
            textField.setText
                    (textField.getText() + " Yes!");
            textField.setEnabled(false);
        } else {
            textField.setText("");
            textField.requestFocus();
        }

        numGuesses++;
        String guessWord =
            (numGuesses == 1) ? " guess" : " guesses";
        label.setText(numGuesses + guessWord);
    }
}
```

To run the code in Listings 16-6 and 16-7, you need an HTML file:

```html
<applet code="GameApplet" width=225 height=50></applet>
```

Figures 16-3 and 16-4 show you what happens when you run this section's listings. It's pretty much the same as what happens when you run the code in Listing 15-1. The big difference is that the applet appears as part of a web page in a browser window.

Figure 16-3:
An incorrect guess.

C:\Users\bburd\workspaceFeb2

✕ 🖵 Snagit 📇 🕮

8   **Guess**   2 guesses

Figure 16-4:
The correct guess.

C:\Users\bburd\workspaceFe

✕ 🖵 Snagit 📇 🕮

4 Yes!   Guess   6 guesses

Instead of noticing whatever code Listing 16-7 may have, notice what code the listing doesn't have. To change Listing 15-1 to Listing 16-7, I remove several lines.

✔ **I don't bother calling `setLayout`.**

The default layout for an applet is `FlowLayout`, which is just what I want.

If you want info on how `FlowLayout` works, see Chapter 9.

✔ **I don't call the `pack` method.**

The `width` and `height` fields in the HTML applet tag determine the applet's size.

✔ **I don't call the `setVisible` method.**

An applet is visible by default.

The only other significant change is between Listings 15-2 and 16-6. Like many other applets, Listing 16-6 has no `main` method. Instead, Listing 16-6 has an `init` method. You don't need a `main` method because you never need to say `new GameApplet()` anywhere in your code. The web browser says it for you. Then, after the web browser creates an instance of the `GameApplet` class, the browser calls the instance's `init` method. That's the standard scenario for running a Java applet.

Chapter 17

Using Java Database Connectivity

. . . .

In This Chapter

▶ Connecting to a database

▶ Inserting values into a database

▶ Making queries to a database

. . . .

*W*henever I teach Java to professional programmers, I always hear the same old thing. "We don't need to make any cute little characters fly across the screen. No blinking buttons for us. We need to access databases. Yup, just show us how to write Java programs that talk to databases."

So here it is, folks — Java Database Connectivity.

JDBC and Java DB

When I first started working with databases, my toughest problem was connecting to a database. I had written all the Java code. (Well, I had copied all the Java code from some book.) The Java part was easy. The hard part was getting my code to find the database on the system.

Part of the problem was that the way you get your code to talk to the database depends on the kind of system you have and the kind of database that you're running on your system. The books that I was using couldn't be too specific on all the details because the details (having nothing to do with Java) varied from one reader's computer to another. And now I'm writing my own chapter about database connectivity. What's an author to do?

Fortunately, the Java Development Kit (JDK) comes with its own built-in database — *Java DB*. Based on the Apache Derby database, Java DB is secure, lightweight, and standards-based. Java DB runs seamlessly along with the rest of the Java JDK. The Java gurus introduced Java DB with the release of Java 6.

Java DB makes life easier for me by providing a common database that all my readers can use. The database is freely available, and it requires no setup.

And what if you don't use Java DB? What if all your data is stored in other kinds of databases, namely, MySQL, PostgreSQL, SQLite, Oracle, Microsoft Access, DB2, or almost any other database? Then Java has a solution for you! The Java Database Connectivity (JDBC) classes provide common access to most database management systems. Just get a driver for your favorite vendor's system, customize two lines of code in each of this chapter's examples, and you're ready to run the code.

Creating Data

The crux of JDBC is contained in two packages: `java.sql` and `javax.sql`, which are both in the Java API. This chapter's examples use the classes in `java.sql`. The first example is shown in Listing 17-1.

Listing 17-1:   Creating a Database and a Table, and Inserting Data

```java
import java.sql.DriverManager;
import java.sql.Statement;
import java.sql.Connection;
import java.sql.SQLException;

public class CreateTable {

    public static void main(String args[]) {

        final String DRIVER =
            "org.apache.derby.jdbc.EmbeddedDriver";
        final String CONNECTION =
            "jdbc:derby:AccountDatabase;create=true";


        try {
            Class.forName(DRIVER).newInstance();
        } catch (InstantiationException e) {
          e.printStackTrace();
        } catch (IllegalAccessException e) {
          e.printStackTrace();
        } catch (ClassNotFoundException e) {
          e.printStackTrace();
        }


        try (Connection connection =
                DriverManager.getConnection(CONNECTION);
```

```
    Statement statement =
        connection.createStatement()) {

  statement.executeUpdate(
    "create table ACCOUNTS                         "
    + "  (NAME VARCHAR(32) NOT NULL PRIMARY KEY, "
    + "   ADDRESS VARCHAR(32),                    "
    + "   BALANCE FLOAT)                         ");

  statement.executeUpdate(
    "insert into ACCOUNTS values                  "
    + "  ('Barry Burd', '222 Cyber Lane', 24.02)");

  statement.executeUpdate(
    "insert into ACCOUNTS values                  "
    + "  ('Joe Dow', '111 Luddite Street', 55.63)");

  } catch (SQLException e) {
      e.printStackTrace();
  }
  }
}
```

To use MySQL instead of Java DB, make the following changes in Listing 17-1: Change the value of DRIVER to "com.mysql.jdbc.Driver". Change the value of CONNECTION to "jdbc:mysql://localhost/ AccountDatabase;create=true". Make similar changes for DB2, Oracle, and other databases.

To run database code, you must have a file containing a suitable database driver, and that file must be in a place where Java can find it. In this chapter's examples, I connect to a Java DB database, also known as an Apache Derby database. The driver is in a file named derby.jar, which normally lives in the JDK's db/lib directory. To make db/lib/derby.jar available to my Java programs, I add this .jar file to my Java classpath.

The way you add a .jar file to your classpath depends on the kind of IDE you use and possibly on the kind of operating system you use. In Eclipse, I select Project➪Properties➪Java Build Path. Then I click the Add External JARs button and navigate to the db/lib directory. For other IDEs, the steps are slightly different.

When you run the code in Listing 17-1, nothing seems to happen. The program starts running and then stops running. That's about it. The code has no visible output because all the output goes to a database. So, to see the result of running the code in Listing 17-1, you have to look for changes in the database itself. So read on!

In the previous paragraph, I wrote that running Listing 17-1 is terribly uneventful. I wrote that "nothing seems to happen" and that "The code has no visible output." But, if you look closely, you can find some evidence of a run of the Listing 17-1 code. In particular, your hard drive has a few additional files after the first run of this code. One of these files, named `derby.log`, contains text describing the starting and stopping of the Derby database software. You can also find a new folder named `derbyDB`, which contains more log files, a `service.properties` file, and a folder full of `.dat files`. (These `.dat` files contain all the stuff stored in the database.) If you use Eclipse, you can make these new files and folders visible by selecting your project branch in the Package Explorer and then choosing File➪Refresh.

Using SQL commands

In Listing 17-1, the heart of the code lies in three calls to `executeUpdate`. Each `executeUpdate` call contains a string — a normal, Java, double-quoted string of characters. To keep the code readable, I've chopped each string into parts. I separate the parts with plus signs (Java's string concatenation operator).

Java's plus sign does double duty. For numbers, the plus sign performs addition. For strings, the plus sign squishes two strings together, creating one big, combined string.

You can make a double-quoted string as long as you like. When you get to the right edge of your screen, just keep typing. If you want to see the whole string without scrolling, however, you can break the string into pieces, as I did in Listing 17-1. Just separate the pieces with plus signs.

You cannot break a Java string into pieces by just pressing Enter and moving to the next line. When you start a string with the double-quote ("), the ending double-quote must be on the same line of code.

If you're familiar with SQL (Structured Query Language), the command strings in the calls to `executeUpdate` make sense to you. If not, pick up a copy of *SQL For Dummies,* 8th Edition, by Allen G. Taylor. One way or another, don't go fishing around this chapter for explanations of `create table` and `insert into`. You won't find the explanations because these command strings aren't part of Java. These commands are just strings of characters that you feed to the `executeUpdate` method. These strings, which are written in SQL, create a new database table and add rows of data to the table. When you write a Java database program, that's what you do. You write ordinary SQL commands and surround those commands with calls to Java methods.

The code in this chapter adheres strictly to the techniques defined in JDBC version 1.0. Later versions of the JDBC classes support something called *scrollable result sets.* With a scrollable result set, you have methods like `insertRow` — methods that save you the effort of writing complete SQL command strings.

Connecting and disconnecting

Aside from the calls to the `executeUpdate` method, the code in Listing 17-1 is cut-and-paste stuff. Here's a rundown on what each part of the code means:

✔ **`Class.forName`:** Find a database driver.

To talk to a database, you need an intermediary piece of software, or a *database driver*. Drivers come in all shapes and sizes, and many of them are quite expensive. But Listing 17-1 uses a small, freebie driver — the Derby JDBC Embedded driver. The code for the Derby JDBC Embedded driver is kept in the `EmbeddedDriver` class (which is a Java class). This class lives inside the `org.apache.derby.jdbc` package.

To use this `EmbeddedDriver` class, you call the `Class.forName` method. Believe it or not, the Java API has a class named `Class`. The `Class` class contains information about classes that are available to the Java Virtual Machine (JVM). In Listing 17-1, the call to `Class.forName` looks for the `org.apache.derby.jdbc.EmbeddedDriver` class. After an `EmbeddedDriver` instance is loaded, you can proceed to connect with a database.

✔ **`DriverManager.getConnection`:** Establish a session with a particular database.

The `getConnection` method lives in a Java class named `DriverManager`. In Listing 17-1, the call to `getConnection` creates an `AccountDatabase` and opens a connection to that database. Of course, you may already have an `AccountDatabase` before you start running the code in Listing 17-1. If you do, the text `;create=true` string in the `getConnection` call has no effect.

In the parameter for `getConnection` (refer to Listing 17-1), notice the colons. The code doesn't simply name the `AccountDatabase`, it tells the `DriverManager` class what protocols to use to connect with the database. The code `jdbc:derby:` — which is the same as the `http:` in a web address — tells the computer to use the `jdbc` protocol to talk to the `derby` protocol, which in turn talks directly to your `AccountDatabase`.

✔ **`connection.createStatement`:** Make a statement.

It seems strange, but in Java Database Connectivity, you create a single `statement` object. After you've created a `statement` object, you can use that object many times, with many different SQL strings, to issue many different commands to the database. So, before you start calling the `statement.executeUpdate` method, you have to create an actual `statement` object. The call to `connection.createStatement` creates that `statement` object for you.

✔ **`try...catch...`:** Acknowledge exceptions that can be thrown in the code.

If you read Chapter 13, you know that some method calls throw checked exceptions. A *checked exception* is one that has to be acknowledged somewhere in the calling code. Well, a call to `Class.forName` can throw three kinds of exceptions, and just about everything else in Listing 17-1 can throw an SQLException. To acknowledge these exceptions, I add try-catch statements to my code.

✔ **try-with-resources:** Release resources, come what may!

As Ritter always says, you're not being considerate of others if you don't clean up your own messes. Every connection and every database statement lock up some system resources. When you're finished using these resources, you release them.

Java's try-with-resources statement automatically closes and releases your resources at the end of the statement's execution. In addition, try-with-resources takes care of all the messy details associated with failed attempts to catch exceptions gracefully.

For the scoop about try-catch and try-with-resources, see Chapter 13.

Retrieving Data

What good is a database if you can't get data from it? In this section, you query the database that you created in Listing 17-1. The code to issue the query is shown in Listing 17-2.

Listing 17-2:   Making a Query

```java
import static java.lang.System.out;
import java.sql.DriverManager;
import java.sql.Statement;
import java.sql.Connection;
import java.sql.SQLException;
import java.sql.ResultSet;
import java.text.NumberFormat;

public class GetData {

    public static void main(String args[]) {

        NumberFormat currency =
            NumberFormat.getCurrencyInstance();

        final String DRIVER =
            "org.apache.derby.jdbc.EmbeddedDriver";
        final String CONNECTION =
            "jdbc:derby:AccountDatabase";


        try {
            Class.forName(DRIVER).newInstance();
        } catch (InstantiationException e) {
            e.printStackTrace();
```

```
        } catch (IllegalAccessException e) {
          e.printStackTrace();
        } catch (ClassNotFoundException e) {
          e.printStackTrace();
        }


        try (Connection connection =
            DriverManager.getConnection(CONNECTION);

            Statement statement =
              connection.createStatement();

            ResultSet resultset =
              statement.executeQuery(
                              "select * from ACCOUNTS")) {

            while(resultset.next()) {
              out.print(resultset.getString("NAME"));
              out.print(", ");
              out.print(resultset.getString("ADDRESS"));
              out.print(" ");
              out.println(currency.format(
                              resultset.getFloat("BALANCE")));
            }
        } catch (SQLException e) {
          e.printStackTrace();
        }
    }
}
```

To use MySQL instead of Java DB, make the following changes in Listing 17-2: Change the value of DRIVER to `"com.mysql.jdbc.Driver"`. Change the value of CONNECTION to `"jdbc:mysql://localhost/AccountDatabase; create=true"`. Make similar changes for DB2, for Oracle, and for other databases.

A run of the code from Listing 17-2 is shown in Figure 17-1. The code queries the database and then steps through the rows of the database, printing the data from each of the rows.

Figure 17-1:
Getting data
from the
database.

```
Barry Burd, 222 Cyber Lane $24.02
Joe Dow, 111 Luddite Street $55.63
```

Listing 17-2 starts with the usual calls to `forName`, `getConnection`, and `createStatement`. Then the code calls `executeQuery` and supplies the call with an SQL command. For those who know SQL commands, this particular command gets all data from the `ACCOUNTS` table (the table that you create in Listing 17-1).

The thing returned from calling `executeQuery` is of type `java.sql.ResultSet`. (That's the difference between `executeUpdate` and `executeQuery` — `executeQuery` returns a result set, and `executeUpdate` doesn't.) This result set is very much like a database table. Like the original table, the result set is divided into rows and columns. Each row contains the data for one account. Each row has a name, an address, and a balance amount.

After you call `executeQuery` and get your result set, you can step through the result set one row at a time. To do this, you go into a little loop and test the condition `resultset.next()` at the top of each loop iteration. Each time around, the call to `resultset.next()` does two things:

✓ It moves you to the next row of the result set (the next account) if another row exists.

✓ It tells you whether another row exists by returning a boolean value — `true` or `false`.

If the condition `resultset.next()` is true, the result set has another row. The computer moves to that other row, so you can march into the body of the loop and scoop data from that row. On the other hand, if `resultset.next()` is false, the result set doesn't have any more rows. You jump out of the loop and start closing everything.

Now, imagine that the computer is pointing to a row of the result set, and you're inside the loop in Listing 17-2. Then you're retrieving data from the result set's row by calling the result set's `getString` and `getFloat` methods. Back in Listing 17-1, you set up the `ACCOUNTS` table with the columns `NAME`, `ADDRESS`, and `BALANCE`. So, here in Listing 17-2, you're getting data from these columns by calling your `getSomeTypeOrOther` methods and feeding the original column names to these methods. After you have the data, you display the data on the computer screen.

Each Java `ResultSet` instance has several nice `get SomeTypeOrOther` methods. Depending on the type of data you put into a column, you can call methods `getArray`, `getBigDecimal`, `getBlob`, `getInt`, `getObject`, `getTimestamp`, and several others.

Part V
The Part of Tens

A good integrated development environment (IDE) makes writing code a pleasure. The more you know about your IDE, the more you can breeze through tedious typing tasks. Instead of typing line after line, you can concentrate on your coding logic. Discover ten of my favorite Eclipse IDE tricks at www.dummies.com/extras/java.

In this part . . .

✔ Catch common mistakes before you make them.

✔ Explore the best resources for Java on the web.

Chapter 18

Ten Ways to Avoid Mistakes

"**T**he only people who never make mistakes are the people who never do anything at all." One of my college professors said that. I don't remember the professor's name, so I can't give him proper credit. I guess that's my mistake.

Putting Capital Letters Where They Belong

Java is a case-sensitive language, so you really have to mind your *P*s and *Q*s — along with every other letter of the alphabet. Here are some details to keep in mind as you create Java programs:

✔ Java's keywords are all completely lowercase. For instance, in a Java `if` statement, the word *if* can't be *If* or *IF.*

✔ When you use names from the Java API (Application Programming Interface), the case of the names has to match what appears in the API.

✔ You also need to make sure that the names you make up yourself are capitalized the same way throughout your entire program. If you declare a `myAccount` variable, you can't refer to it as `MyAccount`, `myaccount`, or `Myaccount`. If you capitalize the variable name two different ways, Java thinks you're referring to two completely different variables.

For more info on Java's case-sensitivity, see Chapter 3.

Breaking Out of a switch Statement

If you don't break out of a switch statement, you get fall-through. For instance, if the value of verse is 3, the following code prints all three lines — Last refrain, He's a pain, and Has no brain.

```
switch (verse) {
case 3:
    out.print("Last refrain, ");
    out.println("last refrain,");
case 2:
    out.print("He's a pain, ");
    out.println("he's a pain,");
case 1:
    out.print("Has no brain, ");
    out.println("has no brain,");
}
```

For the full story, see Chapter 5.

Comparing Values with a Double Equal Sign

When you compare two values with one another, you use a double equal sign. The line

```
if (inputNumber == randomNumber)
```

is correct, but the line

```
if (inputNumber = randomNumber)
```

is not correct. For a full report, see Chapter 5.

Adding Components to a GUI

Here's a constructor for a Java frame:

```
public SimpleFrame() {
    JButton button = new JButton("Thank you...");
    setTitle("...Connie Santisteban and Brian Walls");
    setLayout(new FlowLayout());
    add(button);
    button.addActionListener(this);
    setSize(300, 100);
    setVisible(true);
}
```

Whatever you do, don't forget the call to the add method. Without this call, you go to all the work of creating a button, but the button doesn't show up on your frame. For an introduction to such issues, see Chapter 9.

Adding Listeners to Handle Events

Look again at the previous section's code to construct a SimpleFrame. If you forget the call to addActionListener, nothing happens when you click the button. Clicking the button harder a second time doesn't help. For the rundown on listeners, see Chapter 15.

Defining the Required Constructors

When you define a constructor with parameters, as in

```
public Temperature(double number)
```

then the computer no longer creates a default parameterless constructor for you. In other words, you can no longer call

```
Temperature roomTemp = new Temperature();
```

unless you explicitly define your own parameterless Temperature constructor. For all the gory details on constructors, see Chapter 9.

Fixing Non-Static References

If you try to compile the following code, you get an error message:

```
class WillNotWork {
    String greeting = "Hello";

    public static void main(String args[]) {
        System.out.println(greeting);
    }
}
```

You get an error message because `main` is static, but `greeting` isn't static. For the complete guide to finding and fixing this problem, see Chapter 10.

Staying within Bounds in an Array

When you declare an array with ten components, the components have indices 0 through 9. In other words, if you declare

```
int guests[] = new int[10];
```

then you can refer to the `guests` array's components by writing `guests[0]`, `guests[1]`, and so on, all the way up to `guests[9]`. You can't write `guests[10]`, because the `guests` array has no component with index 10.

For the latest gossip on arrays, see Chapter 11.

Anticipating Null Pointers

This book's examples aren't prone to throwing the `NullPointerException`, but in real-life Java programming, you see that exception all the time. A `Null PointerException` comes about when you call a method that's supposed to return an object, but instead the method returns nothing. Here's a cheap example:

```
import static java.lang.System.out;
import java.io.File;

class ListMyFiles {

    public static void main(String args[]) {
        File myFile = new File("\\windows");
```

```
        String dir[] = myFile.list();

        for (String fileName : dir) {
            out.println(fileName);
        }
    }
}
```

This program displays a list of all the files in the windows directory. (For clarification on the use of the double backslash in "\\windows", see Chapter 8.)

But what happens if you change \\windows to something else — something that doesn't represent the name of a directory?

```
File myFile = new File("&*%$!!");
```

Then the new File call returns null (a special Java word meaning *nothing*), so the variable myFile has nothing in it. Later in the code, the variable dir refers to nothing, and the attempt to loop through all the dir values fails miserably. You get a big NullPointerException, and the program comes crashing down around you.

To avoid this kind of calamity, check Java's API documentation. If you're calling a method that can return null, add exception-handling code to your program.

For the story on handling exceptions, see Chapter 13. For some advice on reading the API documentation, see Chapter 3 and this book's website (www.allmycode.com/JavaForDummies).

Helping Java Find Its Files

You're compiling Java code, minding your own business, when the computer gives you a NoClassDefFoundError. All kinds of things can be going wrong, but chances are good that the computer can't find a particular Java file. To fix this, you must align all the planets correctly:

- ✔ Your project directory has to contain all the Java files whose names are used in your code.
- ✔ If you use named packages, your project directory has to have appropriately named subdirectories.
- ✔ Your CLASSPATH must be set properly.

For specific guidelines, see Chapter 14 and this book's website (www.allmy code.com/JavaForDummies).

Chapter 19

Ten Websites for Java

In This Chapter

▶ Checking out this book's website

▶ Finding resources from Oracle

▶ Reading more about Java

*N*o wonder the web is so popular. It's both useful and fun. This chapter proves that fact by listing ten useful and fun websites. Each website has resources to help you use Java more effectively. And as far as I know, none of these sites use adware, pop-ups, or other grotesque things.

This Book's Website

For all matters related to the technical content of this book, visit `www.allmycode.com/JavaForDummies`.

For business issues (for example, "How can I purchase 100 more copies of *Java For Dummies*?"), visit `www.dummies.com`.

The Horse's Mouth

The official Oracle website for Java is `www.oracle.com/technetwork/java`.

Consumers of Java technology should visit `www.java.com`.

Programmers and developers interested in sharing Java technology can go to `www.java.net`.

Finding News, Reviews, and Sample Code

For articles by the experts visit InfoQ at www.infoq.com.

For discussion by everyone (including many very smart people), visit JavaRanch at www.javaranch.com.

Looking for Java Jobs

For job listings, visit www.computerwork.com.

Everyone's Favorite Sites

It's true — these two sites aren't devoted exclusively to Java. However, no geek-worthy list of resources would be complete without Slashdot and SourceForge.

- ✔ The Slashdot slogan is "News for nerds, stuff that matters," which says it all. By all means, visit http://slashdot.org.

- ✔ The SourceForge repository (at http://sourceforge.net) houses more than 200,000 free, open-source projects. Check it out!

Index

About the Author

Barry Burd received a Master of Science degree in computer science at Rutgers University and a PhD in mathematics at the University of Illinois. As a teaching assistant in Champaign-Urbana, Illinois, he was elected five times to the university-wide List of Teachers Ranked as Excellent by Their Students.

Since 1980, Dr. Burd has been a professor in the Department of Mathematics and Computer Science at Drew University in Madison, New Jersey. When he's not lecturing at Drew University, Dr. Burd leads training courses for professional programmers in business and industry. He has lectured at conferences in the United States, Europe, Australia, and Asia. He is the author of several articles and books, including *Beginning Programming with Java For Dummies, Java Programming for Android Developers For Dummies*, and *Android Application Development All-in-One For Dummies*, all from Wiley Publishing, Inc.

Dr. Burd lives in Madison, New Jersey, with his wife and two kids (both in their 20s and mostly on their own). In his spare time, he enjoys being a workaholic.

Dedication

for

Jennie, Sam, and Harriet,

Jennie and Benjamin, Katie and Abram,

and Basheva

Author's Acknowledgments

I love having my name on the cover of this book. But honestly, I'm not the only person responsible for the creation of this work. I want to thank everyone involved, with special thanks to Connie Santisteban, Brian Walls, and Virginia Sanders for their work on this 6th edition.

Publisher's Acknowledgments

Acquisitions Editor: Connie Santisteban

Project Editor: Brian Walls

Copy Editor: Virginia Sanders

Technical Editor: John Mueller

Editorial Assistant: Anne Sullivan

Sr. Editorial Assistant: Cherie Case

Project Coordinator: Melissa Cossell

Cover Image: ©ZoneCreative/iStockphoto.com

pple & Mac

ad For Dummies,
h Edition
8-1-118-72306-7

hone For Dummies,
h Edition
8-1-118-69083-3

acs All-in-One
r Dummies, 4th Edition
8-1-118-82210-4

X Mavericks
r Dummies
8-1-118-69188-5

ogging & Social Media

cebook For Dummies,
h Edition
8-1-118-63312-0

ocial Media Engagement
r Dummies
8-1-118-53019-1

ordPress For Dummies,
h Edition
8-1-118-79161-5

usiness

ock Investing
r Dummies, 4th Edition
8-1-118-37678-2

vesting For Dummies,
h Edition
8-0-470-90545-6

Personal Finance
For Dummies, 7th Edition
978-1-118-11785-9

QuickBooks 2014
For Dummies
978-1-118-72005-9

Small Business Marketing
Kit For Dummies,
3rd Edition
978-1-118-31183-7

Careers

Job Interviews
For Dummies, 4th Edition
978-1-118-11290-8

Job Searching with Social
Media For Dummies,
2nd Edition
978-1-118-67856-5

Personal Branding
For Dummies
978-1-118-11792-7

Resumes For Dummies,
6th Edition
978-0-470-87361-8

Starting an Etsy Business
For Dummies, 2nd Edition
978-1-118-59024-9

Diet & Nutrition

Belly Fat Diet For Dummies
978-1-118-34585-6

Mediterranean Diet
For Dummies
978-1-118-71525-3

Nutrition For Dummies,
5th Edition
978-0-470-93231-5

Digital Photography

Digital SLR Photography
All-in-One For Dummies,
2nd Edition
978-1-118-59082-9

Digital SLR Video &
Filmmaking For Dummies
978-1-118-36598-4

Photoshop Elements 12
For Dummies
978-1-118-72714-0

Gardening

Herb Gardening
For Dummies, 2nd Edition
978-0-470-61778-6

Gardening with Free-Range
Chickens For Dummies
978-1-118-54754-0

Health

Boosting Your Immunity
For Dummies
978-1-118-40200-9

Diabetes For Dummies,
4th Edition
978-1-118-29447-5

Living Paleo For Dummies
978-1-118-29405-5

Big Data

Big Data For Dummies
978-1-118-50422-2

Data Visualization
For Dummies
978-1-118-50289-1

Hadoop For Dummies
978-1-118-60755-8

Language & Foreign Language

500 Spanish Verbs
For Dummies
978-1-118-02382-2

English Grammar
For Dummies, 2nd Edition
978-0-470-54664-2

French All-in-One
For Dummies
978-1-118-22815-9

German Essentials
For Dummies
978-1-118-18422-6

Italian For Dummies,
2nd Edition
978-1-118-00465-4

Available in print and e-book formats.

Available wherever books are sold. **For more information or to order direct visit www.dummies.com**

Math & Science

Algebra I For Dummies,
2nd Edition
978-0-470-55964-2

Anatomy and Physiology
For Dummies, 2nd Edition
978-0-470-92326-9

Astronomy For Dummies,
3rd Edition
978-1-118-37697-3

Biology For Dummies,
2nd Edition
978-0-470-59875-7

Chemistry For Dummies,
2nd Edition
978-1-118-00730-3

1001 Algebra II Practice
Problems For Dummies
978-1-118-44662-1

Microsoft Office

Excel 2013 For Dummies
978-1-118-51012-4

Office 2013 All-in-One
For Dummies
978-1-118-51636-2

PowerPoint 2013
For Dummies
978-1-118-50253-2

Word 2013 For Dummies
978-1-118-49123-2

Music

Blues Harmonica
For Dummies
978-1-118-25269-7

Guitar For Dummies,
3rd Edition
978-1-118-11554-1

iPod & iTunes
For Dummies, 10th Edition
978-1-118-50864-0

Programming

Beginning Programming
with C For Dummies
978-1-118-73763-7

Excel VBA Programming
For Dummies, 3rd Edition
978-1-118-49037-2

Java For Dummies,
6th Edition
978-1-118-40780-6

Religion & Inspiration

The Bible For Dummies
978-0-7645-5296-0

Buddhism For Dummies,
2nd Edition
978-1-118-02379-2

Catholicism For Dummies,
2nd Edition
978-1-118-07778-8

Self-Help & Relationships

Beating Sugar Addiction
For Dummies
978-1-118-54645-1

Meditation For Dummies,
3rd Edition
978-1-118-29144-3

Seniors

Laptops For Seniors
For Dummies, 3rd Edition
978-1-118-71105-7

Computers For Seniors
For Dummies, 3rd Edition
978-1-118-11553-4

iPad For Seniors
For Dummies, 6th Edition
978-1-118-72826-0

Social Security
For Dummies
978-1-118-20573-0

Smartphones & Tablets

Android Phones
For Dummies, 2nd Edition
978-1-118-72030-1

Nexus Tablets
For Dummies
978-1-118-77243-0

Samsung Galaxy S 4
For Dummies
978-1-118-64222-1

Samsung Galaxy Tabs
For Dummies
978-1-118-77294-2

Test Prep

ACT For Dummies,
5th Edition
978-1-118-01259-8

ASVAB For Dummies,
3rd Edition
978-0-470-63760-9

GRE For Dummies,
7th Edition
978-0-470-88921-3

Officer Candidate Tests
For Dummies
978-0-470-59876-4

Physician's Assistant Exam
For Dummies
978-1-118-11556-5

Series 7 Exam For Dummie
978-0-470-09932-2

Windows 8

Windows 8.1 All-in-One
For Dummies
978-1-118-82087-2

Windows 8.1 For Dummie
978-1-118-82121-3

Windows 8.1 For Dummie
Book + DVD Bundle
978-1-118-82107-7

e **Available in print and e-book formats.**

Available wherever books are sold. **For more information or to order direct visit www.dummies.com**

Take Dummies with you everywhere you go!

Whether you are excited about e-books, want more from the web, must have your mobile apps, or are swept up in social media, Dummies makes everything easier.

Leverage the Power

For Dummies is the global leader in the reference category and one of the most trusted and highly regarded brands in the world. No longer just focused on books, customers now have access to the For Dummies content they need in the format they want. Let us help you develop a solution that will fit your brand and help you connect with your customers.

Advertising & Sponsorships

Connect with an engaged audience on a powerful multimedia site, and position your message alongside expert how-to content.

Targeted ads • Video • Email marketing • Microsites • Sweepstakes sponsorship

21 Million Monthly Page Views & 13 Million Unique Visitors